科斯文集
Collected Works of Ronald H. Coase

COASE ON LAW AND ECONOMICS

科斯论法律经济学

| 英文版 |

Ronald H. Coase
Edited by Ning Wang

北京大学出版社
PEKING UNIVERSITY PRESS

图书在版编目（CIP）数据

科斯论法律经济学 = Coase on Law and Economics：英文 /（英）罗纳德·科斯著；（英）王宁编. —北京：北京大学出版社，2024.4
ISBN 978-7-301-34541-2

Ⅰ.①科… Ⅱ.①罗… ②王… Ⅲ.①法律经济学 – 研究 – 英文 Ⅳ.① D90-056

中国国家版本馆 CIP 数据核字（2023）第 192910 号

"科斯文集"之《科斯论法律经济学》由芝加哥大学出版社授权北京大学出版社在全球出版英文版。
This English edition is published by arrangement with the University of Chicago Press.

书　　名	Coase on Law and Economics·科斯论法律经济学 Coase on Law and Economics·KESI LUN FALÜ JINGJIXUE
著作责任者	Ronald H. Coase（罗纳德·H. 科斯）　Edited by Ning Wang
责 任 编 辑	黄炜婷
标 准 书 号	ISBN 978-7-301-34541-2
出 版 发 行	北京大学出版社
地　　址	北京市海淀区成府路 205 号　100871
网　　址	http://www.pup.cn
微信公众号	北京大学经管书苑（pupembook）
电 子 邮 箱	编辑部 em@pup.cn　　总编室 zpup@pup.cn
电　　话	邮购部 010-62752015　发行部 010-62750672　编辑部 010-62752926
印 刷 者	天津中印联印务有限公司
经 销 者	新华书店 730 毫米 ×1020 毫米　16 开本　27.5 印张　196 千字 2024 年 4 月第 1 版　2024 年 4 月第 1 次印刷
定　　价	88.00 元

未经许可，不得以任何方式复制或抄袭本书之部分或全部内容。
版权所有，侵权必究
举报电话：010-62752024　电子邮箱：fd@pup.cn
图书如有印装质量问题，请与出版部联系，电话：010-62756370

Contents

Preface and Remembrance: Coase—the Man and His Work / Richard A. Epstein / 1

Introduction: Law in the Economy—the Coasean Law and Economics / Ning Wang / 12

Series I   On the Problem of Social Cost / 001

The Federal Communications Commission and the Broadcasting Industry / 005

The Federal Communications Commission / 031

Testimony to the Federal Communications Commission / 085

The Problem of Social Cost / 092

Notes on the Problem of Social Cost / 151

Comment on Thomas W. Hazlett: Assigning Property Rights to Radio Spectrum Users
  Why Did FCC License Auctions Take 67 Years? / 180

Series II   The Market for Ideas / 185

The Market for Goods and the Market for Ideas / 187

Advertising and Free Speech / 199

Series III   Empirical Study / 245

Payola in Radio and Television Broadcasting / 249

Blackmail / 327

Series IV   History of Law and Economics / 351

Law and Economics and A. W. Brian Simpson / 353

Law and Economics At Chicago / 373

Law and Economics: A Personal Journey / 392

Preface and Remembrance

Coase—the Man and His Work

*Richard A. Epstein**

Mr. Ning Wang has put together this historical collection of essays written by the late Ronald Coase over his long and distinguished academic career, first in England and then in the United States. It is especially fitting that this volume will be published by the Peking University Press, given that Coase, along with Wang, spent much of his last years engaged in research on the transition of China into a capitalist economy, which resulted in 2012 of the publication of their book, *How China Became Capitalist*. In addition to his extensive written work, Coase spoke and organized conferences devoted to this theme. It marks a profound transformation in the life of a man who started in England, moved to the United States and finished his career with a decided Chinese twist.

Wang has asked me to write a preface to this collection, for which he has supplied an introduction. My preface is intended to achieve two related purposes. First, to offer some personal reflections on my own relationship to Ronald Coase, and second,

---

* Laurence A. Tisch Professor of Law, The New York University School of Law, The Peter and Kirsten Bedford Senior Fellow, The Hoover Institution, The James Parker Hall Distinguished Service Professor of Law Emeritus and Senior Lecturer, The University of Chicago. My thanks to Nathaniel Tisa, New York University School of Law, Class of 2019, for his usual impeccable research assistance.

to speak about his influence, not so much on the economics profession, but on the legal profession, which has fully embraced his ideas. Indeed, lawyers continue to use Coase's work to explicate major areas of law that become intelligible only after taking into account the frictions that beset the legal system, which Ronald Coase first systematically identified with the beguilingly obvious term—obvious, that is, only after you figure it out—transactions costs. So much of my own intellectual development has been associated with Coase that it is hard to keep these two prefatory tasks in watertight compartments.

The Man

To start at the beginning, I had never heard of Ronald Coase when I graduated from Yale Law School in the late spring of 1968. His name was mentioned neither at Yale nor at Oxford Law School where I took my first law degree as a pseudo—Englishman in the spring of 1966. My first introduction to Coase came shortly after I arrived at the University of Southern California to begin my own teaching career. The late Michael Levine arrived that same summer, fresh from his one-year fellowship at the University of Chicago Law School, where he worked in depth with Ronald Coase. Our first substantive conversation concerned various theories of liability in the law of tort. It was only a few moments into the discussion before Mike piped up with some reference to "Coase," and I did not know whether the word was a noun, verb, or name. But what followed was an outpouring of discussion about how the system of liability had to take into account transactions costs both between the parties and against the rest of the world. My initial response, like so many others, was that this supposed insight seemed to put the cart before the horse. Transactions costs were always some kind of added extra into a much larger equation, not very relevant to the traditional legal concerns of justice fairness, and equity in the particular case which had long dominated the landscape, just as they had throughout in my own legal education.

It was only a matter of time before the issues that piqued my attention at the

University of Southern California came into sharper relief when I got to the University of Chicago in the fall of 1972, which is when I first met Coase. By that time he was already 61—a lot younger than I am today. It seems clear in retrospect that he had lost some of the fire that characterized his younger behavior. But Coase was always insistent about the soundness of his position, which he defended against one and all. He was more than gracious to me, and, as editor of the *Journal of Law and Economics*, published my article "Unconscionability: A Critical Reappraisal" in 1975, which marked another step in my evolution towards his transactions costs approach. Over the 40 years that I knew Coase he never wavered in his defense of the distinctive nature of his approach.

Several incidents during this period come quickly to mind. At some time in the 1980s Coase, James Buchanan, and myself were asked to attend a small meeting with members of the staff of the Liberty Fund. At that occasion Coase was quite upset at the way in which he thought the world, and most particularly Richard A. Posner, misunderstood and misapplied his work.[1] Coase wanted to use transactions costs to define the operation of the legal system. He did not see that his theory had powerful applications, often implicitly, for the way judges crafted their legal doctrine. Indeed, Coase often thought that lawyers had taken his ideas in directions of which he did not approve. He claimed that he had used the transactions costs language merely to explicate land disputes between neighbors under the law of nuisance.

Ironically, on this point Coase was surely wrong. His work had far greater reach than he supposed, and the legions of scholars that ported his work into different subject matter areas were right to do so given how far-reaching were the applications of the now famous "Coase Theorem" to all aspects of legal and social behavior. Indeed, it is instructive to ask why there is no second theorem by some other scholar with the same breadth as Coase's. I have come to the conclusion that none has emerged in the near sixty years since the publication of his work because none is really needed. Restated modestly, that theorem posits that the correct way to maximize social welfare is to minimize transactions costs, for only this strategy can increase the volume of socially-maximizing transactions. For readers who want to hear Coase talk about these issues in his own words, I had the privilege to conduct a longish interview with him in 2002, which has been been recorded for posterity as "A Conversation with Ronald H. Coase."[2]

Even toward the end of his life Coase was fiercely proud of his individuality. Here are two incidents illustrating this fact.

In 2010 Professor Thomas Hazlett and I planned a conference devoted to the works of Coase. Coase was not able to attend the conference but did record, with some evident difficulty, a few remarks that were played on the occasion. The main topic of those remarks was a provocative essay by Richard A. Posner that pointed out the asserted resemblances between Coase and John Maynard Keynes. Posner emphasized that both men had grand theories that eschewed the use of formal mathematics. Coase would have none of it, so he gave his own account of the interconnections between himself and Keynes that went roughly as follows: "Mr. Keynes and I met on only one occasion shortly after the end of the war. It was at a tea party. Mr. Keynes was sitting down, and I was standing up behind him. He turned to me and asked if I could pour him a cup of tea, which I dutifully did. And that was the influence of Keynes on Coase."

Indeed, Coase is right on this point. His every instinct was to break down complex aggregates into their constituent parts to see how they worked together. Keynes by contrast always moved in the opposite direction, ignoring individual transactions in order to postulate aggregates that can be studied for their macro-economic effects. On this I think that Coase's reductionism of macro to micro is much preferable to Keynesian aggregation from micro to macro, as the latter approach tends to ignore conflicts of interest between members within the aggregate group, which in turn leads one to overlook the public choice problems with government regulation, a dynamic which Coase correctly saw as a stumbling block to the more efficient operation of markets.

The last time I saw Coase was for lunch at his old-folks home. He was then over the age of 101 and obviously labored. Coase had always jealously protected both his reputation and the purity of his economic position in his final years. But on this occasion he was morose. He pronounced that his life had been an academic failure because the world had largely misconstrued his understanding of the role of transactions costs in the economic system, echoing points he had made earlier. Those scholars took the theory to places where it did not belong. I disagreed with him on this gloomy assessment, but got only a small smile when I said to him that he had a huge intellectual advantage—a last name with only one syllable—which he had exploited to the maximum, which happens whenever your name becomes an adjective ... like Coasean.

His Work

The adjectival use of his name is well-deserved because his simple insights were able to upend other conceptual frameworks. Raised as a typical English and American lawyer in the mid-1960s, I was in the midst of my own first legal project, which was to explain how some conception of individual autonomy provided the intellectual glue that held together the diverse common law fields of property, contract, tort, and restitution. Those models worked pretty well for simple two-party transactions, or at least I thought. Those (relatively) simple cases involving disputes between two drivers over an automobile accident, or landlord and tenant over a rental agreement, did not bring the issue of transaction costs to the fore. But once the seed had been planted, it was difficult to erase the Coasean notions from my mind. Coase developed these ideas in "The Problem of Social Cost" initially with cases drawn from the English law of nuisance, chiefly during the late nineteenth century, with which I was familiar from my studies at Oxford. There was something odd about what Coase had to say about them. The point here has less to do with the transactions costs model and more to do with the role of causation in tort law. Coase's view of this subject was to treat the term "causation" as wholly reciprocal, so that it was impossible to say whether the fish died because they ingested pollution or because their lungs were in some way weak or defective.

Viewed in this light the term is largely useless as a way to decide particular cases, which should have been a warning sign to Coase that something was wrong because he generally loathed to disregard longstanding practice in business. Why then should he do so on linguistic matters? Ordinary language stood in stark opposition to the Coasean conception of causation, and the pervasive role of theories of causation in the law of tort offered a loud testament that these issues could not be ignored, which is not to say that I could put together the law's divergent ideas into any cohesive synthesis.

Part of the problem in this analysis stems from a challenge that Ning Wang addresses when he tries to conceive of how to think about a zero transactions costs world. The conceptual issues here are really more difficult than Coase let on for the simple reason that no one has any idea what a zero transactions costs world looks like, any more than they understand how the world looks once one accelerates beyond the speed of light. To put it more concretely, in a world of zero transactions costs there can be no fraud because everyone knows everything. There can be no temporal barriers because all information is incorporated instantaneously in order to avoid the costs of delay. Nor can distances matter because whatever actions do take place also have to be instantaneous. The features of time and space that mark the world as we know it disappear in a world of zero transactions costs. What then do we make of the gap between contract formation and contract performance, or of particular acts and their consequences? What then can be the use of this construct?

The way to escape this puzzle lies in restating the question. We know that we all live in a world that has temporal and spatial dimensions. We also know that information is costly to acquire, which necessarily means that monitoring is imperfect and fraud or opportunism always remain serious threats given the fact that self-interested individuals do not always have the moral fiber Coase found so important in economic affairs—to steer the straight and narrow. At this point, the zero transactions costs model asks this question: suppose that we had all the time in the world at to figure out how to design and organize transactions that take place in a positive transactions costs world. How in our infinite leisure would we structure those transactions from formation to execution to avoid the strains and tension that take place when we leave this intellectual Nirvana—to use one of Harold Demsetz's favorite phrases—and enter into the real world where transactions costs matter for all the obvious reasons?[3]

The answers to this question are quite tractable, and they help explain why Coase thought that as transactions costs tended to zero the question of externalities disappeared. In my own writing about Coase I refer to this as the single-owner approach to thinking about social and legal relationships. Consider any kind of collective endeavor—the formation of a condominium association or the creation of a corporation or a club. All members at the outset are fully aware of the set of laudable and dangerous traits present in individual human beings, and thus the single owner.[4] This single owner knows that he will part with his property, often to multiple parties who then will be neighbors with relationships with each other in a decidedly positive transactions cost environment. That single owner also knows that all benefits and costs are correlative with each other, so that if he grants a set of rights to one potential buyer as against all others, he will get less from them; even as he gets more from the original purchaser, he will get less from those who follow. He therefore has to calculate whether the downstream losses, reduced to present value, exceed the initial set of gains. And that singular calculation has to be undertaken for each of these transactions with each of these parties. The effect of this is to impose an enormous discipline on the way in which these transactions are undertaken, because these concerns effect how to make the sales, what terms to include in contracts between the various parties, how to deal with subsequent sales and leases by the original parties, and so on down the line.

In this world there are by definition no externalities, just as Coase posited when he held that transactions costs were zero. But it was then instructive to see what kinds of obligations were imposed on various parties, which could serve as a template for how to deal with neighbors who did *not* derive their title from a common owner. The simplest approach is to ask which prohibitions on use were imposed as part of the deal by the single owner and then use those findings to develop the law of nuisance that Coase studies so intensely in "The Problem of Social Cost." This point then ties neatly into one of Coase's lifelong obsessions that is often derided by more theoretical economists and lawyers. If you want to understand, Coase always maintained, how people would contract with each other, then by all means look at how they do contract with each other. Far from starting with blackboard economics, as Coase liked to call it, it is much better to get into the nitty-gritty of agreements and use those actual transactions as the baseline to uncover how, for example, neighbors get along with each other.

And once you take Coase's methodology in this light, it turns out that Coase was *incorrect* in thinking that causation should be understood as perfectly reciprocal when in ordinary language it is not. The simplest case of causation is the direct application of force by one person against the person or property of the other. The differentiation between the nominative and accusative in all languages shows how deeply the distinction is built into the universal architecture of the human mind. This notion of causation carries forward in a somewhat attenuated form in the cases to which Coase devoted so much attention in the law of nuisance, which stresses various forms of physical invasion of noise, smells, and solids. These cases are recognized as needing special treatment in all these initial agreements promulgated by the single owner. Emissions are sharply circumscribed in virtually all initial condominium agreements, for example, which are drafted and recorded in ways that make sure that the benefit and burden side of the prohibition descends to all takers, regardless of the order in which they take or the price they pay. The structure has this feature of permanence because the problem is one that is constant over time.

That fixity of vision is decidedly not true on all cases. Thus, these same master agreements contain terms on softer externalities having to do with styles, colors, decor and the like that vary much more with wealth and taste, and thus display a greater degree of diversity. So the common law of nuisance entrenches the first set of rights, and deals very cautiously with the second set of rights. Indeed, with public nuisance from factories and automobiles the concern with pollution is the same as it in the private settings, but once again the notion of transactions costs comes in to explain the different responses to public nuisances, which has been built into the English common law since 1535.[5] The definition of what counts as a nuisance does not switch as the property damaged—we can now use that word—ceases to be a private pond and becomes a public river. But the cost of enforcing rights differs radically given the general rule that for common resources like rivers, open access was the initial rule— all could enter but none could exclude. In these settings private rights of action are very costly to administer relative to the lower amounts at stake to individuals. Hence the common law distinction, which endures to this day, takes the position that those individuals who suffer special, e.g. large and unique, damages can maintain their traditional rights to sue for property damage. By contrast those individuals who suffer only general damages along with their fellow citizens have no private rights of action. But now the state can bring an administrative remedy against the offender, which allows it both to remove the obstacle or clean up the pollution while also fining that party in order to improve the deterrent effect. There are, of course, constant gradations between the two categories that cannot be ignored. But the basic point only shows the power of the Coasean concern with transactions costs, which now receives a much more central role in cases where the numbers of parties seeking redress increases. This simple point helps explain, as no other theory can, the switch from simple lawsuits based on principles of corrective justice to more complex class actions and administrative remedies. And so it is that the law of nuisance slowly turns into environmental law, with a larger role for direct public enforcement of prohibitions in the case of widespread harms of diffuse or multiple origins. All too many people think of these as discrete when in fact they are not. The concern with keeping the entitlements that emerged from the early concerns of the single owner now gives way to greater understanding of the hard remedial choices that develop when the scope of problems increases.

The insistence on the role of transactions costs also influences Coase's first classic article, "The Nature of the Firm"[6] published in 1937 after his trip to study industrial organization in the United States. As ever, the basic observation Coase makes is perfectly obvious—at least after he makes it. As it turns out, the system of voluntary transactions is marked by a mixture of some discrete, or spot, transactions, where a price is paid for the provision of some good or service. But there are also many settings in which informal exchange or the formation of the firm takes hold and puts the sale of goods or services to one side. Coase asked the simple question: why the division between spot transactions and firm formation? His resulting simple answer has survived the test of time. It is not costless to organize an exchange system. There are transactions costs that have to be incurred during negotiation, contract formation, performance, and litigation. In some cases these costs are well worth bearing. But in other settings it turns out that these expenses are too high, so instead the firm arises such that employees are paid not for each discrete act but with a wage for overall services whose content and description is not fully specified in advance. The new strategy also has negotiation and enforcement costs, and it is often harder to monitor work than it is to inspect a good before it is purchased, or to repair work before it is paid for. But there is no general rule to push things in one direction or another, and Coase was right to insist that the notion of transactions costs lies at the differentiation of various forms of organization.

The world is, of course, even more complex than this simple dichotomy implies, so that it is often the case that firms have more complex structures.[7] Workers can receive base pay and a commission, or a bonus at the end of the year. It may be better for them to bear some residual risk along with the employer. Or the employer could become a partnership instead of an individual proprietorship. These permutations are not the work of an economist, but a product of lawyers who address these issues as they draft agreements for the provision of capital and labor. Lawyers also have to ask the hard question of how different members of the firm fit together in order to take into account differences in tastes and competence, which militate against a simple firm design in which all workers have identical roles with respect to management. It is here that the genius of Coase lies. It is not just that he made observations about everyday events that many great minds had missed. It is that all of his work was capable of a principled extension to problems that Coase never addressed. And so it is that work which was always important has become more so over time, and will continue to do so. Coase's preoccupation with transactions costs turns out to unlock many of the secrets of social organization such that familiar notions that were once afterthoughts in legal and social discussion have become the centerpiece of modern social science. Thank you, Ronald Coase.

Notes

[1] On which *see* Ronald H. Coase, Coase on Posner on Coase, 149 *Journal of Institutional and Theoretical Economics.* 96 (1993).

[2] Ronald H. Coase, The intellectual portrait series: A conversation with Ronald H. Coase (2002), available at https://oll.libertyfund.org/titles/coase-the-intellectual-portrait-series-a-conversation-with-ronald-h-coase (last visited Jan. 1, 2019).

[3] Harold Demsetz, Information and efficiency: Another viewpoint, 12 *Journal of Law and Economics.* 1 (1969).

[4] Richard A. Epstein, Holdouts, externalities and the single owner: Another tribute to Ronald Coase, 36 *Journal of Law and Economics.* 553 (1993); as applied to real estate, *see* Richard A. Epstein, Positive and negative externalities in real estate development, 102 *Minnesota Law Review.* 1493 (2018).

[5] Y.B. 27 Hen. 8, fo. 26, pl. 10 (1536)).

[6] R.H. Coase, The nature of the firm, 4 *Economica* (N.S.) 386 (1937).

[7] Richard A. Epstein, Inside the Coasean firm: Why variations in competence and taste matter, 54 *Journal of Law and Economics.* S41 (2011).

Introduction

Law in the Economy—the Coasean Law and Economics

Ning Wang[*]

The modern market economy, from which most of us derive our livelihood and much else, is full of dynamism, creativity, and uncertainty. New and better products and services, from the latest models of cellphones and electric cars to life-saving drugs to online shopping and payment services, are continuously becoming available to consumers everywhere. As new markets, technologies, organizations, industries and economies arise, existing ones are forced to compete, adapt or falter. With its constant flux, unpredictable dynamism, and unrivaled creativity, the market economy constantly raises a host of perplexing puzzles and daunting challenges (e.g., Schumpeter, 1934; Coase and Wang, 2011). Amidst them, stand out two fundamental questions; they drive and shape our imagination and our understanding of the economy, including our own place in it. How does the market economy work? What can be done to make it work better?

---

[*] I'd like to thank Alexandre and Lee Benham, Dean Lueck, Deidre McCloskey, Steven Medema, and Henry Mohrman for their helpful comments and suggestions, which have resulted in many improvements. I am solely responsible for any remaining faults. The choice of articles collected in this volume was first made by Ronald Coase in 2012 after we had convinced him the value of bringing together his articles on law and economics. Later, four more articles were added to his original list, "The Federal Communications Commission and Broadcasting Industry," "Testimony to the FCC," "The Notes on the Problem of Social Cost," and "Law and Economics: A Personal Journey." I'd like to thank Stephen Littlechild and John L. Peterman for their advice.

The two questions capture our insatiable curiosity concerning the world we reside in, including our desire to see beyond the veil of social reality glued and fused together by our own thinking, speaking, and acting, and our continuous ambition to enrich our lives. On them rest the possibility and progress of human civilization. The articles collected in this volume trace one individual's bold and creative efforts to tackle the two questions in his own characteristic Coasean way.

The articles span almost half a century, the earliest one being a lecture Coase delivered in 1958 to celebrate the opening of the Thomas Jefferson Center for Studies in Political Economy at the University of Virginia, and the last one being another lecture Coase presented in 2002, at the University of Chicago Law School as part of its centennial celebration, both published posthumously in *Man and the Economy*, a new journal Coase launched shortly before his death. In between those years, the modern approach to law and economics was born and steadily established itself as a profoundly influential school of thought in American jurisprudence and one of the most exciting developments in economics in the 20th century and beyond.

All the articles have been published before, but they are collected here in a single volume for the first time. Many of them are familiar to most readers, and some have been treasured by generations of students—Steven Cheung once told me that as a Ph.D. student at UCLA in the late 1960s, for a couple of years he always carried a copy of "The Federal Communications Commission" in his pocket and eventually memorized most parts of the 40-page long article. This collection brings to light forcefully, in a way that no single article possibly can, how Coase worked throughout his long career as a "solitary philosopher," with little regard to the changing trends and fashions in the profession, conceiving the subject, approaching problems, and searching for solutions. The two fundamental questions on which Coase focused– how the market economy works and what can be done to improve it–are still with us today. Neither is likely to lose its significance in the foreseeable future. Thanks to Coase's wisdom and humor, we can view both questions in different lights and explore solutions in more fruitful directions. The simple but powerful ideas, which run through the articles, enlarge our toolbox and broaden our horizon. We are thus better equipped, with finer maps in hand and more humility in the heart, to embark on our own intellectual journeys. For those who seek to follow Coase's path, this volume serves well as a signpost and a steppingstone.

1

Coase on Law and Economics contains thirteen articles that Coase wrote on the subject of law and economics. In terms of content, the articles fall into four series.

The first and by far the largest series centers on the problem of social cost, which is Coase's most influential article; The second series of papers focuses on the market for ideas, including "The Market for Goods and the Market for Ideas" and "Advertising and Free Speech"; The third series consists of two empirical papers, "Payola in Radio and Television Broadcasting" and "Blackmail"; The fourth and last series of papers deals with the history of law and economics.

2

Ronald Coase has been widely acclaimed as a founding father of modern law and economics. His paper, "The Problem of Social Cost," the most cited paper in modern legal and economics scholarship, together with Guido Calabresi's (1961) influential article on torts, is largely responsible for the birth of the new discipline (Posner, 2003[1973]).[1] In addition, Coase served for 18 years, from 1964 to 1982, as editor of the *Journal of Law and Economics*, founded at the University of Chicago Law School in 1958 by Aaron Director. Coase used his editorship to inspire, induce, and instruct scholars, particularly junior ones, to study the impact of the law on the economy.

This honor, however, often made the honoree uneasy. Law and economics, as seen by Coase, contains two different and complementary lines of scholarship, each with distinct subject matter and research program. The first and dominant one, as currently taught and practiced, is generally identified as the "economic analysis of law," a term coined and made popular by Richard Posner's (2003[1973]) *Economic Analysis of Law*, the very first textbook in the new subject and now a classic. It applies the basic concepts and principles of modern price theory to analyze the law and make sense of legal rules, institutions, and practices. Thanks to Posner's erudition and exceptional productivity, the economic analysis of law has grown into a well-developed and firmly institutionalized research program in American law schools, with its standard curriculum and regular outlets for scholarship. Law and economics in this regard is an innovation in legal education and in jurisprudence, matters to which Coase did not have much interest or qualification to contribute. Coase, an old-style economist, always felt somewhat uneasy by a sense of exile while teaching in a law school.

Another factor, which probably played a more important part, further distanced Coase's approach from economic analysis of law. In terms of its intellectual origin, economic analysis of law is an enterprise of the "economic imperialism" that has gradually moved modern economics away from a study of man, of wealth, and of social organization in the tradition of Adam Smith (1976[1776]), Alfred Marshall (1920[1890]), and Frank Knight (1951[1933]) and made it a formal science of choice precipitated by scarce means and given ends à la Lionel Robbins (1932) and Gary Becker (1976). A striking and far-reaching consequence of the transformation, which deeply disturbed Coase, is that modern economics has severed (or liberated, depending on the perspective taken) itself from the real-world economy. Having abandoned its traditional subject matter, contemporary economics risks losing its empirical root and measure of relevance. A longtime junior colleague of Robbins at the London School of Economics in his early career and later a colleague of Becker at the University of Chicago, Coase enjoyed a congenial relationship with both. As a scholar, however, Coase stuck to the old-style vision of economics and never joined their path. Coase practiced economics in the spirit of Smith, Marshall, and Knight, holding economics as a study of man creating wealth in society through specialization, organization, and exchange. Coase's unwavering commitment to this intellectual tradition explains his lack of interest in economic imperialism and his insouciance toward economic analysis of law.

Holding such a high hope for economics and embracing such a demanding measure of progress, Coase often felt that too little had been accomplished since the time of Adam Smith and that much had to be done to keep economics relevant and alive. With a sense of urgency, Coase approached law and economics with a different purpose. Instead of analyzing law from an economic perspective, Coase examined law's impact on the working of the economy. What roles does the law play in the origins and development of the market economy? How does it affect the structure of the economy, its performance and evolution over time? How can it be altered to make the economy work better?

Compared with economic imperialism spearheaded by Gary Becker (1976), which extends to the whole terrain of social sciences and beyond, the pre-Becker view of economics as found in Smith, Marshall, and Knight, with its focus on the working of the economy, appears rather narrow. For those who take pride in economics practiced as a universal analytical parlance for social sciences, Coase's vision of economics may well appear anachronistic and unnecessarily self-restricted in focus. At the core of modern economics stands the theory of pricing (e.g., Friedman, 1976; McCloskey, 1985; Stigler, 1987; Cheung, 2017). Economic imperialists apply it to understand human behavior beyond the traditional boundaries of economics, such as the family, the school, the court, and government offices. Travelling in a reverse direction, Coase employed basic economic reasoning to understand the working of the firm and of the market as well as the economic impact of government policy and regulation. Thanks to Coase's persistence, we now have a richer economics that goes beyond resource allocation and price determination and a better understanding of how the economy works. Still, our growth of knowledge in economics, like explorations in the fundamentals elsewhere, only leads us to see farther and clearer what we don't know. Law and economics, Coase believed, could help economists to tackle some of the most intricate and elusive questions about the economy. Unless economics achieves a resounding success in understanding the working of the economy, economic imperialism will face legitimate resistance and even popular revolt in its recently colonized fields.

At this point, it is of interest to compare Coase's approach to law and economics with that of Guido Calabresi, another founder of modern law and economics. In his recent book, *The Future of Law and Economics* (Calabresi, 2016), Calabresi also emphatically separates law and economics from the economic analysis of law. A fellow, Calabresi shares Coase's view that law and economics is not equal to, and has to be more than, economic analysis of law. What bothers Calabresi (2016) is not so much that economic analysis of law examines the legal world from the standpoint of economic theory, but rather "as a result of that examination, [it] confirms, casts doubt upon, and often seeks reform of legal reality," taking existing economic theory— whether it is market or Marxist economics—as the unproblematic Archimedean reference point.

Law and economics, Calabresi explains, "begins with an agnostic acceptance of the world as it is, as the lawyer describes it to be. It then looks to whether economic theory can explain that world" (p. 2). Furthermore, when existing economic theory cannot explain it, rather than dismissing the legal world as irrational, Calabresi (2016) recommends two further questions. First, are we looking at the legal world as it really is? Second, can economic theory be revised and refined so as to explain why the legal world is as it is?

In contrast to the economic analysis of law, which applies existing economic theory to analyze law, both Coase and Calabresi begin with the real world and look for theory to explain what the real world is and why it is what it is. As a legal scholar, Calabresi is understandably more interested in what economics can do for law; as an economist, Coase is more interested in what law does to the economy. Only when Posner and Calabresi meet Coase, can law and economics build a strong reciprocal bilateral relation between law and economics, each informing, inspiring and enriching the other.[2]

3

In the introductory essay to the first collection of his papers, *The Firm, the Market, and the Law*, which shares the same title with the volume, Coase (1988a) emphatically recognized the law as an integral part of the economic system. It is straightforward for economists to recognize the firm and the market as basic components making up the institutional structure of the economy. The law is no less a constituent part of the economy, Coase emphasized, interacting with the firm and market in complex ways that we still poorly understand.

In the first place, law provides the foundation for economic activity. Economics starts with and centers around exchange. But what is exchanged are rights rather than physical entities, rights primarily, though not exclusively, defined and enforced by law. From another perspective, economics is essentially concerned with competition, not the kind of competition conceived in theory of perfect competition, but the act of competing and process of rivalry as commonly understood. But the rules of competition are primarily defined by property rights. Both approaches take us to the same conclusion, a point brought out forcefully in "The Federal Communications Commission" and "The Problem of Social Cost," that the delineation of rights establishes a precondition for the working of the market—this insight is what Steven Cheung (1992) calls the Coase Theorem. Armen Alchian reached the same point when he stated that "in essence, economics is the study of property rights" (1967). When rights are not clearly delineated, as in the case of collective ownership under socialism in China (Coase and Wang, 2012), or rescinded, as in the case of "Payola in Radio and Television Broadcasting," potential acquirers of rights, who believe that they can employ the resources more profitably, are deprived of the opportunities to resolve their conflict through competitive bidding. The market, as a result, becomes incapacitated, giving rise to resource misallocation and rent dissipation. When such oppression of the market becomes widespread throughout the economy and extends over time, its grim consequences go far beyond economic inefficiency; affected economic actors become discouraged and even feel helpless. No economy and society peopled by such demoralized people have a chance to succeed in the long run.

Economists are inclined to imagine the economy as the flow of goods and services that link the households and firms together through markets, joined and facilitated by the flow of money. Think about Frank Knight's (1933) famous "wheel of wealth" (Patinkin, 1973), which is widely popularized by Paul Samuelson's (1948) influential textbook.[3] This, however, is not how legal scholars have been trained to approach the subject. They have long emphasized that what is exchanged in the market are rights rather than physical materials, a viewpoint shared by contemporary sociologists (e.g., Coleman, 1990). The famed 19th century German jurist, Rudolph von Jhering, brought the point home. "The commerce of exchanges, looked at from the legal point of view, is not a circulation of objects; it is a transfer of rights. Isolated from the law which relates to it, the object is deprived of all value. Neither utility nor economic use determines the value of things; that is the result essentially of the circumstances that the use of the object is legally assured and depends on the manner in which it is protected by law. The law is an essential factor in the notion of value; in a revolution all values suffer; they recover when confidence in the certainty of law returns. Legally the transfer of an object signifies the transfer of the right over that object; legally commerce in objects is no other than the establishment of rights, their transfer, their extinction" (quoted from Charles Reinold Noyes, 1936).

That the foundation of economics is anchored to law can be seen from another perspective. Economics, in the tradition of Adam Smith and Alfred Marshall, is essentially a social science of wealth-creation. In a commercial society built on specialization, organization, and exchange, wealth essentially hinges on direct or indirect exchangeability. For example, because voluntary slavery is outlawed today, a person cannot sell himself directly, but he can bring whatever he can produce to the market or sell his service of productivity, making himself for sale indirectly. Without exchange, there would be neither room nor incentive for specialization. Without specialization, there would be little growth in productivity. Since the object of exchange is rights, wealth-creation thus critically depends on rights, their delineation, enforcement, and protection. Wealth can be efficiently employed in a market economy, generating the highest returns to its owner and enriching the society at the same time, only when the laws of contract, property, and tort reduce transaction costs and facilitate the transfer of rights.

Moreover, wealth or the stream of services it generates, unless secured by law and norms, is bound to be squandered, if ever created in the first place. The law of property, which institutes private property rights and induces private entrepreneurship, is the bedrock of civil society. This traditional view of private property, whose rich roots go back to Locke, Hume, and Smith, is further reinforced in the 20th century when radical schemes of nationalization that trample private property have all ended up impoverishing the economy and undermining the dignity of human life, despite noble intentions.

Secondly, law plays a critical role in creating and shaping what Coase (1991) called the "institutional structure of production." The firm—the social organization that transforms input into output—comes into being because of the cost of using the market mechanism. The market is an institution that exists to reduce the cost of carrying out exchange transactions. Because law is intimately involved in exchange, it clearly plays a pervasive role in the setting up of the firm and the market. Moreover, law is a critical component in the institutional environment in which the firm and the market operate. The working of modern markets, particularly, the labor and financial markets, is heavily influenced by a whole range of statute laws and rules of regulation. Business firms also operate in the shadow of the law, including various laws of corporation and of competition. Because law occupies a central and continuously growing role in the modern market economy, unless it is taken fully into account, Coase believed, economics would be severely ill prepared for understanding, let alone to prescribe policies to improve, the working of the market economy. It was this conviction that brought Coase to law.

Thirdly, by changing the rights and duties of personal and corporate actors, and redrawing the line between what is lawful and what is not in business dealings, law can directly and profoundly change how economic actors behave and through them, how the economy operates. In this way, law becomes a valuable policy instrument to be employed to improve the working of the economy. Compared with conventional instruments, like monetary and fiscal policies, law is more direct and focused. It has the potential to be a powerful tool to shape the working of the economic system to our liking.

That this did not happen was a constant source of Coase's critique of modern economics. Two policy choices, strongly favored by economists and commonly adopted by policy-makers, are taxation (e.g., imposing a Pigovian tax to deal with externalities) and direct government regulation (e.g., establishing certain ad hoc regulatory agents, such as the Federal Communication Commission entrusted to manage broadcasting, telephone and telegraph industries). Both are meticulously scrutinized and systematically criticized by Coase (1959, 1960). The reason that Coase favors the use of law to modify the rights and duties of economic actors over taxation and government regulation is not so much that private bargaining always ends up in allocative efficiency, making Pigovian taxation and government regulation unnecessary, a proposition has become known as the popular Coase Theorem (e.g., Farrell, 2016), but that well-defined property rights empower economic actors and induce enterprising initiatives from those who are motivated to discover the most profitable employment for whatever assets or rights they possess. Without such continuous enterprising undertaking from economic actors, the market economy will quickly lose its dynamism and wither away.

For Coase, the study of law in the working of the economy also has a substantial methodological payoff: It ties economics to the real world. In economics, many examples are ingeniously invented to illustrate economic theory; they are meant to provide a convenient empirical footing to otherwise abstract theory. The lighthouse in economics has long been such a canonical example (Coase, 1974); the story of Fisher Body and General Motors is a recent example that Coase (2006) turned his critical eyes to. The "fable of the bees" as investigated by Steve Cheung (1973) is a favorite of Coase, who solicited Cheung to write the paper.[4]

In contrast, legal scholars are trained to rely on real life examples in their reasoning and writings. The basic pattern of common-law reasoning is reasoning by example, that is, reasoning from case to case. The doctrine of precedent in common law is built on close perusal and careful comparison of legal cases. For law school students in the United States, an important part of their training is to memorize classic cases and to learn to think like a lawyer, that is, reason by analogy. Strikingly different from economics, the examples used in law are true and real, not something concocted or fabricated just to make a case. This is an important and apparently unique feature of legal reasoning.[5] Marrying law and economics in the Coasean way helps to bring realism back to economics.

4

A discussion of law in the economy would leave a big lacuna in our understanding of Coasean law and economics unless ethics is taken into account because ethics plays a fundamental role in adjudicating positive law, in regulating right and wrong, and in motivating and judging human behavior.

Ethics and economics have had long and intimate relations since the time of Adam Smith, who started his career as professor of moral philosophy, authored *The Theory of Moral Sentiments* before the *Wealth of Nations*, and revised the former significantly to note down his last thoughts a few months before his death. For Smith, ethics and economics are integral part of what he called the "science of human nature" (1982). Man's natural sociality, his curiosity for order, desire for plenty and esteem, mediated and augmented by his power of imagination, joy of sympathy, and longing for propriety and virtue, mold human instincts into social life. Cultivated, refined, and elevated human nature, made possible by growing wealth extended to all members of the commercial society, promises new venues to develop social institutions. In the pursuit of science of man, the abstract theory of human nature is applied to understand the evolution of morality and law and the progress of politics and commerce. A better understanding of social institutions sheds further light on human nature and provides a firm empirical foundation on which a mature "science of human nature" can be built. The science of man so cumulatively built may well be positioned to inform and even instruct the development of social institutions, in the critical and negative sense of pointing out what is wrong and proscribing what not to do. In this sense, economics, for Smith and Coase alike, is necessarily an applied empirical moral science.

Frank Knight took the same approach to ethics and economics, who had a formative and lasting impact on Coase. Knight (1935) reminded us that "life is not fundamentally a striving for ends, for satisfactions, but rather for bases for further striving … the true achievement is the refinement and elevation of the plane of desires, the cultivation of taste." Man is not a utility-maximizer, not due to the limitation of bounded rationality as emphasized by Herbert Simon (1955), or the lack of information as noted by George Stigler (1961), but rather because man is always explorative and constantly creative, if he remains active at all. Being "the discontented animal, the romantic, argumentative, aspiring animal," man is "interested in changing himself, even to changing the ultimate core of his being" (Knight, 1947). Thus, he can never pre-commit himself to a set of fixed goals; such a strict life would be frustrating if he fails, and boring if he succeeds. Instead of striving for a given end, "the end is always more or less redefined in the course of the action itself, and an interest in this process of redefinition is inherent in the interest in action. The end or ideal which functions in advance of action is rather a sense of direction than an end in the concrete sense" (Knight, 1947). In redefining his end, man may fall prey to the vice of "conspicuous consumption" and other traps, he never totally aborts his striving for a better self. The striving, as Adam Smith (1976) noted, is not driven by "the love of our neighbor" or "the love of mankind," but by a "stronger love, a more powerful affection," that is, "the love of what is honorable and noble, of the grandeur, and dignity, and superiority of our own character."

Unlike Smith and Knight, Coase rarely took on ethics explicitly in his writing.

Nonetheless, he approached economics similarly as a moral science. At the end of "The Problem of Social Cost," Coase (1960) pointed out the limitation of his analysis. "The analysis has been confined, as is usual in this part of economics, to comparisons of the value of production, as measured by the market. But it is, of course, desirable that the choice among different social arrangements for the solution of economic problems should be carried out in broader terms than this and that the total effect of these arrangements in all spheres of life should be taken into account." To close the paragraph, Coase referred to a point stressed by Knight that the problems of economics "must ultimately dissolve into a study of aesthetics and morals" (1960).

Commenting on the wide readership *The Theory of Moral Sentiments* has commanded in present-day China, Coase and Wang (2012) write: "After thirty years of market transformation, China has not only endorsed capitalism as an economic system which facilitates the creation of wealth, but also its moral character and ethical foundation, without which capitalism itself cannot be sustained." To explain the moral character and ethical foundation of capitalism in the Chinese context, they continue, "A traditional Chinese moral precept, 'do not give up a good dead because it is trivial; do not commit a misconduct because it is trivial,' ostensibly contradicts the basic tenet of modern economics. ... This Chinese teaching focuses on an aspect of human nature that is largely ignored in modern economics; that our character is formed gradually and almost imperceptibly by what we do. ... Frank Knight made a valuable point in stressing that a society should be judged more by 'the new wants it generates, the type of character it forms in its people, than by its efficiency in satisfying wants as they exist at the time.' Modern economics takes as given the wants that the choice of resource allocation intends to satisfy and disregard the long-time cumulative impact that choice inevitably has on shaping the wants—it takes a snapshot view of a continuous process. But the economy both satisfies wants and simultaneously sows the seeds of new wants, which in turn drives the next round of economic production and consumption. Any action that promises short-term gains but has a corrupting effect on the moral character of the people dims the long-term future of the market economy."[6]

The ethical feature of Coase's economics is demonstrated most characteristically in his study of the market for ideas and a lifetime commitment to seeking truth in the market for economics ideas. His courage to go his own way and his conviction in the final triumph of truth revealed the courage of his conviction and show us the best way to defend a free market for ideas. Coase's (1991) Nobel lecture ends with the following: "A scholar must be content with the knowledge that what is false in what he says will soon be exposed and as for what is true, he can count on ultimately seeing it accepted, if only he lives long enough." The will to believe in truth, as Frank Knight (1947) told us, is "the foundation of all morality." A free market economy rests on ethical principles of personal autonomy and individual responsibility. The right of everyone to choose and pursue his ends and the duty of everyone to respect the same right in others have long and widely been appreciated as the moral foundation of a market economy. Equally important but far less recognized is the intellectual commitment to seeking truth as a crucial pillar in the moral foundation of a free society (Popper, 1946; Polanyi, 1951), the courage of everyone to express his ideas and pursue what he believes is truth, particularly when he is against the majority view, the obligation of everyone to encourage the same courage in others, and the humility to admit and the grace to come to terms with his ignorance and missteps.

5

Both law and the economy are human institutions; they are products and by-products, intended or not, of human mind and action, subject to human will and error. Their plasticity renders them a fertile field for us to exercise imagination and practice creativity, so long as we are wise enough to attend to the boundaries of what we know and what we can do. Good laws facilitate the working of the economy, the evolution of which induces legal change. The co-evolution of law and the economy makes them a joint human enterprise.

Law figures prominently in a market economy that rests on an extensive division and complex organization of labor and exchange. An open market economy, with a peaceful and bursting communal life, implies law and government of the highest order. Law as general rules, as opposed to customs and commands, and government ruled by law rather than by discretion are essential in establishing order among diversity, including economic order among competing interests. The fundamental role that law plays in the working of the market economy and the complex ways law, ethics, and the economy interact and counteract in co-evolution were appreciated by none other than Adam Smith, the founder of modern economics.[7]

Adam Smith meant the subject he helped to found to be a branch of what he called "the science of a legislator" (1976; see also Haakonssen, 1981), to be joined by ethics (Smith, 1978) and jurisprudence. Though his long-projected treatise on natural jurisprudence was left unfulfilled, Smith's lectures on the subject have survived in the form of student notes (Smith, 1982). In the lectures, Smith endeavored "to trace the gradual progress of jurisprudence, both public and private, from the rudest to the most refined ages, and to point out the effects of those arts which contribute to subsistence, and to the accumulation of property, in producing correspondent improvements or alterations in law and government" (John Stewart, quoted in "Introduction," Smith, 1982). Jurisprudence, which provides "the theory of the rules by which civil government ought to be directed" and shows "the foundation of the different systems of government in different countries" (Smith, 1982), instructs the legislator to govern in accord with natural liberty to allow the invisible hand to work its magic. Natural liberty works, as Smith (1976) emphasized, only in a "well-governed society" which justice is regularly and tolerably administered so that universal opulence "extends itself to the lowest ranks of the people." Natural liberty lasts only when the majority of the population actively participate in and benefit from the wealth it helps to create because "no society can surely be flourishing and happy, of which the far greater part of the members are poor and miserable" (Smith, 1976).

Most of his contemporaries read the *Wealth of Nations,* if read it at all, as a crude, unsophisticated, and imprecise formulation of price theory; their focus is placed squarely, if not exclusively, on what Smith called the "invisible hand." Coase saw in Smith's masterpiece an overwhelming emphasis the author consistently and systematically placed on "the appropriate institutional [and ethical] framework for the working of a pricing system" (Coase, 1977b). Such a framework is neither a derivation from timeless metaphysical foundations nor a deduction of universal abstract theories. Rather, it has to evolve out of historical experiences, full of uncertainty and contingency. The framework is inevitably imperfect, always leaves room for continuous innovation and improvement. Modern institutional economics, which, as envisioned by Coase (1984), "should study man as he is, acting within the constraints imposed by real institutions," and was hoped to be "economics as it ought to be, " continues the classical line of economics started by Smith. For Smith and Coase alike, the market economy is not, and cannot be, populated by atomized economic man, an imaginary species created by economists to work out their theoretical models. Were the atomistic picture true of the market economy, there would be nothing to talk about the institutional structure of production, let alone the legal system or ethics. Law and ethics are critical in fashioning and preserving economic order, exactly because a market economy is not a mechanical system of logic and calculation, but has to rely upon unruly human passion and unbounded human imagination.[8]

6

Coase (1960) is widely regarded as the beginning of economics of property rights and property law (e.g., Demsetz, 1967; Cheung, 1978; Barzel, 1997; Lueck and Miceli, 2007; see also Allen, 1998). For Coase, law is less an authoritarian program of delimiting or fixing rights once and for all than a common framework of reference based on which market order can emerge to coordinate competing interests. Coase did not take right as absolute or inviolable. At the end of "The Problem of Social Cost," he stressed that "a system in which the rights of individuals were unlimited would be one in which there were no rights to acquire." Nor did Coase believe that government infringement of rights must be denounced on an *a priori* basis. In a modern pluralistic society, rights are always subject to government intervention. Indeed, even if it is possible to keep government out, rights are inevitably constrained by each other. In a market economy, "balancing" or tradeoff of rights is not a choice, but an essential feature of social reality.

For this reason, Coase (1960) has often been criticized for sidestepping *in rem* rights (Merrill and Smith, 2001), for overlooking property as the law of things (Smith, 2012), for ignoring property as sequential exchange (Arrunada, 2017) and even charged for undermining private property institutions (Block, 2003). It would take us too afar to address such criticisms. A short defense is that Coase was an economist and he followed a conventional approach which he found helpful and adequate to expose Pigou's fallacy. For an institution as evolved as property and a concept as complex as right, it is unreasonable to expect any single piece of scholarship from an economist to provide a comprehensive treatment. It is certainly not fair to ask Coase to "bear the costs of the limitations in the development of the literature on property rights he spawned" (Lueck, 2017). *In rem* and *in personam* rights, while distinct analytically, can hardly be disjointed in practice. *In rem* property rights secure possession; *in personam* contractual rights maximizes its market value. For *in personam* rights to be of any value, *in rem* rights have to be respected to a sufficient degree. Without the "right to exclude," the "right to use" would be defenseless against any encroachment. Without the "right to use," the "right to exclude" would be less valuable.

The problem of sequential exchanges is common in any market economy where economic resources are valued differentially over time and among a plurality of economic actors and they change hands continually. Writing on the rise of market economy in China, Coase and Wang (2012) notes, "China did not first delineate property rights, specific other relevant institutional rules and then allow market forces to allocate rights to the highest bidder. Instead, what rights economic actors were allocated to have … and what institutional constraints they faced in exercising their rights were delineated when the state released the rights of control to private economic actors." This unconventional practice greatly speeded up the introduction of market competition into China to avoid the cost of delineating rights, which would be prohibitive at the time. In this way, as one reviewer points out, "The state followed the promptings of private business and did not have 'to get the rights right before their economic values were revealed in competition'" (Schwartz, 2014). Moreover, as Coase and Wang (2012) observed, when economic conditions change over time, the value of rights also alters, some rights gain and others lose relevance. In this process, the state "was thus frequently called in to revise and redefine the structure of rights." As a result, while China did not formally sanction *in rem* rights during the first two decades of market reform, *in personam* rights worked through free contracting and subcontracting to activate and take advantage of market competition.

As demonstrated in the Chinese case, Coase's law of the market has worked its magic. The Coasean emphasis on contractual or *in personam* rights, without challenging collective ownership head on at the outset, has proved surprisingly effective in introducing property rights and market forces into the Chinese economy in the early 1980s (e.g., Coase and Wang, 2012; Cheung, 2014). Only after a quarter century of market transformation, during which *in personam* rights had become widely appreciated, did formal *in rem* rights become ratified, with the passing of the Property Law of China in 2007, in which rights to private property are formally recognized for the first time in the history of the People's Republic of China.

7

Coasean law and economics, with its focus on the law's impact, direct or indirect, intended or not, on the working of the economy, sets us on a long-overdue search for appropriate institutional frameworks and ethical underpinnings that make a free market economy not just possible, but viable and resilient. The task has gained more urgency and become even more challenging in our rapidly globalizing economy. With the recent spread of market economies in Asia, Africa, Eastern Europe and Latin America over the past few decades, an unprecedented size of the world's population depends on the division and organization of labor and global trade for their prosperity. Market economies are taking root in societies with different cultures, histories, religions, and political systems. The common fate of humanity has never been so crucially dependent on our understanding of the market, both its unbounded transformative creativity and its inescapable limitations. The development of law and economics in these fledging markets and its continuous evolution in developed economies along the Coasean line require scholars to stand firm on the ground and away from "blackboard economics," engaging real-world problems, discovering and inventing theories that help them understand whatever questions they choose to tackle. For travelers on this long and challenging intellectual journey, *Coase on Law and Economics* will be cherished as a source of inspiration, ideas, and courage.

Notes

[1] At the first annual meeting of the American Law and Economics Association in 1991, Guido Calabresi, Ronald Coase, Henry Manne and Richard Posner were honored as the founders of the new discipline. In 2010, the board of the Association established the Ronald H. Coase Medal to recognize bi-annually major contributions to the field. Richard Posner was its first recipient, followed by Guido Calabresi in 2012.

[2] For his recent coming to terms with Coasean economics, see Posner (2011). After realizing that "Keynes's informal, unrigorous, largely unmathematized analysis of the macroeconomy has provided greater insight into our current economic situation than 75 years of increasingly formal, rigorous, mathematized analysis," Posner is able to appreciate Coase's "stubborn adherence to the illustrious tradition of what might be called commonsense economics."

[3] Knight later dropped this rather mechanic view. In the 1948 preface to *Risk, Uncertainty, and Profit*, Knight wrote that, "the correct picture of production is not that of a 'circular flow' but that of an inclusive organic complex of agents, human and non-human, which continuously maintains itself and yields in addition a return available for consumption or further investment" (Knight, 1964).

[4] These and several other fables of economics can be conveniently found in a collection put together by Daniel Spulber (2001).

[5] Moral reasoning, for example, otherwise quite similar and often deeply related to legal reasoning, does not shun away from made-up moral dilemmas to capture the complexity and intricacy involved in moral

decision-making. Actually, the best-known moral dilemmas are all conceived imaginary examples, such as the prisoner's dilemma, the trolley problem and Sophie's choice.

[6] The lack of personal and institutional trust has seriously inflicted the economy and society and has of late become a public outcry in China (e.g., Li, 1995; He, 2015).

[7] Adam Smith's legacy to the development of law and economics has attracted a fair amount of attention (see for example, MacCormick, 1981; Malloy and Evensky, 1994; Simon, 2013; Mahoney, 2017). Unfortunately, the discussions often take the economic analysis of law as the only way to practice law and economics and fail to notice the distinction between the Coasean law and economics and economic analysis of law (for few exceptions, see McCloskey, 1998; Medema, 2016).

[8] Otherwise, "the science of a legislator" as conceived by Smith would not make any sense. As stressed by Smith, "laws of justice" make a "well-governed state" possible; together they are conducive to and protective of a commercial society. Among contemporary economists, Hayek (1973, 1976, 1979) probably represents the most ambitious effort to restate the "principles of justice and political economy" and revive Smith's "science of a legislator." Efforts of the same spirit should include the Freiburg school of law and economics associated with Walter Eucken (e.g., Vanberg, 2001) and the research program of constitutional political economy (e.g., Brennan and Buchanan, 1985).

References

Alchian, Armen. 1967. *Pricing and Society.* Originally published by Institute of Economic Affairs (London), it can be found in *The Collected Works of Armen Alchian* (2000), Volume 2: Property rights and economic behavior. Indianapolis: Liberty Fund.

Allen, Douglass. 1998. Property rights, transaction costs, and Coase, in *Coasean Economics: Law and Economics and the New Institutional Economics*, edited by Steven G. Medema, pp. 105-118. New York: Kluwer Academic Publishers.

Angrist, Joshua and Jorn-Steffen Pischke. 2010. The credibility revolution in empirical economics: How better research design is taking the con out of econometrics. *Journal of Economic Perspective*, 24(2): 3-30.

Arrunada, Benito. 2017. Property as sequential exchange. *Journal of Institutional Economics,* 13(4): 753-783.

Barzel, Yoram. 1997. *Economic Analysis of Property Rights*. New York: Cambridge University Press.

Becker, Gary. 1976. *The Economic Approach to Human Behavior*. Chicago: University of Chicago Press.

Block, Walter. 2003. Private property rights, economic freedom and Professor Coase. *Harvard Journal of Law & Public Policy,* 26(3): 923-951.

Brennan, Geoffrey and James Buchanan. 1985. *The Reason of Rules*. New York: Cambridge University Press.

Calabresi, Guido. 1961. Some thoughts on risk distribution and the law of torts. *Yale Law Review,* 70 (4): 499-553.

Calabresi, Guido. 2016. *The Future of Law and Economics: Essays in Reform and Recollection*. Yale University Press.

Cheung, Steven NS. 1973. The fable of the bees: an economic investigation. *Journal of Law and Economics,* 16(1): 11-33.

Cheung, Steven NS. 1978. *The Myth of Social Cost.* London: Institute of Economic Affairs.

Cheung, Steven NS. 1992. On the new institutional economics. In *Contract Economics*, edited by L.Werin and H. Wijkander, Basil Blackwell, pp. 48-65.

Cheung, Steven NS. 2014. The economic system of China. *Man and the Economy,* 1(1): 65-113.

Cheung, Steven NS. 2017. *Economic Explanation.* Hong Kong: Arcadia Press.

Coase, Ronald H. 1959. The Federal Communications Commission, *Journal of Law and Economics,* 2(1): 1-40.

Coase, Ronald H. 1960. The problem of social cost, *Journal of Law and Economics,* 3(1): 1-44.

Coase, Ronald H. 1974. The market for goods and the market for ideas, *American Economic Review,* 64(2): 384-391.

Coase, Ronald H. 1974. The lighthouse in economics. *Journal of Law and Economics,* 17(2): 357-376.

Coase, Ronald H. 1977a. Advertising and free speech, *Journal of Legal Studies,* 6(1): 1-34.

Coase, Ronald H. 1977b. The wealth of nations. *Economic Inquiry,* 15(3): 309-325.

Coase, Ronald H. 1979. Payola in radio and television broadcasting, *Journal of Law and Economics,* 22(2): 269-328.

Coase, Ronald H. 1984. The new institutional economics. *Journal of Institutional and Theoretical Economics*, 140: 229-231.

Coase, Ronald H. 1988a. *The Firm, the Market, and the Law.* Chicago: University of Chicago Press.

Coase, Ronald H. 1988b. Blackmail, *Virginia Law Review,* 74(4): 655-676.

Coase, Ronald H. 1988c. The nature of the firm: Meaning. *Journal of Law, Economics and Organization*, 4: 19-32.

Coase, Ronald H. 1991. The Institutional structure of production. The Nobel Lecture. Reprinted in *Essays on Economics and Economists* (1994), Chicago: University of Chicago Press.

Coase, Ronald H. 1993. Law and economics at Chicago, *Journal of Law and Economics,* 36(1): 239-254.

Coase, Ronald H. 1996. Law and economics and A. W. Brian Simpson, *Journal of Legal Studies,* 25(1): 103-119.

Coase, Ronald H. 1998. Comment on Thomas W. Hazlett, assigning property rights to radio spectrum users: Why did FCC license auctions take 67 years? *Journal of Law and Economics,* 41(S2): 577-580.

Coase, Ronald H. 2006. The conduct of economics. *Journal of Economics & Management Strategy,* 15(2): 255-278.

Coase, Ronald H. 2014. Law and economics: A personal journey. *Man and the Economy,* 1(1): 23-32.

Coase, Ronald H. 2015. Testimony to the FCC, *Man and the Economy,* 2(1): 1-6.

Coase, Ronald H. 2017. The Federal Communications Commission and Broadcasting Industry, *Man and the Economy,* 4(1):1-21.

Coase, Ronald and Ning Wang. 2011. The industrial structure of production: A research agenda for innovation in an entrepreneurial Economy. *Entrepreneurship Research Journal,* 1(2): 1-13.

Coase, Ronald and Ning Wang. 2012. *How China Became Capitalist.* London: Palgrave Macmillan.

Coleman, James. 1990. *Foundations of Social Theory.* Cambridge: Harvard University Press.

Deaton, Angus and Nancy Cartwright. 2017. Understanding and misunderstanding randomized controlled trials. *Social Science & Medicine,* https://doi.org/10.1016/j.socscimed.2017.12.005.

Demsetz, Harold. 1967. Toward a theory of property rights. *American Economic Review,* 57(2): 347-359.

Farrell, Joseph. 2016. Some failures of the popular Coase Theorem. in *The Elgar Companion to Ronald H. Coase,* edited by Claude Menard and Elodie Bertrand. Edward Elgar, pp. 333-345.

Friedman, Milton. 1976. *Price Theory.* Chicago: Aldine.

Hayek, Friedrich A. 1937. Economics and knowledge. *Economica,* 4: 33-54.

Hayek, Friedrich A. 1973. *Law, Legislation and Liberty.* Volume 1: Rules and Order. Chicago: University of Chicago Press.

Hayek, Friedrich A. 1976. *Law, Legislation and Liberty.* Volume 2: The Mirage of Social Justice. Chicago: University of Chicago Press.

Hayek, Friedrich A. 1979. *Law, Legislation and Liberty.* Volume 3: The Political Order of a Free People. Chicago: University of Chicago Press.

Haakonssen, Knud. 1981. *The Science of a Legislator: The Natural Jurisprudence of David Hume and Adam Smith.* New York: Cambridge University Press.

He, Huaihong. 2015. *Social Ethics in a Changing China: Moral Decay or Ethical Awakening?* Washington, DC: Brookings Institution Press.

Knight, Frank. 1933. *The Economic Organization.* New York: Augustus M. Kelley.

Knight, Frank. 1935. *The Ethics of Competition and Other Essays.* London: G. Allen & Unwin.

Knight, Frank. 1947. *Freedom and Reform.* New York: Harper & Brothers.

Knight, Frank. 1964[1921]. *Risk, Uncertainty, and Profit.* New York: Augustus M. Kelley.

Leamer, Edward. 1983. Let's take the con out of econometrics. *American Economic Review,* 73(1): 31-43.

Li, Yining. 2015. *Beyond Market and Government: Influence of Ethical Factors on Economy.* Beijing: Springer and Foreign Language Teaching and Research Publishing Co.

Lueck, Dean. 2017. Property rights and the limits of Coase. *Journal of Institutional Economics,* 13(4): 793-800.

Lueck, Dean and Thomas Miceli. 2007. Property law, in *Handbook of Law and Economics,* edited by A. Mitchell Polinsky and Steven Shavell, New York: North-Holland. pp. 186-257.

MacCormick, Neil. 1981. Adam Smith on law, *Valparaiso University Law Review,* 15(2): 243-263.

Mahoney, Paul G. 2017. Adam Smith, prophet of law and economics. *Journal of Legal Studies,* 46(1): 207-236.

Malloy, Robin Paul and Jerry Evensky (eds.). 1994. *Adam Smith and the Philosophy of Law and Economics.* Kluwer Academic Publishers.

Marshall, Alfred. 1920 [1890]. *Principles of Political Economy.* London: Macmillan.

McCloskey, Deirdre. 1985. *The Applied Theory of Price.* New York: Macmillan.

McCloskey, Deirdre. 1998. The good old Coase Theorem and the good old Chicago School, in *Coasean Economics: Law and Economics and the New Institutional Economics,* edited by Steven G. Medema, pp. 239-248. New York: Kluwer Academic Publishers.

Medema, Steven. 2016. Ronald Coase and the legal-economic nexus, in *The Elgar Companion to Ronald H. Coase,* edited by Claude Menard and Elodie Bertrand. Cheltenham, UK: Edward Elgar, pp. 291-304.

Medema, Steven. 2017. The Coase theorem at sixty. Working Paper.

Merrill, Thomas and Henry Smith. 2001. What happened to property in law and economics? *Yale Law Journal,* 111(2): 357-398.

Noyes, C. Reinold. 1936. *The Institution of Property: A Study of the Development, Substance and Arrangement of the System of Property in Modern Anglo-American Law.* New York: Longmans, Green and Co.

Patinkin, Don. 1973. In search of the "wheel of wealth": On the origins of Frank Knight's circular-flow diagram. *American Economic Review,* 63(5): 1037-1046.

Polanyi, Michael. 1950. *The Logic of Liberty.* Chicago: University of Chicago Press.

Popper, Karl. 1946. *Open Society and Its Enemy.* London: Routledge.

Posner, Richard. 2003. *Economic Analysis of Law,* 6th edition. Aspen Publishers. The first edition was published in 1973, by Little, Brown and Company (Boston).

Posner, Richard. 2011. Keynes and Coase. *Journal of Law and Economics,* 54(4): 831-840.

Posner, Richard and Francesco Parisi (eds.). 2013. *The Coase Theorem.* Cheltenham, UK: Edward Elgar.

Robbins, Lionel. 1932. *An Essay on the Nature and Significance of Economic Science.* London: Macmillan.

Samuelson, Paul. 1948. *Economics.* New York: McGraw-Hill. (Its 19th edition was released in 2009, co-authored with William Nordhaus).

Schwartz, Pedro. 2014. Coase looks at China. *Policy,* 30(3): 8-12.

Schumpeter, Joseph. 1934. *The Theory of Economic Development.* Cambridge, MA: Harvard University Press.

Simon, Fabrizio. 2013. Adam Smith and the law, in *The Oxford Handbook of Adam Smith,* edited by Christopher Berry, Maria Pia Paganelli and Graig Smith. New York: Oxford University Press, pp. 393-416.

Smith, Adam. 1976. *The Wealth of Nations.* Chicago: University of Chicago Press.

Smith, Adam. 1978. *Lectures on Jurisprudence.* Indianapolis: Liberty Fund.

Smith, Adam. 1982. *The Theory of Moral Sentiments.* Indianapolis: Liberty Fund.

Smith, Henry. 2012. Property as the law of things. *Harvard Law Review,* 125(7): 1691-1726.

Spulber, Daniel. (ed.). 2001. *Famous Fables of Economics: Myths of Market Failures.* New York: Wiley.

Stigler, George. 1961. The economics of information. *Journal of Political Economy,* 69(3): 213-225.

Stigler, George. 1987. *The Theory of Price,* 4th edition. New York: Macmillan.

Vanberg, Viktor. 2001. *The Constitution of Markets.* New York: Routledge.

Series I

On the Problem of Social Cost

Ning Wang

The first and by far the largest series centers on "The Problem of Social Cost," Coase's most influential article. This article played a critical part in the rise of law and economics and helped Coase to win the 1991 Nobel Memorial Prize in Economics Sciences. Five other closely related articles are included: "The Federal Communications Commission and the Broadcasting Industry," "The Federal Communications Commission" "Testimony to the Federal Communications Commission" "Notes on the Problem of Social Cost," and "Comment on Thomas W. Hazlett: Assigning Property Rights to Radio Spectrum Users—Why Did FCC License Auctions Take 67 Years."

The first piece in the collection, "The Federal Communications Commission and the Broadcasting Industry," was a lecture Coase delivered in 1958 at the University of Virginia while he was still teaching at the University of Buffalo. Careful readers will discover there the seeds of the main arguments that he developed fully and forcefully later in "The Federal Communications

Commission." "Testimony to the Federal Communications Commission" was expert testimony Coase gave in 1959 to a government panel, in which he suggested that the United States government use the pricing mechanism to allocate radio spectrums. "Notes on the Problem of Social Cost" is an expository essay that Coase wrote in 1988 specifically for *The Firm, the Market, and the Law* (Coase, 1988a), the first collection of his articles, to address some of the most important criticisms that had been directed at the original paper and to explain the origin of and controversy over the so called "Coase Theorem," which has played a fundamental role in the birth and development of law and economics [see, for example, the two-volume collection edited by Posner and Parisi (2013), which runs more than twelve hundred pages. See also Medema (2017)]. The last piece in this group is a commentary in which Coase addressed some specific questions related to the FCC and, which is of more interest and importance, revealed some of his convictions about the limitations of reason in human affairs, whose significance has been ignored in modern economics to its peril.

Coase did not take the Coase Theorem, as formulated and popularized by George Stigler (1987[1961]) that "under perfect competition private and social costs will be equal," as the main message of his article on social cost. But he was reluctant to blame, let alone reproach, Stigler for misinterpretation, whom he admired greatly. Still, Coase made his position clear. "My aim ... was not to describe what life would be like in such a world [of zero transaction costs] but to provide a simple setting in which to develop the analysis and, what was even more important, to make clear the fundamental role which transaction costs do, and should, play in the fashioning of the institutions which make up the economic system" (Coase, 1988a). Coase (1991) took great length in his Nobel lecture to expound his view of the Coase Theorem. "I tend to regard the Coase Theorem as a stepping stone on the way to an analysis of an economy with positive transaction costs. The significance to me of the Coase Theorem is that it undermines the Pigovian system. Since standard economic theory assumes transaction costs to be zero, the Coase Theorem demonstrates that the Pigovian solutions are unnecessary in these circumstances. Of course, it does not imply, when transaction costs are positive, that government actions (such as government operation, regulation or taxation, including subsidies) could not produce a better result than relying on negotiations between individuals in the market. Whether this would be so could be discovered not by studying imaginary governments but what real governments actually do."

Once we get the Coase Theorem out of the way, Coase's original message becomes simple and straight. "If rights to perform certain actions can be bought and sold, they will tend to be acquired by those for whom they are most valuable" (Coase, 1988a). This may be called Coase's law of the market, a conclusion Coase reached through examples in "The Federal Communications Commission." "Whether a newly discovered cave belongs to the man who discovered it, the man on whose land the entrance to the cave is located, or the man who owns the surface under which the cave is situated is no doubt dependent on the law of property. But the law merely determines the person which whom it is necessary to make a contract to obtain the use of cave. Whether the cave is used for storing bank records, as a natural gas reservoir, or for growing mushrooms depends, not on the law of property, but on whether the bank, the natural gas corporation, or the mushroom concern will pay the most in order to be able to use the cave" (Coase 1959). Writing at a time when economic collectivism prevailed in various forms, Coase restored our confidence in the market. His law of the market places Smith's "invisible hand" on a simple and firm legal foundation.

"The Federal Communications Commission" was largely overshadowed, if not forgotten after the publication of "The Problem of Social Cost" and the formulation of the Coase Theorem. However, it is a tour-de-force of empirical work in modern social sciences, best exemplifying Coase's way of conducting economic research.[1] It investigates a well-specified real-life question. In the process, it navigates a deep sea of meticulous details and brings out penetrating insights which resolve the problem at hand and shed light on a wide range of seemingly unrelated issues. Its narrative is as captivating as a Sherlock Holmes story, and its conclusion, while unexpected and even counter-intuitive at first sight, is so firmly and systematically reasoned that once it is understood, it falls into the category of truths that can be deemed self-evident. That *The Firm, the Market, and the Law* contains only one empirical article, "The Lighthouse in Economics," the others all being theoretical in nature, conceals from readers Coase's devotion to empirical studies and his unique style and craftsmanship as an empirical economist. Coase is by no means a usual empiricist preoccupied with technicalities, such as endogeneity or instrumental variables, but one whose empirical investigation always engages, enriches, and enlightens basic economic theories. Containing "The Federal Communications Commission" and other empirical papers, the present volume helps to bring to readers the empirical side of Coase's scholarship.

---

[1] Coase's characteristic case method was first developed in his study of public utilities in Britain, a subject he was asked to teach after he joined LSE in 1935 as an assistant lecturer in economics. His book-length investigation of the British Broadcasting Corporation (Coase, 1950) started his interest in the political economy of broadcasting, which led him to study the Federal Communications Commission after he migrated to the United States.

The Federal Communications Commission and the Broadcasting Industry[*]

I am sure I do not have to remind this audience that to an Englishman there is a magic about the name of Virginia. It is therefore a great pleasure for me to have the honor of speaking in the University of Virginia during the inaugural year of the Thomas Jefferson Center for the Study of Political Economy. But my feelings do not arise simply from a feeling of kinship. With the formation of this Center we may indeed be participating in the rebirth of political economy. That this should happen in Virginia is singularly appropriate; for Virginia played a part in the birth of political economy. The first political economy club in the English-speaking world, that founded by Andrew Cochrane in the 1740s in Glasgow, which Adam Smith later joined and from the deliberations of which he drew much information and probably some of his doctrines, was composed to a large extent of Virginia merchants. They were engaged in the tobacco trade, owned plantations and had extensive interests in wholesale and retail trade in Virginia.

It is therefore fitting that political economy should be given its second chance in Virginia, where, as a glance around this campus will confirm, the eighteenth century has lasted rather longer than in the rest of the world. But there are other features which

---

[*] *Man and the Economy*, 2017, 4(1). This was an invited lecture Professor Coase delivered in spring 1958 at the Thomas Jefferson Center for Studies of Political Economy at the University of Virginia, while he was still on the faculty of the University of Buffalo. The powerful ideas later developed in his well-known FCC and social cost articles can be found here as an unpolished gem. We thank the Coase Society for the permission to publish the lecture notes for the first time. All footnotes are added by the editor.

strengthen one's sense of the historical appropriateness of the occasion. It is, I think, of interest that Glasgow, which was to play such an important part in the development of our subject, had, in the middle of the eighteenth century, approximately the same population as Charlottesville now. One of those Virginia merchants, as you would expect, was named Buchanan. He owned tobacco plantations and when, through his grounds in Glasgow, he opened an avenue for gentlemen's houses, he named it Virginia Street and the town house he planned he called Virginia Mansion. Along with his brothers he founded the Buchanan Society for the assistance of apprentices, a sort of eighteenth century fellowship program. The Society also had the task of supporting widows with the name of Buchanan, which must have made Buchanans more attractive as husbands, although not for long.

This Buchanan should not be confused with Professor James Buchanan, who was, of course, a colleague of Adam Smith's at the University of Glasgow. Their association together and the honor they brought to Glasgow was hailed in a poem published in 1783, on which I quote you one verse:

Here great Buchanan learnt to scan
The verse that makes him mair than man!
Cullen and Hunter here began
Their first probation;
And Smith frae Glasgow form'd his plan,
"The Wealth o' Nations!"

It will not come as a surprise to you to lean that when Ricardo came to study Adam Smith, it was Buchanan's edition that he used. This was another Buchanan, David, who was, naturally enough, an expert in public finance. After this the Buchanans seem to have adopted the sanguine but incorrect view that the subject had been successfully launched and could now get on without them, with what dire consequences we all know. You can therefore imagine my relief when I learnt that a Buchanan was to be the first Director of the Thomas Jefferson Center. All in all, I cannot believe that any institution ever started with more favorable omens than this Center.

I am, as you know, engaged in a study of the political economy of radio and television, a study which is being financed by the Ford Foundation. In this connection, the Foundation has asked me, when acknowledging the assistance that they are rendering, to state that they do not necessarily agree with any views which I may express. For the sake of completeness I would like to add that I do not necessarily agree with the views of the Ford Foundation. Incidentally, if you look at that part of the Annual Report of the Foundation which mentions my study, you will find that the fine old term political economy has been put within quotation marks as if to indicate that it is a term no longer used in polite society. This disavowing of the name is I think symptomatic of what has happened to the subject and serves to show that when I spoke of this Center as bringing about a rebirth of political economy, I was not indulging in an undue exaggeration.

It had not originally been my intention to speak about the Federal Communications Commission since the detailed study of the Commission is something I will be taking up later in my investigations. But recent events in Washington have focused our attention on the work (if such it can be called) of the Commission and I thought you might be interested in some preliminary views which I have formed even though further study will no doubt bring some important modifications.

The first thing that needs to be realized about the Federal Communications Commission is that it is a very extraordinary institution, particularly so because it is found here in the United States. It is a body set up and run by the Federal Government to regulate an industry which disseminates news and opinion. It is therefore an organization whose very existence runs counter to our notions of freedom of the press. Yet, and this is a paradoxical situation, support for the work of the FCC is widespread in the United States among students of public affairs, and not least among those who are most vigilant in their defense of personal freedom and civil liberties. Indeed, I think it would not be untrue to say that those who are most active in supporting free speech and freedom of the press are particularly prone to argue that the powers of the FCC to regulate the radio be more consistently and more vigorously exercised. We are often told of the evils of Government censorship and of the need to resist encroachments on our freedoms. I quote a recent statement of this point of view:

> The Orwellian super-state of 1984 is the veritable censor's paradise. Yet it is not only extreme totalitarianism that Orwell's nightmare allegorizes. 1984 is the extreme case; but there certainly are varying degrees of a similar tendency present in the world of today. It may be that the censorship of our time will never attain the extent of intensity which Orwell foresaw. The way to ensure that is, however, by constantly struggling against extensions of the censor's domain, while we are able effectively to do so. It will be too late to begin the struggle in 1984.[1]

These obviously true words were written in 1953 by Professor Bernard Schwartz of the New York University School of Law, who has recently devoted himself, beyond the call of duty, to the task of improving the efficiency with which the FCC carries out its regulation of the radio and television industries.

The peculiarity of the position occupied by those who support the policies of the FCC is immediately apparent if we think of what the reaction would be if the same policies accepted as proper for the radio and television industries were applied to books, newspapers and periodicals. Government regulation of radio and television to make sure that there is a fair representation of the various points of view is accepted without misgiving. But a proposal that the Government should be allowed to regulate newspapers to promote a more balanced presentation of the various points of view would certainly encounter fierce opposition. An attempt to stop newspapers from editorializing would hardly be taken seriously; although this was the rule in radio and television until comparatively recently and editorializing is still only possible under restrictions. Suppose that it was suggested that a newspaper which had published certain opinions (whether expressed by the newspaper as such or in the form of reports) should be compelled to give equal space in a subsequent issue to those holding a contrary point of view on the same topic. Do you think that such a proposal would be accepted, although something like this is the rule for radio and television? Or assume that it was proposed that some Government authority should be given power to decide for every community in the United States which persons were fit to publish a newspaper. We can be sure that such a proposal would be rejected in short order. Yet this is what is done in the case of radio and television. It is quite clear that there is a greater abridgment of freedom of operation in the case of radio and television than there is in case of books, newspapers and periodicals.

This difference in policy may be due to technical considerations but I think there is something more involved. Professor Chafee has pointed out that the newer media of communications have been made subject to a stricter control than the old. This is what he says: "Newspapers, books, pamphlets, and large meetings were for many centuries the only means of public discussion, so that the need for their protection had long been generally realized. On the other hand, when additional methods for spreading facts and ideas were introduced or greatly improved by modern inventions, writers and judges had not got into the habit of being solicitous about guarding their freedom. And so we have tolerated censorship of the mails, the importation of foreign books, the stage, the motion picture, and the radio."[2] And in Britain, the form of organization which was imposed until recently on radio and television, with its high degree of centralized control, was not due to technical considerations but was due to the acceptance of an authoritarian political philosophy. I have little doubt that, had radio been invented in the fifteenth century and the printing press in the twentieth, we should now have in Great Britain a privately owned radio system and a British Press Corporation with a monopoly of the publication of books, newspapers and periodicals, while in the United States we should have a free radio and television system and a press regulated by the Federal Press Commission. Perhaps I exaggerate; but I wonder if I do.

But now let us look at the technical considerations which have led many to think of radio and television as requiring very special treatment. In transmitting radio and television signals, use is made of wavelengths or frequencies (need I say that quite literally I don't know what I am talking about). A station cannot transmit a signal without using a frequency and this denies its use to some other station. This fact is usually considered to make it necessary to have some Government regulation of the radio and television industry. I will give as an example of this point of view (I would add, the dominant point of view) the following extract from an opinion of Justice Frankfurter, speaking for the majority of the Supreme Court, in one of the leading cases on radio law:

> The plight into which radio fell prior to 1927 was attributable to certain basic facts about radio as a means of communication that its facilities are limited; they are not available to all who may wish to use them; the radio spectrum simply is not large enough to accommodate everybody. There is a fixed natural number of stations that can operate without interfering with one another. Regulation of radio was therefore as vital to its development as traffic control was to the development of the automobile. In enacting the Radio Act of 1927, the first comprehensive scheme of control over radio communication, Congress acted upon the knowledge that if the potentialities of radio were not to be wasted, regulation was essential.[3]

The events which preceded Government regulation have been described very vividly by Professor Charles A. Siepmann, a, perhaps the, leading authority in the United States on the social aspects of radio and television:

> The chaos that developed as more and more enthusiastic pioneers entered the field of radio was indescribable. Amateurs crossed signals with professional broadcasters. Many of the professionals broadcast on the same wavelength and either came to a gentleman's agreement to divide the hours of broadcasting or blithely set about cutting one another's throats by broadcasting simultaneously. Listeners thus experienced the annoyance of trying to hear one program against the raucous background of another.

Ship-to-shore communication in Morse code added its pulsing dots and dashes to the silly symphony of sound.

Professor Siepmann sums up the situation in the following words: "Private enterprise, over seven long years, failed to set its own house in order. Cutthroat competition at once retarded radio's orderly development and subject listeners to intolerable strain and inconvenience."[4]

Notwithstanding the general acceptance of these arguments and the eminence of the authorities who expound them, it is my opinion that such views as I have quoted to you exhibit a certain confusion of thought. Had these gentlemen been more familiar with economics, they would have realized that for a resource to be limited in quantity and scarce, in that people would like to use more of it than exists, is true not simply of radio and television frequencies but of almost all resources used in the economic system. Land, Labor and Capital are all scarce but this, of itself, does not call for Government regulation. It is true that some mechanism has to be employed to decide who, out of the many claimants, should be allowed to use the scarce resource. But the mechanism usually employed is the price mechanism and this allocates resources to users without the need for Government regulation. What has to be shown is that the price mechanism would work so badly in allocating radio and television frequencies that Government regulation would be preferable. But the case for Government regulation has appeared to be so self-evident that it has not seemed necessary to examine this possibility at all seriously.

Professor Siepmann seems to ascribe the confusion which existed before Government regulation to a failure of private enterprise and the competitive system. But the real cause of the trouble was that no property rights were created in these scarce frequencies. We know from our ordinary experience that land can be allocated to land users without the need for Government regulation, by using the price mechanism. But if no property rights were created in hand, so that everyone could use a tract of land and there were no exclusive rights to the land, it is clear that there would be considerable confusion and that the price mechanism could not work because there would not be any property rights that could be acquired. If one person could use land for growing a crop and then another person could come along and build a house on the land used for the crop and the anther could come along, tear down the house and build his own, confusion would be too mild a word to describe what would be likely to ensure. This problem is normally solved by creating property rights in resources and then someone wishing to use a resource has to pay the owner to obtain it. Confusion disappears; and so does the Government except that a legal system to define property rights, interpret contracts and arbitrate dispute is, of course, necessary. But there is no need for Government regulation of the type described by Justice Frankfurter and Professor Siepmann and which we find in operation in the case of the American radio and television industry.

Let us consider how we might use the price mechanism to allocate television frequencies. The obvious course would be for the Federal Communications Commission, or whoever was appointed by the Government as the custodian of frequencies, to sell or lease frequencies to the highest bidder. Actually, with the law as it is, it would seem that leasing would be the only possible course since it is specifically provided in the Communications Act of 1934 that there shall be no private ownership of frequencies (or channels as they are described in the Act). Ownership of these frequencies is vested in the Government of the United States. But even without repealing this provision, it would appear that it would be possible to lease frequencies to the highest bidder. Use of the frequencies would then be determined by the price mechanism.

But this is not the way things are done. And since the allocation of frequencies is not to be done by means of the price mechanism, the FCC has had to devise other criteria. The position was described by Justice Frankfurter in that opinion from which I have already read you an extract:

> ...we are asked to regard the Commission as a kind of traffic officer, policing the wave lengths to prevent stations from interfering with each other. But the Act does

not restrict the Commission merely to the supervision of traffic. It puts upon the Commission the burden of determining the composition of that traffic. The facilities of radio are not large enough to accommodate all who wish to use them. Methods must be devised for choosing from among the many who apply. And since Congress itself could not do this, it committed the task to the Commission. The Commission was, however, not left at large in performing this duty. The touchstone provided by Congress was the "public interest, convenience or necessity" ...The facilities of radio are limited and therefore precious; they cannot be left to wasteful use without detriment to the public interest ...The Commission's licensing function cannot be discharged, therefore, merely by finding that there are no technological objections to the granting of a license. If the criterion of "public interest" were limited to such matters, how could the Commission choose between two applicants for the same facilities, each of whom is financially and technically qualified to operate a station? Since the very inception of federal regulation of radio, comparative considerations as to the services to be rendered have governed the application of the standard of "public interest, convenience or necessity."[5]

What has been established in the United States is a system in which power to control the service provided by radio and television stations is vested, in the last analysis, in the Federal Government. One commentator has described the position as it had been reached by 1946: "The Commission had travelled far from its original role of airwaves traffic policeman. Control over radio had become more than regulation based on technological necessity; it had become regulation of conduct, and the basis was but emerging."[6] It is, I think, clear that the ability of the Government to choose those who can use radio and television frequencies on the basis of their actual or proposed programs poses a potential threat to free speech and to the doctrine of freedom of the press in its application to radio and television.

Justice Frankfurter spoke, in the opinion that I have just quoted, of the phrase "public interest, convenience or necessity" as a "touchstone" provided for the Commission.

But this is an extremely vague phrase and whatever meaning the phrase may have acquired so far as the radio and television industries are concerned it is only to be discovered from a study of the actions of the Commission itself. A recent Chairman of the Commission explained the factors which influence the Commissioners in choosing between applicants for frequencies. "Proposed programming and policies, local ownership, integration of ownership and management, participation in civic activities, record of past broadcast performance, broadcast experience, relative likelihood of effectuation of proposals as shown by the contacts made with local groups and similar efforts, carefulness of operational planning for television, staffing, diversification of the background of the persons controlling, diversification of control of the mediums of mass communications."[7] This is not, of course, a complete list of all the factors which influence the Commissioners. Furthermore, since these criteria are almost certain to conflict, it is never easy to say what factors were of crucial importance in influencing Commissioners in making their decisions (as is evident from the examination of the procedure in the recent Miami Channel 10 case). But the whole procedure, which involves choosing between applicants on the basis, among other things, of their programming promises and records, is clearly a dangerous one. And this is particularly so because the control exercised by the FCC can in fact extend from radio and television to the press itself. For example, when the applicant for a radio or television license is a newspaper owner, the editorial policy of the newspaper becomes a factor which the Commission may take into account. And if the grant of a license is much desired (and often it is), then a wish to accommodate the FCC may well lead to a very real abridgment of the freedom of the press in its original sense.

These consequences were more or less inevitable once it was decided to make these frequencies (or channels) public property. It is most improbable that a Government which has to distribute any resource will simply be guided by market forces and will not attempt to serve some social purposes, purposes, that is, favored by the political organization. But the decision not to charge for frequencies made it certain that the Government would have to choose among the applicants for frequencies on some other basis. The desire to preserve Government ownership of the frequencies plus the unwillingness to require any payment for the use of these frequencies has had results which one might have thought would have annoyed those who favored public control of radio and television. A station operator who is granted a license to use a particular frequency in a particular place may in fact be granted a very valuable right, one for which he would be willing to pay a large sum of money. But he is not asked to pay anything. As part of a scheme designed to avoid a "giveaway" of public property, it has been quite acceptable to include a "giveaway" of the use of public property. It would require a very detailed investigation to determine the extent to which private operators of radio and television stations have been enriched as a result of this policy. But part of the extremely high return on the capital invested in some radio and television stations has been due to this factor. And occasionally one gets an idea of what may be involved when a station is sold. Strictly, of course, all that can be sold is the station and its organization; the frequency as you know is public property and the grant of a license gives no rights of any sort in that frequency. Furthermore, transfers of ownership of radio and television stations have to be approved by the FCC. However, the FCC almost always approves such negotiated transfers and when these take place there can be little doubt that usually the greater part of the purchase price of the station is in fact payment for the use of the frequency. Thus, when a few weeks ago station WATV in New Jersey was sold for over $ 3 million, I feel quite sure that it would have been possible to duplicate the transmitter and studio equipment and furniture of WATV for considerably less than $ 3 million. The difference would be payment for the use of the frequency. That this sort of thing happens is well known and is often referred to in the literature. But I have often wondered why this feature of the present-day allocation scheme has not been made the subject of more vigorous criticism. Could it be that many of those who dislike this feature also realize that if the Government once began to charge for the use of frequencies, the case for the existing public control of radio and television would be considerably weakened?

Just how sensitive people are to a suggestion that users of frequencies should pay for them can be gauged from the way in which a proposal that radio and television licensees should pay a fee to cover the costs of the licensing process (that is, the costs of the FCC) was treated. Very quickly the Senate Committee on Interstate and Foreign Commerce adopted a resolution suggesting that the FCC should suspend consideration of this proposal since "the proposal for license fees for broadcasting stations raises basic questions with regard to the fundamental philosophy of regulation under the Communications Act." Since then the proposal has remained in abeyance. The Senate Committee resolution to which I referred was passed in March, 1954. Of course, the recent investigation into the Federal Communications Commission and also that into the proposal for pay television has led a number of people to raise the possibility of there being a charge for frequencies. Earlier this year during a Congressional enquiry, Mr. Frank Stanton, President of CBS, was asked his opinion of such a proposal. Mr. Stanton, as you know, is one of the best informed men in the industry and his reply was masterly. This is what he said: "This is a novel theory and one to which I have not addressed myself during my operating career."[8] After this, there was little the Congressmen could do except to pass on to some other subject. The trade paper, "Broadcasting," did not display the same wisdom and in an issue just two months ago, commented on the proposal. This is what "Broadcasting" said: "In the TV field, lip service is given to a proposal that television 'franchises' be awarded to the 'highest bidder' among those who may be qualified. This is ridiculous on its face, since it would mean that choice outlets in prime markets would go to those with the most money."[9] It is not easy to know what to say about a statement which both misunderstands and rejects a market economy, the basis of the American economic system and that by which newspapers and periodicals, including "Broadcasting", are now published. However, I must observe that resources do not go, in our economic system, to those with the most money but to those who are willing to pay the most for them. The result is that in the struggle for particular resources, men who earn $ 5,000 a year are every day outbidding those who earn $ 50,000 a year. The same system which enables a man with $ 1 million to obtain a $ 1 million's worth of resources enables a man with $ 1,000 to obtain a $ 1,000's worth of resources. The reason why many firms would not wish to invest their funds in radio and television is simply that they could use them more efficiently elsewhere. But just as the distribution of expenditure by an individual business is not arbitrary but is based on the profitability of different lines of expenditure so the distribution of funds between businesses is not fixed by the stars but is determined by the efficiency with which businesses use their funds. Those who use funds profitably find it easy to get more; those who do not find it difficult. A private enterprise market economy is not really so ridiculous or the case for Socialism so strong as the comment in "Broadcasting" would seem to suggest. Furthermore, I would ask you not to be misled by romantic notions simply because so many choice outlets in prime markets have been awarded by the FCC to little fellows like the Radio Corporation of America or the Columbia Broadcasting System, not to mention National Airlines.

I should perhaps add that I do not mean to suggest that some Government action may not be necessary to prevent monopoly. I think it may well be the case that action should be taken to curb newspaper ownership of radio and television stations in certain cases. And perhaps there should be some control exercised over the relations of the networks to their affiliates. I haven't made any investigation of this question, but it would seem to me that what we are faced with here is simply a special case of the general antitrust problem. However, what has been brought about in the case of the radio and television industries is a situation in which the antitrust law actually applied is not simply the law on the statute book but also, and more importantly, a law invented by the FCC itself. The Commission explained the position in 1941 in the following words: "While many of the network practices raise serious question under the anti trust laws, our jurisdiction does not depend on showing that they do in fact constitute a violation of the antitrust laws. It is not our function to apply the antitrust laws as such. It is our duty, however, to refuse licenses or renewals to any person who engages or proposes to engage in practices which will prevent either himself or other licensees or both from making the fullest use of radio facilities."[10] I have not given this problem any close thought but the question I think can be raised of whether it is desirable to have a special antitrust law for the radio and television industry, particularly one which arises from the deliberations of an independent administrative agency.

The FCC has, up to the present, been rather cautious in its regulation of the radio and television services. Some stations have certainly been denied renewal of their licenses. But there have been very few such cases. There have, of course, been a vast number of cases in which applicants for licenses have been denied the facilities because they were granted to someone else. But I have no knowledge of what the overall effect has been on the service provided. My impression is that the unwillingness of the Commission to deny a renewal of the license, once it has been granted, has led to a crystallizing of the status quo. I think it likely that the use of frequencies is very different from what it would have been had the alternative of leasing frequencies to the highest bidder been adopted by the FCC. Certainly the history of subscription television would have been very different if bidding for frequencies had been allowed since we should have had a trial of the system by now. But it is not easy to say what the overall effect of the FCC's policy has been. To do so, it would be necessary actually to possess that knowledge which the planners claim to have.

I should mention two major attempts on the part of the FCC to influence program content. The first was the *Mayflower* decision of 1941 which forbade operators of radio stations to editorialize.[11] This was later modified by the Report on Editorializing of 1949 which allowed editorializing but subject to the criterion of "overall fairness."[12] I think you will be interested in the statement by the majority of the Commission on the nature of the regulation which they exercised, at that time, over the radio industry. "Any regulation of radio, especially a system of limited licenses, is in a real sense an abridgement of the inherent freedom of persons to express themselves by means of radio communication. It is, however, a necessary and constitutional abridgement in order to prevent chaotic interference from destroying ... this medium ... The most significant meaning of freedom of the radio is the right of the American people to listen free from any governmental dictation as to what they can or cannot hear and free alike from similar restraints by private licensees."[13] A literal interpretation of this passage might lead us to conclude that the regulation of radio programs in the United States had been placed in the hands of some heavenly power, since clearly someone has to decide what should be transmitted. But as the Commission also maintains "that freedom of speech can best be protected in radio by effective government controls, and that these controls are but a means by which to secure a more effective freedom," this is probably not a correct interpretation.

The second attempt to influence program content came with the issue in 1946 of the so-called "Blue Book," entitled *Public Service Responsibilities of Broadcast Licensees*. This document set out programming principles which operators of radio stations ought to follow.

> In issuing and in reviewing the licenses of broadcast stations the Commission proposes to give particular consideration to four program service factors relevant to the public interest. These are: (1)the carrying of sustaining programs, including network sustaining programs, with particular reference to the retention by licensees of a proper discretion and responsibility for maintaining a well-balanced program structure, (2)the carrying of local live programs, (3)the carrying of programs devoted to the discussion of public issues, (4) the elimination of advertising excesses.

In the case of sustaining programs, it was suggested that they should be used with a view to "(a) maintaining an overall program balance, (b)providing time for programs inappropriate for sponsorship, (c)providing time for programs serving particular minority tastes and interests, (d)providing time for nonprofit organizations, religious, civic, agricultural, labor, educational etc., and (e)providing time for experiment and for unfettered artistic self-expression."

It is a question how effective such statements of policy have been in influencing the behavior of station operators. Opinions differ on the subject. Personally, I would be inclined to guess that the effect has not been great. But I have been assured by people in the industry that the wishes of the FCC are given great weight and I may be wrong in this. Certainly the complete compliance of the industry to the *Mayflower* decision may be cited as evidence of the effectiveness of the Commission's decisions.

I should now like to draw your attention to a discussion of this subject which took place in the *University of Chicago Law Review* a few years ago. In 1951, a suggestion was made in a comment by a student-author, Mr. Leo Herzel, for a change in the FCC's methods of allocating frequencies.[14] In brief, Mr. Herzel proposed that frequencies should be leased to the highest bidder, thus allowing private enterprise to operate in the radio and television industry without the kind of Government regulation to which it is now subject. As useful as the original article and perhaps more so, was the fact that it led to a reply by Professor Dallas Smythe, Professor of Economics at the University of Illinois and formerly chief economist of the Federal Communications Commission.

Professor Dallas Smythe opened with a general reproof to Mr Herzel.[15] Professor Smythe thought that Mr. Herzel's comment "offers a graphic illustration of the hazards of applying in sweeping fashion a general body of economic theory for an industry whose facts do not conform to the premises of the theory." He added: "The public importance of the issues is too great for the matter to be dropped at this point, and a thoughtful review of the facts and logic of the Comment seems useful." This "thoughtful review" was presumably to be provided by Professor Smythe's article.

First of all, Professor Smythe pointed out that commercial broadcasting is not a "dominant user of spectrum space" but "a minor claimant on it." He noted use of this spectrum space (whatever it is) by the military, law enforcement agencies, fire fighting authorities, the Weather Bureau, the Forestry Service, and the radio amateurs, the "hams," adding, "the last of which by definition could hardly be expected to pay for frequency use." I found this last comment rather confusing. I gather that Professor Smythe thinks an amateur is someone who doesn't pay for the things he uses. But maybe this is the modern definition.

Professor Smythe went on to point out that there were many commercial users other than broadcasters. There were the common carriers, radio-telegraph and radio-telephone, transportation agencies, vessels on the higher seas, railroads, street railways, buses, trucks, harbor craft and taxis. Then there are various specialized users, such as electric power, gas and water concerns, the oil industry (which uses radio waves for communication and also for geophysical exploration), the motion picture industry (for work on location), and so on. Professor Smythe commented: "Surely it is not seriously intended that the noncommercial radio users (such as police), the non-broadcast common carriers (such as radio-telegraph) and the non-broadcast commercial users (such as the oil industry) should compete with dollar bids against the broadcast users for channel allocations."

I'm afraid the effect on me of this account of the myriad uses of radio waves was rather different from what Professor Smythe intended. When I learned that the FCC had undertaken the task of deciding whether it was more important that a particular frequency should be used by the police, or for a radio-telephone, or for a taxi-service, for by an oil company for geophysical exploration, or by a motion picture company to keep in touch with a film star, I could not but feel certain that the allocation would be better if they made use of the price mechanism. I have rarely come across a stronger case. The allocation of the steel output of the country among the various users without the use of the price mechanism would seem as easy to perform as the task which the FCC has set itself. In the circumstances, I found Mr. Herzel's rejoinder on this point extremely mild.[16]

He pointed out that these various users of radio waves "compete for all other kinds of equipment or else they don't get them."

That the present system of allocating frequencies is subject to the kinds of inefficiencies that one would expect to find in a Government allocation scheme of this kind seems clear. One often hears of the strain on the staff of the FCC. And decisions on policy come only after long delays, if at all. Occasionally one gets a glimpse of what is going on, as, for example, in a speech made last year by a gentleman who bears a name which will live in glory long after the problems of the FCC have been forgotten. I am, of course, referring to Commissioner Robert E. Lee. Commissioner Lee said that the question of an allocation study of assignments below 890mc was being pondered, but whether this would be undertaken was still uncertain. "There is considerable discussion of such a move within and without the Commission. The examination of the more crowded spectrum below 890mc presents an extremely difficult administrative problem. While this should be no excuse, I hope that all will appreciate the limitations of our overburdened staff which, as a practical matter, must be given great weight."[17] And then, after referring to a possible change in the method of allocation, he added: "I am finding it increasingly difficult to explain why a steel company in a large community, desperate for additional frequency space cannot use a frequency assigned, let us say, to the forest service in an area where there are no trees."

In the exchange to which I have been referring, Mr. Herzel also dealt with another strand of thought which seemed to be involved in Professor Smythe's argument, namely that we wouldn't wish to have the police, or fire fighting organizations, or the military compete with other users for these scarce frequencies. Mr. Herzel commented: "If the illusory comfort of free service to government is considered essential, then it would still be possible to treat differently the broadcasting and other segments of the radio spectrum. The result would be that the Government would be saved from the self-knowledge of what such services cost and, unlike other consumers, would not have to decide whether they were really worth it in comparison with available substitutes."

But Professor Smythe introduced an argument of quite a different character to suggest that the price mechanism is an inappropriate method of allocation to use in the case of radio and television. "A second broad postulate which seems to underlie proposals such as that advanced in the Comment is politico-economic in nature; that the public weal will be served if broadcasting, like grocery stores, used the conventional business organization, subject only to general legal restraints on its profit-seeking activity. This postulate carries with it, usually, the parallel assumption that the educational and cultural responsibilities of broadcast station operators ought to be no more substantial at the most than those of operators of newspapers and magazines. The author of the Comment does accept the former of these assumptions but he neither avows nor disavows the latter assumption. The acceptance or rejection of these twin assumptions by an individual is ultimately a matter of taste ...Despite the extensive use made of these two assumptions by business organizations for propaganda purposes, there is a powerful tradition in the United States that the economic, educational and cultural rights and responsibilities of broadcasting are unique."[18]

In this extract, Professor Smythe revealed that his objection to the use of the price mechanism for allocation of radio and television frequencies was in part due to the fact that it would make it more difficult to impose educational and cultural responsibilities on the operators of radio and television stations; in short, that it would make more difficult Government regulation of the operation of radio and television stations. This is a long step from the doctrine of the freedom of the press. Professor Smythe made this clear when he indicated that he thought that regulation of radio and television stations ought to go further than regulation of the press. The responsibilities of the operators of broadcasting stations are, according to Professor Smythe, unique. But what really is the difference between broadcasting and the press? Merely, as I suggested earlier, that the Press came into existence before the century of the common man, that broadcasting has always been regulated and that we are used to the idea. It is, I think, a measure of the unfamiliarity of people in the industry with the idea that there might be a charge for frequencies that the *Journal of the Federal Communications Bar Association*, commenting on the exchange between Mr. Herzel and Professor Smythe, said that this discussion would "be above the heads of most readers."[19]

However, I would not wish to leave you with the impression that I would advocate a substitution here and now of a system under which frequencies were allocated by means of the price mechanism for the one which we now have. There are a number of factors about which I would like to have more information or to which I would like to give more thought before coming to a final conclusion, much as I would like that conclusion to be that no special Government regulation is necessary.

First of all, there are the international aspects. The use of frequencies is not something which can be confined within national boundaries. Use of a frequency within a country does not only deny it to others in that country but also to others outside that country. The allocation has to be on an international basis. This is certainly true in Europe and applies also to the Americas. It is possible to imagine an international auction of frequencies with the nationals of the various countries bidding for the frequencies (or the countries bidding on behalf of their nationals), with the proceeds being divided up among the countries in some pre-determined way. But it would be quite unrealistic to suppose that there could be any international agreement at the present time on such a procedure. It will not come as a surprise to you to learn that the arguments which have been so successful in obstructing the use of the price mechanism in the United States are even more widely believed outside the United States. So I think we have to accept the fact that there will be an international allocating machinery which will not use the price mechanism.

It also needs to be taken into account that the international allocating machinery is likely to assign certain frequencies for use in particular ways and this, although it need not prevent the use of the price mechanism altogether, will at any rate limit the scope of its use. An additional factor is that use of the price mechanism might well reduce the bargaining power of a country in its international negotiations. Consider which of the following arguments would be most likely to persuade an international conference. This one: "Our country is gravely handicapped by lack of frequencies. Ours is a narrow, mountainous country, whose people speak three languages, who are poor and derive much of their entertainment from the radio, and, being unable to read, can only learn about the many beneficient policies carried out on their behalf by the Government if they can listen to the radio." Or this: "We are not too sure what this frequency is used for but it certainly sells at a very high price." I know that these factors would be of considerable importance if one were thinking of the position in Europe. Whether the geographical location and power of the United States makes it equally important here I do not know. Possibly the only effect of these international complications would be to restrict somewhat the use of the price mechanism. But I would need to satisfy myself before deciding exactly what policy to advocate.

Another factor that needs to be taken into account is the market for the services which the frequencies are used to produce. These frequencies are used in so many different ways that there is no reason to suppose that these markets are any worse than markets in general. However, for reasons connected with the very peculiar method of finance now used for commercial radio and television, namely finance by revenue from advertisements, it is my view that the supply of broadcast services may well differ from the optimum. The market for frequencies will reflect the underlying market for broadcast services; and this, I believe, works in a manner which is by no means perfect with commercial radio and television. However, as the Government allocating machinery will also work in a way which be far from perfect, this does not settle the matter. Furthermore, I think that the sale of frequencies would probably lead to improvements in the market for broadcast services through the introduction of subscription radio and television. But I would prefer to reserve judgment on this problem for the time being.

There are also some technical problems which need to be taken into account. A single frequency can be used simultaneously by several users provided that the power, location and, no doubt, other technical aspects are appropriately regulated to prevent interference (or more accurately to take account of interference). And many alternative arrangements are possible. The straightforward answer, as Mr. Herzel indicated, is to lease a frequency to a single person, who will then sub-let rights to other in such a way as to maximize his income. But Professor Smythe would appear to suggest the way in which a single frequency is used can affect the use to which other frequencies can be put. In which case, it can be argued that the primary landlord for all frequencies should be a single organization, presumably the FCC, which would determine the conditions attaching to the use of any given frequency. I would not like this conclusion but it may be what one is forced to. Of course, this need not prevent the FCC disposing of the facilities which it carves out of the available frequencies to the persons willing to pay the highest prices. But I am afraid that in practice the facilities created will be affected by social and political ends.

Mr. Herzel suggested that the FCC should sub-divide the frequencies in such a way as to make its income a maximum. It would be a good rule if applied to an individual landowner. But it would hardly be a good rule for a State land monopoly. Or for the FCC in its handling of frequencies. By manipulating the width of the frequencies, the terms of leases, and, no doubt, in other ways I have not thought of, the authority monopolizing the frequencies could restrict the number of frequencies available for certain purposes and by this means could, in certain circumstances, raise the income to be derived from their disposal. I do not wish to suggest that the income of the FCC would in fact be increased by such manipulations. But the temptation to undertake them if the FCC had the explicit goal of maximizing income would, I think, be too difficult to resist. A series of State agencies would, of course, be better than one, if it could be arranged. It might, indeed, be better to put up with a certain amount of interference resulting from the private control of individual frequencies (or even a lot of interference). Of course, it may be that, on examination, these technical problems will prove to be rather unimportant. Sometimes opponents of the market exaggerate the difficulties of bringing one into existence.

I don't know what the solution is to all these problems, or even how serious they are. This is something I will have to examine as part of my investigation. But I feel certain that the right solution should be one adopted with due regard to the efficiency of the market and the dangers inherent in Government intervention. Technological obstacles to the easy working of the market have to be accepted; but they should not be an excuse for adopting solutions which are inimical to the efficient working of the economic system and, in the long run, to our freedom. Technological problems should serve as a challenge to liberal economists to devise institutional arrangements which overcome them without sacrificing either efficiency or freedom.

Can we say that the recent investigations in Washington are likely to produce an improvement in the operations of the FCC? On the whole, I think that the answer is no. Here and there, simple-minded souls have wondered why we couldn't rely on the market. But in general people have looked elsewhere for a solution to the problems of the FCC. Some have urged that the FCC ought to follow more judicial procedures. Well, if you're going to be hanged it is very nice to have a fair trial first, but judicial procedures are no solution if the basic law is wrong. Nor am I much excited by the suggestion that the FCC should draw up a code of ethics to govern their actions, although it might have been of some help to their mothers some fifty or sixty years ago. In this connection, I could not join whole-heartedly in the general satisfaction over the resignation of Commissioner Mack. Strange though this may sound, in many ways he represented as fine a type of man for the job as we're likely to get. Consider why it is that this institution, with its great potentialities for evil, has in fact been relatively so innocuous. Surely the answer must lie, in part, in the character of the Commissioners that have been appointed. It is now suggested that a different type of Commissioner should be appointed men who are honest, anxious to serve the public interest, who know and care about social problems, who would draw up criteria by which applicants for frequencies were to be appraised and would apply them fearlessly and consistently, who would check up on their performance in broadcasting before renewing their licenses (and would examine all their other activities too to make sure that they were worthy of their public trust). I must say that the prospect strikes me with horror. Just imagine what would happen if the Federal Communications Commission consisted entirely of men like Professor Bernard Schwartz. Freedom of the press would be dead so far as radio and television were concerned. In Government, private virtue becomes public vice. It is a melancholy truth that with the present system, maintenance of our freedoms in the sphere of radio and television depends on our retaining Commissioners similar to those which we now have. Perhaps they should be a little more careful in money matters but certainly not more energetic or socially conscious.

Some people have tried to find a way out of the present dilemma which would not involve any fundamental change in the present system. One proposal is to allocate so many frequencies to broadcasting that they are no longer scarce and therefore no problem of allocation would arise. I gather that some of those who advocate shifting all television to UHF have this in mind as one of the results. It has to be seen whether such a scheme is technically possible. I have to confess that I am skeptical. It is not simply a question of making more frequencies available for broadcasting. As additional frequencies are made available they would have to possess characteristics which make theme as valuable as those already available; otherwise, an allocation problem would remain. Furthermore, if such a plan were possible, it would produce freedom from one sort of Government intervention by tightening it elsewhere and also at the cost of an inefficient use of frequencies since the frequencies which were treated as a free good so far as broadcasting was concerned would in fact be scarce for other users. The result would be that some frequencies would be used for broadcasting although their value elsewhere was greater.

I remain firm in my conviction that the only solution to the problems of the FCC is to rely on the market and the institution of private property. And although I have indicated to you some of the difficulties such an approach would have to overcome, I am really quite confident that these obstacles are not insurmountable. The problem which we face in broadcasting is, I think, but an example of a type which is likely to be encountered more often in future with the development of the new technologies. Consider the exploitation of space, the control of weather and similar developments. Who owns an orbit? Who owns a cloud? It seems inevitable that there will be some international agreements determining the use of these new resources. But it would be a tragedy if the emergence of a form of international Socialism led to the imposition of a Socialist system within the United States itself. In protecting us from such a fate, it is good to know that in future we will be able to rely on the watchful eyes of the workers at the Thomas Jefferson Center for the Study of Political Economy.

Notes

[1] While the editor has failed to locate this specific reference, the following paragraph is found instead, which contains a similar point of view: "In an age of ever-expanding State authority, it is essential that law have its basis in more than mere governmental fiat. Government was, after all, but one of many competing power structures in the State of half a century ago. The individual was affected less by it than by the private institutions with which he normally dealt. In the State toward which we appear to be evolving, on the other hand, government tends either to take over or strictly to regulate the functions performed by these inferior institutions. George Orwell may have been unduly pessimistic in his description of the State of the future in his novel 1984. The State of tomorrow need not necessarily be the Orwellian super State, with all authority vested in its all-powerful administration. But the Orwellian nightmare can be avoided only if, in the present transitional period, the bases of a sound system of administrative law can be laid. And such a system cannot be sound if it ignores the principles of right and justice upon which our public law has heretofore rested. The present is surely the time for ensuring that these principles remain firmly established in our positive law. It will be too late to do so in 1984." Bernard Schwartz, "Administrative Procedure and Natural Law," *Notre Dame Law Review* 28(2), 1953, pp. 197-198.

[2] Z. Chafee, *Free Speech in the United States*, 381 (1942).

[3] *National Broadcasting Co. v. United States*, 319 U.S. 190, 213 (1943).

[4] Id.

[5] *National Broadcasting Co. v. United States*, 319 U.S. 190, 215–217 (1943).

[6] Old Standards in New context: A comparative analysis of FCC regulations, 18 *University of Chicago Law Review*, 78, 83 (1950).

[7] Network Broadcasting, H.R. Rep. No. 1297, 85th Cong., 2nd Sess., at 62 n. 44 (1958). Citing letter of Aug. 30, 1956 from George C. McConnaughy, the FCC Chairman, to Chairman Warren G. Magnuson of the Interstate and Foreign Commerce Committee.

[8] Hearing on subscription television before the House Committee on interstate and foreign commerce, 85th Cong., 2nd Sess. 434 (1958).

[9] *Broadcasting,* February 24, 1958, p. 200.

[10] Report on Chain Broadcasting, U.S. Federal Communications Commissions, May 1941, pp. 80-87.

[11] Mayflower Broadcasting Corp., 8 F.C.C. 333 (1941).

[12] FCC, Report on Editorializing by Licensees (1949).

[13] Editorializing by Broadcast Licensees, 13 F.C.C. 1246, 1257 (1949). Cf. Mayflower Broadcasting Corp., 8 F.C.C. 333 (1941).

[14] "Public interest" and the market in color television regulation, 18 *University of Chicago Law Review* (1951).

[15] Smythe (1952).

[16] Facing facts about the broadcast business, 20 *University of Chicago Law Review,* 96 (1952).

[17] R. E. Lee, *Broadcasting*, February 4, 1957, p. 96.

[18] Id.

[19] Recent articles, 13 *Journal of the Federal Communication Bar Association,* 89 (1953).

References

Herzel, L. 1952. Rejoinder. *University of Chicago Law Review,* 20:106.

Schwartz, B. 1953. Administrative procedure and natural law. *Notre Dame Law Review,* 28(2): 197-198.

Siepmann, C. A. 1950. *Radio, Television and Society*, 5-6. New York: Oxford University Press.

Smythe, D.W. 1952. Facing facts about the broadcast business. *University of Chicago Law Review,* 20: 96.

The Federal Communications Commission*

I. The Development of Government Regulation

In The United States no one may operate a broadcasting station unless he first obtains a license from the Federal Communications Commission. These licenses are not issued automatically but are granted or withheld at the discretion of the Commission, which is thus in a position to choose those who shall operate radio and television stations. How did the Commission come to acquire this power?

About the turn of the century, radio began to be used commercially, mainly for ship-to-shore and ship-to-ship communication.[1] This led to various proposals for legislation. Some of these were concerned with the promotion of safety at sea, requiring the installation of radio equipment on ships, the employment of skilled operators, and the like. Others, and it is these in which we are interested, were designed to bring about government control of the operations of the industry as a whole.

The reason behind such proposals can be seen from a letter dated March 30, 1910, from the Department of the Navy to the Senate Committee on Commerce, which

---

* *Journal of Law and Economics*, 1959, 2(2), 1-40.(Also appeared in *The Firm. the Market, and the Law*) This article constitutes part of a study of the Political Economy of Broadcasting, the research expenses for which are being met out of a grant from the Ford Foundation. In acknowledging this financial assistance, I should make clear that the Ford Foundation does not necessarily agree with any of the views I express. This article was largely written at the Center for Advanced Study in the Behavioral Sciences, and I am greatly indebted to Mrs. Barbara Anderson for research assistance.

described, "clearly and succinctly" according to the Committee, the purpose of the bill to regulate radio communication which was then under discussion. The Department of the Navy explained that each radio station

> considers itself independent and claims the right to send forth its electric waves through the ether at any time that it may desire, with the result that there exists in many places a state of chaos. Public business is hindered to the great embarrassment of the Navy Department. Calls of distress from vessels in peril on the sea go unheeded or are drowned out in the etheric bedlam produced by numerous stations all trying to communicate at once. Mischievous and irresponsible operators seem to take great delight in impersonating other stations and in sending out false calls. It is not putting the case too strongly to state that the situation is intolerable, and is continually growing worse.

The letter went on to point out that the Department of the Navy, in cooperation with other Government departments,

> has for years sought the enactment of legislation that would bring some sort of order out of the turbulent condition of radio communication, and while it would favor the passage of a law placing all wireless stations under the control of the Government, at the same time recognizes that such a law passed at the present time might not be acceptable to the people of this country.[2]

The bill to which this letter referred was passed by the Senate but was not acted upon by the House of Representatives. Toward the end of 1911 the same bill was reintroduced in the Senate. A subcommittee concluded that it "bestowed too great powers upon the departments of Government and gave too great privileges to military and naval stations, while it did not accurately define the limitations and conditions under which commercial enterprises could be conducted."[3] In consequence, a substitute bill was introduced, and this secured the approval both of the Senate and of the House of Representatives and became law on August 13, 1912. The Act provided that anyone operating a radio station must have a license issued by the Secretary of Commerce. This license would include details of the ownership and location of the station, the wave length or wave lengths authorized for use, the hours for which the station was licensed for work, etc. Regulations, which could be waived by the Secretary of Commerce, required the station to designate a normal wave length (which had to be less than 600 or more than 1,600 meters), but the station could use other wave lengths, provided that they were outside the limits already indicated. Amateurs were not to use a wave length exceeding 200 meters. Various other technical requirements were included in the Act. The main difference between the bill introduced in 1910 and the Act as passed was that specific regulations were set out in the Act, whereas originally power had been given to the Secretary of Commerce to make regulations and to prevent interference to "signals relating to vessels in distress or of naval and military stations by private and commercial stations"; power to make regulations was also given to the President.[4]

It was not long before attempts were made to change the law. The proposal that the Secretary of Commerce should have power to make regulations was revived. A bill was even introduced to create a Post Office monopoly of electrical communications. In 1917 and 1918, bills were introduced which would have given control of the radio industry to the Department of the Navy. Indeed, the 1918 bill was described, quite accurately, by Josephus Daniels, the Secretary of the Navy, as one which "would give the Navy Department the ownership, the exclusive ownership, of all wireless communication for commercial purposes." Mr. Daniels explained that radio was "the only method of communication which must be dominated by one power to prevent interference. ...The question of interference does not come in at all in the matter of cables or telegraphs but only in wireless." Some members of the House Committee to which Mr. Daniels was giving evidence asked whether it would not be sufficient to regulate the hours of operation and the wave lengths used by radio stations, while leaving them in private hands. But Mr. Daniels was not to be moved from his position:

My judgment is that in this particular method of communication the government ought to have a monopoly, just like it has with the mails—and even more so because other people could carry the mails on trains without interference, but they cannot use the air without interference.

Later Mr. Daniels explained: "There are only two methods of operating the wireless: either by the government or for it to license one corporation—there is no other safe or possible method of operating the wireless." That led one of the Committee to ask: "That is because of the interference in the ether, is it?" Mr. Daniels replied: "There is a certain amount of ether, and you cannot divide it up among the people as they choose to use it; one hand must control it." Later, Commander Hooper, one of Mr. Daniels, advisers, told the Committee:

... radio, by virtue of the interferences, is a natural monopoly; either the government must exercise that monopoly by owning the stations, or it must place the ownership of these stations in the hands of one concern and let the government keep out of it.[5]

The Navy in 1918 was in a much stronger position to press its claim than in the period before the 1912 Act. It had controlled the radio industry during the war and, as a result of building stations and the acquisition by purchase of certain private stations, owned 111 of the 127 existing American commercial shore stations. Nevertheless, the House Committee does not appear to have been convinced by the Navy Department's argument, and no further action was taken on this bill. Nor was this proposal ever to be raised again. The emergence of the broadcasting industry was to make it impossible in the future to think of the radio industry solely in terms of point-to-point communication and as a matter largely of concern to the Department of the Navy.

The broadcasting industry came into being in the early 1920's. Some broadcasting stations were operating in 1920 and 1921, but a big increase in the number of stations occurred in 1922. On March 1, 1922, there were 60 broadcasting stations in the United States. By November 1, the number was 564.[6] Mr. Herbert Hoover, as Secretary of Commerce, was responsible for the administration of the 1912 Act, and he faced the task of preventing the signals of these new stations from interfering with each other and with those of existing stations. In February, 1922, Mr. Hoover invited representatives of various government departments and of the radio industry to the first Radio Conference. The Conference recommended that the powers of the Secretary of Commerce to control the establishment of radio stations should be strengthened and proposed an allocation of wave bands for the various classes of service. Other conferences followed in 1923, 1924, and 1925.[7] Bills were introduced in Congress embodying the recommendations of these conferences, but none passed into law. The Secretary of Commerce attempted to carry out their recommendations by inserting detailed conditions into the licenses. However, his power to regulate radio stations in this way was destroyed by court decisions interpreting the 1912 Act.

In 1921, Mr. Hoover declined to renew the license of a telegraph company, the Intercity Radio Company, on the ground that its use of any available wave length would interfere with the signals of other stations. The company took legal action, and in February, 1923, a court decision held that the Secretary of Commerce had no discretion to refuse a license.[8] This meant, of course, that the Secretary had no control over the number of stations that could be established. However, the wording of the court decision seemed to imply that the Secretary had power to choose the wave length which a licensee could use. A later decision was to deny him even this power. In 1925 the Zenith Radio Corporation was assigned the wave length of 332.4 meters, with hours of operation limited from 10:00 to 12:00 p.m. on Thursday and then only when this period was not wanted by the General Electric Company's Denver station. These terms indicate the highly restrictive conditions which Mr. Hoover felt himself obliged to impose at this time. Not unnaturally, the Zenith Company was not happy with what was proposed and, in fact, broadcast on wave lengths and at times not allowed by the license. Criminal proceedings were then taken against the Zenith Company for violation of the 1912 Act. But in a decision rendered in April, 1926, it was held that the Act did not give the Secretary of Commerce power to make regulations and that he was required to issue a license subject only to the regulations in the Act itself.[9] As we have seen, these merely required that the wave length used should be less than 600 or more than 1,600 meters. The decision in the Zenith case appeared in certain respects to be in conflict with that in the Intercity Radio Company case, and the Secretary of Commerce asked the Attorney General for an opinion. His opinion upheld the decision in the Zenith case.[10] This meant that the Secretary of Commerce was compelled to issue licenses to anyone who applied, and the licensees were then free to decide on the power of their station, its hours of operation, and the wave length they would use (outside the limits mentioned in the Act). The period which followed has often been described as one of "chaos in broadcasting." More than two hundred stations were established in the next nine months. These stations used whatever power or wave length they wished, while many of the existing stations ceased to observe the conditions which the Secretary of Commerce had inserted in their licenses.

For a number of years Congress had been studying various proposals for regulating radio communication. The Zenith decision added very considerably to the pressure for new legislation. In July, 1926, as a stop-gap measure designed to prevent licensees establishing property rights in frequencies, the two houses of Congress passed a joint resolution providing that no license should be granted for more than ninety days for a broadcasting station or for more than two years for any other type of station. Furthermore, no one was to be granted a license unless he executed "a waiver of any right or of any claim to any right, as against the United States, to any wave length or to the use of the ether in radio transmission..." This echoed an earlier Senate resolution (passed in 1925), in which the ether and the use thereof had been declared to be "the inalienable possession of the people of the United States..." When Congress reconvened in December, 1926, the House and Senate quickly agreed on a comprehensive measure for the regulation of the radio industry, which became law in February, 1927.

This Act brought into existence the Federal Radio Commission. The Commission, among other things, was required to classify radio stations, prescribe the nature of the service, assign wave lengths, determine the power and location of the transmitters, regulate the kind of apparatus used, and make regulations to prevent interference. It was provided that those wanting licenses to operate radio stations had to make a written application which was to include such facts as the Commission

> may prescribe as to the citizenship, character, and financial, technical, and other qualifications of the applicant to operate the station; the ownership and location of the proposed station and of the stations, if any, with which it is proposed to communicate; the frequencies or wave lengths and the power desired to be used; the hours of the day or other periods of time during which it is proposed to operate the station; the purposes for which the station is to be used, and such other information as it may require.

The Commission was authorized to issue a license if the "public interest, necessity or convenience would be served" by so doing. Once the license was granted, it could not be transferred to anyone else without the approval of the Commission. And, incorporating the sense of the 1926 joint resolution, licensees were required to sign a waiver of any claim to the use of a wave length or the ether.

The Commission was thus provided with massive powers to regulate the radio industry. But it was prohibited from censoring programs:

> Nothing in this Act shall be understood or construed to give the licensing authority the power of censorship over the radio communications or signals transmitted by any radio station, and no regulation or condition shall be promulgated or fixed by the licensing authority which shall interfere with the right of free speech by means of radio communications.

Nonetheless, the Act did impose some restrictions on a station's programing. Obscene, indecent, or profane language was prohibited. A station was not allowed to rebroadcast programs without the permission of the originating station. The names of people paying for or furnishing programs had to be announced. Finally, it was provided that, if a licensee permitted a legally qualified candidate for public office to broadcast, equal opportunities had to be offered to all other candidates.

The regulatory powers of the Federal Radio Commission did not extend to radio stations operated by the federal government, except when the signals transmitted did not relate to government business. These government stations were subject to the authority of the President. In fact, the allocation of frequencies for government use was carried out under the auspices of the Interdepartment Radio Advisory Committee, which had originally been formed in 1922 but which continued in existence after the establishment of the Federal Radio Commission.

In 1934 the powers exercised by the Federal Radio Commission were transferred to the Federal Communications Commission, which was also made responsible for the regulation of the telephone and telegraph industries. This change in the administrative machinery made little difference to the relations between the regulatory authority and the radio industry. Indeed, the sections of the 1934 Act dealing with the radio industry very largely reproduced the 1927 Act.[11] Amendments have been made to the 1934 Act from time to time, but these have related mainly to procedural matters, and the main structure has been unaffected.[12] In all essentials, the system as it exists today is that established in 1927.

II. The Clash with the Doctrine of Freedom of the Press

The situation in the American broadcasting industry is not essentially different in character from that which would be found if a commission appointed by the federal government had the task of selecting those who were to be allowed to publish newspapers and periodicals in each city, town, and village of the United States. A proposal to do this would, of course, be rejected out of hand as inconsistent with the doctrine of freedom of the press. But the broadcasting industry is a source of news and opinion of comparable importance with newspapers or books and, in fact, nowadays is commonly included with the press, so far as the doctrine of freedom of the press is concerned. The Commission on Freedom of the Press, under the chairmanship of Mr. Robert M. Hutchins, used the term "press" to include "all means of communicating to the public news and opinions, emotions and beliefs, whether by newspapers, magazines, or books, by radio broadcasts, by television, or by films."[13] Professor Zechariah Chafee had little doubt that the broadcasting industry came within the protection of the First Amendment.[14] A dictum in the Supreme Court expressed a similar view: "We have no doubt that moving pictures, like newspapers and radio, are included in the press whose freedom is guaranteed by the First Amendment."[15] Yet, as Mr. Louis G. Caldwell has pointed out,

> A broadcasting station can be put out of existence and its owner deprived of his investment and means of livelihood, for the oral dissemination of language which, if printed in a newspaper, is protected by the First Amendment to the Constitution against exactly the same sort of repression.[16]

In the discussions preceding the formation of the Federal Radio Commission, Mr. Hoover distinguished between two problems: the prevention of interference and the choice of those who would operate the stations:

> ... The ideal situation, as I view it, would be traffic regulation by Federal Government to the extent of the allotment of wave lengths and control of power and the policing of interference, leaving to each community a large voice in determining who are to occupy the wave lengths assigned to that community.[17]

But, as we have seen, both of these tasks were given to the Federal Radio Commission. Some interpreted the fact that the Commission was denied the power of censorship as meaning that it would not concern itself with programing but would simply act as "the traffic policeman of the ether". But the Commission maintained and in this it has been sustained by the courts that, to decide whether the "public interest, convenience or necessity" would be served by granting or renewing a license, it had to take into account proposed or past programing. One commentator remarked, that by 1949, the "Commission had travelled far from its original role of airwaves traffic policeman. Control over radio had become more than regulation based on technological necessity; it had become regulation of conduct, and the basis was but emerging." [18]

The Commission is instructed to grant or renew a license if this would serve the "public interest, convenience or necessity." This phrase, taken from public utility legislation, lacks any definite meaning. It "means about as little as any phrase that the drafters of the Act could have used and still comply with the constitutional requirement that there be some standard to guide the administrative wisdom of the licensing authority." [19] Furthermore, the many inconsistencies in Commission decisions have made it impossible for the phrase to acquire a definite meaning in the process of regulation. The character of the program proposals of an applicant for a frequency or channel is, of course, one of the factors taken into account by the Commission, and any applicant with a good lawyer will find that his proposals include live programs with local performers and programs in which public issues are discussed (these being program types which appear to be favored by the Commission). And when the time comes for renewal of the license, which at the present time is every three years, the past programing of the station is reviewed.[20]

A good illustration of the difference between the position of the owner of a broadcasting station and the publisher of a newspaper is provided by the case of Mr. Baker, who operated a radio station in Iowa and was denied a renewal of his license in 1931 because he broadcast bitter personal attacks on persons and institutions he did not like. The Commission said:

This Commission holds no brief for the Medical Associations and other parties whom Mr. Baker does not like. Their alleged sins may be at times of public importance, to be called to the attention of the public over the air in the right way. But this record discloses that Mr. Baker does not do so in any high-minded way. It shows that he continually and erratically over the air rides a personal hobby, his cancer cure ideas and his likes and dislikes of certain persons and things. Surely his infliction of all this on the listeners is not the proper use of a broadcasting license. Many of his utterances are vulgar, if not indeed indecent. Assuredly they are not uplifting or entertaining.

Though we may not censor, it is our duty to see that broadcasting licenses do not afford mere personal organs, and also to see that a standard of refinement fitting our day and generation is maintained.[21]

It is hardly surprising that this decision has been described as "in spirit pure censorship."[22]

The Commission's attempts to influence programing have met with little opposition, except on two occasions, when the broadcasting industry made vigorous protests. The first arose out of the so-called *Mayflower* decision of 1940. A Boston station had broadcast editorials urging the election of certain candidates for public office and expressing views on controversial questions. The Commission criticized the station for doing this and renewed its license only after receiving assurances that the station would no longer broadcast editorials. In 1948 the Commission re-examined the question and issued a report which, while not explicitly repudiating the *Mayflower* doctrine, nevertheless expressed approval of editorializing subject to the criterion of "overall fairness." The Commission agreed that its ruling involved an abridgment of freedom but that this was necessary:

Any regulation of radio, especially a system of limited licensees, is in a real sense an abridgment of the inherent freedom of persons to express themselves by means of radio communications. It is howerever, a necessary and constitutional abridgment in order to prevent chaotic interference from destroying the great potential of this medium for public enlightment and entertainment.

The Commission then went on:

The most significant meaning of freedom of the radio is the right of the American people to listen to this great medium of communications free from any governmental dictation as to what they can or cannot hear and free alike from similar restraints by private licensees.

It is not clear to me what the Commission meant by this. It could hardly have been the intention of the Commission to pay a tribute to the "invisible hand." [23]

The second controversy arose out of the publication of the so-called Blue Book by the Federal Communications Commission in 1946, entitled *Public Service Responsibility of Broadcast Licensees*. In this report the Commission indicated that it was going to pay closer attention to questions of programming and that those stations which carried sustaining programs, local live programs, and programs devoted to the discussion of public issues and which avoided "advertising excesses" would be more likely to have their licenses renewed. In the case of sustaining programs, it was suggested that they should be used with a view to

(a) maintaining an overall program balance, (b) providing time for programs inappropriate for sponsorship, (c) providing time for programs serving particular minority tastes and interests, (d) providing time for non-profit organizations—religious, civic, agricultural, labor, educational, etc., and (e) providing time for experiment and for unfettered artistic self-expression.[24]

It was argued (by Justin Miller, of the National Association of Broadcasters, among others) that the publication of the Blue Book was unconstitutional, as being contrary to the First Amendment, but on this the courts have not given an opinion.

The examination by the Commission of the past activities of applicants has at times posed a threat to other freedoms. One example is furnished by the proceedings in the *Daily News* case. The publishers of the New York *Daily News* applied for permission to construct an FM station. The American Jewish Congress intervened, arguing that the application should be denied because the *Daily News* had

> evidenced bias against minority groups, particularly Jews and Negroes, and has published irresponsible and defamatory news items and editorials concerning such minorities... the News had thus demonstrated ... that it is unqualified to be the licensee of a radio station because it could not be relied upon to operate its station with fairness to all groups and points of view in the community.

The admissibility of such evidence was questioned, but the Commission held that it could be received, although pronouncing it inconclusive in this case. The application of the owners of the *Daily News* was finally rejected on other grounds, although it has been suggested that the evidence of the American Jewish Congress in fact played a part in bringing about the decision. What seems clear is that a newspaper which has an editorial policy approved of by the Commission is more likely to obtain a radio or television license than one that does not. The threat to freedom of the press in its strictest sense is evident.[25] Another case involved the political activities of an owner of a radio station, Mr. Edward Lamb. In earlier hearings, Mr. Lamb had denied having Communist associations. When the license of his station came up for renewal in 1954, the Commission charged that his previous statements were false. According to Professor Ralph S. Brown, the Broadcast Bureau of the Commission "produced in support of its charge as sorry a collection of unreliable and mendacious witnesses as have appeared in any recent political case." Finally, after lengthy proceedings, the license was renewed, but the Commission in its decision rejected the view that it "had no right to inquire into past associations, activities, and beliefs. ..."[26]

If we ask why it is that the Commission's policies have met with so little opposition, the answer, without any doubt, is that the Commission has been exremely hesitant about imposing its views on the broadcasting industry. Sometimes licenses have been renewed on condition that the programs to which the Commission objected were not broadcast in the future. Some operators have not had their licenses renewed largely or wholly because of objections to the programs transmitted. But the number of such cases is not large, and the programs to which objection was taken were devoted to such topics as fortune-telling, horse-racing results, or medical advice or involved attacks on public officials, medical associations, or religious organizations.[27]

It is difficult for someone outside the broadcasting industry to assess the extent to which programing has been affected by the views and actions of the Commission. On the face of it, it would seem improbable that the Commission's cautious approach would intimidate many station operators. However, the complete compliance of the industry to the *Mayflower* decision may be cited as evidence of the power of the Commission. Furthermore, the Commission has many favors to give, and few people with any substantial interests in the broadcasting industry would want to flout too flagrantly the wishes of the Commission.

III. The Rationale of the Present System

Professor Chafee has pointed out that the newer media of communication have been subjected to a stricter control than the old:

> Newspapers, books, pamphlets, and large meetings were for many centuries the only means of public discussion, so that the need for their protection has long been generally realized. On the other hand, when additional methods for spreading facts and ideas were introduced or greatly improved by modern inventions, writers and judges had not got into the habit of being solicitous about guarding their freedom. And so we have tolerated censorship of the mails, the importation of foreign books, the stage, the motion picture, and the radio.[28]

It is no doubt true that the difference between the position occupied by the press and the broadcasting industry is in part due to the fact that the printing press was invented in the fifteenth and broadcasting in the twentieth century. But this is by no means the whole story. Many of those who have acquiesced in this abridgment of freedom of the press in broadcasting have done so reluctantly, the situation being accepted as a necessary, if unfortunate, consequence of the peculiar technology of the industry.

Mr. Justice Frankfurter, in delivering the opinion of the Supreme Court in one of the leading cases on radio law, gave an account of the rationale of the present system:

> The plight into which radio fell prior to 1927 was attributable to certain basic facts about radio as a means of communication—its facilities are limited; they are not available to all who may wish to use them; the radio spectrum simply is not large enough to accommodate everybody. There is a fixed natural limitation upon the number of stations that can operate without interfering with one another. Regulation of radio was therefore as vital to its development as traffic control was to the development of the automobile. In enacting the Radio Act of 1927, the first comprehensive scheme of control over radio communication, Congress acted upon the knowledge that if the potentialities of radio were not to be wasted, regulation was essential.

To those who argued that we should "regard the Commission as a kind of traffic officer, policing the wave lengths to prevent stations from interfering with each other." Mr. Justice Frankfurter answered:

> But the Act does not restrict the Commission merely to supervision of traffic. It puts upon the Commission the burden of determining the composition of that traffic. The facilities of radio are not large enough to accommodate all who wish to use them. Methods must be devised for choosing from among the many who apply. And since Congress itself could not do this, it committed the task to the Commission.

The Commission was, however, not left at large in performing this duty. The touchstone provided by Congress was the "public interest, convenience or necessity."

...The facilities of radio are limited and therefore precious; they cannot be left to wasteful use without detriment to the public interest ...The Commission's licensing function cannot be discharged, therefore, merely by finding that there are no technological objections to the granting of a license. If the criterion of "public interest" were limited to such matters, how could the Commission choose between two applicants for the same facilities, each of whom is financially and technically qualified to operate a station? Since the very inception of federal regulation of radio, comparative considerations as to the services to be rendered have governed the application of the standard of "public interest, convenience or necessity."[29]

The events which preceded government regulation have been described very vividly by Professor Charles A. Siepmann:

The chaos that developed as more and more enthusiastic pioneers entered the field of radio was indescribable. Amateurs crossed signals with professional broadcasters. Many of the professionals broadcast on the same wave length and either came to a gentleman's agreement to divide the hours of broadcasting or blithely set about cutting one another's throats by broadcasting simultaneously. Listeners thus experienced the annoyance of trying to hear one program against the raucous background of another. Ship-to-shore communication in Morse code added its pulsing dots and dashes to the silly symphony of sound.

Professor Siepmann sums up the situation in the following words: "Private enterprise, over seven long years, failed to set its own house in order. Cutthroat competition at once retarded radio's orderly development and subjected listeners to intolerable strain and inconvenience."[30]

Notwithstanding the general acceptance of these arguments and the eminence of the authorities who expound them, the views which have just been quoted are based on a misunderstanding of the nature of the problem. Mr. Justice Frankfurter seems to believe that federal regulation is needed because radio frequencies are limited in number and people want to use more of them than are available. But it is a commonplace of economics that almost all resources used in the economic system (and not simply radio and television frequencies) are limited in amount and scarce, in that people would like to use more than exists. Land, labor, and capital are all scarce, but this, of itself, does not call for government regulation. It is true that some mechanism has to be employed to decide who, out of the many claimants, should be allowed to use the scarce resource. But the way this is usually done in the American economic system is to employ the price mechanism, and this allocates resources to users without the need for government regulation.

Professor Siepmann seems to ascribe the confusion which existed before government regulation to a failure of private enterprise and the competitive system. But the real cause of the trouble was that no property rights were created in these scarce frequencies. We know from our ordinary experience that land can be allocated to land users without the need for government regulation by using the price mechanism. But if no property rights were created in land, so that everyone could use a tract of land, it is clear that there would be considerable confusion and that the price mechanism could not work because there would not be any property rights that could be acquired. If one person could use a piece of land for growing a crop, and then another person could come along and build a house on the land used for the crop, and then another could come along, tear down the house, and use the space as a parking lot, it would no doubt be accurate to describe the resulting situation as chaos. But it would be wrong to blame this on private enterprise and the competitive system. A private-enterprise system cannot function properly unless property rights are created in resources, and, when this is done, someone wishing to use a resource has to pay the owner to obtain it. Chaos disappears; and so does the government except that a legal system to define property rights and to arbitrate disputes is, of course, necessary. But there is certainly no need for the kind of regulation which we now find in the American radio and television industry.

In 1951, in the course of a comment dealing with the problem of standards in color television, Mr. Leo Herzel proposed that the price mechanism should be used to allocate frequencies. He said:

> The most important function of radio regulation is the allocation of a scarce factor of production—frequency channels. The FCC has to determine who will get the limited number of channels available at any one time. This is essentially an economic decision, not a policing decision.

And later, Mr. Herzel suggested that channels should be leased to the highest bidder.[31] This article brought a reply from Professor Dallas W. Smythe of the Institute of Communications Research of the University of Illinois and formerly chief economist of the Federal Communications Commission. In his article, Professor Smythe presented the case against the use of the price mechanism in broadcasting.[32]

First of all, Professor Smythe pointed out that commercial broadcasting was not a "dominant user of spectrum space" but "a minor claimant on it." He explained that, "the radio spectrum up to at least 1,000,000 Kc is susceptible of commercial exploitation, technologically. On this basis, the exclusive use of frequencies by broadcasters represents 2.3 per cent of the total and the shared use, 7.2 per cent." But, according to Professor Smythe, even these percentages may overstate the importance of broadcasting. "The FCC has allocated the spectrum to different users as far as 30,000,000 Kc. And on this basis commercial broadcasters use exclusively less than one tenth of one per cent, and, on a shared basis, two tenths of one per cent."[33]

Professor Smythe then went on to explain who it was that used most of the radio spectrum. First, there were the military, the law-enforcement agencies, the fire-fighting agencies, the Weather Bureau, the Forestry Service, and the radio amateurs, "the last of which by definition could hardly be expected to pay for frequency use." This is, of course, in accordance with the modern view that an amateur is someone who does not pay for the things he uses. Then there were many commercial users other than broadcasters. There were the common carriers, radiotelegraph and radiotelephone; transportation agencies, vessels on the high seas, railroads, street railways, busses, trucks, harbor craft, and taxis. There were also various specialized users, such as electric power, gas and water concerns, the oil industry (which used radio waves for communication and also for geophysical exploration), the motion-picture industry (for work on location), and so on. Professor Smythe commented:

> Surely it is not seriously intended that the non-commercial radio users (such as police), the non-broadcast common carriers (such as radio-telegraph) and the non-broadcast commercial users (such as the oil industry) should compete with dollar bids against the broadcast users for channel allocations.

To this Mr. Herzel replied:

> It certainly is seriously suggested. Such users compete for all other kinds of equipment or else they don't get it. I should think the more interesting question is, why is it seriously suggested that they shouldn't compete for radio frequencies?

Certainly, it is not clear why we should have to rely on the Federal Communications Commission rather than the ordinary pricing mechanism to decide whether a particular frequency should be used by the police, or for a radiotelephone, or for a taxi service, or for an oil company for geophysical exploration, or by a motion-picture company to keep in touch with its film stars or for a broadcasting station. Indeed, the multiplicity of these varied uses would suggest that the advantages to be derived from relying on the pricing mechanism would be especially great in this case.

Professor Smythe also argued that the use of market controls depends on "the economic assumption that there is substantially perfect competition in the electronics field." This is a somewhat extreme view. An allocation scheme costs something to administer, will itself lead to a malallocation of resources, and may encourage some monopolistic tendencies—all of which might well make us willing to tolerate a considerable amount of imperfect competition before substituting an allocation scheme for market controls. Nonetheless, the problem of monopoly is clearly one to be taken seriously. But this does not mean that frequencies should not be allocated by means of the market or that we should employ a special organization, the Federal Communications Commission, for monopoly control in the broadcasting industry rather than the normal procedure. In fact, the antitrust laws do apply to broadcasting, and recently we have seen the Department of Justice taking action in a case in which the Federal Communications Commission had not thought it necessary to act.[34] The situation is not simply one in which there are two organizations to carry out one law. There are, in effect, two laws. The Federal Communications Commission is not bound by the antitrust laws and may refuse an application for a license because of the monopolistic practices of the applicant, even though these may not have been illegal under the antitrust laws. Thus, the broadcasting industry, while subject to the antitrust laws, is also subject to another not on the statute book but one invented by the Commission.[35]

It may be wondered whether such an involved system is required for the broadcasting industry, but this is not the question with which I am mainly concerned. To increase the competitiveness of the system, it may be that certain firms should not be allowed to operate broadcasting stations (or more than a certain number) and that certain practices should be prohibited; but this does not mean that those regarded as eligible to operate broadcasting stations ought not to pay for the frequencies they use. It is no doubt desirable to regulate monopolistic practices in the oil industry, but to do this it is not necessary that oil companies be presented with oil fields for nothing. Control of monopoly is a separate problem.

IV. The Pricing System and the Allocation of Frequencies

There can be little doubt that the idea of using private property and the pricing system in the allocation of frequencies is one which is completely unfamiliar to most of those concerned with broadcasting policy. Consider, for example, the comment on the articles by Mr. Herzel and Professor Smythe (discussed in the previous section) which appeared in the Journal of the Federal Communications Bar Association and which was therefore addressed to the group with the greatest knowledge of the problems of broadcasting regulation in the United States: "The whole discussion will be over the heads of most readers."[36] Or consider the answers given by Mr. Frank Stanton, president of Columbia Broadcasting System and one of the most experienced and able men in the broadcasting industry, when Representative Rogers in a congressional inquiry raised the possibility of disposing of television channels by putting them up for the highest bids:

> *Mr. Rogers.* Doctor, what would you think about a proposition of the Government taking all of these channels and opening them to competitive bidding and let the highest bidder take them at the best price the taxpayers could get out of it?
>
> *Mr. Stanton.* This is a novel theory and one to which I have not addressed myself during my operating career. This is certainly entirely contrary to what the Communication Act was in 1927 and as it was later amended.
>
> *Mr. Rogers.* I know, but if the Government owns a tract of land on which you raise cattle, they charge a man for the use of the land.
>
> Why would it not be just as reasonable to charge a man to use the avenues of the air as it would be to use that pasture? Why should the people be giving one group something free and charging another group for something that is comparable?
>
> *Mr. Stanton.* This is a new and novel concept. I think it would have to be applied broadly to all uses of the spectrum and not just confined to television, if you will.
>
> *Mr. Rogers.* I understand that. Do you not think that would really be free enterprise

where the taxpayer would be getting the proceeds?

Mr. Stanton. You have obviously given some thought to this and you are hitting me for the first time with it.[37]

This "novel theory" (novel with Adam Smith) is, of course, that the allocation of resources should be determined by the forces of the market rather than as a result of government decisions. Quite apart from the malallocations which are the result of political pressures, an administrative agency which attempts to perform the function normally carried out by the pricing mechanism operates under two handicaps. First of all, it lacks the precise monetary measure of benefit and cost provided by the market. Second, it cannot, by the nature of things, be in possession of all the relevant information possessed by the managers of every business which uses or might use radio frequencies, to say nothing of the preferences of consumers for the various goods and services in the production of which radio frequencies could be used. In fact, lengthy investigations are required to uncover part of this information, and decisions of the Federal Communications Commission emerge only after long delays, often extending to years.[38] To simplify the task, the Federal Communications Commission adopts arbitrary rules. For example, it allocates certain ranges of frequencies (and only these) for certain specified uses. The situation in which the Commission finds itself was described in a recent speech by Commissioner Robert E. Lee. He explained that the question of undertaking a study of assignments below 890mc was being considered, but whether this would be done was uncertain.

There is considerable discussion of such a move within and without the Commission ... The examination of the more crowded spectrum below 890mc presents an extremely difficult administrative problem. While this should be no excuse, I hope that all will appreciate the limitations of our overburdened staff, which, as a practical matter, must be given great weight.

And, after referring to a possible change in procedure, he added:

I am finding it increasingly difficult to explain why a steel company in a large community, desperate for additional frequency space cannot use a frequency assigned, let us say, to the forest service in an area where there are no trees.[39]

This discussion should not be taken to imply that an administrative allocation of resources is inevitably worse than an allocation by means of the price mechanism. The operation of a market is not itself costless, and, if the costs of operating the market exceeded the costs of running the agency by a sufficiently large amount, we might be willing to acquiesce in the malallocation of resources resulting from the agency's lack of knowledge, inflexibility, and exposure to political pressure. But in the United States few people think that this would be so in most industries, and there is nothing about the broadcasting industry which would lead us to believe that the allocation of frequencies constitutes an exceptional case.

An example of how the nature of the pricing system is misunderstood in current discussions of broadcasting policy in the United States is furnished by a recent comment which appeared in the trade journal *Broadcasting*:

In the TV field, lip service is given to a proposal that television "franchises" be awarded to the highest bidder among those who may be qualified. This is ridiculous on its face, since it would mean that choice outlets in prime markets would go to those with the most money.[40]

First of all, it must be observed that resources do not go, in the American economic system, to those with the most money but to those who are willing to pay the most for them. The result is that, in the struggle for particular resources, men who earn $5,000 per annum are every day outbidding those who earn $50,000 per annum. To be convinced that this is so, we need only imagine a situation occurring in which all those who earned $50,000 or more per annum arrived at the stores one morning and, at the prices quoted, were able to buy everything in stock, with nothing left over for those with lower incomes. Next day we may be sure that the prices quoted would be higher and that those with higher incomes would be forced to reduce their purchases—a process which would continue as long as those with lower incomes were unable to spend all they wanted. The same system which enables a man with $1 million to obtain $1 million's worth of resources enables a man with $1,000 to obtain a $1, 000's worth of resources. Of course, the existence of a pricing system does not insure that the distribution of money between persons (or families) is satisfactory. But this is not a question we need to consider in dealing with broadcasting policy. Insofar as the ability to pay for frequencies or channels depends on the distribution of funds, it is the distribution not between persons but between firms which is relevant. And here the ethical problem does not arise. All that matters is whether the distribution of funds contributes to efficiency, and there is every reason to suppose that, broadly speaking, it does. Those firms which use funds profitably find it easy to get more; those which do not, find it difficult. The capital market does not work perfectly, but the general tendency is clear. In any case, it is doubtful whether the Federal Communications Commission has, in general, awarded frequencies to firms Which are in a relatively unfavorable position from the point of view of raising capital. The inquiries which the Commission conducts into the financial qualifications of applicants must, in fact, tend in the opposite direction.[41]

And if we take as examples of "choice outlets in prime markets" network- affiliated television stations in the six largest metropolitan areas in the United States on the basis of population (New York, Chicago, Los Angeles, Philadelphia, Detroit, and San Francisco), we find that five stations are owned by American Broadcasting-Paramount Theatres, Inc., four by the National Broadcasting Company (a subsidiary of the Radio Corporation of America), four by the Columbia Broadcasting System, Inc., and one each by the Westinghouse Broadcasting Company (a subsidiary of the Westinghouse Electric Corporation), the Storer Broadcasting Company, and three newspaper publishing concerns.[42] It would be difficult to argue that these are firms which have been unduly handicapped in their growth by their inability to raise capital.

The Supreme Court appears to have assumed that it was impossible to use the pricing mechanism when dealing with a resource which was in limited supply. This is not true. Despite all the efforts of art dealers, the number of Rembrandts existing at a given time is limited; yet such paintings are commonly disposed of by auction. But the works of dead painters are not unique in being in fixed supply. If we take a broad enough view, the supply of all factors of production is seen to be fixed (the amount of land, the size of the population, etc.). Of course, this is not the way we think of the supply of land or labor. Since we are usually concerned with a particular problem, we think not in terms of the total supply but rather of the supply available for a particular use. Such a procedure is not only practically more useful; it also tells us more about the processes of adjustment at work in the market. Although the quantity of a resource may be limited in total, the quantity that can be made available to a particular use is variable. Producers in a particular industry can obtain more of any resource they require by buying it on the market, although they are unlikely to be able to obtain considerable additional quantities unless they bid up the price, thereby inducing firms in other industries to curtail their use of the resource. This is the mechanism which governs the allocation of factors of production in almost all industries. Notwithstanding the almost unanimous contrary view, there is nothing in the technology of the broadcasting industry which prevents the use of the same mechanism. Indeed, use of the pricing system is made particularly easy by a circumstance to which Professor Smythe draws our special attention, namely, that the broadcasting industry uses but a small proportion of "spectrum space." A broadcasting industry, forced to bid for frequencies, could draw them away from other industries by raising the price it was willing to pay. It is impossible to say whether the result of introducing the pricing system would be that the broadcasting industry would obtain more frequencies than are allocated to it by the Federal Communications Commission. Not having had, in the past, a market for frequencies, we do not know what these various industries would pay for them. Similarly, we do not know for what frequencies the broadcasting industry would be willing to outbid these other industries. All we can say is that the broadcasting industry would be able to obtain all the existing frequencies it now uses (and more) if it were willing to pay a price equal to the contribution which they could make to production elsewhere. This is saying nothing more than that the broadcasting industry would be able to obtain frequencies on the same basis as it now obtains its labor, buildings, land, and equipment.

A thoroughgoing employment of the pricing mechanism for the allocation of radio frequencies would, of course, mean that the various governmental authorities, which are at present such heavy users of these frequencies, would also be required to pay for them. This may appear to be unnecessary, since payment would have to be made to some other government agency appointed to act as custodian of frequencies. What was paid out of one government pocket would simply go into another. It may also seem inappropriate that the allocation of resources for such purposes as national defense or the preservation of human life should be subjected to a monetary test. While it would be entirely possible to exclude from the pricing process all frequencies which government departments consider they need and to confine pricing to frequencies available for the private sector, there would seem to be compelling reasons for not doing so. A government department, in making up its mind whether or not to undertake a particular activity, should weigh against the benefits this would confer, the costs which are also involved: That is, the value of the production elsewhere which would otherwise be enjoyed. In the case of a government activity which is regarded as so essential as to justify any sacrifice, it is still desirable to minimize the cost of any particular project. If the use of a frequency which if used industrially would contribute goods worth $1 million could be avoided by the construction of a wire system or the purchase of reserve vehicles costing $100,000, it is better that the frequency should not be used, however essential the project. It is the merit of the pricing system that, in these circumstances, a government department (unless very badly managed) would not use the frequency if made to pay for it. Some hesitation in accepting this argument may come from the thought that, though it might be better to provide government departments with the funds necessary to purchase the resources they need, it by no means follows that Congress will do this. Consequently, it might be better to accept the waste inherent in the present system rather than suffer the disadvantages which would come from government departments having inadequate funds to pay for frequencies. This, of course, assumes that government departments are, in general, denied adequate funds by Congress, but it is not clear that this is true, above all for the defense departments, which, at present, use the bulk of the frequencies. Furthermore, it has to be remembered that a pricing scheme for frequencies would not involve any budgetary strain, since all government payments would be exactly balanced by the receipts of the agency responsible for disposing of frequencies, and there would be a net gain from the payments by private firms. In any case, such considerations do not apply to the introduction of pricing in the private sector and, in particular, for the broadcasting industry.

The desire to preserve government ownership of radio frequencies coupled with an unwillingness to require any payment for the use of these frequencies has had one consequence which has caused some uneasiness. A station operator who is granted a license to use a particular frequency in a particular place may, in fact, be granted a very valuable right, one for which he would be willing to pay a large sum of money and which he would be forced to pay if others could bid for the frequency. This provision of a valuable resource without charge naturally raises the income of station operators above what it would have been in competitive conditions. It would require a very detailed investigation to determine the extent to which private operators of radio and television stations have been enriched as a result of this policy. But part of the extremely high return on the capital invested in certain radio and television stations has undoubtedly been due to this failure to charge for the use of the frequency. Occasionally, when a station is sold, it is possible to glimpse what is involved. Strictly, of course, all that can be sold is the station and its organization; the frequency is public property, and the grant of a license gives no rights of any sort in that frequency.

Furthermore, transfers of the ownership of radio and television stations have to be approved by the Federal Communications Commission. However, the Commission almost always approves such negotiated transfers, and, when these take place, there can be little doubt that often a great part of the purchase price is in fact payment for obtaining the use of the frequency. Thus when WNEW in New York City was sold in 1957 for $5 million or WDTV in Pittsburgh in 1955 for $10 million or WCAV (AM, FM, and TV) in Philadelphia in 1958 for $20 million, it is possible to doubt that it would cost $5 million or $10 million or $20 million to duplicate the transmitter, studio equipment, furniture, and the organization, which nominally is what is being purchased.[43] The result of sales at such prices is, of course, to reduce the return earned by the new owners to (or at any rate nearer to) the competitive level. When, as happened in the early days of radio regulation but less often since the Commission refused to sanction transfers at a price much more than the value of the physical assets and the organization being acquired, the effect was simply to distribute the benefits derived from this free use of public property more widely among the business community: To enable the new as well as the old owners to share in it. I do not wish to discuss whether such a redistribution of the gain is socially desirable. My point is different: There is no reason why there should be any gain to redistribute.

The extraordinary gain accruing to radio and television station operators as a result of the present system of allocating frequencies becomes apparent when stations are sold.[44] Even before the 1927 Act was passed, it was recognized that stations were transferred from one owner to another at prices which implied that the right to a license was being sold.[45] Occasionally, references to this problem are found in the literature, but the subject has not been discussed extensively. In part, I think this derives from the fact that the only solution to the problem of excessive profits was thought to be rate regulation or profit control.[46] Such solutions were unlikely to gain support for a number of reasons. Although in the early days of the broadcasting industry it was commonly thought that it would be treated as another public utility, this view was later largely abandoned. An attempt to make broadcasters common carriers failed. And broadcasting has come to be thought of, so far as its business operations are concerned, as an unregulated industry. As the Supreme Court has said: "... the field of broadcasting is one of free competition."[47] In any case, the determination of the rates to be charged or the level of profits to be allowed would not seem an easy matter, although it has been claimed that "it should be possible for resource and tax economists to develop norms for levying such special franchise taxes."[48] Furthermore, rate or profit regulation with the concomitant need for control of the quality of the programs is hardly an attractive prospect.

It is an odd fact that the obvious way out of these difficulties, which is to make those wishing to use frequencies bid for them (allowing the profits earned to be determined not by a regulatory commission but by the forces of competition), received no attention in the literature, so far as I know, until comparatively recently. Mr. Herzel's article contains the first reference I have found. More recently, the suggestion has been mentioned on a number of occasions. In 1958 the proposal for bidding made its appearance in a bill introduced by Representative Henry S. Reuss. This bill would have established an order of priority for the various categories of applicants for radio and television licenses but contained the provision that, where there was more than one applicant falling into the highest category, the Federal Communications Commission would then grant the license to the highest bidder in that category, with the money to be "deposited in the Treasury of the United States to the credit of miscellaneous receipts." The same procedure would be applied when a license was transferred. Representative Reuss explained: "The airwaves are the public domain, and under such circumstances a decision should be made in favor of the taxpayers, just as it is when the government takes bids for the logging franchise on public timberland."[49]

It is to be expected that even so modest a suggestion for bidding as that of Representative Reuss would not be welcomed. From the earliest days of radio regulation suggestions have been made that those holding radio licenses should pay a fee to the regulating authority, but this has never been incorporated in the law. When, a few years ago, the Federal Communications Commission announced that it was considering a proposal that radio and television licenses should pay a fee to cover the costs of the licensing process (that is, the cost of the Federal Communications Commission), the Senate Committee on Interstate and Foreign Commerce quickly adopted a resolution suggesting that the Commission should suspend consideration of this proposal for the time being, since "the proposal for license fees for broadcasting stations raises basic questions with regard to the fundamental philosophy of regulation under the Communications Act."[50]

It is not easy to understand the feeling of hostility to the idea that people should pay for the facilities they use. It is true that this attitude has been supposed by the argument that it was technologically impossible to charge for the use of frequencies, but this is clearly wrong. It is difficult to avoid the conclusion that the widespread opposition to the use of the pricing system for the allocation of frequencies can be explained only by the fact that the possibility of using it has never been seriously faced.

V. Private Property and the Allocation of Frequencies

If the right to use a frequency is to be sold, the nature of that right would have to be precisely defined. A simple answer would be to leave the situation essentially as it is now: The broadcaster would buy the right to use, for a certain period, an assigned frequency to transmit signals at a given power for certain hours from a transmitter located in a particular place. This would simply superimpose a payment on to the present system. It would certainly make it possible for the person or firm who is to use a frequency to be determined in the market. But the enforcement of such detailed regulations for the operation of stations as are now imposed by the Federal Communications Commission would severely limit the extent to which the way the frequency was used could be determined by the forces of the market.

It might be argued that this is by no means an unusual situation, since the rights acquired when one buys, say, a piece of land, are determined not by the forces of supply and demand but by the law of property in land. But this is by no means the whole truth. Whether a newly discovered cave belongs to the man who discovered it, the man on whose land the entrance to the cave is located, or the man who owns the surface under which the cave is situated is no doubt dependent on the law of property. But the law merely determines the person with whom it is necessary to make a contract to obtain the use of the cave. Whether the cave is used for storing bank records, as a natural gas reservoir, or for growing mushrooms depends, not on the law of property, but on whether the bank, the natural gas corporation, or the mushroom concern will pay the most in order to be able to use the cave. One of the purposes of the legal system is to establish that clear delimitation of rights on the basis of which the transfer and recombination of rights can take place through the market. In the case of radio, it should be possible for someone who is granted the use of a frequency to arrange to share it with someone else, with whatever adjustments to hours of operation, power, location and kind of transmitter, etc., as may be mutually agreed upon; or when the right initially acquired is the shared use of a frequency (and in certain cases the FCC has permitted only shared usage), it should not be made impossible for one user to buy out the rights of the other users so as to obtain an exclusive usage.

The main reason for government regulation of the radio industry was to prevent interference. It is clear that, if signals are transmitted simultaneously on a given frequency by several people, the signals would interfere with each other and would make reception of the messages transmitted by any one person difficult, if not impossible. The use of a piece of land simultaneously for growing wheat and as a parking lot would produce similar results. As we have seen in an earlier section, the way this situation is avoided is to create property rights (rights, that is, to exclusive use) in land. The creation of similar rights in the use of frequencies would enable the problem to be solved in the same way in the radio industry.

The advantage of establishing exclusive rights to use a resource when that use does not harm others (apart from the fact that they are excluded from using it) is easily understood. However, the case appears to be different when it concerns an action which harms others directly. For example, a radio operator may use a frequency in such a way as to cause interference to those using adjacent frequencies.

Let us start our analysis of this situation by considering the case of *Sturges v. Bridgman*[51], which illustrates the basic issues. A confectioner had used certain premises for his business for a great many years. When a doctor came and occupied a neighboring property, the working of the confectioner's machinery caused the doctor no harm until, some eight years later, he built a consulting room at the end of his garden, right against the confectioner's premises. Then it was found that noise and vibrations caused by the machinery disturbed the doctor in his work. The doctor then brought an action and succeeded in securing an injunction preventing the confectioner from using his machinery. What the courts had, in fact, to decide was whether the doctor had the right to impose additional costs on the confectioner through compelling him to install new machinery, or move to a new location, or whether the confectioner had the right to impose additional costs on the doctor through compelling him to do his consulting somewhere else on his premises or at another location.[52] What this example shows is that there is no analytical difference between the right to use a resource without direct harm to others and the right to conduct operations in such a way as to produce direct harm to others. In each case something is denied to others: In one case, use of a resource; in the other, use of a mode of operation.[53] This example also brings out the reciprocal nature of the relationship which tends to be ignored by economists who, following Pigou, approach the problem in terms of a difference between private and social products but fail to make clear that the suppression of the harm which A inflicts on B inevitably inflicts harm on A. The problem is to avoid the more serious harm. This aspect is clearly brought out in *Sturges v. Bridgman*, and the case would not have been different in essentials if the doctor's complaint had been about smoke pollution rather than noise and vibrations.

Once the legal rights of the parties are established, negotiation is possible to modify the arrangements envisaged in the legal ruling, if the likelihood of being able to do so makes it worthwhile to incur the costs involved in negotiation. The doctor would be willing to waive his right if the confectioner would pay him a sum of money greater than the additional costs he would have incurred in carrying out his consulting at another location (which we will assume to be $200) . The confectioner would be willing to pay up to an amount slightly less than the additional costs imposed on him by the decision of the court in order to induce the doctor to waive his rights (which we will assume to be $100). With the figures given, the doctor would not accept less than $200, and the confectioner would not pay more than $100, and the doctor would not waive his right. But consider the situation if the confectioner had won the case (as well he might). In these circumstances the confectioner would be willing to waive his right if he could obtain more than $100, and the doctor would be willing to pay slightly less than $200 to induce the confectioner to do so. Thus it should be possible to strike a bargain which would result in the confectioner's waiving his right. This hypothetical example shows that the delimitation of rights is an essential prelude to market transactions; but the ultimate result (which maximizes the value of production) is independent of the legal decision.[54]

What this analysis demonstrates, so far as the radio industry is concerned, is that there is no analytical difference between the problem of interference between operators on a single frequency and that of interference between operators on adjacent frequencies. The latter problem, like the former, can be solved by delimiting the rights of operators to transmit signals which interfere, or might potentially interfere, with those of others. Once this is done, it can be left to market transactions to bring an optimum utilization of rights. It is sometimes implied that the aim of regulation in the radio industry should be to minimize interference. But this would be wrong. The aim should be to maximize output. All property rights interfere with the ability of people to use resources. What has to be insured is that the gain from interference more than offsets the harm it produces. There is no reason to suppose that the optimum situation is one in which there is no interference. In general, as the distance from a radio station increases, it becomes more and more difficult to receive its signals. At some point, people will decide that it is not worthwhile to incur costs involved in receiving the station's signals. A local station operating on the same frequency might be easily received by these same people. But if this station operated simultaneously with the first one, people living in some region intermediate between the stations may be unable to receive signals from either station. These people would be better off if either station stopped operating and there was no interference; but then those living in the neighborhood of one of these other stations would suffer. It is not clear that the solution in which there is no interference is necessarily preferable.

In some circumstances it has been suggested that cost considerations may lead to a minimizing of interference. Thus it has been said of mobile radio:

> Dollar discipline is a very effective force which prevents unwarranted overdesign of land mobile communications system. Vehicular communication is a business tool and like any other tool, the return on investment suffers if excessive overcapacity is provided. Experience has shown that land mobile station licensees are not willing to pay for equipment to provide coverage significantly in excess of their requirements. This attitude serves to effectively reduce adjacent area, co-channel interference to a minimum.[55]

But cost considerations alone cannot always be relied upon to bring about such happy results. The reduction of interference on adjacent frequencies may require costly improvements in equipment, and operators on one frequency could hardly be expected to incur such costs for the benefit of others if the rights of those operating on adjacent frequencies have not been determined. The institution of private property plus the pricing system would resolve these conflicts. The operator whose signals were interfered with, if he had the right to stop such interference, would be willing to forego this right if he were paid more than the amount by which the value of his service was decreased by this interference or the costs which he would have to incur to offset it. The other operator would be willing to pay, in order to be allowed to interfere, an amount up to the costs of suppressing the interference or the decrease in the value of the service he could provide if unable to use his transmitter in a way which resulted in interference. Or, alternatively, if this operator had the right to cause interference, he would be willing to desist if he were paid more than the costs of suppressing the interference or the decrease in the value of the service he could provide if interference were barred. And the operator whose signals were interfered with would be willing to pay to stop this interference an amount up to the decrease in the value of his service which it causes or the costs he has to incur to offset the interference. Either way, the result would be the same. It is the problem of the confectioner's noise and vibrations all over again.

The fact that actions might have harmful effects on others has been shown to be no obstacle to the introduction of property rights. But it was possible to reach this unequivocal result because the conflicts of interest were between individuals. When large numbers of people are involved, the argument for the institution of property rights is weakened and that for general regulations becomes stronger. The example commonly given by economists, again following Pigou, of a situation which calls for such regulation is that created by smoke pollution. Of course, if there were only one source of smoke and only one person were harmed, no new complication would be involved; it would not differ from the vibration case discussed earlier. But if many people are harmed and there are several sources of pollution, it is more difficult to reach a satisfactory solution through the market. When the transfer of rights has to come about as a result of market transactions carried out between large numbers of people or organizations acting jointly, the process of negotiation may be so difficult and time-consuming as to make such transfers a practical impossibility. Even the enforcement of rights through the courts may not be easy. It may be costly to discover who it is that is causing the trouble. And, when it is not in the interest of any single person or organization to bring suit, the problems involved in arranging joint actions represent a further obstacle. As a practical matter, the market may become too costly to operate.

In these circumstances it may be preferable to impose special regulations (whether embodied in a statute or brought about as a result of the rulings of an administrative agency). Such regulations state what people must or must not do. When this is done, the law directly determines the location of economic activities, methods of production, and so on. Thus the problem of smoke pollution may be dealt with by regulations which specify the kind of heating and power equipment which can be used in houses and factories or which confine manufacturing establishments to certain districts by zoning arrangements. The aim of such regulation should not, of course, be to eliminate smoke pollution but to bring about the optimum amount of smoke pollution. The gains from reducing it have to be matched with the loss in production due to the restrictions in choice of methods of production, etc. The conditions which make such regulation desirable do not change the nature of the problem. And, in principle, the solution to be sought is that which would have been achieved if the institution of private property and the pricing mechanism were working well. Of course, as the making of such special regulations is dependent on the political organization, the regulatory process will suffer from the disadvantages mentioned in the previous section. But this merely means that, before turning to special regulations, one should tolerate a worse functioning market than would otherwise be the case. It does not mean that there should be no such regulation. Nor should it be thought that, because some rights are determined by regulation, there cannot be others which can be modified by contract. That zoning and other regulations apply to houses does not mean that there should not be private property in houses. Businessmen usually find themselves both subject to regulation and possessed of rights which may be transferred or modified by contracts with others.

There is no reason why users of radio frequencies should not be in the same position as other businessmen. There would not appear, for example, to be any need to regulate the relations between users of the same frequency. Once the rights of potential users have been determined initially, the rearrangement of rights could be left to the market. The simplest way of doing this would undoubtedly be to dispose of the use of a frequency to the highest bidder, thus leaving the subdivision of the use of the frequency to subsequent market transactions. Nor is it clear that the relations between users of adjacent frequencies will necessarily call for special regulation. It may well be that several people would normally be involved in a single transaction if conflicts of interests between users of adjacent frequencies are to be settled through the market. But, though an increase in the number of people involved increases the cost of carrying out a transaction, we know from experience that it is quite practicable to have market transactions which involve a multiplicity of parties. Whether the number of parties normally involved in transactions involving users of adjacent frequencies would be unduly large and call for special regulation, only experience could show. Some special regulation would certainly be required. For example, some types of medical equipment can apparently be operated in such a way as to cause interference on many frequencies and over long distances. In such a case, a regulation limiting the power of the equipment and requiring shielding would probably be desirable. It is also true that the need for wide bands of frequencies for certain purposes may require the exercise of the power of eminent domain; but this does not raise a problem different from that encountered in other fields. It is easy to embrace the idea that the interconnections between the ways in which frequencies are used raise special problems not found elsewhere or, at least, not to the same degree. But this view is not likely to survive the study of a book on the law of torts or on the law of property in which will be found set out the many (and often extraordinary) ways in which one person's actions can affect the use which others can make of their property.

If the problems faced in the broadcasting industry are not out of the ordinary, it may be asked why was not the usual solution (a mixture of transferable rights plus regulation) adopted for this industry? There can be little doubt that, left to themselves, the courts would have solved the problems of the radio industry in much the same way as they had solved similar problems in other industries. In the early discussions of radio law an attempt was made to bring the problems within the main corpus of existing law. The problem of radio interference was examined by analogy with electric-wire interference, water rights, trade marks, noise nuisances, the problem of acquiring title to ice from public ponds, and so on. It was, for example, pointed out that a "receiving set is merely a device for decoying to the human ear signals which otherwise would not reach it," and an analogy was drawn with a case in which one man had maintained a decoy for wild ducks but another on neighboring land had frightened the ducks away by shooting, so that they avoided the decoy. Some of the analogies were no doubt fanciful, but most of them presented essentially the same problem as that posed by radio interference. And when the problem came before the courts, there seems to have been little difficulty in reaching a decision.[56] No doubt, in time, statutes prescribing some special regulation would also have been required. But this line of development was stopped by the passage of the 1927 Act, which established a complete regulatory system.[57]

Support for the 1927 Act came, in part, from a belief that no other solution was possible, and, as we have seen, the rationale which has developed since certainly largely reflects this view. But some of those who favored government regulation in the early 1920's did so in order to prevent the establishment of property rights in frequencies. Their reasons for wanting government regulation were vividly expressed by Mr. Walter S. Rogers:

> There is no question that certain private radio companies believe that by something analogous to what we call "Squatters' Rights" they can secure an actual out-and-out ownership of the right to use wave lengths, and they do not want to get the right to use wave lengths through a license from any government or as a result of any international agreement. They want to hold completely the right to the use of wave lengths which they employ in their services. In a certain sense the development of radio has opened up a new domain comparable to the discovery of a hitherto unknown continent. No one can foresee with certitude the possible development of the transmission of energy through space. Really great stakes are being gambled for. And private interests are trying to obtain control of wave lengths and establish private property claims to them

precisely as though a new continent were opened up to them and they were securing great tracts of land in outright ownership.[58]

Similar views were held in Congress. Mr. Harry P. Warner has explained that, during the period before the 1927 Act,

> the gravest fears were expressed by legislators, and those generally charged with the administration of communications ... that government regulation of an effective sort might be permanently prevented through the accrual of property rights in licenses or means of access, and that thus franchises of the value of millions of dollars might be established for all time.[59]

It may be that in some cases these views reflected a dislike of the institution of private property as such, but in the main what seems to have been feared is that private persons and organizations might establish property rights in frequencies without making any payment for appropriating what was called "the last of the public domain." The view that property rights in frequencies should be acquired in an orderly fashion and that those acquiring these rights should be required to pay for them is clearly one which commands respect. But this is not what happened as a result of the 1927 Act. In fact, government regulation brought about the very results which some of its supporters had sought to avoid. Because no charge has been made for the use of frequencies, franchises worth millions of dollars have been created, have been bought and sold, and have served to enrich those to whom they were first granted. Intertwined with the dislike of property rights acquired by priority of use was the fear that monopolies might be established. But, as we have seen (although in discussions of broadcasting policy it is often overlooked), it is not necessary to abolish the institution of private property in order to control the growth of monopolies.

When we contemplate the simple misunderstandings which are rife in discussions of government policy toward the radio industry, it is difficult to resist the conclusion that one factor that has helped to bring this about is terminological in character.[60] I have spoken, following the normal usage, of the allocation of frequencies (or the use of frequencies) and of the establishment of property rights in frequencies (or the use of frequencies). But this way of speaking is liable to mislead. Every regular wave motion may be described as a frequency. The various musical notes correspond to frequencies in sound waves; the various colors correspond to frequencies in light waves. But it has not been thought necessary to allocate to different persons or to create property rights in the notes of the musical scale or the colors of the rainbow. To handle the problem arising because one person's use of a sound or light wave may have effects on others, we establish the rights which people have to make sounds which others may hear or to do things which others may see.

Clarity of thought is even more difficult to achieve when we speak not of ownership of frequencies but of ownership of the ether, the medium through which the wave travels. Mr. James G. McCain has argued that the "radio wave [should] be clearly distinguished from the medium through which it is transmitted. Metaphorically, it is the difference between a train and a tunnel." His reason for making this distinction is that it affords the "most satisfactory" basis for holding radio communication to be interstate commerce. His argument, briefly, is that the ether by reason of its omnipresence and the use to which it is devoted constitutes a natural channel for interstate commerce, thus making federal regulation of radio communication constitutional under the commerce clause.[61] The Senate once declared the ether or its use to be "the inalienable possession" of the United States, and today all those to whom radio or television licenses are granted have to sign a waiver of any right not only to the use of a frequency but also to the use of the ether. This attempt to nationalize the ether has not been without its critics. There is some doubt whether the ether exists. Certainly, its properties correspond exactly to those of something which does not exist, a tunnel without any edges. And Mr. Stephen Davis has remarked: "Whoever claims ownership of a thing or substance may very properly be required to prove existence before discussing title."[62]

What does not seem to have been understood is that what is being allocated by the Federal Communications Commission, or, if there were a market, what would be sold, is the right to use a piece of equipment to transmit signals in a particular way. Once the question is looked at in this way, it is unnecessary to think in terms of ownership of frequencies or the ether. Earlier we discussed a case in which it had to be decided whether a confectioner had the right to use machinery which caused noise and vibrations in a neighboring house. It would not have facilitated our analysis of the case if it had been discussed in terms of who owned sound waves or vibrations or the medium (whatever it is) through which sound waves or vibrations travel. Yet this is essentially what is done in the radio industry. The reason why this way of thinking has become so dominant in discussions of radio law is that it seems to have developed by using the analogy of the law of airspace. In fact, the law of radio and television has commonly been treated as part of the law of the air.[63] It is not suggested that this approach need lead to the wrong answers, but it tends to obscure the question that is being decided. Thus, whether we have the right to shoot over another man's land has been thought of as depending on who owns the airspace over the land.[64] It would be simpler to discuss what we should be allowed to do with a gun. As we saw earlier, we cannot shoot a gun even on our own land when the effect is to frighten ducks that a neighbor is engaged in decoying. And we all know that there are many other restrictions on the uses of a gun. The problem confronting the radio industry is that signals transmitted by one person may interfere with those transmitted by another. It can be solved by delimiting the rights which various persons possess. How far this delimitation of rights should come about as a result of a strict regulation and how far as a result of transactions on the market is a question that can be answered only on the basis of practical experience. But there is good reason to believe that the present system, which relies exclusively on regulation and in which private property and the pricing system play no part, is not the best solution.

In defining property rights, it would be necessary to take into account the existence of international agreements on the use of radio frequencies.[65] Such agreements do not, of course, prevent bidding by individuals and firms for the facilities which have been allocated to the United States. But, to the extent that the ways in which frequencies can be used are specified in the agreements, the transfer and recombination of rights through the market are restricted. However, the reservation contained in the present agreements by which frequencies can be used "in derogation of the table of frequency allocations" when this does not cause harmful interference to stations in foreign countries operating in conformity with the table would seem to permit considerable flexibility in the way frequencies are used. (There is no legal restriction on military use of radio frequencies.)[66] The aim of the United States government should be to secure the maximum freedom for countries to use radio frequencies as they wish. To read the intentions of a government from the proceedings of an international conference is obviously hazardous. But on the surface it is not clear that the United States government wished to secure this maximum of freedom. In the conference of 1947, the group of countries led by the United States "wanted to take the frequency requirements of all the countries of the world and fit them 'by engineering principles' into the available frequency spectrum." The group led by the Soviet Union "wanted to use the old international frequency list as a point of departure, assigning frequencies on the basis of dates of notification."[67] In effect, the Soviet Union seemed to want the establishment of international property rights based on priority. Since the Soviet Union had registered notifications of claim to large parts of the radio spectrum, it is probably true that the acceptance of their proposals would have given the Soviet Union advantages. But it also seems clear from the conference proceedings that the Soviet Union was unwilling to give the details required for an assessment of its needs and did not wish to be bound in its internal arrangements by the decisions of an international conference.[68] In the National Missile Conference held in Washington in May, 1959, two scientists (British and American) called for "the creation of an international communications commission to administer and police future myriad uses of the electronics spectrum in space communications, overseas space television, weather reports and other activities."[69] If this international body is to be patterned after the the Federal Communications Commission, there are obvious dangers in this proposal. It would not be wise for the United States to press (possibly against Russian opposition) for the establishment of an international planning system which would make it difficult or impossible to operate a free-enterprise system in the United States.

VI. The Present Position

The Federal Communications Commission has recently come into public prominence as a result of disclosures before the House Subcommittee on Legislative Oversight, concerning the extent to which pressure is brought to bear on the Commission by politicians and businessmen (who often use methods of dubious propriety) with a view to influencing its decisions.[70] That this should be happening is hardly surprising. When rights, worth millions of dollars, are awarded to one businessman and denied to others, it is no wonder if some applicants become overanxious and attempt to use whatever influence they have (political and otherwise), particularly as they can never be sure what pressure the other applicants may be exerting. Some of the suggestions for improving the situation—for example, the enactment of a statutory code of ethics—may have merit in themselves. Others, such as the creation of administrative courts, may secure greater honesty at the expense of efficiency. But what needs to be emphasized is that the problem, so far as the Federal Communications Commission is concerned, largely arises because of a failure to charge for the rights granted. If these rights were disposed of to the highest bidder, the main reason for these improper activities would disappear. In the panel discussion on the Administrative Process and Ethical Questions held by the Subcommittee, a similar point of view was expressed by Professor Clark Byse of the Harvard Law School:

A TV license in some areas often is worth millions of dollars. The Administrative agency dispensing this bonanza operates under the broadest type of congressional direction. The agency is told to grant an application if public convenience, interest, or necessity will be served. It is true that the Commission has developed a number of criteria to govern its exercise of this broad grant of power. But the criteria are so general and numerous that it is often difficult to determine whether Commission action is the product of reasoned deliberation or of caprice. Would it not have been better if Congress had established some basic criteria concerning competence, diversification of mass communication media, and monopoly, and then had provided that the licenses should go to the highest bidder? There may be drawbacks to this suggestion in the TV area, and the device of automatic criteria perhaps cannot be widely adopted. But certainly the goal should be to limit discretion to the narrowest legitimate limits, particularly when the legislation authorizes distribution of a bonanza or contemplates the substitution of an administrative decision for a decision which would otherwise be determined by the forces of competition.[71]

At the present time the idea of using the pricing mechanism in the radio industry is coldly received, and it is not surprising that Professor Byse's suggestion was not taken up in the report of the Subcommittee. In part, this hostile attitude is a reflection of the misunderstandings which have been discussed in previous sections;[72] but there is more to it than that. When Professor Smythe had completed his economic case against using the pricing system (in the article discussed earlier), he introduced an argument of a quite different character. He said that

> A second broad postulate which seems to underlie proposals such as that advanced (by Mr. Herzel) is politico-economic in nature: that the public weal will be served if broadcasting, like grocery stores, uses the conventional business organization, subject only to general legal restraints on its profit-seeking activity. This postulate carries with

it, usually, the parallel assumption that the educational and cultural responsibilities of broadcast station operators ought to be no more substantial at the most than those of the operators of the newspapers and magazines.

...Despite the extensive use made of these two assumptions by business organizations for propaganda purposes, there is a powerful tradition in the United States that the economic, educational and cultural rights and responsibilities of broadcasting are unique.[73]

Professor Smythe's position would seem to be that broadcasting plays (or should play) a more important role, educationally and culturally, than newspapers and magazines (and, I assume he would add, books) and that, therefore, there ought to be stricter governmental regulation of what is broadcast than of what is printed. It is possible to dispute both parts of this argument. But Professor Smythe is right to claim that this view (or something like it) has been long and firmly held by most of those concerned with broadcasting policy in the United States. Thus Mr. Hoover in 1924 said:

Radio communication is not to be considered as merely a business carried on for private gain, for private advertisement, or for entertainment of the curious. It is a public concern impressed with the public trust and to be considered primarily from the standpoint of public interest in the same extent and upon the basis of the same general principles as our other public utilities.[74]

And the present chairman of the Federal Communications Commission, Mr. John C. Doerfer, in 1959, said that regulation of programing

stems from the potential power inherent in broadcasting to influence the minds of men and the concomitant scarcity of the available frequencies. The conjunction ... of potentially great persuasive powers and the insufficiency of desirable spectrum space, has been the mainspring of all actions: legislative, administrative or court, which has qualified those freedoms generally enjoyed by the journalist, the artist and the minister.[75]

If the aim of government regulation of broadcasting is to influence programing, it is irrelevant to discuss whether regulation is necessitated by the technology of the industry. The question does, of course, arise as to whether such regulation is compatible with the doctrine of freedom of speech and of the press. In general, this is not a question which has disturbed those who wished to see the Federal Communications Commission control programing, largely because they thought a dear distinction could be drawn between broadcasting and the publication of newspapers, periodicals, and books (for which few would advocate similar regulation).[76] Thus, in a comment on the *Mayflower* doctrine, we read:

> ... radio is unique. It involves a medium which, while quantitatively limited, has almost infinite capacities as a means for mass communication of ideas, and which is essentially unthinkable as a subject of any but public ownership. To draw an analogy to freedom of the individual or of the press is fruitless in this area.[77]

The Supreme Court made the distinction between broadcasting and the publication of newspapers rest on the fact that a resource used in broadcasting is limited in amount and scarce. But, as we have seen, this argument is invalid. Another common argument is that, since broadcasters are making use of public property, the government has a right to see that such public resources are used "in the public interest." "Radio is a public domain to which licensees have only conditional and temporary access. Its 'landlord' is the public. Licensees are 'tenant farmers.' The public's 'factor' is the FCC."[78] This would seem to give the government the right to influence what is printed in newspapers, periodicals, and books if one of the resources used were public property or subject to government allocation. Mr. Justin Miller, the president of the National Association of Broadcasters, in evidence to a Senate subcommittee in 1947, pointed out that government regulation of what a newspaper could print would be held unconstitutional. But broadcasting also came within the protection of the First Amendment, and therefore, he argued, regulation designed to influence the programing of broadcasting stations was unconstitutional. The senators seem to have been completely unconvinced by Mr. Miller's arguments. Senator McFarland said:

... there is a difference between the press and the radio. You can compare them but you can not assume they are alike. You are granting frequencies in the radio field. Once a license is granted, it is worth a lot of money. That is not true with the press at all. That is where you people get off base, in my opinion.

And Senator White said:

I just do not get at all the idea that there is a complete analogy between a broadcast license, which comes from the Government and is an exercise of power by Government, and the right of anybody to start a newspaper, anybody who wants to, without any let or permission or hindrance from the Government... It is pretty difficult for me to see how a regulatory body can say that a licensee is or is not rendering a public service if it may not take a look and take into account the character of the program being broadcast by that licensee.[79]

These comments point clearly to the misunderstanding involved in this defense of the present system. The argument moves from the existence of public property in frequencies to the assertion of the right which this gives to influence programing. But, as we have seen, there is no reason why there should not be private property in frequencies.[80] If regulation of programing is desirable, it has to be advocated on its own merits; it cannot be justified simply as a by-product of particular economic arrangements. To say that resources should be used in the public interest does not settle the issue. Since it is generally agreed that the use of private property and the pricing system is in the public interest in other fields, why should it not also be in broadcasting?

Mr. William Howard Taft, who was Chief Justice of the Supreme Court during the critical formative period of the broadcasting industry, is reported to have said: "I have always dodged this radio question. I have refused to grant writs and have told the other justices that I hope to avoid passing on this subject as long as possible." Pressed to explain why, he answered:

> ... interpreting the law on this subject is something like trying to interpret the law of the occult. It seems like dealing with something supernatural. I want to put it off as long as possible in the hope that it becomes more understandable before the court passes on the questions involved.[81]

It was indeed in the shadows cast by a mysterious technology that our views on broadcasting policy were formed. It has been the burden of this article to show that the problems posed by the broadcasting industry do not call for any fundamental changes in the legal and economic arrangements which serve other industries. But the belief that broadcasting industry is unique and requires regulation of a kind which would be unthinkable in the other media of communication is now so firmly held as perhaps to be beyond the reach of critical examination. The history of regulation in the broadcasting industry demonstrates the crucial importance of events in the early days of a new development in determining long-run governmental policy. It also suggests that lawyers and economists should not be so overwhelmed by the emergence of new technologies as to change the existing legal and economic system without first making quite certain that this is required.

Notes

[1] This short account of the development of radio regulation does not call for extensive documentation, but sources are given for all quotations and in other cases where they might be difficult to identify. I found the following books and the references therein particularly helpful: H. P. Warner, Radio and Television Law (1948), and L. F. Schmeckebier, The Federal Radio Commission (1932).

[2] S. Rep. No. 659, 61st Cong., 2d Sess. 4 (1910).

[3] S. Rep. No. 698, 62d Cong., 2d Sess. 3 (1912).

[4] Mention should also be made of one bill (S. 5630, 62d Cong. [1912]) which gave the task of regulating radio communication to the Interstate Commerce Commission and another (H.R. 23716, 62d Cong. [1912]) which provided for government ownership of wireless telegraphs.

[5] Hearings on H.R. 13159, A Bill to Further Regulate Radio Communication, before the House Committee on the Merchant Marine and Fisheries, 65th Cong., 3d Sess. (1918).

[6] See Schmeckebier, op. cit. supra note 1, at 4.

[7] For details of these conferences, see Schmeckebier, op. cit. supra note 1, at 6-12.

[8] Hoover v. Intercity Radio Co., 286 Fed. 1003 (App. D.C., 1923).

[9] United States v. Zenith Radio Corp., 12 F.2d 614 (N.D. Ill., 1926).

[10] 35 Ops. Att'y Gen. 126 (1926). The question was submitted on June 4, 1926, and the opinion rendered on July 8, 1926.

[11] The main difference between these two acts was the insertion in the 1934 Act of two new provisions. One was a prohibition against the advertisement or conduct of lotteries (Section 316, presently Title 18, U.S.C. § 1304). The other required anyone maintaining studios to supply programs (whether by wire or otherwise) for foreign stations which could be heard in the United States to obtain a permit from the Commission (Section 325(b)).

[12] The Davis Amendment of 1928 which directed the Commission to make an equal allocation of broadcasting facilities among five zones of the United States and an equitable distribution, according to population, among the states in each zone was incorporated in the 1934 Act. But in 1936 the original wording of the 1927 Act, which merely required the Commission to make "a fair, efficient and equitable distribution" was reinstated.

[13] The Commission on Freedom of the Press, A Free and Responsible Press 109 (1947).

[14] Z. Chafee, Government and Mass Communications 235-241 (1947).

[15] United States v. Paramount Pictures, Inc., 334 U.S. 131, 166 (1948).

[16] Caldwell, Freedom of Speech and Radio Broadcasting, 177 Annals 179, 203 (1935).

[17] Opening Address of Herbert Hoover before the Fourth Annual Radio Conference (1925). Reproduced in Hearings on S. 1 and S. 1754, Radio Control, before the Senate Committee on Interstate Commerce, 69th Cong., 1st Sess. 50, 57-58 (1926).

[18] Old Standards in New Context: A Comparative Analysis of FCC Regulation, 18 U. of Chi. L. Rev. 78, 83 (1950).

[19] Caldwell, The Standard of Public Interest, Convenience or Necessity as Used in the Radio Act of 1927, 1 Air L. Rev. 295, 296 (1930).

[20] It is unnecessary for my purpose to review the policies of the Federal Radio Commission and the Federal Communications Commission in choosing among applicants and passing on the renewal of licenses. For discussions of such questions, the reader is referred to Warner, op. cit. supra note 1; J. M. Edelman, The Licensing of Radio Services in the United States, 1927 to 1947 (1950); Federal Communications Commission, Report of the Network Study Staff on Network Broadcasting (1957), particularly Chapter 3, "Performance in the Public Interest."

[21] Decisions of the FCC, Docket No. 967, June S, 1931. Quoted from Caldwell, Censorship of Radio Programs, 1 J. Radio Law 441, 473 (1931).

[22] Id.

[23] Editorializing by Broadcast Licensees, 13 F.C.C. 1246, 1257 (1949). Cf. *Mayflower* Broadcasting Corp., 8 FCC 333 (1940).

[24] Federal Communications Commission, Public Service Responsibility of Broadcast Licensees 55 (1946).

[25] See WBNX Broadcasting Co., 12 FCC. 805 (1948). For the view that this evidence may have had some effect on the Commission's decision, see Radio Program Controls: A Network of Inadequacy, 57 Yale L. J. 275 (1947).

[26] R. S. Brown, Jr., Loyalty and Security: Employment Tests in the United States, 371-372 (1958). For further details of this case and the questions it raises, see an article by the same author, Character and Candor Requirements for FCC Licensees, 22 Law & Contemp. Prob. 644 (1957).

[27] See the Report of the Network Study Staff on Network Broadcasting, op. cit. supra note 20, at 150-151. The exact number of cases in which the failure to renew a license was due to past programing (that is, in which the renewal would have been made had the programing been different) is uncertain. See E. E. Smead, Freedom of Speech by Radio and Television I23 n. 7 (1959).

[28] Z. Chafee, Free Speech in the United States 381 (1942).

[29] *National Broadcasting Co. v. United States*, 319 U.S. 190, 213, 215-217 (1943).

[30] C. A. Siepmann, Radio, Television and Society 5-6 (1950).

[31] "Public Interest" and the Market in Color Television Regulation, 18 U. of Chi. L. Rev. 802, 809 (1951).

[32] Smythe, Facing Facts about the Broadcast Business, 20 U. of Chi. L. Rev. 96 (1952), and a Rejoinder by the student author, Mr. Leo Herzel, which appeared in 20 U. of Chi. L. Rev. 106 (1952).

[33] Of course not all these frequencies would be equally desirable for use in the broadcasting industry.

[34] See United States v. Radio Corp. of America, 358 U.S. 334 (1959).

[35] Compare the statement of the court in Mansfield Journal Co. v. FCC, 180 F.2d 28, 33 (App.D.C., 1950): "Whether Mansfield's activities do or do not amount to a positive violation of law, and neither this court nor the Federal Communications Commission is determining that question, they still may impair Mansfield's ability to serve the public. Thus, whether Mansfield's competitive practices were legal or illegal, in the strict sense, is not conclusive here. Monopoly in the mass communication of news and advertising is contrary to the public interest, even if not in terms proscribed by the antitrust laws."

[36] Recent Articles, 13 Fed. Com. B J. 89 (1953).

[37] Hearings on Subscription Television before the House Committee on Interstate and Foreign Commerce, 85th Cong., 2d Sess. 434 (1958).

[38] A former chairman of the Federal Communications Commission argued that it could not be intelligent in its regulation "if... [the Commission's] information lags behind the latest developments and policies of the industry—if the industry knows more than the government does." Edelman, op. cit. supra note 20, at 20. But it is inevitable that the industry will know more than the Commission.
[39] Broadcasting, February 4, 1957, p. 96.
[40] Broadcasting, February 24, 1958, p. 200.
[41] On the Commission's policies with regard to financial qualifications, consult Edelman, op. cit. supra note 20, at 62-64, and Warner, op. cit. supra note 1, § 22a.
[42] The first four firms are so well known as not to require any notation. The Storer Broadcasting Company owns television stations in Toledo, Cleveland, Detroit, Atlanta, and Wilmington and radio stations in Toledo, Cleveland, Detroit, Philadelphia, Wheeling, Atlanta, and Miami. Of the three stations owned by newspaper publishing concerns, one in Philadelphia is owned by Triangle Publications (which publishes the Philadelphia Inquirer and other papers, owns four other television stations and some radio stations), one in Detroit is owned by the publisher of the Detroit News, and one in San Francisco is owned by the publisher of the San Francisco Chronicle.
[43] See the Annual Report of the Federal Communications Commission for 1957 at p. 123, and for 1958, at p. 121.
[44] See Radio and Television Station Transfers: Adequacy of Supervision under the Federal Communications Act, 30 Ind. L. J. 351 (1955), and Warner, op. cit. supra note 1, Chapter V, "The Transfer and Assignment of Broadcasting Licenses." Compare C. C. Dill, Radio Law 208-209 (1938).
[45] See Hearings on S. 1 and S. 1754, Radio Control, before the Senate Committee on Interstate Commerce, 69th Cong, 1st Sess. 38-47 (1926).
[46] Consult Stewart, The Public Control of Radio, 8 Air L. Rev. 131 (1937) ; Hettinger, The Economic Factor in Radio Regulation, 9 Air L. Rev. 115 (1939); Salsbury, The Transfer of Broadcast Rights, 11 Air L. Rev. 113 (1940); Lissner, Public Control of Radio, 5 Am. J. Econ. & Soc. 552 (1946).
[47] FCC v. Sanders Bros. Radio Station, 309 U.S. 470, 474 (1940).
[48] Lissner, op. cit. supra note 46.
[49] Press release dated April 14, 1958, from the office of Congressman Henry S. Reuss. See H.R. 11893, 85th Cong., 2d Sess. (1958).
[50] 100 Cong. Rec. 3783 (1954).
[51] 11 Ch. D. 852 (1879).
[52] Another possibility is that the doctor or confectioner might abandon his activity altogether.
[53] In the case of *Sturges v. Bridgman*, the situation would not have been analytically different had the dispute concerned the ownership of a piece of land lying between the two premises on which either the doctor could have installed his laboratory or the confectioner could have installed his machinery.
[54] It is, of course, true that the distribution of wealth as between the doctor and the confectioner was affected by the decision, which is why questions of equity bulk so largely in such cases. Indeed, if the efficiency with which the economic system worked was completely independent of the legal position, this would be all that mattered. But this is not so. First of all, the law may be such as to make certain desirable market transactions impossible. This is, indeed, my chief criticism of the present American

law of radio communication. Second, it may impose costly and time-consuming procedures. Third, the legal delimitation of rights provides the starting point for the rearrangement of rights through market transactions. Such transactions are not costless, with a result that the initial delimitation of rights may be maintained even though some other would be more efficient. Or, even if the original position is modified, the most efficient delimitation of rights may not be attained. Finally, a waste of resources may occur when the criteria used by the courts to delimit rights result in resources being employed solely to establish a claim.

[55] Testimony of Motorola Inc., Statutory Inquiry into the Allocation of Frequencies to the Various Non-Government Services in the Radio Spectrum between 25 mc and 890 mc, FCC Docket No. 11997, March 30, 1959, at p. 29.

[56] See S. Davis, The Law of Radio Communication (1927), particularly Chapter VII, "Conflicting Rights in Reception and Transmission." Articles dealing with this question are: Rowley, Problems in the Law of Radio Communication, 1 U. of Cinc. L. Rev. 1 (1927); Taugher, The Law of Radio Communication with Particular Reference to a Property Right in a Radio Wave Length, 12 Marq. L. Rev. 179, 299 (1928); Dyer, Radio Interference as a Tort, 17 St. Louis L. Rev. 125 (1932). In the case of Tribune Co. v. Oak Leaves Broadcasting Station (Cir. Ct., Cook County, Illinois, 1926), reproduced in 68 Cong. Rec. 216 (1926), it was held that the operator of an existing station had a sufficient property right, acquired by priority, to enjoin a newcomer from using a frequency so as to cause any material interference.

[57] Although attempts were made to assert property rights in frequencies after the establishment of the Federal Radio Commission, such claims were not sustained. See Warner, op. cit. supra note 1, at 543.

[58] Rogers, Air as a Raw Material, 112 Annals 251, 254 (1924). Mr. Rogers was adviser to the American Delegation to the Peace Conference in Paris, 1919. Compare Childs, Problems in the Radio Industry, 14 *The American Economics Review*, 520 (1924).

[59] Warner, op. cit. supra note 1, at 540.

[60] In the development of my ideas on this subject, I was greatly helped by an article by Segal and Warner, "Ownership" of Broadcasting "Frequencies": A Review, 19 Rocky Mt. L. Rev. 111 (1947).

[61] McCain, The Medium through which the Radio Wave Is Transmitted as a Natural Channel of Interstate Commerce, 11 *Air Law Review*. 144 (1940). The grounds on which radio communication has been held to be interstate commerce are not those advanced by Mr. McCain. As he explains, the reasons given by the courts for holding radio communication to be interstate commerce are that radio waves cross state lines (even though the communication is intrastate) and potentially interfere with interstate communication. The advantage of Mr. McCain's approach would appear to be that it would allow federal regulation of intrastate communication which interferes with no one. Other articles dealing with this question are: Fletcher, The Interstate Character of Radio Broadcasting: An Opinion, 11 *Air Law Review*. 345 (1940), and Kennedy, Radio and the Commerce Clause, 3 *Air Law Review*. 16 (1932).

[62] Davis, op. cit. supra note 56, at 15. See also the article by Segal and Warner, op. cit. supra note 60, at 112-114.

[63] See, e.g., Jome, Property in the Air as Affected by the Airplane and the Radio, 4 *Journal of Land and Public Utility Economics*. 257 (1928). The *Air Law Review* dealt with radio law and aviation law. And law books, for example, Manion, *Law of the Air* (1950), are often organized in the same way.

[64] See Ball, The Vertical Extent of Ownership in Land, 76 *University of Pennsylvania Law Review and American Law Register*. 631 (1928); Niles, The Present Status of the Ownership of Airspace, 5 *Air Law Review*. 132 (1934) ; and W. L. Prosser, *Law of Torts* 85 (1941).

[65] For a detailed discussion of international agreements on the use of radio frequencies, see G. A. Codding, Jr., The International Telecommunication Union (1952), and an article by the same author, The International Law of Radio, 14 Fed. Com. B.J. 85 (1955).

[66] See Codding, The International Law of Radio, 14 Fed. Com. B.J. 85, 91-92, 97-98 (1955).

[67] Id., at 94 n. 40.

[68] See Codding, The International Telecommunication Union 380 (1952).

[69] *Broadcasting*, June 1,1959, p. 79.

[70] See Hearings on Investigation of Regulatory Commissions and Agencies before the Special Subcommittee and Agencies before the Special Subcommittee on Legislative Oversight of the House Committee on Interstate and Foreign Commerce, 85th Cong., 2d Sess. (1958). The Subcommittee was not simply concerned with the Federal Communications Commission but with the operations of all the independent regulatory commissions. The publicity received and the emphasis on improper personal conduct in the hearings was due to the activities of Dr. Bernard Schwartz, chief counsel of the Subcommittee, who exerted himself with a zeal which went beyond the call of duty and whose services with the Subcommittee were finally terminated. See B. Schwartz, The Professor and the Commissions (1959).

[71] See the panel discussion by representatives of law schools, of the government, and of the bar, in Hearings, op. cit. supra note 70, at 166-167. A similar point was raised by Professor Arthur S. Miller of Emory University Law School. Id., at 172.

[72] During the Hearings Representative Moulder asked Professor Byse whether his proposal would not lead the Commission to "award the license not to the most competent, but to the one who has the most money?" Id., at 186.

[73] Smythe, Facing Facts about the Broadcast Business, 20 *University of Chicago Law Review*. 96, 104 (1952). See note 32 supra.

[74] Hearings on H.R. 7357, To Regulate Radio Communication, before the House Committee on the Merchant Marine and Fisheries, 68th Cong., 1st Sess. 10 (1924).

[75] Address by John C. Doerfer at Chicago before the National Association of Broadcasters (March 17,1959).

[76] There have been some who interpret the doctrine of freedom of speech and of the press not as an absolute prohibition of certain types of government action but as being "permissive and ... subject (under due proces of law) to forfeiture," if it results in "serious damage to some aspect of the public interest" (Siepmann, op. cit. supra note 30, at 231). The establishment of a Federal Press Commission with powers similar to those of the Federal Communications Commission would presumably be compatible with this interpretation of the meaning of freedom of speech and of the press.

[77] Radio Editorials and the *Mayflower* Doctrine, 48 *Columbia Law Review*. 785, 788 (1948).

[78] Siepmann, op. cit. supra note 30, at 222.

[79] Hearings on S. 1333, to Amend the Communications Act of 1934, before the Senate Committee on

Interstate and Foreign Commerce, 80th Cong., 1st Sess. 120, 123 (1947). Mr. Miller's statement will also be found in National Association of Broadcasters, Broadcasting and the Bill of Rights 1-35 (1947). This interchange between Mr. Miller and the Senators is discussed in Regulation of Broadcasting: Half a Century of Government Regulation of Broadcasting and the Need for Further Legislative Action, a study by Mr. Robert S. McMahon, for the House Subcommittee on Legislative Oversight, 85th Cong., 2d Sess. (1958).

[80] It was a weakness of Mr. Miller's presentation that he accepted the need for government allocation of frequencies and apparently was unaware of the possibility of disposing of frequencies by using the pricing mechanism. Mr. Miller attempted to bring the Senators to see the validity of his analogy between broadcasting and the publication of newspapers, so far as the First Amendment was concerned, by citing a hypothetical example. He said that there was a shortage of newsprint and that "some of these days we may have a government agency authorized to make allotments of newsprint. ...Would it be proper, under such circumstances, for such a government body to impose the sort of abridgments upon freedom of the press that are now imposed on radio broadcasting? The question would seem to answer itself." But if the government allocated newsprint to users without charge, there can be little doubt that it would take into account what the newsprint was being used to produce. The obvious way to avoid the government's doing this would be to sell the newsprint at a price which equated demand to supply.

[81] C. C. Dill, Radio Law 1-2 (1938). Mr. Taft was Chief Justice of the Supreme Court from 1921 to 1930. So far as I can discover, the Supreme Court did not consider any radio case while Mr. Taft was Chief Justice.

Testimony to the Federal Communications Commission[*]

I appear before you with a strong conviction and a bold proposal. My conviction is that the principles under which the American economic system generally operates are fundamentally sound. My proposal is that the American broadcasting industry adopt those principles.

In presenting my case, I suffer from the disadvantage that, at the outset, I must attack a position which, although I am convinced it is erroneous, is none the less firmly held by many of those most knowledgeable about the broadcasting industry. Most authorities argue that the administrative assignment of radio and television frequencies by the Commission is called for by the technology of the industry. The number of frequencies, we are told, is limited. If I might quote a passage with which you are all

---

[*] *Man and the Economy*, 2015, 2(1),1-6. This testimony was given by Professor Ronald Coase on December 11, 1959 to the Federal Communication Commission, in which he suggested that the US government use the pricing mechanism to allocate radio spectrums. The simplicity and cogency of his message did not save Coase from ridicule at the hearing. The very first question Coase received from the panel, after giving his testimony, was "Are you spoofing us? Is this all a big joke?" While not prepared for such blatant hostility, Coase managed to reply, "Is it a joke to believe in the American economic system?" Eventually, it took more than three decades for the FCC to adopt spectrum auctions. In 1993, US Congress authorized the FCC to use competitive bidding to resolve mutual exclusivity among spectrum license applicants. In the following year, the FCC adopted its initial regulations governing general auctioning structure. In 2003, Coase won the Economist's Innovation Award in the category of "No Boundaries" for proposing the use of pricing mechanisms in allocating spectrums. Professor Coase referred to this testimony a number of times in his writing, but it has never been published. With the permission of the Coase Society, we are now pleased to make it available to the public.

familiar, Mr. Justice Frankfurter said in the NBC case[1] in 1943: "The facilities of radio are not large enough to accommodate all who wish to use them. Methods must be devised for choosing among the many who apply. And since Congress itself could not do this, it committed the task to the Commission." In short, the argument is that the selection of broadcast station operators by the Commission is needed because radio frequencies are limited in number and people want to use more of them than are available. But the situation described by Mr. Justice Frankfurter is in no sense peculiar to the broadcasting industry. All resources used in the economic systems are limited in amount and are scarce in that people want to use more of them than exists. This is so whether we think of labor, land or capital. However, we do not ordinarily consider that this situation calls for government regulation. It is true that some mechanism has to be employed to decide who, out of the many claimants, should be allowed to use the scarce resources. But the usual way of handling this problem in the American economic system is to employ the pricing mechanism, and this allocates resources to users without the need for government regulation. This is the system under which broadcasting concerns obtain the labor, land and capital equipment they require. There is no reason why the same system could not be adopted for radio and television frequencies. If these were disposed of by selling or leasing them to the highest bidder, there would be no need to use such criteria as proposed or past programming as a basis for the selection of broadcast station operators. Such a system would require a delimitation of the property rights acquired and there would almost certainly also have to be some general regulation of a technical character. But such regulation would not preclude the existence of private rights in frequencies, just as zoning and other regulations do not preclude the existence of private property in houses.

Such a use of pricing mechanism would bring the same advantages to the radio and television industry as its use confers on the rests of the American economy. It would avoid the need for much of the costly and time-consuming procedures involved in the assignment of frequencies by the Commission. It would rule out inefficient use of frequencies by bringing any proposal for the use of such frequencies up against the test of the market, with its precise monetary measure of cost and benefit. It would avoid the threat to freedom of the press in its widest sense which is inherent in present procedures, weak though the threat may be at the moment. And it would avoid that arbitrary enrichment of private operators of radio and television stations which inevitably follows from the present system. A station operator who is granted a license to use a particular frequency in a particular place may be granted a very valuable right, one for which he would be willing to pay millions of dollars and which he would be forced to pay if others could bid for the frequency. We sometimes hear denunciations of giveaways and their corrupting influence. You, gentlemen, who are administering what must be one of the biggest giveaways of all, must surely have been very uneasy at this aspect of your work. I have not made any detailed calculations, but it would be surprising to me if the extent of this enrichment of private individuals did not amount to hundreds of millions of dollars; and this could be too low a figure. All this is unnecessary. It could be avoided by charging for the use of frequencies.

It has been my experience that such a suggestion as I have made horrifies my listeners. I am told that it is necessary to choose those who should operate radio and television stations to make sure that the public interest is served and that programs of the right kind are transmitted. But, put this way, the case for governmental selection of broadcast station operators represents a significant shift of position from that which justifies it on technological grounds. It is, of course, a tenable position. But if the object of the selection is, in part, directly or indirectly, to influence programming, we have to face squarely the issue of freedom of the press so far as broadcasting is concerned. It may be doubted whether regulation designed to influence programming, and which was instituted for that purpose alone, would be constitutional, but on this a lawyer's opinion would be more valuable than mine.

But in any case it may be doubted whether an indirect attempt to influence programming through the selection of broadcast station operators could ever be very effective. For over 30 years the Federal Communications Commission and your predecessor, the Federal Radio Commission, have been selecting broadcast station operators on the basis, among other things, of their good character and their devotion to the public interest. By now one would expect the broadcasting industry to be a beacon of virtue, shining out in a wicked world. Such, I am afraid, is not the case. I do not wish to claim that the ethical standards of the broadcasting industry are lower than in the rest of American business. It is enough for my purpose that, in spite of the selective process, it is not obvious that the standards are significantly higher. This is not really surprising. Most people have presumably invested in the broadcasting industry because they thought it would be more profitable than any alternative investment open to them; and the list of occupations of broadcast station owners published by the Commission show them to represent a cross-section of American business. Of course, it might be argued that the Commission should show more zeal in future, but I would not urge this upon you. I think it is the cautious approach of the present, and past, Commission which has made the existing system tolerable. Imagine what would happen if the Commission really determined to enquire into an applicant's morals, beliefs, association, fair-mindedness, devotion to truth and to the public interest. The situation that would arise would be intolerable, and you may be sure that it would not long continue.

In saying this, I do not mean to imply that it is not of supreme importance to maintain high moral standards. It obviously is. But I am doubtful whether it is possible to do much to raise moral standards by governmental regulation. The recent disclosures of widespread deceit, and possibly fraud, in the broadcasting industry is shocking. But perhaps the most shocking aspect of the whole business has been to find that there are many people who cannot see anything wrong with an act if there is no law against it. This attitude, which recognizes no moral restraints, by its very nature cannot be touched by any change in the law. Furthermore, without moral standards the law itself is largely ineffective. It matters little what the law says if those who administer it can be bribed. Nor is it possible to enforce a law unless most people feel it to be morally justified. The major problem posed by recent events is not one for the Commission but for parents, educational institutions and religious bodies. It may be that there are some loopholes in the law relating to fraud, but this is a very minor aspect of the whole question. If we rule out, as I think we must, governmental regulation of programming on both constitutional and practical grounds, and also because it cannot touch the basic issue of morality, we can but hope that the changes now being put into effect by the broadcasting industry are not simply an attempt to offset public criticism but represent a new awareness of what right conduct is.

As an economist I cannot but be aware that the nature of the problem has just forced me into a discussion of questions on which I have little professional competence. But part of the dissatisfaction with the performance of the broadcasting industry stems from something which falls squarely within the domain of an economist. The American broadcasting system is financed by revenue from advertisements. The essence of a commercial broadcasting system is that the operator of a radio or television station is paid for making broadcasts or allowing them to be made. But he is not paid by those who listen to or view the programs. He is paid by those who wish listeners to receive a particular message—the advertisement, or commercial. However, simply to broadcast the commercial will not usually lead people to listen or view. A program, therefore, has to be broadcast to induce people to listen or view. In a commercial broadcasting system, the object of the program is to attract an audience for the commercials. With such a system what program will be broadcast? They are the programs which maximize the difference between the profits yielded by broadcast advertising and the costs of the program. If programs were supplied in the way which is normal in the American economic system, the program which would be broadcast would be those which maximize the difference between the amount people would pay to hear or see the program and the cost of the program. It is easy to see that these are completely different ways of determining what programs to transmit and that a broadcasting system organized as other industries are (with revenue accruing directly from the consumers) would lead to a very different structure of programs. But how different and in what ways? This is a difficult problem (it happens to be one on which I will be working during the next few months)—and it is difficult precisely because the systems are so very different. The best I can do now is to indicate some of the ways in which these two systems will lead to different results. It is clear that some programs which people would be willing to pay for will have costs which are higher than the profits that would accrue from any commercials that might be associated with them and that therefore they would not be made available with the commercial system. Again, with commercial broadcasting, a program which attracts a larger audience may be chosen even though viewers or listeners in total would pay more for one which would attract a smaller audience. The result of all this is that commercial broadcasting leaves some sectors of the public with the feeling that they are not being catered for. And this is true. This result is particularly bad because it is often the educated classes who feel that their wants are not being satisfied and because they are apt to conclude that this is the inevitable result of the working of a private enterprise market economy.

This, of course, is not the case. I need not here go into the rationale of the competitive system, which treats all money demands equally and operates in such a way as to maximize the value of output. But it will hardly come as a surprise to you that, holding these views, I urge you to do all you can to bring about the introduction of subscription television (and subscription radio, too, if possible). There may be practical difficulties standing in the way of subscription television. But I am convinced that there are no substantial objections to subscription television in principle. Much is made of the fact that with commercial television the service is free. The argument is essentially the same as that for socialism and the welfare state. What is being attacked is the price mechanism. The factors of production used in television are not made available for nothing. They will be paid for by someone: The Government out of the proceeds of taxation, by the advertiser or by the consumer. What is important is that factors of production should be used where their output is most valuable, and this is most likely to happen if the use of factors of production is determined by what consumers are willing to pay. The objection to a "free" system is that it is not really "free" and it is less efficient. It has been pointed out that, with subscription television, programs will only be seen by those who have the money to pay for them. But if reliance on ability to pay is so unfortunate when applied to television programs, how much worse it must be when applied to food, or clothing, or housing or even to television sets and phonograph records. The arguments of the opponents of pay-television should not convince anyone who believes in the capitalist system.

One final point. It is clear that we can rely on the competitive system remaining competitive only if the Government takes actions to curb monopolistic tendencies and to prevent agreements in restraint of trade. This is as true for the broadcasting industry as for others. In this regard, I would like to draw the Commission's attention to an area in which it seems to me there has been, as yet, insufficient investigation and in which there may well be practices which restrain trade and obstruct the efficient working of the broadcasting industry. I refer to the structure of programming. A great deal is known about the practices of the networks and their relations with their affiliates. But, perhaps because it stretches out into the entertainments industry, there seems to be very little information available about how programming is organized. I had hoped that the supplement on programming, about which we were told in the Barrow Report[2], would have been completed by now and made available for public study. But, for reasons which I do not know, nothing has appeared. It seems to me that the relations between the networks and stations and the independent program producers, talent and the talent agencies may well affect significantly the performance of the broadcasting industry, and that publication of the results of work conducted within the Federal Communications Commission in this area would greatly assist in bringing about an informed public opinion.

Notes

[1] *National Broadcasting Co. v. United States,* 319 U.S. 190 (1943). The opinion of the Supreme Court was delivered by Justice Felix Frankfurter.
[2] Network Broadcasting, Report of the Network Study Staff to the Network Study Committee (1957), authored by Roscoe L. Barrow.

The Problem of Social Cost[*]

I. The Problem to Be Examined[1]

This paper is concerned with those actions of business firms which have harmful effects on others. The standard example is that of a factory the smoke from which has harmful effects on those occupying neighbouring properties. The economic analysis of such a situation has usually proceeded in terms of a divergence between the private and social product of the factory, in which economists have largely followed the treatment of Pigou in *The Economics of Welfare*. The conclusions to which this kind of analysis seems to have led most economists is that it would be desirable to make the owner of the factory liable for the damage caused to those injured by the smoke, or alternatively, to place a tax on the factory owner varying with the amount of smoke produced and equivalent in money terms to the damage it would cause, or finally, to exclude the factory from residential districts (and presumably from other areas in which the emission of smoke would have harmful effects on others). It is my contention that the suggested courses of action are inappropriate, in that they lead to results which are not necessarily, or even usually, desirable.

---

[*] *Journal of Law and Economics*, 1960, 3(2), 1-44.

II. The Reciprocal Nature of the Problem

The traditional approach has tended to obscure the nature of the choice that has to be made. The question is commonly thought of as one in which A inflicts harm on B and what has to be decided is: how should we restrain A? But this is wrong. We are dealing with a problem of a reciprocal nature. To avoid the harm to B would inflict harm on A. The real question that has to be decided is: should A be allowed to harm B or should B be allowed to harm A? The problem is to avoid the more serious harm. I instanced in my previous article[2] the case of a confectioner the noise and vibrations from whose machinery disturbed a doctor in his work. To avoid harming the doctor would inflict harm on the confectioner. The problem posed by this case was essentially whether it was worth while, as a result of restricting the methods of production which could be used by the confectioner, to secure more doctoring at the cost of a reduced supply of confectionery products. Another example is afforded by the problem of straying cattle which destroy crops on neighbouring land. If it is inevitable that some cattle will stray, an increase in the supply of meat can only be obtained at the expense of a decrease in the supply of crops. The nature of the choice is clear: meat or crops. What answer should be given is, of course, not clear unless we know the value of what is obtained as well as the value of what is sacrificed to obtain it. To give another example, Professor George J. Stigler instances the contamination of a stream.[3] If we assume that the harmful effect of the pollution is that it kills the fish, the question to be decided is: Is the value of the fish lost greater or less than the value of the product which the contamination of the stream makes possible? It goes almost without saying that this problem has to be looked at in total and at the margin.

III. The Pricing System with Liability for Damage

I propose to start my analysis by examining a case in which most economists would presumably agree that the problem would be solved in a completely satisfactory manner: When the damaging business has to pay for all damage caused *and* the pricing system works smoothly (strictly this means that the operation of a pricing system is without cost).

A good example of the problem under discussion is afforded by the case of straying cattle which destroy crops growing on neighbouring land. Let us suppose that a fanner and a cattle-raiser are operating on neighbouring properties. Let us further suppose that, without any fencing between the properties, an increase in the size of the cattle-raiser's herd increases the total damage to the farmer's crops. What happens to the marginal damage as the size of the herd increases is another matter. This depends on whether the cattle tend to follow one another or to roam side by side, on whether they tend to be more or less restless as the size of the herd increases and on other similar factors. For my immediate purpose, it is immaterial what assumption is made about marginal damage as the size of the herd increases.

To simplify the argument, I propose to use an arithmetical example. I shall assume that the annual cost of fencing the farmer's property is $9 and that the price of the crop is $1 per ton. Also, I assume that the relation between the number of cattle in the herd and the annual crop loss is as follows:

number in herd (steers)	annual crop loss (tons)	crop loss per additional steer (tons)
1	1	1
2	3	2
3	6	3
4	10	4

Given that the cattle-raiser is liable for the damage caused, the additional annual cost imposed on the cattle-raiser if he increased his herd from, say, 2 to 3 steers is $3 and in deciding on the size of the herd, he will take this into account along with his other costs. That is, he will not increase the size of the herd unless the value of the additional meat produced (assuming that the cattle-raiser slaughters the cattle), is greater than the additional costs that this will entail, including the value of the additional crops destroyed. Of course, if, by the employment of dogs, herdsmen, aeroplanes, mobile radio and other means, the amount of damage can be reduced, these means will be adopted when their cost is less than the value of the crop which they prevent being lost. Given that the annual cost of fencing is $9, the cattle-raiser who wished to have a herd with steers or more would pay for fencing to be erected and maintained, assuming that other means of attaining the same end would not do so more cheaply. When the fence is erected, the marginal cost due to the liability for damage becomes zero, except to the extent that an increase in the size of the herd necessitates a stronger and therefore more expensive fence because more steers are liable to lean against it at the same time. But, of course, it may be cheaper for the cattle-raiser not to fence and to pay for the damaged crops, as in my arithmetical example, with 3 or fewer steers.

It might be thought that the fact that the cattle-raiser would pay for all crops damaged would lead the farmer to increase his planting if a cattle-raiser came to occupy the neighbouring property. But this is not so. If the crop was previously sold in conditions of perfect competition, marginal cost was equal to price for the amount of planting undertaken and any expansion would have reduced the profits of the farmer. In the new situation, the existence of crop damage would mean that the farmer would sell less on the open market but his receipts for a given production would remain the same, since the cattle-raiser would pay the market price for any crop damaged. Of course, if cattle-raising commonly involved the destruction of crops, the coming into existence of a cattle-raising industry might raise the price of the crops involved and farmers would then extend their planting. But I wish to confine my attention to the individual farmer.

I have said that the occupation of a neighbouring property by a cattle-raiser would not cause the amount of production, or perhaps more exactly the amount of planting, by the farmer to increase. In fact, if the cattle-raising has any effect, it will be to decrease the amount of planting. The reason for this is that, for any given tract of land, if the value of the crop damaged is so great that the receipts from the sale of the undamaged crop are less than the total costs of cultivating that tract of land, it will be profitable for the farmer and the cattle-raiser to make a bargain whereby that tract of land is left uncultivated. This can be made clear by means of an arithmetical example. Assume initially that the value of the crop obtained from cultivating a given tract of land is $12 and that the cost incurred in cultivating this tract of land is $10, the net gain from cultivating the land being $2. I assume for purposes of simplicity that the farmer owns the land. Now assume that the cattle-raiser starts operations on the neighbouring property and that the value of the crops damaged is $1. In this case $11 is obtained by the farmer from sale on the market and $1 is obtained from the cattle-raiser for damage suffered and the net gain remains $2. Now suppose that the cattle-raiser finds it profitable to increase the size of his herd, even though the amount of damage rises to $3; which means that the value of the additional meat production is greater than the additional costs, including the additional $2 payment for damage. But the total payment for damage is now $3. The net gain to the farmer from cultivating the land is still $2. The cattle-raiser would be better off if the farmer would agree not to cultivate his land for any payment less than $3. The farmer would be agreeable to not cultivating the land for any payment greater than $2. There is clearly room for a mutually satisfactory bargain which would lead to the abandonment of cultivation.[4] But the same argument applies not only to the whole tract cultivated by the farmer but also to any subdivision of it. Suppose, for example, that the cattle have a well-defined route, say, to a brook or to a shady area. In these circumstances, the amount of damage to the crop along the route may well be great and if so, it could be that the farmer and the cattle-raiser would find it profitable to make a bargain whereby the farmer would agree not to cultivate this strip of land.

But this raises a further possibility. Suppose that there is such a well-defined route. Suppose further that the value of the crop that would be obtained by cultivating this strip of land is $10 but that the cost of cultivation is $11. In the absence of the cattle-raiser, the land would not be cultivated. However, given the presence of the cattle-raiser, it could well be that if the strip was cultivated, the whole crop would be destroyed by the cattle. In which case, the cattle-raiser would be forced to pay $10 to the farmer. It is true that the farmer would lose $1. But the cattle-raiser would lose $10. Clearly this is a situation which is not likely to last indefinitely since neither party would want this to happen. The aim of the farmer would be to induce the cattle-raiser to make a payment in return for an agreement to leave this land uncultivated. The farmer would not be able to obtain a payment greater than the cost of fencing off this piece of land nor so high as to lead the cattle-raiser to abandon the use of the neighbouring property. What payment would in fact be made would depend on the shrewdness of the farmer and the cattle-raiser as bargainers. But as the payment would not be so high as to cause the cattle-raiser to abandon this location and as it would not vary with the size of the herd, such an agreement would not affect the allocation of resources but would merely alter the distribution of income and wealth as between the cattle-raiser and the farmer.

I think it is clear that if the cattle-raiser is liable for damage caused and the pricing system works smoothly, the reduction in the value of production elsewhere will be taken into account in computing the additional cost involved in increasing the size of the herd. This cost will be weighed against the value of the additional meat production and, given perfect competition in the cattle industry, the allocation of resources in cattle-raising will be optimal. What needs to be emphasized is that the fall in the value of production elsewhere which would be taken into account in the costs of the cattle-raiser may well be less than the damage which the cattle would cause to the crops in the ordinary course of events. This is because it is possible, as a result of market transactions, to discontinue cultivation of the land. This is desirable in all cases in which the damage that the cattle would cause, and for which the cattle-raiser would be willing to pay, exceeds the amount which the farmer would pay for use of the land. In conditions of perfect competition, the amount which the fanner would pay for the use of the land is equal to the difference between the value of the total production when the factors are employed on this land and the value of the additional product yielded in their next best use (which would be what the farmer would have to pay for the factors). If damage exceeds the amount the farmer would pay for the use of the land, the value of the additional product of the factors employed elsewhere would exceed the value of the total product in this use after damage is taken into account. It follows that it would be desirable to abandon cultivation of the land and to release the factors employed for production elsewhere, A procedure which merely provided for payment for damage to the crop caused by the cattle but which did not allow for the possibility of cultivation being discontinued would result in too small an employment of factors of production in cattle-raising and too large an employment of factors in cultivation of the crop. But given the possibility of market transactions, a situation in which damage to crops exceeded the rent of the land would not endure. Whether the cattle-raiser pays the farmer to leave the land uncultivated or himself rents the land by paying the land-owner an amount slightly greater than the farmer would pay (if the farmer was himself renting the land), the final result would be the same and would maximise the value of production. Even when the farmer is induced to plant crops which it would not be profitable to cultivate for sale on the market, this will be a purely short-term phenomenon and may be expected to lead to an agreement under which the planting will cease. The cattle-raiser will remain in that location and the marginal cost of meat production will be the same as before, thus having no long-run effect on the allocation of resources.

IV. The Pricing System with No Liability for Damage

I now turn to the case in which, although the pricing system is assumed to work smoothly (that is, costlessly), the damaging business is not liable for any of the damage which it causes. This business does not have to make a payment to those damaged by its actions. I propose to show that the allocation of resource will be the same in this case as it was when the damaging business was liable for damage caused. As I showed in the previous case that the allocation of resources was optimal, it will not be necessary to repeat this part of the argument.

I return to the case of the farmer and the cattle-raiser. The farmer would suffer increased damage to his crop as the size of the herd increased. Suppose that the size of the cattle-raiser's herd is 3 steers (and that this is the size of the herd that would be maintained if crop damage was not taken into account). Then the farmer would be willing to pay up to $3 if the cattle-raiser would reduce his herd to 2 steers, up to $5 if the herd were reduced to 1 steer and would pay up to $6 if cattle-raising was abandoned. The cattle-raiser would therefore receive $3 from the farmer if he kept 2 steers instead of 3. This $3 foregone is therefore part of the cost incurred in keeping the third steer. Whether the $3 is a payment which the cattle-raiser has to make if he adds the third steer to his herd (which it would be if the cattle-raiser was liable to the farmer for damage caused to the crop) or whether it is a sum of money which he would have received if he did not keep a third steer (which it would be if the cattle-raiser was not liable to the farmer for damage caused to the crop) does not affect the final result. In both cases $3 is part of the cost of adding a third steer, to be included along with the other costs. If the increase in the value of production in cattle-raising through increasing the size of the herd from 2 to 3 is greater than the additional costs that have to be incurred (including the $3 damage to crops), the size of the herd will be increased. Otherwise, it will not. The size of the herd will be the same whether the cattle-raiser is liable for damage caused to the crop or not.

It may be argued that the assumed starting point—a herd of 3 steers—was arbitrary. And this is true. But the farmer would not wish to pay to avoid crop damage which the cattle-raiser would not be able to cause. For example, the maximum annual payment which the farmer could be induced to pay could not exceed $9, the annual cost of fencing. And the farmer would only be willing to pay this sum if it did not reduce his earnings to a level that would cause him to abandon cultivation of this particular tract of land. Furthermore, the farmer would only be willing to pay this amount if he believed that, in the absence of any payment by him, the size of the herd maintained by the cattle raiser would be 4 or more steers. Let us assume that this is the case. Then the farmer would be willing to pay up to $3 if the cattle raiser would reduce his herd to

3 steers, up to $6 if the herd were reduced to 2 steers, up to $8 if one steer only were kept and up to $9 if cattle-raising were abandoned. It will be noticed that the change in the starting point has not altered the amount which would accrue to the cattle-raiser if he reduced the size of his herd by any given amount. It is still true that the cattle-raiser could receive an additional $3 from the farmer if he agreed to reduce his herd from 3 steers to 2 and that the $3 represents the value of the crop that would be destroyed by adding the third steer to the herd. Although a different belief on the part of the farmer (whether justified or not) about the size of the herd that the cattle-raiser would maintain in the absence of payments from him may affect the total payment he can be induced to pay, it is not true that this different belief would have any effect on the size of the herd that the cattle-raiser will actually keep. This will be the same as it would be if the cattle-raiser had to pay for damage caused by his cattle, since a receipt foregone of a given amount is the equivalent of a payment of the same amount.

It might be thought that it would pay the cattle-raiser to increase his herd above the size that he would wish to maintain once a bargain had been made, in order to induce the farmer to make a larger total payment. And this may be true. It is similar in nature to the action of the farmer (when the cattle-raiser was liable for damage) in cultivating land on which, as a result of an agreement with the cattle-raiser, planting would subsequently be abandoned (including land which would not be cultivated at all in the absence of cattle-raising). But such manoeuvres are preliminaries to an agreement and do not affect the long-run equilibrium position, which is the same whether or not the cattle-raiser is held responsible for the crop damage brought about by his cattle.

It is necessary to know whether the damaging business is liable or not for damage caused since without the establishment of this initial delimitation of rights there can be no market transactions to transfer and recombine them. But the ultimate result (which maximises the value of production) is independent of the legal position if the pricing system is assumed to work without cost.

V. The Problem Illustrated Anew

The harmful effects of the activities of a business can assume a wide variety of forms. An early English case concerned a building which, by obstructing currents of air, hindered the operation of a windmill.[5] A recent case in Florida concerned a building which cast a shadow on the cabana, swimming pool and sunbathing areas of a neighbouring hotel.[6] The problem of straying cattle and the damaging of crops which was the subject of detailed examination in the two preceding sections, although it may have appeared to be rather a special case, is in fact but one example of a problem which arises in many different guises. To clarify the nature of my argument and to demonstrate its general applicability, I propose to illustrate it anew by reference to four actual cases.

Let us first reconsider the case of *Sturges v. Bridgman*[7] which I used as an illustration of the general problem in my article on "The Federal Communications Commission." In this case, a confectioner (in Wigmore Street) used two mortars and pestles in connection with his business (one had been in operation in the same position for more than 60 years and the other for more than 26 years). A doctor then came to occupy neighbouring premises (in Wimpole Street). The confectioner's machinery caused the doctor no harm until, eight years after he had first occupied the premises, he built a consulting room at the end of his garden right against the confectioner's kitchen. It was then found that the noise and vibration caused by the confectioner's machinery made it difficult for the doctor to use his new consulting room. "In particular... the noise prevented him from examining his patients by auscultation[8] for diseases of the chest. He also found it impossible to engage with effect in any occupation which required thought and attention." The doctor therefore brought a legal action to force the confectioner to stop using his machinery. The courts had little difficulty in granting the doctor the injunction he sought. "Individual cases of hardship may occur in the strict carrying out of the principle upon which we found our judgment, but the negation of the principle would lead even more to individual hardship, and would at the same time produce a prejudicial effect upon the development of land for residential purposes."

The court's decision established that the doctor had the right to prevent the confectioner from using his machinery. But, of course, it would have been possible to modify the arrangements envisaged in the legal ruling by means of a bargain between the parties. The doctor would have been willing to waive his right and allow the machinery to continue in operation if the confectioner would have paid him a sum of money which was greater than the loss of income which he would suffer from having to move to a more costly or less convenient location or from having to curtail his activities at this location or, as was suggested as a possibility, from having to build a separate wall which would deaden the noise and vibration. The confectioner would have been willing to do this if the amount he would have to pay the doctor was less than the fall in income he would suffer if he had to change his mode of operation at this location, abandon his operation or move his confectionery business to some other location. The solution of the problem depends essentially on whether the continued use of the machinery adds more to the confectioner's income than it subtracts from the doctor's.[9] But now consider the situation if the confectioner had won the case. The confectioner would then have had the right to continue operating his noise and vibration-generating machinery without having to pay anything to the doctor. The boot would have been on the other foot: The doctor would have had to pay the confectioner to induce him to stop using the machinery. If the doctor's income would have fallen more through continuance of the use of this machinery than it added to the income of the confectioner, there would clearly be room for a bargain whereby the doctor paid the confectioner to stop using the machinery. That is to say, the circumstances in which it would not pay the confectioner to continue to use the machinery and to compensate the doctor for the losses that this would bring (if the doctor had the right to prevent the confectioner's using his machinery) would be those in which it would be in the interest of the doctor to make a payment to the confectioner which would induce him to discontinue the use of the machinery (if the confectioner had the right to operate the machinery). The basic conditions are exactly the same in this case as they were in the example of the cattle which destroyed crops. With costless market transactions, the decision of the courts concerning liability for damage would be without effect on the allocation of resources. It was of course the view of the judges that they were affecting the working of the economic system—and in a desirable direction. Any other decision would have had "a prejudicial effect upon the development of land for residential purposes," an argument which was elaborated by examining the example of a forge operating on a barren moor, which was later developed for residual purposes. The judges' view that they were settling how the land was to be used would be true only in the case in which the costs of carrying out the necessary market transactions exceeded the gain which might be achieved by any rearrangement of rights. And it would be desirable to preserve the areas (Wimpole Street or the moor) for residential or professional use (by giving non-industrial users the right to stop the noise, vibration, smoke, etc., by injunction) only if the value of the additional residential facilities obtained was greater than the value of cakes or iron lost. But of this the judges seem to have been unaware.

Another example of the same problem is furnished by the case of *Cooke v. Forbes*.[10] One process in the weaving of cocoa-nut fibre matting was to immerse it in bleaching liquids after which it was hung out to dry. Fumes from a manufacturer of sulphate of ammonia had the effect of turning the matting from a bright to a dull and blackish colour. The reason for this was that the bleaching liquid contained chloride of tin, which, when affected by sulphuretted hydrogen, is turned to a darker colour. An injunction was sought to stop the manufacturer from emitting the fumes. The lawyers for the defendant argued that if the plaintiff "were not to use ... a particular bleaching liquid, their fibre would not be affected; that their process is unusual, not according to the custom of the trade, and even damaging to their own fabrics." The judge commented: "... It appears to me quite plain that a person has a right to carry on upon his own property a manufacturing process in which he uses chloride of tin, or any sort of metallic dye, and that his neighbour is not at liberty to pour in gas which will interfere with his manufacture. If it can be traced to the neighbour, then, I apprehend, clearly he will have a right to come here and ask for relief." But in view of the fact that the damage was accidental and occasional, that careful precautions were taken and that there was no exceptional risk, an injunction was refused, leaving the plaintiff to bring an action for damages if he wished. What the subsequent developments were I do not know. But it is clear that the situation is essentially the same as that found in *Sturges v. Bridgman*, except that the cocoanut fibre matting manufacturer could not secure an injunction but would have to seek damages from the sulphate of ammonia manufacturer. The economic analysis of the situation is exactly the same as with the cattle which destroyed crops. To avoid the damage, the sulphate of ammonia manufacturer could increase his precautions or move to another location. Either course would presumably increase his costs. Alternatively he could pay for the damage. This he would do if the payments for damage were less than the additional costs that would have to be incurred to avoid the damage. The payments for damage would then become part of the cost of production of sulphate of ammonia. Of course, if, as was suggested in the legal proceedings, the amount of damage could be eliminated by changing the bleaching agent (which would presumably increase the costs of the matting manufacturer) and if the additional cost was less than the damage that would otherwise occur, it should be possible for the two manufacturers to make a mutually satisfactory bargain whereby the new bleaching agent was used. Had the court decided against the matting manufacturer, as a consequence of which he would have had to suffer the damage without compensation, the allocation of resources would not have been affected. It would pay the matting manufacturer to change his bleaching agent if the additional cost involved was less than the reduction in damage. And since the matting manufacturer would be willing to pay the sulphate of ammonia manufacturer an amount up to his loss of income (the increase in costs or the damage suffered) if he would cease his activities, this loss of income would remain a cost of production for the manufacturer of sulphate of ammonia. This case is indeed analytically exactly the same as the cattle example.

Bryant v. Lefever[11] raised the problem of the smoke nuisance in a novel form. The plaintiff and the defendants were occupiers of adjoining houses, which were of about the same height.

Before 1876 the plaintiff was able to light a fire in any room of his house without the chimneys smoking; the two houses had remained in the same condition some thirty or forty years. In 1876 the defendants took down their house, and began to rebuild it. They carried up a wall by the side of the plaintiff's chimneys much beyond its original height, and stacked timber on the roof of their house, and thereby caused the plaintiffs chimneys to smoke whenever he lighted fires.

The reason, of course, why the chimneys smoked was that the erection of the wall and the stacking of the timber prevented the free circulation of air. In a trial before a jury, the plaintiff was awarded damages of £40. The case then went to the Court of Appeals where the judgment was reversed. Bramwell, L.J., argued:

...It is said, and the jury have found, that the defendants have done that which caused a nuisance to the plaintiffs house. We think there is no evidence of this. No doubt there is a nuisance, but it is not of the defendant's causing. They have done nothing in causing the nuisance. Their house and their timber are harmless enough. It is the plaintiff who causes the nuisance by lighting a coal fire in a place the chimney of which is placed so near the defendants' wall, that the smoke does not escape, but comes into the house. Let the plaintiff cease to light his fire, let him move his chimney, let him carry it higher, and there would be no nuisance. Who then, causes it? It would be very clear that the plaintiff did, if he had built his house or chimney after the defendants had put up the timber on theirs, and it is really the same though he did so before the timber was there. But (what is in truth the same answer), if the defendants cause the nuisance, they have a right to do so. If the plaintiff has not the right to the passage of air, except subject to the defendants' right to build or put timber on their house, then his right is subject to their right, and though a nuisance follows from the exercise of their right, they are not liable.

And Cotton, L.J., said:

Here it is found that the erection of the defendants' wall has sensibly and materially interfered with the comfort of human existence in the plaintiff's house, and it is said this is a nuisance for which the defendants are liable. Ordinarily this is so, but the defendants have done so, not by sending on to the plaintiff's property any smoke or noxious vapour, but by interrupting the egress of smoke from the plaintiff's house in a way to which ... the plaintiff has no legal right. The plaintiff creates the smoke, which interferes with his comfort. Unless he has ... a right to get rid of this in a particular way which has been interfered with by the defendants, he cannot sue the defendants, because the smoke made by himself, for which he has not provided any effectual means of escape, causes him annoyance. It is as if a man tried to get rid of liquid filth arising on his own land by a drain into his neighbour's land. Until a right had been acquired by user, the neighbour might stop the drain without incurring liability by so doing. No doubt great inconvenience would be caused to the owner of the property on which the liquid filth arises. But the act of his neighbour would be a lawful act, and he would not be liable for the consequences attributable to the fact that the man had accumulated filth without providing any effectual means of getting rid of it.

I do not propose to show that any subsequent modification of the situation, as a result of bargains between the parties (conditioned by the cost of stacking the timber elsewhere, the cost of extending the chimney higher, etc.), would have exactly the same result whatever decision the courts had come to since this point has already been adequately dealt with in the discussion of the cattle example and the two previous cases. What I shall discuss is the argument of the judges in the Court of Appeals that the smoke nuisance was not caused by the man who erected the wall but by the man who lit the fires. The novelty of the situation is that the smoke nuisance was suffered by the man who lit the fires and not by some third person. The question is not a trivial one since it lies at the heart of the problem under discussion. Who caused the smoke nuisance? The answer seems fairly clear. The smoke nuisance was caused both by the man who built the wall *and* by the man who lit the fires. Given the fires, there would have been no smoke nuisance without the wall; given the wall, there would have been no smoke nuisance without the fires. Eliminate the wall *or* the fires and the smoke nuisance would disappear. On the marginal principle it is clear that *both* were responsible and *both* should be forced to include the loss of amenity due to the smoke as a cost in deciding whether to continue the activity which gives rise to the smoke. And given the possibility of market transactions, this is what would in fact happen. Although the wall-builder was not liable legally for the nuisance, as the man with the smoking chimneys would presumably be willing to pay a sum equal to the monetary worth to him of eliminating the smoke, this sum would therefore become for the wall-builder, a cost of continuing to have the high wall with the timber stacked on the roof.

The judges' contention that it was the man who lit the fires who alone caused the smoke nuisance is true only if we assume that the wall is the given factor. This is what the judges did by deciding that the man who erected the higher wall had a legal right to do so. The case would have been even more interesting if the smoke from the chimneys had injured the timber. Then it would have been the wall-builder who suffered the damage. The case would then have closely paralleled *Sturges v. Bridgman* and there can be little doubt that the man who lit the fires would have been liable for the ensuing damage to the timber, in spite of the fact that no damage had occurred until the high wall was built by the man who owned the timber.

Judges have to decide on legal liability but this should not confuse economists about the nature of the economic problem involved. In the case of the cattle and the crops, it is true that there would be no crop damage without the cattle. It is equally true that there would be no crop damage without the crops. The doctor's work would not have been disturbed if the confectioner had not worked his machinery; but the machinery would have disturbed no one if the doctor had not set up his consulting room in that particular place. The matting was blackened by the fumes from the sulphate of ammonia manufacturer; but no damage would have occurred if the matting manufacturer had not chosen to hang out his matting in a particular place and to use a particular bleaching agent. If we are to discuss the problem in terms of causation, both parties cause the damage. If we are to attain an optimum allocation of resources, it is therefore desirable that both parties should take the harmful effect (the nuisance) into account in deciding on their course of action. It is one of the beauties of a smoothly operating pricing system that, as has already been explained, the fall in the value of production due to the harmful effect would be a cost for both parties.

Bass v. Gregory[12] will serve as an excellent final illustration of the problem. The plaintiffs were the owners and tenant of a public house called the Jolly Anglers. The defendant was the owner of some cottages and a yard adjoining the Jolly Anglers. Under the public house was a cellar excavated in the rock. From the cellar, a hole or shaft had been cut into an old well situated in the defendant's yard. The well therefore became the ventilating shaft for the cellar. The cellar "had been used for a particular purpose in the process of brewing, which, without ventilation, could not be carried on." The cause of the action was that the defendant removed a grating from the mouth of the well, "so as to stop or prevent the free passage of air from [the] cellar upwards through the well..." What caused the defendant to take this step is not clear from the report of the case. Perhaps "the air... impregnated by the brewing operations" which "passed up the well and out into the open air" was offensive to him. At any rate, he preferred to have the well in his yard stopped up. The court had first to determine whether the owners of the public house could have a legal right to a current of air. If they were to have such a right, this case would have to be distinguished from *Bryant v. Lefever* (already considered). This, however, presented no difficulty. In this case, the current of air was confined to "a strictly defined channel." In the case of *Bryant v. Lefever*, what was involved was "the general current of air common to all mankind." The judge therefore held that the owners of the public house could have the right to a current of air whereas the owner of the private house in *Bryant v. Lefever* could not. An economist might be tempted to add "but the air moved all the same." However, all that had been decided at this stage of the argument was that there could be a legal right, not that the owners of the public house possessed it. But evidence showed that the shaft from the cellar to the well had existed for over forty years and that the use of the well as a ventilating shaft must have been known to the owners of the yard since the air, when it emerged, smelt of the brewing operations. The judge therefore held that the public house had such a right by the "doctrine of lost grant." This doctrine states "that if a legal right is proved to have existed and been exercised for a number of years the law ought to presume that it had a legal origin."[13] So the owner of the cottages and yard had to unstop the well and endure the smell.

The reasoning employed by the courts in determining legal rights will often seem strange to an economist because many of the factors on which the decision turns are, to an economist, irrelevant. Because of this, situations which are, from an economic point of view, identical will be treated quite differently by the courts. The economic problem in all cases of harmful effects is how to maximise the value of production. In the case of *Bass v. Gregory* fresh air was drawn in through the well which facilitated the production of beer but foul air was expelled through the well which made life in the adjoining houses less pleasant. The economic problem was to decide which to choose: A lower cost of beer and worsened amenities in adjoining houses or a higher cost of beer and improved amenities. In deciding this question, the "doctrine of lost grant" is about as relevant as the colour of the judge's eyes. But it has to be remembered that the immediate question faced by the courts is not what shall be done by whom but who has the legal right to do what. It is always possible to modify by transactions on the market the initial legal delimitation of rights. And, of course, if such market transactions are costless, such a rearrangement of rights will always take place if it would lead to an increase in the value of production.

VI. The Cost of Market Transactions Taken into Account

The argument has proceeded up to this point on the assumption (explicit in Sections III and IV and tacit in Section V) that there were no costs involved in carrying out market transactions. This is, of course, a very unrealistic assumption. In order to carry out a market transaction it is necessary to discover who it is that one wishes to deal with, to inform people that one wishes to deal and on what terms, to conduct negotiations leading up to a bargain, to draw up the contract, to undertake the inspection needed to make sure that the terms of the contract are being observed, and so on. These operations are often extremely costly, sufficiently costly at any rate to prevent many transactions that would be carried out in a world in which the pricing system worked without cost.

In earlier sections, when dealing with the problem of the rearrangement of legal rights through the market, it was argued that such a rearrangement would be made through the market whenever this would lead to an increase in the value of production. But this assumed costless market transactions. Once the costs of carrying out market transactions are taken into account it is clear that such a rearrangement of rights will only be undertaken when the increase in the value of production consequent upon the rearrangement is greater than the costs which would be involved in bringing it about. When it is less, the granting of an injunction (or the knowledge that it would be granted) or the liability to pay damages may result in an activity being discontinued (or may prevent its being started) which would be undertaken if market transactions were costless. In these conditions the initial delimitation of legal rights does have an effect on the efficiency with which the economic system operates. One arrangement of rights may bring about a greater value of production than any other. But unless this is the arrangement of rights established by the legal system, the costs of reaching the same result by altering and combining rights through the market may be so great that this optimal arrangement of rights, and the greater value of production which it would bring, may never be achieved. The part played by economic considerations in the process of delimiting legal rights will be discussed in the next section. In this section, I will take the initial delimitation of rights and the costs of carrying out market transactions as given.

It is clear that an alternative form of economic organisation which could achieve the same result at less cost than would be incurred by using the market would enable the value of production to be raised. As I explained many years ago, the firm represents such an alternative to organising production through market transactions.[14] Within the firm individual bargains between the various cooperating factors of production are eliminated and for a market transaction is substituted an administrative decision. The rearrangement of production then takes place without the need for bargains between the owners of the factors of production. A landowner who has control of a large tract of land may devote his land to various uses taking into account the effect that the interrelations of the various activities will have on the net return of the land, thus rendering unnecessary bargains between those undertaking the various activities. Owners of a large building or of several adjoining properties in a given area may act in much the same way. In effect, using our earlier terminology, the firm would acquire the legal rights of all the parties and the rearrangement of activities would not follow on a rearrangement of rights by contract, but as a result of an administrative decision as to how the rights should be used.

It does not, of course, follow that the administrative costs of organising a transaction through a firm are inevitably less than the costs of the market transactions which are superseded. But where contracts are peculiarly difficult to draw up and an attempt to describe what the parties have agreed to do or not to do (e.g. the amount and kind of a smell or noise that they may make or will not make) would necessitate a lengthy and highly involved document, and, where, as is probable, a long-term contract would be desirable;[15] it would be hardly surprising if the emergence of a firm or the extension of the activities of an existing firm was not the solution adopted on many occasions to deal with the problem of harmful effects. This solution would be adopted whenever the administrative costs of the firm were less than the costs of the market transactions that it supersedes and the gains which would result from the rearrangement of activities greater than the firm's costs of organising them. I do not need to examine in great detail the character of this solution since I have explained what is involved in my earlier article.

But the firm is not the only possible answer to this problem. The administrative costs of organising transactions within the firm may also be high, and particularly so when many diverse activities are brought within the control of a single organisation. In the standard case of a smoke nuisance, which may affect a vast number of people engaged in a wide variety of activities, the administrative costs might well be so high as to make any attempt to deal with the problem within the confines of a single firm impossible. An alternative solution is direct Government regulation. Instead of instituting a legal system of rights which can be modified by transactions on the market, the government may impose regulations which state what people must or must not do and which have to be obeyed. Thus, the government (by statute or perhaps more likely through an administrative agency) may, to deal with the problem of smoke nuisance, decree that certain methods of production should or should not be used (e.g. that smoke preventing devices should be installed or that coal or oil should not be burned) or may confine certain types of business to certain districts (zoning regulations).

The government is, in a sense, a super-firm (but of a very special kind) since it is able to influence the use of factors of production by administrative decision. But the ordinary firm is subject to checks in its operations because of the competition of other firms, which might administer the same activities at lower cost and also because there is always the alternative of market transactions as against organisation within the firm if the administrative costs become too great. The government is able, if it wishes, to avoid the market altogether, which a firm can never do. The firm has to make market agreements with the owners of the factors of production that it uses. Just as the government can conscript or seize property, so it can decree that factors of production should only be used in such-and-such a way. Such authoritarian methods save a lot of trouble (for those doing the organising). Furthermore, the government has at its disposal the police and the other law enforcement agencies to make sure that its regulations are carried out.

It is clear that the government has powers which might enable it to get some things done at a lower cost than could a private organisation (or at any rate one without special governmental powers). But the governmental administrative machine is not itself costless. It can, in fact, on occasion be extremely costly. Furthermore, there is no reason to suppose that the restrictive and zoning regulations, made by a fallible administration subject to political pressures and operating without any competitive check, will necessarily always be those which increase the efficiency with which the economic system operates. Furthermore, such general regulations which must apply to a wide variety of cases will be enforced in some cases in which they are clearly inappropriate. From these considerations it follows that direct governmental regulation will not necessarily give better results than leaving the problem to be solved by the market or the firm. But equally there is no reason why, on occasion, such governmental administrative regulation should not lead to an improvement in economic efficiency. This would seem particularly likely when, as is normally the case with the smoke nuisance, a large number of people are involved and in which therefore the costs of handling the problem through the market or the firm may be high.

There is, of course, a further alternative, which is to do nothing about the problem at all. And given that the costs involved in solving the problem by regulations issued by the governmental administrative machine will often be heavy (particularly if the costs are interpreted to include all the consequences which follow from the Government engaging in this kind of activity), it will no doubt be commonly the case that the gain which would come from regulating the actions which give rise to the harmful effects will be less than the costs involved in Government regulation.

The discussion of the problem of harmful effects in this section (when the costs of market transactions are taken into account) is extremely inadequate. But at least it has made clear that the problem is one of choosing the appropriate social arrangement for dealing with the harmful effects. All solutions have costs and there is no reason to suppose that government regulation is called for simply because the problem is not well handled by the market or the firm. Satisfactory views on policy can only come from a patient study of how, in practice, the market, firms and governments handle the problem of harmful effects. Economists need to study the work of the broker in bringing parties together, the effectiveness of restrictive covenants, the problems of the large-scale real estate development company, the operation of Government zoning and other regulating activities. It is my belief that economists, and policymakers generally, have tended to over-estimate the advantages which come from governmental regulation. But this belief, even if justified, does not do more than suggest that government regulation should be curtailed. It does not tell us where the boundary line should be drawn. This, it seems to me, has to come from a detailed investigation of the actual results of handling the problem in different ways. But it would be unfortunate if this investigation were undertaken with the aid of a faulty economic analysis. The aim of this article is to indicate what the economic approach to the problem should be.

VII. The Legal Delimitation of Rights and the Economic Problem

The discussion in Section V not only served to illustrate the argument but also afforded a glimpse at the legal approach to the problem of harmful effects. The cases considered were all English but a similar selection of American cases could easily be made and the character of the reasoning would have been the same. Of course, if market transactions were costless, all that matters (questions of equity apart) is that the rights of the various parties should be well-defined and the results of legal actions easy to forecast. But as we have seen, the situation is quite different when market transactions are so costly as to make it difficult to change the arrangement of rights established by the law. In such cases, the courts directly influence economic activity. It would therefore seem desirable that the courts should understand the economic consequences of their decisions and should, insofar as this is possible without creating too much uncertainty about the legal position itself, take these consequences into account when making their decisions. Even when it is possible to change the legal delimitation of rights through market transactions, it is obviously desirable to reduce the need for such transactions and thus reduce the employment of resources in carrying them out.

A thorough examination of the presuppositions of the courts in trying such cases would be of great interest but I have not been able to attempt it. Nevertheless it is clear from a cursory study that the courts have often recognized the economic implications of their decisions and are aware (as many economists are not) of the reciprocal nature of the problem. Furthermore, from time to time, they take these economic implications into account, along with other factors, in arriving at their decisions. The American writers on this subject refer to the question in a more explicit fashion than do the British. Thus, to quote Prosser on Torts:

> A person may make use of his own property or ... conduct his own affairs at the expense of some harm to his neighbors. He may operate a factory whose noise and smoke cause some discomfort to others, so long as he keeps within reasonable bounds. It is only when his conduct is unreasonable, *in the light of its utility and the harm which results* [italics added], that it becomes a nuisance ... As it was said in an ancient case in regard to candle-making in a town, "Le utility del chose excusera le noisomeness del stink."
> The world must have factories, smelters, oil refineries, noisy machinery and blasting, even at the expense of some inconvenience to those in the vicinity and the plaintiff may be required to accept some not unreasonable discomfort for the general good.[16]

The standard British writers do not state as explicitly as this that a comparison between the utility and harm produced is an element in deciding whether a harmful effect should be considered a nuisance. But similar views, if less strongly expressed, are to be found.[17] The doctrine that the harmful effect must be substantial before the court will act is, no doubt, in part a reflection of the fact that there will almost always be some gain to offset the harm. And in the reports of individual cases, it is clear that the judges have had in mind what would be lost as well as what would be gained in deciding whether to grant an injunction or award damages. Thus, in refusing to prevent the destruction of a prospect by a new building, the judge stated:

I know no general rule of common law, which ... says, that building so as to stop another's prospect is a nuisance. Was that the case, there could be no great towns; and I must grant injunctions to all the new buildings in this town.[18]

In *Webb v. Bird* [19] it was decided that it was not a nuisance to build a schoolhouse so near a windmill as to obstruct currents of air and hinder the working of the mill. An early case seems to have been decided in an opposite direction. Gale commented:

In old maps of London a row of windmills appears on the heights to the north of London. Probably in the time of King James it was thought an alarming circumstance, as affecting the supply of food to the city, that anyone should build so near them as to take the wind out from their sails.[20]

In one of the cases discussed in section V, *Sturges v. Bridgman*, it seems clear that the judges were thinking of the economic consequences of alternative decisions. To the argument that if the principle that:

They seemed to be following were carried out to its logical consequences, it would result in the most serious practical inconveniences, for a man might go—say into the midst of the tanneries of *Bermondsey*, or into any other locality devoted to any particular trade or manufacture of a noisy or unsavoury character, and by building a private residence upon a vacant piece of land put a stop to such trade or manufacture altogether,

The judges answered that:

Whether anything is a nuisance or not is a question to be determined, not merely by an abstract consideration of the thing itself, but in reference to its circumstances; What would be a nuisance in *Belgrave Square* would not necessarily be so in *Bermondsey;*

and where a locality is devoted to a particular trade or manufacture carried on by the traders or manufacturers in a particular and established manner not constituting a public nuisance, Judges and juries would be justified in finding, and may be trusted to find, that the trade or manufacture so carried on in that locality is not a private or actionable wrong.[21]

That the character of the neighborhood is relevant in deciding whether something is, or is not, a nuisance, is definitely established.

He who dislikes the noise of traffic must not set up his abode in the heart of a great city. He who loves peace and quiet must not live in a locality devoted to the business of making boilers or steamships.[22]

What has emerged has been described as "planning and zoning by the judiciary."[23] Of course there are sometimes considerable difficulties in applying the criteria.[24]

An interesting example of the problem is found in *Adams v. Ursell*[25] in which a fried fish shop in a predominantly working-class district was set up near houses of "a much better character." England without fish-and-chips is a contradiction in terms and the case was clearly one of high importance. The judge commented:

It was urged that an injunction would cause great hardship to the defendant and to the poor people who get food at his shop. The answer to that is that it does not follow that the defendant cannot carry on his business in another more suitable place somewhere in the neighbourhood. It by no means follows that because a fried fish shop is a nuisance in one place it is a nuisance in another.

In fact, the injunction which restrained Mr. Ursell from running his shop did not even extend to the whole street. So he was presumably able to move to other premises near houses of "a much worse character", the inhabitants of which would no doubt consider the availability of fish-and-chips to outweigh the pervading odour and "fog or mist" so graphically described by the plaintiff. Had there been no other more suitable place in the neighbourhood, the case would have been more difficult and the decision might have been different. What would "the poor people" have had for food? No English judge would have said: "Let them eat cake."

The courts do not always refer very clearly to the economic problem posed by the cases brought before them but it seems probable that in the interpretation of words and phrases like "reasonable" or "common or ordinary use" there is some recognition, perhaps largely unconscious and certainly not very explicit, of the economic aspects of the questions at issue. A good example of this would seem to be the judgment in the Court of Appeals in *Andreae v. Selfridge and Company Ltd.*[26] In this case, a hotel (in Wigmore Street) was situated on part of an island site. The remainder of the site was acquired by Selfridges which demolished the existing buildings in order to erect another in their place. The hotel suffered a loss of custom in consequence of the noise and dust caused by the demolition. The owner of the hotel brought an action against Selfridges for damages. In the lower court, the hotel was awarded £4,500 damages. The case was then taken on appeal. The judge who had found for the hotel proprietor in the lower court said:

> I cannot regard what the defendants did on the site of the first operation as having been commonly done in the ordinary use and occupation of land or houses. It is neither usual nor common, in this country, for people to excavate a site to a depth of 60 feet and then to erect upon that site a steel framework and fasten the steel frames together with rivets. ... Nor is it, I think, a common or ordinary use of land, in this country, to act as the defendants did when they were dealing with the site of their second operation—namely, to demolish all the houses that they had to demolish, five or six of them I think, if not more, and to use for the Purpose of demolishing them pneumatic hammers.

Sir Wilfred Greene, M.R., speaking for the Court of Appeals, first noted:

That when one is dealing with temporary operations, such as demolition and rebuilding, everybody has to put up with a certain amount of discomfort, because operations of that kind cannot be carried on at all without a certain amount of noise and a certain amount of dust. Therefore, the rule with regard to interference must be read subject to this qualification.

He then referred to the previous judgment:

With great respect to the learned judge, I take the view that he has not approached this matter from the correct angle. It seems to me that it is not possible to say ... that the type of demolition, excavation and construction in which the defendant company was engaged in the course of these operations was of such an abnormal and unusual nature as to prevent the qualification to which I have referred coming into operation. It seems to me that, when the rule speaks of the common or ordinary use of land, it does not mean that the methods of using land and building on it are in some way to be stabilised for ever. As time goes on new inventions or new methods enable land to be more profitably used, either by digging down into the earth or by mounting up into the skies. Whether, from other points of view, that is a matter which is desirable for humanity is neither here nor there; but it is part of the normal use of land, to make use upon your land, in the matter of construction, of what particular type and what particular depth of foundations and particular height of building may be reasonable, in the circumstances, and in view of the developments of the day. ... Guests at hotels are very easily upset. People coming to this hotel, who were accustomed to a quiet outlook at the back, coming back and finding demolition and building going on, may very well have taken the view that the particular merit of this hotel no longer existed. That would be a misfortune for the plaintiff; but assuming that there was nothing wrong in the defendant company's works, assuming the defendant company was carrying on the demolition and its building, productive of noise though it might be, with all reasonable skill, and taking all reasonable precautions not to cause annoyance to its neighbors, then the plaintiff might lose all her clients in the hotel because they have lost the amenities of an open and quiet place behind, but she would have no cause of complaint. ... But those who say that their interference with the comfort of their neighbors is justified because their operations are normal and usual and conducted with proper care and skill are under a specific duty ... to use that reasonable and proper care and skill. It is not a correct attitude to take to say: "We will go on and do what we like until somebody complains!"...Their duty is to take proper precautions and to see that the nuisance is reduced to a minimum. It is no answer for them to say: "But this would mean that we should have to do the work more slowly than we would like to do it, or it would involve putting us to some extra expense." All these questions are matters of common sense and degree, and quite clearly it would be unreasonable to expect people to conduct their work so slowly or so expensively, for the purpose of preventing a transient inconvenience, that the cost and trouble would be prohibitive. ... In this case, the defendant company's attitude seems to have been to go on until somebody complained, and, further, that its desire to hurry its work and conduct it according to its own ideas and its own convenience was to prevail if there was a real conflict between it and the comfort of its neighbors. That is not carrying out the obligation of using reasonable care and skill. ... The effect comes to this ... the plaintiff suffered an actionable nuisance; she is entitled, not to a nominal sum, but to a substantial sum, based upon those principles but in arriving at the sum ... I have discounted any loss of custom ... which might be due to the general loss of amenities owing to what was going on at the back.

The upshot was that the damages awarded were reduced from £4,500 to £1,000.

The discussion in this section has, up to this point, been concerned with court decisions arising out of the common law relating to nuisance. Delimitation of rights in this area also comes about because of statutory enactments. Most economists would appear to assume that the aim of governmental action in this field is to extend the scope of the law of nuisance by designating as nuisances activities which would not be recognized as such by the common law. And there can be no doubt that some statutes, for example, the Public Health Acts, have had this effect. But not all Government enactments are of this kind. The effect of much of the legislation in this area is to protect businesses from the claims of those they have harmed by their actions. There is a long list of legalized nuisances.

The position has been summarized in *Halsbury's Laws of England* as follows:

Where the legislature directs that a thing shall in all events be done or authorises certain works at a particular place for a specific purposes or grants powers with the intention that they shall be exercised, although leaving some discretion as to the mode of exercise, no action will lie at common law for nuisance or damage which is the inevitable result of carrying out the statutory powers so conferred. This is so whether the act causing the damage is authorised for public purposes or private profit. Acts done under powers granted by persons to whom Parliament has delegated authority to grant such powers, for example, under provisional orders of the Board of Trade, are regarded as having been done under statutory authority. In the absence of negligence it seems that a body exercising statutory powers will not be liable to an action merely because it might, by acting in a different way, have minimised an injury.

Instances are next given of freedom from liability for acts authorized:

An action has been held not to be against a body exercising its statutory powers without negligence in respect of the flooding of land by water escaping from water courses, from water pipes, from drains, or from a canal; the escape of fumes from sewers; the escape of sewage: The subsidence of a road over a sewer; vibration or noise caused by a railway; fires caused by authorised acts; the pollution of a stream where statutory requirements to use the best known method of purifying before discharging the effluent have been satisfied; interference with a telephone or telegraph system by an eletric tramway; the insertion of poles for tramways in the subsoil;

annoyance caused by things reasonably necessary for the excavation of authorised works; accidental damage caused by the placing of a grating in a roadway; the escape of tar acid; or interference with the access of a frontager by a street shelter or safety railings on the edge of a pavement.[27]

The legal position in the United States would seem to be essentially the same as in England, except that the power of the legislatures to authorize what would otherwise be nuisances under the common law, at least without giving compensation to the person harmed, is somewhat more limited, as it is subject to constitutional restrictions.[28] Nonetheless, the power is there and cases more or less identical with the English cases can be found. The question has arisen in an acute form in connection with airports and the operation of aeroplanes. The case of *Delta Air Corporation v. Kersey, Kersey v. City of Atlanta*[29] is a good example. Mr. Kersey bought land and built a house on it. Some years later the City of Atlanta constructed an airport on land immediately adjoining that of Mr. Kersey. It was explained that his property was "a quiet, peaceful and proper location for a home before the airport was built, but dust, noises and low flying of airplanes caused by the operation of the airport have rendered his property unsuitable as a home." A state of affairs which was described in the report of the case with a wealth of distressing detail. The judge first referred to an earlier case, *Thrasher v. City of Atlanta* [30] in which it was noted that the City of Atlanta had been expressly authorized to operate an airport.

> By this franchise aviation was recognised as a lawful business and also as an enterprise affected with a public interest ... all persons using [the airport] in the manner contemplated by law are within the protection and immunity of the franchise granted by the municipality. An airport is not a nuisance per se, although it might become such from the manner of its construction or operation.

Since aviation was a lawful business affected with a public interest and the construction of the airport was authorized by statute, the judge next referred to *Georgia Railroad and Banking Co. v. Maddox* [31] in which it was said:

> Where a railroad terminal yard is located and its construction authorized, under statutory powers, if it be constructed and operated in a proper manner, it cannot be adjudged a nuisance. Accordingly, injuries and inconveniences to persons residing near such a yard, from noises of locomotives, rumbling of cars, vibrations produced thereby, and smoke, cinders, soot and the like, which result from the ordinary and necessary, therefore proper, use and operation of such a yard, are not nuisances, but are the necessary concomitants of the franchise granted.

In view of this, the judge decided that the noise and dust complained of by Mr. Kersey "may be deemed to be incidental to the proper operation of an airport, and as such they cannot be said to constitute a nuisance." But the complaint against low flying was different:

> Can it be said that flights ... at such a low height [25 to 50 feet above Mr. Kersey's house] as to be imminently dangerous to life and health are a necessary concomitant of an airport? We do not think this question can be answered in the affirmative. No reason appears why the city could not obtain lands of an area [sufficiently large]...as not to require such low flights. ... For the sake of public convenience adjoining property owners must suffer such inconvenience from noise and dust as result from the usual and proper operation of an airport, but their private rights are entitled to preference in the eyes of the law where the inconvenience is not one demanded by a properly constructed and operated airport.

Of course this assumed that the City of Atlanta could prevent the low flying and continue to operate the airport. The judge therefore added:

From all that appears, the conditions causing the low flying may be remedied; but if on the trial it should appear that it is indispensable to the public interest that the airport should continue to be operated in its present condition, it may be said that the petitioner should be denied injunctive relief.

In the course of another aviation case, *Smith v. New England Aircraft Co.,*[32] the court surveyed the law in the United States regarding the legalizing of nuisances and it is apparent that, in the broad, it is very similar to that found in England:

It is the proper function of the legislative department of government in the exercise of the police power to consider the problems and risks that arise from the use of new inventions and endeavor to adjust private rights and harmonics conflicting interests by comprehensive statutes for the public welfare. ... There are ... analogies where the invasion of the airspace over underlying land by noise, smoke, vibration, dust and disagreeable odors, having been authorized by the legislative department of government and not being in effect a condemnation of the property although in some measure depreciating its market value, must be borne by the landowner without compensation or remedy. Legislative sanction makes that lawful which otherwise might be a nuisance. Examples of this are damages to adjacent land arising from smoke, vibration and noise in the operation of a railroad ...; the noise of ringing factory bells; the abatement of nuisances; the erection of steam engines and furnaces; unpleasant odors connected with sewers, oil refining and storage of naphtha.

Most economists seem to be unaware of all this. When they are prevented from sleeping at night by the roar of jet planes overhead (publicly authorized and perhaps publicly operated), are unable to think (or rest) in the day because of the noise and vibration from passing trains (publicly authorized and perhaps publicly operated), find it difficult to breathe because of the odour from a local sewage farm (publicly authorized and perhaps publicly operated) and are unable to escape because their driveways are blocked by a road obstruction (without any doubt, publicly devised), their nerves frayed and mental balance disturbed, they proceed to declaim about the disadvantages of private enterprise and the need for Government regulation.

While most economists seem to be under a misapprehension concerning the character of the situation with which they are dealing, it is also the case that the activities which they would like to see stopped or curtailed may well be socially justified. It is all a question of weighing up the gains that would accrue from eliminating these harmful effects against the gains that accrue from allowing them to continue. Of course, it is likely that an extension of Government economic activity will often lead to this protection against action for nuisance being pushed further than is desirable. For one thing, the Government is likely to look with a benevolent eye on enterprises which it is itself promoting. For another, it is possible to describe the committing of a nuisance by public enterprise in a much more pleasant way than when the same thing is done by private enterprise. In the words of Lord Justice Sir Alfred Denning:

> The significance of the social revolution of today is that, whereas in the past the balance was much too heavily in favor of the rights of property and freedom of contract. Parliament has repeatedly intervened so as to give the public good its proper place.[33]

There can be little doubt that the Welfare State is likely to bring an extension of that immunity from liability for damage, which economists have been in the habit of condemning (although they have tended to assume that this immunity was a sign of too little Government intervention in the economic system). For example, in Britain, the powers of local authorities are regarded as being either absolute or conditional. In the first category, the local authority has no discretion in exercising the power conferred on it. "The absolute power may be said to cover all the necessary consequences of its direct operation even if such consequences amount to nuisance." On the other hand, a conditional power may only be exercised in such a way that the consequences do not constitute a nuisance.

> It is the intention of the legislature which determines whether a power is absolute or conditional. ... As there is the possibility that the social policy of the legislature may change from time to time, a power which in one era would be construed as being conditional, might in another era be interpreted as being absolute in order to further the policy of the Welfare State. This point is one which should be borne in mind when considering some of the older cases upon this aspect of the law of nuisance.[34]

It would seem desirable to summarize the burden of this long section. The problem which we face in dealing with actions which have harmful effects is not simply one of restraining those responsible for them. What has to be decided is whether the gain from preventing the harm is greater than the loss which would be suffered elsewhere as a result of stopping the action which produces the harm. In a world in which there are costs of rearranging the rights established by the legal system, the courts, in cases relating to nuisance, are, in effect, making a decision on the economic problem and determining how resources are to be employed. It was argued that the courts are conscious of this and that they often make, although not always in a very explicit fashion, a comparison between what would be gained and what lost by preventing actions which have harmful effects. But the delimitation of rights is also the result of statutory enactments. Here we also find evidence of an appreciation of the reciprocal nature of the problem. While statutory enactments add to the list of nuisances, action is also taken to legalize what would otherwise be nuisances under the common law. The kind of situation which economists are prone to consider as requiring corrective Government action is, in fact, often the result of Government action. Such action is not necessarily unwise. But there is a real danger that extensive Government intervention in the economic system may lead to the protection of those responsible for harmful effects being carried too far.

VIII. Pigou's Treatment in the *Economics of Welfare*

The fountainhead for the modern economic analysis of the problem discussed in this article is Pigou's *Economics of Welfare* and, in particular, that section of Part II which deals with divergences between social and private net products which come about because,

> one person A, in the course of rendering some service, for which payment is made, to a second person B, incidentally also renders services or disservices to other persons (not producers of like services), of such a sort that payment cannot be exacted from the benefited parties or compensation enforced on behalf of the injured parties.[35]

Pigou tells us that,

> His aim in Part II of *The Economics of Welfare* is to ascertain how far the free play of self-interest, acting under the existing legal system, tends to distribute the country's resources in the way most favorable to the production of a large national dividend, and how far it is feasible for State action to improve upon "natural" tendencies.[36]

To judge from the first part of this statement, Pigou's purpose is to discover whether any improvements could be made in the existing arrangements which determine the use of resources. Since Pigou's conclusion is that improvements could be made, one might have expected him to continue by saying that he proposed to set out the changes required to bring them about. Instead, Pigou adds a phrase which contrasts "natural" tendencies with State action, which seems in some sense to equate the present arrangements with "natural" tendencies and to imply that what is required to bring about these improvements is State action (if feasible). That this is more or less Pigou's position is evident from Chapter I of Part II.[37] Pigou starts by referring to "optimistic followers of the classical economists"[38] who have argued that the value of production would be maximised if the Government refrained from any interference in the economic system and the economic arrangements were those which came about "naturally." Pigou goes on to say that if self-interest does promote economic welfare, it is because human institutions have been devised to make it so. (This part of Pigou's argument, which he develops with the aid of a quotation from Cannan, seems to me to be essentially correct.) Pigou concludes:

> But even in the most advanced States there are failures and imperfections. ... There are many obstacles that prevent a community's resources from being distributed in the most efficient way. The study of these constitutes our present problem. ... Its purposes is essentially practical. It seeks to bring into clearer light some of the ways in which it now is, or eventually may become, feasible for governments to control the play of economic forces in such wise as to promote the economic welfare, and through that, the total welfare, of their citizens as a whole.[39]

Pigou's underlying thought would appear to be: Some have argued that no State action is needed. But the system has performed as well as it has because of State action. Nonetheless, there are still imperfections. What additional State action is required?

If this is a correct summary of Pigou's position, its inadequacy can be demonstrated by examining the first example he gives of a divergence between private and social products.

> It might happen...that costs are thrown upon people not directly concerned, through, say, uncompensated damage done to surrounding woods by sparks from railway engines. All such effects must be included some of them will be positive, others negative elements—in reckoning up the social net product of the marginal increment of any volume of resources turned into any use or place.[40]

The example used by Pigou refers to a real situation. In Britain, a railway does not normally have to compensate those who suffer damage by fire caused by sparks from an engine. Taken in conjunction with what he says in Chapter 9 of Part II, I take Pigou's policy recommendations to be, first, that there should be State action to correct this "natural" situation and, second, that the railways should be forced to compensate those whose woods are burnt. If this is a correct interpretation of Pigou's position, I would argue that the first recommendation is based on a misapprehension of the facts and that the second is not necessarily desirable.

Let us consider the legal position. Under the heading "Sparks from engines", we find the following in *Halsbury's Laws of England*:

> If railway undertakers use steam engines on their railway without express statutory authority to do so, they are liable, irrespective of any negligence on their part, for fires caused by sparks from engines. Railway undertakers are, however, generally given statutory authority to use steam engines on their railway; accordingly, if an engine is constructed with the precautions which science suggests against fire and is used without negligence, they are not responsible at common law for any damage which may be done by sparks. ... In the construction of an engine the undertaker is bound to use all the discoveries which science has put within its reach in order to avoid doing harm, provided they are such as it is reasonable to require the company to adopt, having proper regard to the likelihood of the damage and to the cost and convenience of the remedy; but it is not negligence on the part of an undertaker if it refuses to use an apparatus the efficiency of which is open to bona fide doubt.

To this general rule, there is a statutory exception arising from the Railway (Fires) Act, 1905, as amended in 1923. This concerns agricultural land or agricultural crops.

> In such a case the fact that the engine was used under statutory powers does not affect the liability of the company in an action for the damage. ... These provisions, however,

only apply where the claim for damage ... does not exceed £200, [£100 in the 1905 act] and where written notice of the occurrence of the fire and the intention to claim has been sent to the company within seven days of the occurrence of the damage and particulars of the damage in writing showing the amount of the claim in money not exceeding £200 have been sent to the company within twenty-one days.

Agricultural land does not include moorland or buildings and agricultural crops do not include those led away or stacked.[41] I have not made a close study of the parliamentary history of this statutory exception, but to judge from debates in the House of Commons in 1922 and 1923, this exception was probably designed to help the smallholder.[42]

Let us return to Pigou's example of uncompensated damage to surrounding woods caused by sparks from railway engines. This is presumably intended to show how it is possible "for State action to improve on 'natural' tendencies." If we treat Pigou's example as referring to the position before 1905, or as being an arbitrary example (in that he might just as well have written "surrounding buildings" instead of "surrounding woods"), then it is clear that the reason why compensation was not paid must have been that the railway had statutory authority to run steam engines (which relieved it of liability for fires caused by sparks). That this was the legal position was established in 1860, in a case, oddly enough, which concerned the burning of surrounding woods by a railway,[43] and the law on this point has not been changed (apart from the one exception) by a century of railway legislation, including nationalisation. If we treat Pigou's example of "uncompensated damage done to surrounding woods by sparks from railway engines" literally, and assume that it refers to the period after 1905, then it is clear that the reason why compensation was not paid must have been that the damage was more than £100 (in the first edition of *The Economics of Welfare*) or more than £200 (in later editions) or that the owner of the wood failed to notify the railway in writing within seven days of the fire or did not send particulars of the damage, in writing, within twenty-one days. In the real world, Pigou's example could only exist as a result of a deliberate choice of the legislature. It is not, of course, easy to imagine the construction of a railway in a state of nature. The nearest one can get to this is presumably a railway which uses steam engines "without express statutory authority." However, in this case the railway would be obliged to compensate those whose woods it burnt down. That is to say, compensation would be paid in the absence of Government action. The only circumstances in which compensation would not be paid would be those in which there had been Government action. It is strange that Pigou, who clearly thought it desirable that compensation should be paid, should have chosen this particular example to demonstrate how it is possible "for State action to improve on 'natural' tendencies."

Pigou seems to have had a faulty view of the facts of the situation. But it also seems likely that he was mistaken in his economic analysis. It is not necessarily desirable that the railway should be required to compensate those who suffer damage by fires caused by railway engines. I need not show here that, if the railway could make a bargain with everyone having property adjoining the railway line and there were no costs involved in making such bargains, it would not matter whether the railway was liable for damage caused by fires or not. This question has been treated at length in earlier sections. The problem is whether it would be desirable to make the railway liable in conditions in which it is too expensive for such bargains to be made. Pigou clearly thought it was desirable to force the railway to pay compensation and it is easy to see the kind of argument that would have led him to this conclusion. Suppose a railway is considering whether to run an additional train or to increase the speed of an existing train or to install spark-preventing devices on its engines. If the railway were not liable for fire damage, then, when making these decisions, it would not take into account as a cost the increase in damage resulting from the additional train or the faster train or the failure to install spark-preventing devices. This is the source of the divergence between private and social net products. It results in the railway performing acts which will lower the value of total production—and which it would not do if it were liable for the damage. This can be shown by means of an arithmetical example.

Consider a railway, which is not liable for damage by fires caused by sparks from its engines, which runs two trains per day on a certain line. Suppose that running one train per day would enable the railway to perform services worth $150 per annum and running two trains a day would enable the railway to perform services worth $250 per annum. Suppose further that the cost of running one train is $50 per annum and two trains $100 per annum. Assuming perfect competition, the cost equals the fall in the value of production elsewhere due to the employment of additional factors of production by the railway. Clearly the railway would find it profitable to run two trains per day. But suppose that running one train per day would destroy by fire crops worth (on an average over the year) $60 and two trains a day would result in the destruction of crops worth $120. In these circumstances running one train per day would raise the value of total production but the running of a second train would reduce the value of total production. The second train would enable additional railway services worth $100 per annum to be performed. But the fall in the value of production elsewhere would be $110 per annum; $50 as a result of the employment of additional factors of production and $60 as a result of the destruction of crops. Since it would be better if the second train were not run and since it would not run if the railway were liable for damage caused to crops, the conclusion that the railway should be made liable for the damage seems irresistable. Undoubtedly it is this kind of reasoning which underlies the Pigovian position.

The conclusion that it would be better if the second train did not run is correct. The conclusion that it is desirable that the railway should be made liable for the damage it causes is wrong. Let us change our assumption concerning the rule of liability. Suppose that the railway is liable for damage from fires caused by sparks from the engine. A farmer on lands adjoining the railway is then in the position that, if his crop is destroyed by fires caused by the railway, he will receive the market price from the railway; but if his crop is not damaged, he will receive the market price by sale. It therefore becomes a matter of indifference to him whether his crop is damaged by fire or not. The position is very different when the railway is not liable. Any crop destruction through railway-caused fires would then reduce the receipts of the farmer. He would therefore take out of cultivation any land for which the damage is likely to be greater than the net return of the land (for reasons explained at length in Section III). A change from a regime in which the railway is not liable for damage to one in which it is liable is likely therefore to lead to an increase in the amount of cultivation on lands adjoining the railway. It will also, of course, lead to an increase in the amount of crop destruction due to railway-caused fires.

Let us return to our arithmetical example. Assume that, with the changed rule of liability, there is a doubling in the amount of crop destruction due to railway-caused fires. With one train per day, crops worth $120 would be destroyed each year and two trains per day would lead to the destruction of crops worth $240. We saw previously that it would not be profitable to run the second train if the railway had to pay $60 per annum as compensation for damage. With damage at $120 per annum the loss from running the second train would be $60 greater. But now let us consider the first train. The value of the transport services furnished by the first train is $150. The cost of running the train is $50. The amount that the railway would have to pay out as compensation for damage is $120. It follows that it would not be profitable to run any trains. With the figures in our example we reach the following result: If the railway is not liable for fire-damage, two trains per day would be run; if the railway is liable for fire-damage, it would cease operations altogether. Does this mean that it is better that there should be no railway? This question can be resolved by considering what would happen to the value of total production if it were decided to exempt the railway from liability for fire-damage, thus bringing it into operation (with two trains per day).

The operation of the railway would enable transport services worth $250 to be performed. It would also mean the employment of factors of production which would reduce the value of production elsewhere by $100. Furthermore it would mean the destruction of crops worth $120. The coming of the railway will also have led to the abandonment of cultivation of some land. Since we know that, had this land been cultivated, the value of the crops destroyed by fire would have been $120, and since it is unlikely that the total crop on this land would have been destroyed, it seems reasonable to suppose that the value of the crop yield on this land would have been higher than this. Assume it would have been $160. But the abandonment of cultivation would have released factors of production for employment elsewhere. All we know is that the amount by which the value of production elsewhere will increase will be less than $160. Suppose that it is $150. Then the gain from operating the railway would be $250 (the value of the transport services) minus $100 (the cost of the factors of production) minus $120 (the value of crops destroyed by fire) minus $160 (the fall in the value of crop production due to the abandonment of cultivation) plus $150 (the value of production elsewhere of the released factors of production). Overall, operating the railway will increase the value of total production by $20. With these figures it is clear that it is better that the railway should not be liable for the damage it causes, thus enabling it to operate profitably. Of course, by altering the figures, it could be shown that there are other cases in which it would be desirable that the railway should be liable for the damage it causes. It is enough for my purpose to show that, from an economic point of view, a situation in which there is "uncompensated damage done to surrounding woods by sparks from railway engines" is not necessarily undesirable. Whether it is desirable or not depends on the particular circumstances.

How is it that the Pigovian analysis seems to give the wrong answer? The reason is that Pigou does not seem to have noticed that his analysis is dealing with an entirely different question. The analysis as such is correct. But it is quite illegitimate for Pigou to draw the particular conclusion he does. The question at issue is not whether it is desirable to run an additional train or a faster train or to install smoke-preventing devices; the question at issue is whether it is desirable to have a system in which the railway has to compensate those who suffer damage from the fires which it causes or one in which the railway does not have to compensate them. When an economist is comparing alternative social arrangements, the proper procedure is to compare the total social product yielded by these different arrangements. The comparison of private and social products is neither here nor there. A simple example will demonstrate this.

Imagine a town in which there are traffic lights. A motorist approaches an intersection and stops because the light is red. There are no cars approaching the intersection on the other street. If the motorist ignored the red signal, no accident would occur and the total product would increase because the motorist would arrive earlier at his destination. Why does he not do this? The reason is that if he ignored the light he would be fined. The private product from crossing the street is less than the social product. Should we conclude from this that the total product would be greater if there were no fines for failing to obey traffic signals? The Pigovian analysis shows us that it is possible to conceive of better worlds than the one in which we live. But the problem is to devise practical arrangements which will correct defects in one part of the system without causing more serious harm in other parts.

I have examined in considerable detail one example of a divergence between private and social products and I do not propose to make any further examination of Pigou's analytical system. But the main discussion of the problem considered in this article is to be found in that part of Chapter 9 in Part II which deals with Pigou's second class of divergence and it is of interest to see how Pigou develops his argument. Pigou's own description of this second class of divergence was quoted at the beginning of this section. Pigou distinguishes between the case in which a person renders services for which he receives no payment and the case in which a person renders disservices and compensation is not given to the injured parties. Our main attention has, of course, centred on this second case. It is therefore rather astonishing to find, as was pointed out to me by Professor Francesco Forte, that the problem of the smoking chimney—the "stock instance" [44] or "class-room example"[45] of the second case—is used by Pigou as an example of the first case (services rendered without payment) and is never mentioned, at any rate explicitly, in connection with the second case.[46] Pigou points out that factory owners who devote resources to preventing their chimneys from smoking render services for which they receive no payment. The implication, in the light of Pigou's discussion later in the chapter, is that a factory owner with a smokey chimney should be given a bounty to induce him to install smoke-preventing devices.

Most modern economists would suggest that the owner of the factory with the smokey chimney should be taxed. It seems a pity that economists (apart from Professor Forte) do not seem to have noticed this feature of Pigou's treatment since a realisation that the problem could be tackled in either of these two ways would probably have led to an explicit recognition of its reciprocal nature.

In discussing the second case (disservices without compensation to those damaged), Pigou says that they are rendered "When the owner of a site in a residential quarter of a city builds a factory there and so destroys a great part of the amenities of neighbouring sites; or, in a less degree, when he uses his site in such a way as to spoil the lighting of the house opposite; or when he invests resources in erecting buildings in a crowded centre, which by contracting the air-space and the playing room of the neighbourhood, tend to injure the health and efficiency of the families living there."[47] Pigou is, of course, quite right to describe such actions as "uncharged disservices". But he is wrong when he describes these actions as "anti-social."[48] They may or may not be. It is necessary to weigh the harm against the good that will result. Nothing could be more "anti-social" than to oppose any action which causes any harm to anyone.

The example with which Pigou opens his discussion of "uncharged disservices" is not, as I have indicated, the case of the smokey chimney but the case of the overrunning rabbits: "... Incidental uncharged disservices are rendered to third parties when the game-preserving activities of one occupier involve the overrunning of a neighbouring occupier's land by rabbits..." This example is of extraordinary interest, not so much because the economic analysis of the case is essentially any different from that of the other examples, but because of the peculiarities of the legal position and the light it throws on the part which economics can play in what is apparently the purely legal question of the delimitation of rights.

The problem of legal liability for the actions of rabbits is part of the general subject of liability for animals.[49] I will, although with reluctance, confine my discussion to rabbits. The early cases relating to rabbits concerned the relations between the lord of the manor and commoners, since, from the thirteenth century on, it became usual for the lord of the manor to stock the commons with conies (rabbits), both for the sake of the meat and the fur. But in 1597, in *Boulston's* case, an action was brought by one landowner against a neighbouring landowner, alleging that the defendant had made coney-burrows and that the conies had increased and had destroyed the plaintiff's corn. The action failed for the reason that

> ... As soon as the coneys come on his neighbor's land he may kill them, for they are ferae naturae, and he who makes the coney-burrows has no property in them, and he shall not be punished for the damage which the coneys do in which he has no property, and which the other may lawfully kill.[50]

As *Boulston's* case has been treated as binding—Bray, J., in 1919, said that he was not aware that *Boulston's* case has ever been overruled or questioned[51]— Pigou's rabbit example undoubtedly represented the legal position at the time *The Economics of Welfare* was written.[52] And in this case, it is not far from the truth to say that the state of affairs which Pigou describes came about because of an absence of Government action (at any rate in the form of statutory enactments) and was the result of "natural" tendencies.

Nonetheless, *Boulsion's* case is something of a legal curiousity and Professor Williams makes no secret of his distaste for this decision:

> The conception of liability in nuisance as being based upon ownership is the result, apparently, of a confusion with the action of cattle-trespass, and runs counter both to principle and to the medieval authorities on the escape of water, smoke and filth. ... The prerequisite of any satisfactory treatment of the subject is the final abandonment of the pernicious doctrine in *Boulston's* case. ... Once *Boulston's* case disappears, the way will be clear for a rational restatement of the whole subject, on lines that will harmonize with the principles prevailing in the rest of the law of nuisance.[53]

The judges in *Boulston's* case were, of course, aware that their view of the matter depended on distinguishing this case from one involving nuisance:

This cause is not like to the cases put, on the other side, of erecting a lime-kiln, dye-house, or the like; for there the annoyance is by the act of the parties who make them; but it is not so here, for the conies of themselves went into the plaintiff's land, and he might take them when they came upon his land, and make profit of them.[54]

Professor Williams comments:

Once more the atavistic idea is emerging that the animals are guilty and not the landowner. It is not, of course, a satisfactory principle to introduce into a modern law of nuisance. If A erects a house or plants a tree so that the rain runs or drips from it on to B's land, this is A's act for which he is liable; but if A introduces rabbits into his land so that they escape from it into B's, this is the act of the rabbits for which A is not liable—such is the specious distinction resulting from *Boulston's* case.[55]

It has to be admitted that the decision in *Boulston's* case seems a little odd. A man may be liable for damage caused by smoke or unpleasant smells, without it being necessary to determine whether he owns the smoke or the smell. And the rule in *Botdston's* case has not always been followed in cases dealing with other animals. For example, in *Bland v. Yates*,[56] it was decided that an injunction could be granted to prevent someone from keeping an *unusual and excessive* collection of manure in which flies bred and which infested a neighbour's house. The question of who owned the flies was not raised. An economist would not wish to object because legal reasoning sometimes appears a little odd. But there is a sound economic reason for supporting Professor Williams' view that the problem of liability for animals (and particularly rabbits) should be brought within the ordinary law of nuisance. The reason is not that the man who harbours rabbits is solely responsible for the damage;

the man whose crops are eaten is equally responsible. And given that the costs of market transactions make a rearrangement of rights impossible, unless we know the particular circumstances, we cannot say whether it is desirable or not to make the man who harbours rabbits responsible for the damage committed by the rabbits on neighbouring properties. The objection to the rule in *Boulston's* case is that, under it, the harbourer of rabbits can *never* be liable. It fixes the rule of liability at one pole: and this is as undesirable, from an economic point of view, as fixing the rule at the other pole and making the harbourer of rabbits always liable. But, as we saw in Section VII, the law of nuisance, as it is in fact handled by the courts, is flexible and allows for a comparison of the utility of an act with the harm it produces. As Professor Williams says: "The whole law of nuisance is an attempt to reconcile and compromise between conflicting interests."[57] To bring the problem of rabbits within the ordinary law of nuisance would not mean *inevitably* making the harbourer of rabbits liable for damage committed by the rabbits. This is not to say that the sole task of the courts in such cases is to make a comparison between the harm and the utility of an act. Nor is it to be expected that the courts will always decide correctly after making such a comparison. But unless the courts act very foolishly, the ordinary law of nuisance would seem likely to give economically more satisfactory results than adopting a rigid rule. Pigou's case of the overrunning rabbits affords an excellent example of how problems of law and economics are interrelated, even though the correct policy to follow would seem to be different from that envisioned by Pigou.

Pigou allows one exception to his conclusion that there is a divergence between private and social products in the rabbit example. He adds: "Unless the two occupiers stand in the relation of landlord and tenant, so that compensation is given in an adjustment of the rent."[58] This qualification is rather surprising since Pigou's first class of divergence is largely concerned with the difficulties of drawing up satisfactory contracts between landlords and tenants. In fact, all the recent cases on the problem of rabbits cited by Professor Williams involved disputes between landlords and tenants concerning sporting rights.[59] Pigou seems to make a distinction between the case in which no contract is possible (the second class) and that in which the contract is unsatisfactory (the first class). Thus he says that the second class of divergences between private and social net product cannot, like divergences due to tenancy laws, be mitigated by a modification of the contractual relation between any two contracting parties, because the divergence arises out of a service or disservice rendered to persons other than the contracting parties.[60]

But the reason why some activities are not the subject of contracts is exactly the same as the reason why some contracts are commonly unsatisfactory—it would cost too much to put the matter right. Indeed, the two cases are really the same since the contracts are unsatisfactory because they do not cover certain activities. The exact bearing of the discussion of the first class of divergence on Pigou's main argument is difficult to discover. He shows that in some circumstances contractual relations between landlord and tenant may result in a divergence between private and social products.[61] But he also goes on to show that Government-enforced compensation schemes and rent-controls will also produce divergences.[62] Furthermore, he shows that, when the Government is in a similar position to a private landlord, e.g. when granting a franchise to a public utility, exactly the same difficulties arise as when private individuals are involved.[63] The discussion is interesting but I have been unable to discover what general conclusions about economic policy, if any, Pigou expects us to draw from it.

Indeed, Pigou's treatment of the problems considered in this article is extremely elusive and the discussion of his views raises almost insuperable difficulties of interpretation. Consequently it is impossible to be sure that one has understood what Pigou really meant. Nevertheless, it is difficult to resist the conclusion, extraordinary though this may be in an economist of Pigou's stature, that the main source of this obscurity is that Pigou had not thought his position through.

IX. The Pigovian Tradition

It is strange that a doctrine as faulty as that developed by Pigou should have been so influential, although part of its success has probably been due to the lack of clarity in the exposition. Not being clear, it was never clearly wrong. Curiously enough, this obscurity in the source has not prevented the emergence of a fairly well-defined oral tradition. What economists think they learn from Pigou, and what they tell their students, which I term the Pigovian tradition, is reasonably clear. I propose to show the inadequacy of this Pigovian tradition by demonstrating that both the analysis and the policy conclusions which it supports are incorrect.

I do not propose to justify my view as to the prevailing opinion by copious references to the literature. I do this partly because the treatment in the literature is usually so fragmentary, often involving little more than a reference to Pigou plus some explanatory comment, that detailed examination would be inappropriate. But the main reason for this lack of reference is that the doctrine, although based on Pigou, must have been largely the product of an oral tradition. Certainly economists with whom I have discussed these problems have shown a unanimity of opinion which is quite remarkable considering the meagre treatment accorded this subject in the literature. No doubt there are some economists who do not share the usual view but they must represent a small minority of the profession.

The approach to the problems under discussion is through an examination of the value of physical production. The private product is the value of the additional product resulting from a particular activity of a business. The social product equals the private product minus the fall in the value of production elsewhere for which no compensation is paid by the business. Thus, if 10 units of a factor (and no other factors) are used by a business to make a certain product with a value of $105; and the owner of this factor is not compensated for their use, which he is unable to prevent; and these 10 units of the factor would yield products in their best alternative use worth $100; then, the social product is $105 minus $100 or $5. If the business now pays for one unit of the factor and its price equals the value of its marginal product, then the social product rises to $15. If two units are paid for, the social product rises to $25 and so on until it reaches $105 when all units of the factor are paid for. It is not difficult to see why economists have so readily accepted this rather odd procedure. The analysis focusses on the individual business decision and since the use of certain resources is not allowed for in costs, receipts are reduced by the same amount. But, of course, this means that the value of the social product has no social significance whatsoever. It seems to me preferable to use the opportunity cost concept and to approach these problems by comparing the value of the product yielded by factors in alternative uses or by alternative arrangements. The main advantage of a pricing system is that it leads to the employment of factors in places where the value of the product yielded is greatest and does so at less cost than alternative systems (I leave aside that a pricing system also eases the problem of the redistribution of income). But if through some God-given natural harmony factors flowed to the places where the value of the product yielded was greatest without any use of the pricing system and consequently there was no compensation, I would find it a source of surprise rather than a cause for dismay.

The definition of the social product is queer but this does not mean that the conclusions for policy drawn from the analysis are necessarily wrong. However, there are bound to be dangers in an approach which diverts attention from the basic issues and there can be little doubt that it has been responsible for some of the errors in current doctrine. The belief that it is desirable that the business which causes harmful effects should be forced to compensate those who suffer damage (which was exhaustively discussed in section VIII in connection with Pigou's railway sparks example) is undoubtedly the result of not comparing the total product obtainable with alternative social arrangements.

The same fault is to be found in proposals for solving the problem of harmful effects by the use of taxes or bounties. Pigou lays considerable stress on this solution although he is, as usual, lacking in detail and qualified in his support.[64] Modern economists tend to think exclusively in terms of taxes and in a very precise way. The tax should be equal to the damage done and should therefore vary with the amount of the harmful effect. As it is not proposed that the proceeds of the tax should be paid to those suffering the damage, this solution is not the same as that which would force a business to pay compensation to those damaged by its actions, although economists generally do not seem to have noticed this and tend to treat the two solutions as being identical.

Assume that a factory which emits smoke is set up in a district previously free from smoke pollution, causing damage valued at $100 per annum. Assume that the taxation solution is adopted and that the factory owner is taxed $100 per annum as long as the factory emits the smoke. Assume further that a smoke-preventing device costing $90 per annum to run is available. In these circumstances, the smoke-preventing device would be installed. Damage of $100 would have been avoided at an expenditure of $90 and the factory-owner would be better off by $10 per annum. Yet the position achieved may not be optimal. Suppose that those who suffer the damage could avoid it by moving to other locations or by taking various precautions which would cost them, or be equivalent to a loss in income of, $40 per annum. Then there would be a gain in the value of production of $50 if the factory continued to emit its smoke and those now in the district moved elsewhere or made other adjustments to avoid the damage. If the factory owner is to be made to pay a tax equal to the damage caused, it would clearly be desirable to institute a double tax system and to make residents of the district pay an amount equal to the additional cost incurred by the factory owner (or the consumers of his products) in order to avoid the damage. In these conditions, people would not stay in the district or would take other measures to prevent the damage from occurring, when the costs of doing so were less than the costs that would be incurred by the producer to reduce the damage (the producer's object, of course, being not so much to reduce the damage as to reduce the tax payments). A tax system which was confined to a tax on the producer for damage caused would tend to lead to unduly high costs being incurred for the prevention of damage. Of course this could be avoided if it were possible to base the tax, not on the damage caused, but on the fall in the value of production (in its widest sense) resulting from the emission of smoke. But to do so would require a detailed knowledge of individual preferences and I am unable to imagine how the data needed for such a taxation system could be assembled. Indeed, the proposal to solve the smoke-pollution and similar problems by the use of taxes bristles with difficulties: The problem of calculation, the difference between average and marginal damage, the interrelations between the damage suffered on different properties, etc. But it is unnecessary to examine these problems here. It is enough for my purpose to show that, even if the tax is exactly adjusted to equal the damage that would be done to neighboring properties as a result of the emission of each additional puff of smoke, the tax would not necessarily bring about optimal conditions. An increase in the number of people living or of business operating in the vicinity of the smoke-emitting factory will increase the amount of harm produced by a given emission of smoke. The tax that would be imposed would therefore increase with an increase in the number of those in the vicinity. This will tend to lead to a decrease in the value of production of the factors employed by the factory, either because a reduction in production due to the tax will result in factors being used elsewhere in ways which are less valuable, or because factors will be diverted to produce means for reducing the amount of smoke emitted. But people deciding to establish themselves in the vicinity of the factory will not take into account this fall in the value of production which results from their presence. This failure to take into account costs imposed on others is comparable to the action of a factory-owner in not taking into account the harm resulting from his emission of smoke. Without the tax, there may be too much smoke and too few people in the vicinity of the factory; but with the tax there may be too little smoke and too many people in the vicinity of the factory. There is no reason to suppose that one of these results is necessarily preferable.

I need not devote much space to discussing the similar error involved in the suggestion that smoke producing factories should, by means of zoning regulations, be removed from the districts in which the smoke causes harmful effects. When the change in the location of the factory results in a reduction in production, this obviously needs to be taken into account and weighed against the harm which would result from the factory remaining in that location. The aim of such regulation should not be to eliminate smoke pollution but rather to secure the optimum amount of smoke pollution, this being the amount which will maximise the value of production.

X. A Change of Approach

It is my belief that the failure of economists to reach correct conclusions about the treatment of harmful effects cannot be ascribed simply to a few slips in analysis. It stems from basic defects in the current approach to problems of welfare economics. What is needed is a change of approach.

Analysis in terms of divergencies between private and social products concentrates attention on particular deficiencies in the system and tends to nourish the belief that any measure which will remove the deficiency is necessarily desirable. It diverts attention from those other changes in the system which are inevitably associated with the corrective measure, changes which may well produce more harm than the original deficiency. In the preceding sections of this article, we have seen many examples of this. But it is not necessary to approach the problem in this way. Economists who study problems of the firm habitually use an opportunity cost approach and compare the receipts obtained from a given combination of factors with alternative business arrangements. It would seem desirable to use a similar approach when dealing with questions of economic policy and to compare the total product yielded by alternative social arrangements. In this article, the analysis has been confined, as is usual in this part of economics, to comparisons of the value of production, as measured by the market. But it is, of course, desirable that the choice between different social arrangements for the solution of economic problems should be carried out in broader terms than this and that the total effect of these arrangements in all spheres of life should be taken into account. As Frank H. Knight has so often emphasized, problems of welfare economics must ultimately dissolve into a study of aesthetics and morals.

A second feature of the usual treatment of the problems discussed in this article is that the analysis proceeds in terms of a comparison between a state of laissez faire and some kind of ideal world. This approach inevitably leads to a looseness of thought since the nature of the alternatives being compared is never clear. In a state of laissez faire, is there a monetary, a legal or a political system and if so, what are they? In an ideal world, would there be a monetary, a legal or a political system and if so, what would they be? The answers to all these questions are shrouded in mystery and every man is free to draw whatever conclusions he likes. Actually very little analysis is required to show that an ideal world is better than a state of laissez faire, unless the definitions of a state of laissez faire and an ideal world happen to be the same. But the whole discussion is largely irrelevant for questions of economic policy since whatever we may have in mind as our ideal world, it is clear that we have not yet discovered how to get to it from where we are. A better approach would seem to be to start our analysis with a situation approximating that which actually exists, to examine the effects of a proposed policy change and to attempt to decide whether the new situation would be, in total, better or worse than the original one. In this way, conclusions for policy would have some relevance to the actual situation.

A final reason for the failure to develop a theory adequate to handle the problem of harmful effects stems from a faulty concept of a factor of production. This is usually thought of as a physical entity which the businessman acquires and uses (an acre of land, a ton of fertiliser) instead of as a right to perform certain (physical) actions. We may speak of a person owning land and using it as a factor of production but what the land-owner in fact possesses is the right to carry out a circumscribed list of actions. The rights of a land-owner are not unlimited. It is not even always possible for him to remove the land to another place, for instance, by quarrying it. And although it may be possible for him to exclude some people from using "his" land, this may not be true of others. For example, some people may have the right to cross the land. Furthermore, it may or may not be possible to erect certain types of buildings or to grow certain crops or to use particular drainage systems on the land. This does not come about simply because of Government regulation. It would be equally true under the common law. In fact it would be true under any system of law. A system in which the rights of individuals were unlimited would be one in which there were no rights to acquire.

If factors of production are thought of as rights, it becomes easier to understand that the right to do something which has a harmful effect (such as the creation of smoke, noise, smells, etc.) is also a factor of production. Just as we may use a piece of land in such a way as to prevent someone else from crossing it, or parking his car, or building his house upon it, so we may use it in such a way as to deny him a view or quiet or unpolluted air. The cost of exercising a right (of using a factor of production) is always the loss which is suffered elsewhere in consequence of the exercise of that right—the inability to cross land, to park a car, to build a house, to enjoy a view, to have peace and quiet or to breathe clean air.

It would clearly be desirable if the only actions performed were those in which what was gained was worth more than what was lost. But in choosing between social arrangements within the context of which individual decisions are made, we have to bear in mind that a change in the existing system which will lead to an improvement in some decisions may well lead to a worsening of others. Furthermore we have to take into account the costs involved in operating the various social arrangements (whether it be the working of a market or of a government department), as well as the costs involved in moving to a new system. In devising and choosing between social arrangements we should have regard for the total effect. This, above all, is the change in approach which I am advocating.

Notes

[1] This article, although concerned with a technical problem of economic analysis, arose out of the study of the Political Economy of Broadcasting which I am now conducting. The argument of the present article was implicit in a previous article dealing with the problem of allocating radio and television frequencies (The Federal Communications Commission, 2 *Journal of Law and Economics* [1959]) but comments which I have received seemed to suggest that it would be desirable to deal with the question in a more explicit way and without reference to the original problem for the solution of which the analysis was developed.

[2] Coase, The Federal Communications Commission, 2 *Journal of Law and Economics*. 26-27 (1959).

[3] G. J. Stigler, *The Theory of Price* 105 (1952).

[4] The argument in the text has proceeded on the assumption that the alternative to cultivation of the crop is abandonment of cultivation altogether. But this need not be so. There may be crops which are less liable to damage by cattle but which would not be as profitable as the crop grown in the absence of damage. Thus, if the cultivation of a new crop would yield a return to the farmer of $1 instead of $2, and the size of the herd which would cause $3 damage with the old crop would cause $1 damage with the new crop, it would be profitable to the cattle-raiser to pay any sum less than $2 to induce the farmer to change his crop (since this would reduce damage liability from $3 to $1) and it would be profitable for the farmer to do so if the amount received was more than $1 (the reduction in his return caused by switching crops). In fact, there would be room for a mutually satisfactory bargain in all cases in which a change of crop would reduce the amount of damage by more than it reduces the value of the crop (excluding damage)—in all cases, that is, in which a change in the crop cultivated would lead to an increase in the value of production.

[5] See *Gale on Easements,* 237-239 (13th ed. M. Bowles 1959).

[6] See *Fontainebleu Hotel Corp. v. Forty-Five Twenty-Five, Inc.*, 114 So. 2d 357 (1959).

[7] 11 Ch. D. 852 (1879).

[8] Auscultation is the act of listening by ear or stethoscope in order to judge by sound the condition of the body.

[9] Note that what is taken into account is the change in income after allowing for alterations in methods of production, location, character of product, etc.

[10] L. R. 5 Eq. 166 (1867-1868).

[11] 4 C.P.D. 172 (1878-1879).

[12] 25 Q.B.D. 481 (1890).

[13] it may be asked why a lost grant could not also be presumed in the case of the confectioner who had operated one mortar for more than 60 years. The answer is that until the doctor built the consulting room at the end of his garden there was no nuisance. So the nuisance had not continued for many years. It is true that the confectioner in his affidavit referred to "an invalid lady who occupied the house upon one occasion, about thirty years before" who "requested him if possible to discontinue the use of the mortars before eight o'clock in the morning" and that there was some evidence that the garden wall had been subjected to vibration. But the court had little difficulty in disposing of this line of argument: "... this vibration, even if it existed at all, was so slight, and the complaint, if it can be called a complaint, of the invalid lady ... was of so trifling a character, that...the Defendant's acts would not have given rise to any proceeding either at law or in equity" (11 Ch.D. 863). That is, the confectioner had not committed a nuisance until the doctor built his consulting room.

[14] See Coase, The Nature of the Firm, 4 *Economica*, New Series, 386 (1937). Reprinted in *Readings in Price Theory*, 331 (1952).

[15] For reasons explained in my earlier article, see *Readings in Price Theory*, n. 14 at 337.

[16] See W. L. Prosser, *The Law of Torts,* 398-399, 412 (2d ed. 1955). The quotation about the ancient case concerning candle-making is taken from Sir James Fitzjames Stephen, *A General View of the Criminal*

Law of England, 106 (1890). Sir James Stephen gives no reference. He perhaps had in mind *Rex. v. Ronkett*, included in Seavey, Keeton and Thurston, *Cases on Torts*, 604 (1950). A similar view to that expressed by Prosser is to be found in F. V. Harper and F. James, *The Law of Torts*, 67-74 (1956); Restatement, Torts, 826, 827 and 828.

[17] See *Winfield on Torts*, 541-548 (6th ed. T. E. Lewis 1954); *Salmond on the Law of Torts*, 181-190 (12th ed. R.F.V. Heuston 1957); H. Street, *The Law of Torts*, 221-229 (1959).

[18] Attorney *General v. Doughty*, 2 Ves. Sen. 453, 28 Eng. Rep. 290 (Ch. 1752). Compare in this connection the statement of an American judge, quoted in Prosser, op. cit. supra n.16 at 413 n.54: "Without smoke, Pittsburgh would have remained a very pretty village," Musmanno, J., in *Versailles Borough v. McKeesport Coal & Coke Co.*, 1935, 83 Pitts. Leg. J. 379, 385.

[19] 10 C.B. (N.S.) 268, 142 Eng. Rep. 445 (1861); 13 C.B. (N.S.) 841, 143 Eng. Rep. 332 (1863).

[20] See *Gale on Easements*, 238, n. 6 (13th ed. M. Bowles 1959).

[21] 11 Ch.D. 865 (1879).

[22] *Salmond on the Law of Torts*, 182 (12th ed. R.F.V. Heuston 1957).

[23] C. M. Haar, *Land-Use Planning, A Casebook on the Use, Misuse, and Reuse of Urban Land*, 95 (1959).

[24] See, for example, *Rushmer v. Polsue and Alfieri, Ltd.* [1906] 1 Ch. 234, which deals with the case of a house in a quiet situation in a noisy district.

[25] [1913] 1 Ch. 269.

[26] [1938] 1 Ch. 1.

[27] See *Halsbury, Law of England*, 690-691 (3d ed. 1960), Article on Public Authorities and Public Officers.

[28] See Prosser, op. cit. supra n. 16 at 421; Harper and James, op. cit. supra n. 16 at 86-87.

[29] Supreme Court of Georgia. 193 Ga. 862, 20 S.E. 2d 245 (1942).

[30] 178 Ga. 514, 173 S.E. 817 (1934).

[31] 116 Ga. 64, 42 S.E. 315 (1902).

[32] 270 Mass. 511, 523, 170 N.E. 385, 390 (1930).

[33] See Sir Alfred Denning, *Freedom Under the Law*, 71 (1949).

[34] M. B. Cairns, *The Law of Tort in Local Government*, 28-32 (1954).

[35] A. C. Pigou, *Economics of Welfare*, 183 (4th ed. 1932). My references will all be to the fourth edition but the argument and examples examined in this article remained substantially unchanged from the first edition in 1920 to the fourth in 1932. A large part (but not all) of this analysis had appeared previously in *Wealth and Welfare* (1912).

[36] Id. at xii.

[37] Id. at 127-130.

[38] In *Wealth and Welfare*, Pigou attributes the "optimism" to Adam Smith himself and not to his followers. He there refers to the "highly optimistic theory of Adam Smith that the national dividend, in given circumstances of demand and supply, tends 'naturally' to a maximum."

[39] Pigou, op. cit. supra n. 35 at 129-130.

[40] Id. at 134.

[41] See 31 *Halsbury, Laws of England*, 474-475 (3d ed. 1960), Article on railways and canals, from which

this summary of the legal position, and all quotations, are taken.

[42] See 152 H.C. Deb. 2622-2663 (1922); 161 H.C. Deb. 2935-2955 (1923).

[43] *Vaughan v. Taff Vale Railway Co.*, 3 H. and N. 743 (Ex. 1858) and 5 H. and N. 679 (Ex. 1860).

[44] Sir Dennis Robertson, *I Lectures on Economic Principles,* 162 (1957).

[45] E. J. Mishan, The Meaning of Efficiency in Economics, *The Bankers' Magazine,* 482 (June 1960).

[46] Pigou, op. cit. supra n. 35 at 184.

[47] Id. at 185-186.

[48] Id. at 186 n.1. For similar unqualified statements see Pigou's lecture "Some Aspects of the Housing Problem" in B. S. Rowntree and A. C. Pigou, Lectures on housing, in 18 Manchester Univ. Lectures (1914).

[49] See G. L. Williams, Liability for animals: An Account of the development and present Law of Tortious Liability for Animals, Distress Damage Feasant and the Duty to Fence, in *Great Britain, Northern Ireland and the Common Law Dominions* (1939). Part Four, The action of nuisance, in relation to liability for animals, 236-262, is especially relevant to our discussion. The problem of liability for rabbits is discussed in this part, 238-247. I do not know how far the common law in the United State regarding liability for animals has diverged from that in Britain. In some Western States of the United States, the English common law regarding the duty to fence has not been followed, in part because "the considerable amount of open, uncleared land made it a matter of public policy to allow cattle to run at large" (Williams, op. cit. supra 227). This affords a good example of how a different set of circumstances may make it economically desirable to change the legal rule regarding the delimitation of rights.

[50] 5 Coke (Vol. 3) 104 b. 77 Eng. Rep., 216, 217.

[51] See *Stearn v. Prentice Bros. Ltd.,* (1919) 1 K.B., 395, 397.

[52] I have not looked into recent cases. The legal position has also been modified by statutory enactments.

[53] Williams, op. cit. supra n. 49 at 242, 258.

[54] *Boulston v. Hardy, Corp. Eliz.*, 547, 548, 77 Eng. Rep. 216.

[55] Williams, op. cit. supra n. 49 at 243.

[56] 58 Sol.J. 612 (1913-1914).

[57] Williams, op. cit. supra n. 49 at 259.

[58] Pigou, op. cit. supra n. 35 at 185.

[59] Williams, op. cit. supra n. 49 at 244-247.

[60] Pigou, op. cit. supra n. 35 at 192.

[61] Id. 174-175.

[62] Id. 177-183.

[63] Id. 175-177.

[64] Id. 192-194, 381 *Public Finance,* 94-100 (3d ed. 1947).

Notes on the Problem of Social Cost*

I. The Coase Theorem

I did not originate the phrase, the "Coase Theorem," nor its precise formulation, both of which we owe to Stigler. However, it is true that his statement of the theorem is based on work of mine in which the same thought is found, although expressed rather differently. I first advanced the proposition which has been transformed into the Coase Theorem in an article on "The Federal Communications Commission." I there said: "Whether a newly discovered cave belongs to the man who discovered it, the man on whose land the entrance to the cave is located, or the man who owns the surface under which the cave is situated is no doubt dependent on the law of property. But the law merely determines the person with whom it is necessary to make a contract to obtain the use of a cave. Whether the cave is used for storing bank records, as a natural gas reservoir, or for growing mushrooms depends, not on the law of property, but on whether the bank, the natural gas corporation, or the mushroom concern will pay the most in order to be able to use the cave."[1] I then indicated that this proposition, which seems difficult to dispute when it relates to the right to use a cave, could also be applied to the right to emit electrical radiations (or to generate smoke pollution), and I illustrated my argument by considering the case of *Sturges v.*

---

[1] *The Firm, the Market, and the Law*, 1988, 157-185, the University of Chicago Press.

Bridgman, which involved a doctor disturbed by noise and vibration resulting from the operation of a confectioner's machinery. Using a line of argument which must now be quite familiar, I showed that, whether or not the confectioner had the right to make the noise or vibration, that right would in fact be acquired by the party to whom it was most valuable (just as would be the case with the newly discovered cave). I summed up by saying that while "The delimitation of rights is an essential prelude to market transactions ... the ultimate result (which maximizes the value of production) is independent of the legal decision."[2] This is the essence of the Coase Theorem. I repeated the argument at greater length in "The Problem of Social Cost," making clear that this result was dependent on the assumption of zero transaction costs.

Stigler states the Coase Theorem in the following words: "...Under perfect competition private and social costs will be equal."[3] Since, with zero transaction costs, as Stigler also points out, monopolies would be induced to "act like competitors,"[4] it is perhaps enough to say that, with zero transaction costs, private and social costs will be equal. It will be observed that Stigler's statement of the Coase Theorem differs from the way I expressed the same thought in my article. There I spoke of the value of production being maximized. There is, however, no inconsistency. Social cost represents the greatest value that factors of production would yield in an alternative use. Producers, however, who are normally only interested in maximizing their own incomes, are not concerned with social cost and will only undertake an activity if the value of the product of the factors employed is greater than their private cost (the amount these factors would *earn* in their best alternative employment). But if private cost is equal to social cost, it follows that producers will only engage in an activity if the value of the product of the factors employed is greater than the value which they would yield in their best alternative use. That is to say, with zero transaction costs, the value of production would be maximized.

The discussion of the Coase Theorem in the economics literature has been very extensive and I cannot hope to deal with all the points that have been raised. Some of the criticisms, however, strike at the heart of my argument and have been so persistently made, often by extremely able economists, that it is meet that I should deal with them, particularly since these criticisms are, in my view, for the most part, either invalid, unimportant or irrelevant. Even those sympathetic to my point of view have often misunderstood my argument, a result which I ascribe to the extraordinary hold which Pigou's approach has had on the minds of modern economists. I can only hope that these notes will help to weaken that hold. Whether I am right or not, they will at least serve to make clear the character of my argument.

II. Will Wealth Be Maximized?

A fundamental point is whether it is reasonable to assume, as I did, that, when there are zero transaction costs, negotiations will lead to an agreement which maximizes wealth. It has been argued that this is an erroneous assumption, an objection which has added weight because it has been advanced by, among others, Samuelson. He makes but two references to "The Problem of Social Cost," both in footnotes, but his point is essentially the same on both occasions. In the first he says: "Unconstrained self-interest will in such cases [negotiations over smoke nuisances and the like] lead to the insoluble bilateral monopoly problem with all its indeterminacies and nonoptimalities."[5] And in the second he says: "... A problem of pricing two or more inputs that can be used in common is not solved by reducing it to a determinate maximized total whose allocation among the parts is an indeterminate problem in multilateral monopoly."[6]

Samuelson's comments embody a view which he has long held and which was originally used to criticize the analysis of a more formidable adversary. Edgeworth had argued in *Mathematical Psychics* (1881) that two individuals engaged in exchanging goods would end on the "contract curve" because, if they did not, there would remain positions to which they could move by exchange which would make both of them better off. Edgeworth implicitly assumed that there was costless "contracting" and "recontracting"; and I have often thought that a subconscious memory of the argument in *Mathematical Psychics*, which I studied more than fifty years ago, may have played a part in leading me to formulate the proposition which has come to be termed the "Coase Theorem." Samuelson says this of Edgeworth's argument in his *Foundations of Economic Analysis:* "... From any point off the contract curve there exists a movement toward it which would be beneficial to both individuals. This is not the same thing as to say, with Edgeworth, that exchange will in fact necessarily cease somewhere on the contract curve; for in many types of bilateral monopoly a final equilibrium may be reached off the contract curve."[7] Later Samuelson adds this: "...Our experience with man as a social animal suggests that one [cannot] safely predict, as a factual matter, that educated and intelligent men of good will, in point of fact tend to move to the generalized contract locus. As an empirical statement of fact we cannot agree with the assertion of Edgeworth that bilateral monopolists must end up somewhere on the contract curve. They may end up elsewhere, because one or both is unwilling to discuss the possibility of making a mutually favorable movement for fear that the discussion may imperil the existing tolerable *status quo*."[8] Samuelson's explanation in the *Foundations* of why two individuals may fail to end up on the contract curve is that they may be unwilling to initiate negotiations leading to an exchange which could make both of them better off, because to do so may have as its result an agreement which leaves one or both of them worse off than they were before. This contention is not easy to understand. If there already existed a contract between the parties, so that mutual agreement was required for its modification, there would seem to be no obstacle hindering the opening of negotiations. And if there were no contract, there is no *status quo* to imperil. For exchange to take place, there has to be an agreement about the terms of the exchange, and given that this is so, I would not expect the parties to choose terms which make both of them worse off than they need be. Perhaps what Samuelson had in mind was that there may be no contract and no exchange because the parties cannot agree on the terms, given that this affects their respective gains from the exchange. This seems to have been Samuelson's position in 1967. He then said that, "The rational self-interest of each of two free wills does not necessitate that there will emerge, even in the most idealized game- theoretic situation, a Pareto-optimal solution that maximizes the sum of two opponent's profits, *in advance of and without regard to how that maximized profit is to be divided up among them.* Except by fiat of the economic analyst or by his tautologically redefining what constitutes 'nonrational' behavior we cannot rule out a non-Pareto-optimal outcome." (italics in original)[9]

It is certainly true that we cannot rule out such an outcome if the parties are unable to agree on the terms of exchange, and it is therefore impossible to argue that two individuals negotiating an exchange *must* end up on the contract curve, even in a world of zero transaction costs in which the parties have, in effect, an eternity in which to bargain. However, there is good reason to suppose that the proportion of cases in which no agreement is reached will be small.

As Samuelson himself points out, situations in which the price at which a supplier is willing to sell is less than the price at which a demander is willing to buy, and in which the parties therefore have to reach an agreement on the price, are "ubiquitous in real life."[10] Samuelson gives an example: "If my secretary has been trained to my ways and I have been trained to hers, there is a range of indeterminacy to the imputation of our joint product. Without her I can find some kind of substitute but not necessarily, per dollar of cost, a close substitute. On the other hand, were I to turn tomorrow to a career in plumbing, her considerable investment in mastering the vocabulary of my peculiar kind of economics might become totally valueless. If I were poised on the margin of indifference it might pay her to make me side payments to tempt me to eschew a career with the monkey wrench."[11]

This is a fanciful example of a very common situation, whether we are considering purchases of raw materials, machinery, land, buildings, or labour services. Of course, the competition of substitutes normally very much narrows the range within which the agreed price must fall, but it must be very rare indeed for both the buyer and the seller to be indifferent as to whether a transaction goes through. And yet we observe that raw materials, machinery, land, and buildings are bought and sold and even professors manage to have secretaries. We do not usually seem to let the problem of the division of the gain stand in the way of making an agreement. Nor is this surprising. Those who find it impossible to conclude agreements will find that they neither buy nor sell and consequently will usually have no income. Traits which lead to such an outcome have little survival value, and we may assume (certainly I do) that normally human beings do not possess them and are willing to "split the difference." Samuelson asserts as "an empirical statement of fact" that people, in the situation analyzed by Edgeworth, will not necessarily end up somewhere on the contract curve. This is no doubt correct, but a fact of even more significance is that normally we would expect them to end up there. Samuelson, discussing the hypothetical example in which he is considering taking up plumbing, points out that "it might pay" his secretary "to make me side payments to tempt me to eschew a career with the monkey wrench." It is certainly true that his secretary might not agree to make these side payments, or, what comes to the same thing, to accept a reduction in salary even though this would make her (and Samuelson) better off; or Samuelson might worsen his situation (and hers) by taking up plumbing because in his view she was not willing to reduce her salary enough; but I would regard such outcomes as being, in these circumstances, most unlikely, particularly in a regime of zero transaction costs.

Samuelson also lays stress on the indeterminacy of the final result. While this is true for purchases of all kinds and therefore applies to all of economic analysis, the existence of indeterminacy, as Edgeworth showed, does not of itself imply that the result is non-optimal. Furthermore, that the respective gains of the two parties are indeterminate is irrelevant to the problem I was discussing in "The Problem of Social Cost," the assignment to individuals and firms of rights to perform certain actions and its effect on what is produced and sold. In any case, there is no reason to suppose that the degree of indeterminacy over the sharing of the gains would be greater in negotiations over the rights to emit smoke than in transactions which economists are more accustomed to handle, such as the purchase of a house.

III. The Coase Theorem and Rents

Most objections to the Coase Theorem seem to underestimate what costless transacting could accomplish. But some criticisms raise questions of a more general character. For example, it is said that the Coase Theorem fails to take into account the crucial role played by the existence or non-existence of rents. The term "rent" in this context is used to denote the difference between what a factor of production earns in the activity under discussion and what it could otherwise earn. I had analyzed the problem by considering what happened to the net return to the land. But there is no difficulty in rephrasing the argument in terms of rent. It does little more than restate in other words my original argument, but some economists may find this approach more congenial.

The relation of the existence of rents to my analysis was first discussed by Wellisz.[12] This way of looking at things has since been used as the basis for arguing that my conclusion is wrong by Regan[13] and Auten, among others. The point is stated succinctly by Auten: "In Coase's examples the results will ... vary with liability depending on the Ricardian rents of polluters and receptors. If both polluter and receptor operate on marginal land the polluter must cease operations in the long run if liable, and the receptor will be driven out if liable."[14] The contention is plausible. The land is marginal and earns no return, while the other factors employed are in perfectly elastic supply and do not earn more in this use than in some alternative use. In these circumstances it would seem obvious that, if those responsible for the pollution have to pay compensation for the damage caused, the factors of production (other than land) used in the activity which pollutes will leave this employment, since any payment for the damage caused would reduce their earnings below what they would be elsewhere. But suppose that those polluting are not liable. Those who suffer the damage resulting from the pollution will find that, taking the damage into account, they now earn less than they would in an alternative employment and will therefore be better off by moving elsewhere. All this would seem to suggest, contrary to what I had said, that the legal position does affect the outcome. Auten's argument, though plausible, I believe, is wrong. Since in these conditions no one's income could be increased by possession of the right to pollute, no one would pay anything for it. The price would therefore be zero. How can one say that someone does not have the right to pollute when for a zero price he can acquire it? How can one say that someone must suffer damage when for a zero price he can avoid it? Liability and nonliability are interchangeable at will. Polluters and receptors, to use Auten's terms, are equally likely to stay or leave. What will happen is completely unaffected by the initial legal position.

Rent consists of the difference between what a factor of production earns in a given activity and what it could earn in the best alternative activity. The factors engaged in an activity would be willing, if need be, to pay an amount of money up to slightly less than the sum of their rents to allow their employment in that activity to continue, because, even after taking this payment into account, they would be better off than if they had to move to their best alternative. Similarly, they would be willing to abandon an activity in return for any payment greater than the sum of their rents, since, including this payment, they would be better off by moving to their best alternative than by continuing in this activity. Given that this is so, it becomes easy to show that, with zero transaction costs, the allocation of resources will remain the same whatever the legal position regarding liability for damage. To simplify the discussion, I will call the sum of the rents of the factors engaged in an activity the "rents" and will examine the same example as in my original article, that of cattle which roam and destroy crops. I will call the factors of production which are engaged in raising cattle the "ranchers" and the factors of production which are engaged in cultivating crops the "farmers."

Since the rents represent the increase in the value of production (and therefore of incomes) from undertaking a particular activity rather than the best alternative, it follows that the value of production, as measured on the market, is maximized when rents are maximized. If the farmers cultivated their crops (and there were no ranchers), the increase in the value of production resulting from their operations would be measured by the rents of the factors engaged in farming. If the ranchers raised their cattle, (and there were no farmers) the increase in the value of production resulting from their operations would be measured by the rents of the factors engaged in ranching. If there were both ranchers and farmers but no damage to crops as a result of the roaming of the cattle, the increase in the value of production would be measured by the sum of the rents of the farmers and ranchers. However, suppose that, given ranching, some crops would be destroyed by the roaming of the cattle. In this case, when farming and ranching are carried on simultaneously, the increase in the value of production is measured by the sum of the rents of both the farmers and the ranchers (as defined) minus the value of the crops destroyed by the cattle.

Suppose first that the damage to the crops with simultaneous ranching and farming is valued at less than either the rents of the ranchers or the rents of the farmers. If the ranchers were liable for the damage inflicted by their cattle, they could compensate the farmers and continue their operations and still be better off than if they abandoned ranching by an amount equal to their rents minus the value of the damage. If the ranchers were not liable, the maximum the farmers would pay to induce the ranchers to stop their operations would be the value of the destroyed crops. This is less than the additional sum the ranchers could earn by continuing to operate rather than moving to their best alternative employment. The farmers would therefore be unable to induce the ranchers to stop their operations. As the rents of the farmers are greater than the value of the destroyed crops, the farmers would still enjoy a net gain from continuing to farm. Whatever the legal position, both ranchers and farmers would continue to operate. It is easy to show that this will maximize the value of production. If the farmers' rents are $100 and the ranchers' rents are also $100 and the value of the crops destroyed is $50, the value of production will be greater than it would otherwise be if both farmers and ranchers continue to operate. In these conditions the increase in the value of production would be $150 (the sum of the rents minus the value of the crops destroyed). If either the farmers or the ranchers discontinued operations, the increase in the value of productions would fall to $100.

Now consider what would happen if the damage to the crops were valued at less than the rents of the ranchers but more than the rents of the farmers. Assume first that the ranchers are liable for the damage brought about by their cattle. If the ranchers compensated the farmers for their crop loss (which they could do since their rents are greater than the value of the crop damage), the farmers would earn the same amount as if the damage had not occurred (payment by the ranchers for the crops destroyed would be substituted for sale on the market). But the rents of the farmers are less than the value of the crops destroyed. The farmers would agree not to cultivate for any payment which is greater than their rents. The ranchers would be better off if they induced the farmers not to grow their crops (and thus bring to an end crop destruction) by making a payment which is less than the value of crop damage. In the assumed circumstances a bargain would be struck by which, for a payment by the ranchers greater than the farmers' rents but less than the value of the crop damage, the farmers would not engage in cultivation. Now assume that the ranchers are not liable for crop damage. As the damage that the farmers would suffer would be greater than their rents, the farmers would earn less than in their best alternative activity if they cultivated their crops and they would therefore not engage in cultivation unless they could induce the ranchers to give up their operations. But the maximum amount which the farmers would pay to bring this about would be slightly less than their rents. As the ranchers' rents from continuing their activities (with its attendant crop destruction) are greater than the farmers' rents, the farmers would be unable to make a payment sufficiently great to induce the ranchers to cease their operations. In these circumstances, just as was true when the ranchers were liable for crop damage, crop cultivation would not take place, the farmers would engage in their best alternative occupation, while the ranchers would continue to operate. As before, a change in the legal position is without effect on the allocation of resources. Furthermore, the resulting allocation is the one which maximizes the value of production. Assume that the rents of the ranchers are $100, the value of the crop damage $50, and the rents of the farmers $25. If the ranchers and farmers both continued their operations, the increase in the value of production would be $75 ($100 plus $25 minus $50). If the ranchers discontinued their operations, the increase in the value of production would be $25 (the rents of the farmers), while if the ranchers alone continued to operate, the increase in the value of production would be $100 (the rents of the ranchers).

Let us now reverse the situation which we have just discussed and consider what would happen if the value of the crop damage is greater than the rents of the ranchers but less than the rents of the farmers. Assume first that the ranchers are liable for the damage. Since the amount the ranchers would have to pay to compensate the farmers would be more than their rents, ranching would not take place and the farmers would continue their cultivation. Now assume that the ranchers are not liable. If the ranchers continued to operate, the farmers would be willing, if they had to, to endure the crop damage since this is less than their rents. But there is a preferable alternative open to them. The rents of the ranchers are less than the value of the damage which their cattle inflict on the farmers' crops. The ranchers would be willing to cease operations in return for any payment greater than their rents. The farmers would be willing to make such a payment, providing that it was less than the value of the crop damage. But this is what the conditions are assumed to be. It follows that a bargain would be made by which the ranchers would not undertake their operations. As before, the outcome remains the same whatever the legal position. And once again, the value of production is maximized. Assume that the rents of the ranchers are $25, the value of crop damage $50, and the rents of the farmers $100. If the ranchers and farmers both continued their operations, the increase in the value of production would be $75 ($25 plus $100 minus $50). If the ranchers alone continued their operations, the increase in the value of production would be $25 (the rents of the ranchers) while if the farmers alone continued to operate, the increase would be $100 (the rents of the farmers).

Let us now consider the case in which the value of the damage to the crops is greater than the rents of either the ranchers or the farmers. Assume first that the rents of the ranchers are greater than the rents of the farmers. If the ranchers were liable for the crop damage caused by their cattle and had to compensate the farmers, it is clear that the ranchers would have to abandon their operations. But this is not the only course open to them. The farmers would be happy not to grow their crops for a payment greater than their rents. In these circumstances the ranchers would be willing to pay the farmers an amount greater than the farmers' rents (but less than their own rents) to induce the farmers not to cultivate, which would bring to an end crop destruction, eliminate the need for compensation from the ranchers, and leave the ranchers better off. If the ranchers were not liable for damage, the value of crop damage would exceed the rents of the farmers, who would not therefore engage in crop cultivation but would choose their best alternative, unless they could induce the ranchers to stop their operations. The maximum the farmers could offer to accomplish this and still be better off would be slightly less than their own rents. But as the rents of the ranchers are greater than the rents of the farmers, the ranchers would be unwilling to accept such an offer. The farmers therefore would not cultivate the land. The outcome, once again, would be the same whatever the legal position. Furthermore, the outcome would be such as maximized the value of production. Assume the rents of the ranchers were $40, the value of crops destroyed $50, and the rents of the farmers $30. If both ranchers and farmers continued to operate, the increase in the value of production over what it would otherwise be would be $20 ($40 plus $30 minus $50). If the farmers alone continued to operate, the increase would be $30 (the rents of the farmers) while if the ranchers alone continued to operate, the increase would be $40 (the rents of the ranchers).

Finally, we may consider the case in which the value of the damage to the crops is greater than the rents of either the farmers or the ranchers, but the rents of the farmers are greater than the rents of the ranchers. Assume first that the ranchers are liable for crop damage. In this case the ranchers would be unable to compensate the farmers for crop destruction and continue their operations. They would also be unable to induce the farmers to cease cultivation, since the maximum the ranchers could pay is slightly less than their own rents, while the farmers would not be willing to cease cultivation unless they received slightly more than their own rents (which are greater than the ranchers' rents). Assume now that the ranchers are not liable for the damage. In these circumstances, the farmers could avoid the damage (whose continuation would force them to abandon cultivation) by making a payment which was greater than the ranchers' rents to induce them to move to their best alternative (and therefore stop the crop damage). This the farmers could do and still be better off than if they ceased to cultivate their crops, given that the farmers' rents are greater than the ranchers' rents. Whatever the rule of liability, the result would be that the farmers would continue to cultivate their land while the ranchers would not engage in cattle raising. A calculation similar to that in the immediately preceding example would also demonstrate that this allocation of resources was such as maximized the value of production.

The examination of all these cases has been tedious, but the results are conclusive. The allocation of resources remains the same in all circumstances, whatever the legal position. Furthermore, the result in each case maximizes the value of production as measured on the market, that is, it maximizes the sum of the ranchers' rents and the farmers' rents minus the value of the crops destroyed. Damage to crops will only persist if it is less in value than the rents of both the ranchers and the farmers. If damage is greater than the rents of either the ranchers or the farmers, but not of both, the activity in which rents are less than the damage will not be undertaken. And if damage is greater than the rents of both the ranchers and the farmers, the activity will not take place which yields the lower rent. Whatever the circumstances, the value of total production will be maximized. These results would remain essentially unchanged if, instead of the question being solely whether there would be ranching or not or farming or not, it had also allowed for the possibility that there could be more or less cattle raising and more or less cultivation of crops, but the calculations would have been even more tedious.

IV. The Assignment of Rights and the Distribution of Wealth

In section III of these notes it was demonstrated that, in a regime of zero transaction costs, the allocation of resources remains the same whatever the legal position regarding liability for harmful effects. However, many economists have argued that this conclusion is wrong, since, even in a regime of zero transaction costs, a change in the legal position affects the distribution of wealth. This will lead to alterations in the demands for goods and services, including—and this is the heart of the matter—those produced by the activity generating the harmful effects and those produced by the activities affected by them. Thus, if we return to the example of the previous section, it would appear that the farmers are always better off and the ranchers worse off if the ranchers are made liable for the damage brought about by their cattle than if they are not. If the ranchers are made liable, they pay the farmers a sum of money to compensate them for the damage, or they pay them not to produce (so there is no damage), or they avoid creating damage by not ranching and choosing instead to work in their next best employment, in which case they receive a lower income. When there is no liability for damage, the farmers receive no compensation when there is damage and continue farming with a reduced income, or they themselves have to pay the ranchers not to operate (so that there is no damage), or they move to their next best employment and receive a lower income. These changes in the wealth of the ranchers and farmers will lead, it is said, to changes in their demands and will thus bring about a change in the allocation of resources.

I consider this argument to be wrong, since a change in the liability rule will not lead to any alteration in the distribution of wealth. There are therefore no subsequent effects on demands to be taken into account. Let us see why. In section III of these notes, I spoke of the group of factors engaged in ranching as "ranchers" and the group of factors engaged in farming as "farmers." Let us separate the group of factors called "ranchers" into ranchers and ranching land and the group of factors called "farmers" into farmers and farming land, and let us furthermore make the perhaps not very unrealistic assumption that only the ranching land and the farming land earn "rents" as defined in section III. Assume also that the land is leased by the ranchers and farmers.

Let us confine ourselves to the simple case in which the damage inflicted by the cattle is less than the "rents" of either the ranching land or the farming land. Consider the effect of the rule of liability on the terms of the contracts entered into by those engaged in ranching and farming. If the rancher has to compensate the farmer for the damage inflicted by his cattle, the amount he would pay for leasing the land would be lower by the sum he would have to pay as compensation than it would be if he did not have to make such a payment, while the farmer would pay a price for leasing his land higher by the same sum than he would if he did not receive any compensation for damage. The wealth of the ranchers and farmers would remain the same whatever the legal position regarding liability for the damage inflicted by the cattle. But what of the land-owners? If compensation has to be paid for damage to crops, the price for leasing the ranching land will be less, and that for the farming land will be more than if compensation does not have to be paid. However, if the rule of liability is known, the amount that will have been paid to acquire the land will reflect this, less being paid for the ranching land and more for the farming land when compensation has to be paid than when it does not have to be paid. The wealth of the land-owners would thus remain the same, changes in the amount paid for the land offsetting the changes in the flow of payments brought about by a difference in the legal position regarding liability for damage. There is no change in the distribution of wealth associated with the choice of a different legal rule and therefore no subsequent changes in demand, the effects of which need to be taken into account. While I have only considered the case in which damage was less than the "rents" of both the ranching land and the farming land, a similar argument would lead to the same conclusion in all the cases discussed in section III.

It may be thought that this analysis of the effects of a difference in the legal position, if it is assumed in each case that all parties are fully adjusted to it, is not applicable when there is a change from one rule of law to another. This is not so. The conclusion that there will be no redistribution of wealth when there are zero transaction costs is unaffected, although this result is reached by a somewhat different route. Remember that with zero transaction costs it costs nothing to make a contract more elaborate. Given that this is so, contracts would be drawn up specifying how payments were to vary with changes in the legal position. In the example we have just discussed, it would be provided that if, for example, the rule of law changed from one in which the ranchers were not liable for the damage inflicted by their cattle to one in which they were liable, the amount which the ranchers would pay for the lease of their land would decrease and owners of ranching land would receive a rebate from those from whom they bought the land, while farmers would have to pay more for the lease of their land and owners of farming land would be required to make an additional payment to those from whom they bought the land. The distribution of wealth would remain the same.

Whether a difference in the law will affect the allocation of resources is not so easily settled in the case of previously unrecognized rights. Different criteria for assigning ownership of these rights would seem in this case to lead inevitably to a different distribution of wealth. It might, of course, be argued that since, with zero transaction costs, it costs nothing to make a contract more elaborate, all contingencies will be provided for and therefore no redistribution of wealth could occur. But it would be unreasonable to assume that people could include in contracts a reference to rights of which they were unable to conceive. The question which then has to be considered is whether, through its influence on demand, a change in the criteria for assigning ownership to previously unrecognized rights could bring about a different allocation of resources. I first advanced the proposition now known as the "Coase Theorem" in my article on "The Federal Communications Commission." As was explained earlier, the example used to illustrate my argument concerned the ownership of a newly discovered cave. I concluded: "Whether the cave is used for storing bank records, as a natural gas reservoir, or for growing mushrooms depends, not on the law of property, but on whether the bank, the natural gas corporation, or the mushroom concern will pay the most in order to be able to use the cave."[15] It never entered my head to add the qualification that if the demand for mushrooms of the possible claimants to the cave differed and if their expenditure on mushrooms (or banking services or natural gas) was an important item in their budgets, and if their consumption of these products was a significant part of total consumption, the decision concerning ownership of a newly discovered cave would affect the demand for banking services, natural gas, and mushrooms. As a result the relative prices of banking services, natural gas, and mushrooms would change; such a change might affect the amount which the various businesses concerned would be willing to pay for the use of the cave, and this might possibly affect the way in which the cave was used. It cannot be denied that it is conceivable that a change in the criteria for assigning ownership to previously unrecognized rights may lead to changes in demand which in turn lead to a difference in the allocation of resources, but, apart from such cataclysmic events as the abolition of slavery, these effects will normally be so insignificant that they can safely be neglected. This is also true of those changes in the distribution of wealth which accompany a change in the law when there are positive transaction costs and it is too costly for the contracts to cover all contingencies. Thus, in considering the legal case of *Sturges v. Bridgman,* it may well be, given the form of the contracts into which they had entered, that the legal decision affected the relative wealth of the doctor and confectioner (and perhaps had similar effects on the wealth of those occupying neighbouring premises), but it is inconceivable to me that this could have any noticeable effect on the demand for cakes or medical services.

V. The Influence of Transaction Costs

The world of zero transaction costs has often been described as a Coasian world. Nothing could be further from the truth. It is the world of modern economic theory, one which I was hoping to persuade economists to leave. What I did in "The Problem of Social Cost" was simply to bring to light some of its properties. I argued that in such a world the allocation of resources would be independent of the legal position, a result which Stigler dubbed the "Coase Theorem": "...Under perfect competition private and social costs will be equal."[16] For reasons given earlier, it would seem that even the qualifying phrase "under perfect competition" can be omitted. Economists, following Pigou whose work has dominated thought in this area, have consequently been engaged in an attempt to explain why there were divergences between private and social costs and what should be done about it, using a theory in which private and social costs were necessarily always equal. It is therefore hardly surprising that the conclusions reached were often incorrect. The reason why economists went wrong was that their theoretical system did not take into account a factor which is essential if one wishes to analyze the effect of a change in the law on the allocation of resources. This missing factor is the existence of transaction costs.

With zero transaction costs, producers would make whatever set of contractual arrangements was necessary to maximize the value of production. If there were actions that could be taken which cost less than the reduction in damage that they would bring, and they were the least costly means available to accomplish such a reduction, they would be undertaken. Action might be required by a single producer or by several in combination. As I indicated in "The Problem of Social Cost" in discussing the cattle-crop example, these measures include such actions as, for the farmer, taking all or part of the crop-land out of cultivation or planting another crop less susceptible to damage; for the rancher, reducing the size of the herd or the kind of cattle raised, or employing herdsmen or dogs, or tethering the cattle; or, on the part of either the farmer or the rancher, the erection of fencing. One can even imagine more unusual measures, such as the farmer keeping a pet tiger whose scent would suffice to keep the cattle away from the crops. Both the farmer and the rancher would have an incentive to employ any measure known to them (including joint actions) which would raise the value of production, since each producer would share in the resulting increase in income.

However, once transaction costs are taken into account, many of these measures will not be undertaken because making the contractual arrangements necessary to bring them into existence would cost more than the gain they make possible. To simplify the discussion, assume that *all* contractual arrangements aimed at reducing the amount of damage are too costly. The result would be, in our example, that if the ranchers are liable to pay compensation for the damage caused by their cattle, the farmers would have no reason to modify their arrangements, since compensation for crops damaged or destroyed would always substitute for sale on the market. The ranchers, however, are in a different position. They have an incentive to change their mode of operating whenever this raises their costs by an amount which is less than the resulting reduction in the compensation paid to the farmers. Suppose, however, that the ranchers are not liable. They now have no incentive to change their arrangements. It is the farmers who will take steps to reduce damage when the gain from the additional crops that become available for sale exceeds the cost incurred to bring this result about. It is easy to show that, in these circumstances, the value of production may be greater if the ranchers are not made liable for the damage to the crops caused by their cattle than if they are. Assume that, if the ranchers were liable, they would find it in their interest to take steps which would completely eliminate the damage, and that the farmers would take action with the same effect if the ranchers were not liable. Assume further that the cost of eliminating the damage is $80 for the ranchers and $50 for the farmers. If the ranchers were not liable, it will be the farmers who take steps to eliminate the damage. The cost to them would be $50. Had the ranchers been liable for the crop damage brought about by their cattle, they would have done what was necessary to eliminate the damage. The cost to them would have been $80. It follows that the value of production is greater by $30 ($80−$50) if the ranchers are not liable. The purpose of this illustration is not to suggest that those generating harmful effects should never be made liable to compensate those harmed. By interchanging the costs of eliminating the damage for the ranchers and farmers, we would have an example of a situation in which the value of production would be greater if the ranchers were made liable for the damage brought about by their cattle. What these examples show is that whether the value of production will be greater when the ranchers are liable or when they are not liable depends on the circumstances of the particular case.

It has been suggested that my argument needs modification to take account of the fact that, at least in common law countries, damages must be mitigated. I assumed that the ranchers, if not liable, and the farmers, if the ranchers were liable, had no incentive to incur costs to reduce damage. It has been pointed out that, in common law countries, to collect compensation for damage when the ranchers are liable, the farmers must take reasonable steps to mitigate the damage, while the ranchers, if they are not liable, must do the same thing if they are to avoid a claim against them. This is no doubt important for those engaged in analyzing the working of a common law system, but it does not change the point that I was making.

While the existence of such a doctrine may lead the ranchers and the farmers to undertake some expenditures which otherwise they would not, the courts are not likely to consider that such expenditures should be incurred unless it is abundantly clear that they would reduce damage by a greater amount, and, what is just as important, that the actions required to bring about this reduction in damage are known to them. It is impossible for me to believe that the doctrine of mitigation of damages would lead the ranchers to take all the measures to reduce damage that they would take if they were liable to compensate the farmers, or that it would lead the farmers to take all the measures to reduce damage that they would take if the ranchers were not liable. If this is true, my conclusion is unaffected. If, after the mitigation of damages, the ranchers would have to incur costs of $70 to eliminate the damage (the remaining damage being more than $70) and the farmers could do this for $20, the value of production would clearly be greater by $50 if the ranchers were not liable for damage and it was therefore the farmers who were forced to take action to prevent the damage. Of course, with other figures a situation could be created in which the value of production would be greater if the ranchers were liable.

It has also been suggested by Zerbe that my conclusion is incorrect because the liability rule which I use in my analysis is not optimal.[17] This objection is based on a misunderstanding of the character of my argument, which is that, in the presence of transaction costs, the liability rule cannot be optimal. In a zero transaction cost world in which all parties have an incentive to discover and disclose all those adjustments which would have the effect of increasing the value of production, the information needed to calculate the optimal liability rule can be imagined to be available, although it would also be superfluous since, in these circumstances, the value of production would be maximized whatever the rule of liability. But once we take transaction costs into account, the various parties have no incentive (or a reduced incentive) to disclose the information needed to formulate an optimal liability rule. Indeed, this information may not even be known to them, since those who have no incentive to disclose information have no reason for discovering what it is. Information needed for transactions which cannot be carried out will not be collected.

The same approach which, with zero transaction costs, demonstrates that the allocation of resources remains the same whatever the legal position, also shows that, with positive transaction costs, the law plays a crucial role in determining how resources are used. But it does more than this. With zero transaction costs, the same result is reached because contractual arrangements will be made to modify the rights and duties of the parties so as to make it in their interest to undertake those actions which maximize the value of production. With positive transaction costs, some or all of these contractual arrangements become too costly to carry out. The incentives to take some of the actions which would have maximized the value of production disappear. What incentives will be lacking depends on what the law is, since this determines what contractual arrangements will have to be made to bring about those actions which maximize the value of production. The result brought about by different legal rules is not intuitively obvious and depends on the facts of each particular case. It may be, for example, as was shown earlier in this section, that the value of production will be greater if those generating harmful effects are not liable to compensate those who suffer the harm they cause.

VI. Pigovian Taxes

Up to the time of the publication of "The Problem of Social Cost", the effect of different liability rules on the allocation of resources was very little discussed in the economics literature. Economists, following Pigou, spoke of uncompensated disservices and implied that those responsible for these harmful effects ought to be liable to compensate those they harmed, but the subject of liability rules was not something to which economists gave much attention. Most economists have thought that the problems arising from the producers' actions which had harmful effects on others were best handled by instituting an appropriate system of taxes and subsidies, with the emphasis being placed on the use of taxes. Thus, in the introduction to a recent article it is said: "It is an established result of economic theory that the achievement of efficiency in a competitive economy requires taxes (subsidies) on commodities generating negative (positive) economic effects."[18] Whatever its merits as a means of regulating the generation of harmful effects, the use of taxes had the added attraction that it could be analyzed by existing price theory, that the schemes devised looked impressive on a blackboard or in articles, and that it required no knowledge of the subject.

I argued towards the end of my article on "The Problem of Social Cost" that a taxing system could not be assumed to produce an optimal allocation of resources, even if the authorities wished to do so. My argument, however, was apparently not well expressed, since even as sympathetic a critic as Baumol failed to understand it. Baumol's criticisms were directed at a position that I did not, and do not, hold. What I will therefore do is to set out my argument more clearly, expanding on those points in which compression or poor exposition may have led my critics astray. Many of those who have written on the use of taxation to deal with harmful effects have accepted Baumol's interpretation of my argument, but confining my comments to Baumol's contribution will be enough to make my own position clear.[19]

I started my argument by saying that I was assuming that the tax would equal the value of the damage caused. The example I used to illustrate my argument was that of a factory whose smoke would cause damage of $100 per annum but in which a smoke-prevention device could be installed for $90. Since emitting smoke would involve the owner of the factory in paying taxes of $100, he would install the smoke-prevention device, thereby saving $10 per annum. Nevertheless the situation may not be optimal. Assume that those who would suffer the damage could avoid it by taking steps which would cost $40 per annum. In this case, if there were no tax and the factory emitted the smoke, the value of production would be greater by $50 per annum ($90 minus $40). Later I noted that an increase in the number of people or businesses locating near the factory would increase the amount of damage produced by a given emission of smoke. This would result in higher taxes if the smoke emissions continued, and consequently the factory would be willing to incur greater costs for smoke prevention than it would previously in order to avoid paying the higher taxes. Those deciding to locate near the factory would not take into account these additional costs. This is easily illustrated using the same figures. Suppose initially that no one was located near the factory. There would be smoke but no damage, and therefore no taxes. Now suppose that a developer decides to build a new subdivision in the vicinity of the factory and that in consequence the value of the damage occasioned by the smoke becomes $100 per annum. The developer could count on the factory-owner installing the smoke-prevention device costing $90 per annum, since this would enable him to avoid a tax of $100. Those settling near the factory will not suffer any damage from smoke, which will not now exist. But the situation may not be optimal. The developer might have been able to choose another location equally satisfactory and without smoke for an additional cost of $40 per annum. Once again, the value of production would have been greater by $50 per annum if there had been no tax and the factory had continued to emit its smoke.

I also said that if "The factory-owner is to be made to pay a tax equal to the damage caused, it would clearly be desirable to institute a double tax system and to make residents of the district pay an amount equal to the additional cost incurred by the factory-owner ... in order to avoid the damage."[20] This is easily shown. The additional cost that would be incurred by the factory-owner in our example is $90 per annum. Assume that a tax of $90 is laid on the residents of the subdivision. In this case the developer would prefer to build his subdivision elsewhere, incurring an additional cost of $40 per annum but avoiding the tax of $90 per annum, with the result that the factory would continue to emit smoke and the value of production would be maximized.

It would be wrong to conclude that I was advocating the introduction of a double tax system or indeed any tax system for that matter. I merely pointed out that if there is a tax based on *damage,* it would also be desirable to tax those whose presence imposes costs on the firm responsible for the harmful effects. But as I said in "The Problem of Social Cost," any tax system bristles with difficulties and what is desirable may be impossible.

Baumol, who discussed my views at length in his article, said that his main purpose was "to show that, taken on its own grounds, the conclusions of the Pigovian tradition are, in fact, impeccable."[21] He argues that, in the case of the smoke nuisance, "An appropriately chosen tax, levied only on the factory (without payment of compensation to local residents) is precisely what is needed for optimal resource allocation under pure competition."[22] He argued further that a double tax (such as I suggested) is unnecessary and claimed that my belief that a taxing system could result in too many people locating near the factory comes from confusing a pecuniary externality with a technological externality. An examination of my arithmetic earlier in this section will, however, demonstrate that my conclusions are correct. Why do Baumol and I reach different answers? The reason is that in my article I assumed that the tax which is to be imposed is equal to the *damage caused,* whereas Baumol's tax is not. I would not deny that Baumol's taxing system is conceivable and that if put into practice it would have the results he describes. My objection, which I stated in my article, is that it could not be put into practice. I thought I had made this clear. This is what I said in "The Problem of Social Cost": "A tax system which was confined to a tax on the producer for damage caused would tend to lead to unduly high costs being incurred for the prevention of damage. Of course, this could be avoided if it were possible to base the tax, not on the damage caused, but on the fall in the value of production (in its widest sense) resulting from the emission of smoke. But to do so would require a detailed knowledge of individual preferences, and I am unable to imagine how the data needed for such a taxation system could be assembled."[23]

What I had in mind becomes clear if we consider how the Pigovian tax scheme would be implemented. Note that it is intended to apply, as Baumol points out, to the "large numbers" case. In our example, therefore, many people and/or businesses must be presumed to be affected by the smoke from the factory. Note also that none of the tax receipts is to be given as compensation to those harmed by the smoke. They would thus have an incentive to adopt measures which reduce the value of damage whenever they could do so at a lower cost. The costs of such measures, together with the value of the remaining damage, would be calculated and totalled for all those affected (or who might be affected) by the smoke. A new calculation would have to be made for each level of smoke emission, or at least for enough of them so that a schedule could be drawn up showing the fall in the value of production resulting from the smoke for each level of smoke emission. The tax would be set for each level of smoke emission equal to the fall in value of production which it brought about. The factory-owner would then be presented with this schedule and he would choose his method of production and the amount of smoke that would be emitted, taking into account the taxes that he would have to pay. He would reduce smoke emission whenever the additional costs he would incur to do this were less than the taxes that would be saved. Since the tax is equal to the fall in the value of production elsewhere occasioned by the smoke, and the increased costs due to the change in methods represents the fall in the value of production in the smoke- producing activity, the factory-owner, in choosing whether to incur additional costs or pay the tax, would make that decision which maximizes the value of production. It is in this sense that the tax system may be said to be optimal.

The position is, however, much more complicated than this. The factory-owner would not normally wish to conduct his business in such a way that the level of smoke emission remained constant over time, but would wish to operate in a way which resulted in variations in the amount of smoke emitted. The extent and timing of these fluctuations in smoke emission would affect the adjustments that those in the vicinity of the factory would find it profitable to make. There is an infinite number of possible patterns of smoke emission, but no doubt it would be thought sufficient to obtain from those in the vicinity of the factory (or those elsewhere who might settle there) what their responses would be to a somewhat smaller number of patterns of smoke emission in order to procure the data from which to devise an appropriate taxing scheme. Of course, as the measures which it would be profitable to take to offset the effects of the smoke emissions would depend on their duration, data would need to be gathered for many years into the future.

As is obvious, even this is a highly simplified account of a very complicated process, but it gives some idea of what would have to be done to implement the Pigovian tax scheme. All those in the area affected by the smoke (or an adequate sample of them) would have to disclose what damage they would suffer from the smoke, what steps they would take to avoid or reduce the damage, and what it would cost them with different patterns of smoke emission from the factory. Similar enquiries would also have to be made of those not in the area but who might come into it if the level of smoke emission were reduced sufficiently (we must assume, of course, that they could be identified). The information which is being sought from this large number of people is information which, if they possessed it, they could have no interest in disclosing and which, for the most part, they would not know. There is, as I see it, no way in which the information required for the Pigovian tax scheme could be collected.

The tax system which I discussed in "The Problem of Social Cost" was one in which the tax was equal to the damage caused. While this requires much less information to be collected than is needed for the Pigovian tax scheme, it cannot easily be obtained and, in any case, as I explained, the results obtained are not optimal. My main purpose was to show this. I added that if the factory-owner has to pay a tax based on damage, it would also be desirable to make those who would suffer the damage from the smoke pay a tax equal to the costs incurred by the factory-owner to avoid causing the damage. My reason was that if the tax is based on damage, it could be that people and businesses would establish themselves in the vicinity of the factory and in consequence the factory-owner would install smoke-prevention devices even though the cost would be lower if those situated near the factory chose another location. Baumol argues that this would not happen because "the externalities (the smoke) keep down the size of the nearby population."[24] However, he assumes that the Pigovian tax system is in operation, which is not what I was assuming. The tax system I was discussing was one in which the tax was based on damage. With this tax system, the factory-owner has an incentive to install a smoke-prevention device in circumstances which would not exist with the Pigovian tax scheme. Once the smoke-prevention device is installed, there would be no smoke and therefore nothing to deter those who wish to locate near the factory; and given the amount of damage, they can count on the smoke-prevention device being installed. The object of the double tax would be to deter people and businesses from locating near the factory and adding to its costs when it would be less costly if they located somewhere else. However, I do not wish to debate the relative merits of these various tax systems which would take us into a thicket of complicated argumentation and, so far as I am concerned, to no purpose. All these tax systems have extremely serious flaws and would certainly not produce results which economists would consider to be optimal. Whether some tax system, however defective, might, in some circumstances, be better than any alternative (including inaction) is another matter, and on this I express no opinion.

Later in his article, Baumol makes what is essentially the same point. He says: "All in all, we are left with little reason for confidence in the applicability of the Pigovian approach, literally interpreted. We do not know how to calculate the required taxes and subsidies and we do not know how to approximate them by trial and error."[25]

Apparently what Baumol meant by saying that, "taken on its own grounds, the conclusions of the Pigovian tradition are, in fact, impeccable" was that its logic was impeccable and that, if its taxation proposals were carried out, which they cannot be, the allocation of resources would be optimal. This I have never denied. My point was simply that such tax proposals are the stuff that dreams are made of. In my youth it was said that what was too silly to be said may be sung. In modern economics it may be put into mathematics.

Notes

[1] R. H. Coase, The Federal Communications Commission. *The Journal of Law and Economics* (October 1959): 25.

[2] Ibid., 27.

[3] George J. Stigler, *The Theory of Price*, 3rd ed. (New York: Macmillan Co., 1966), 113.

[4] George J. Stigler, The law and economics of public policy: A plea to the scholars. *Journal of Legal Studies*, no. 1 (1972): 12.

[5] Paul A. Samuelson. Modern economics realities and individualism, *The Texas Quarterly* (Summer 1963): 128; reprinted in *The Collected Scientific Papers of Paul A. Samuelson,* vol. 2 (Cambridge, Mass.: MIT Press, 1966), 1411.

[6] Paul A. Samuelson, The monopolistic competition revolution , in *Monopolistic Competition Theory: Studies in Impact; Essays in Honor of Edward H. Chamberlin,* ed. Robert E. Kuenne (New York: Wiley, 1967), 105; reprinted in *The Collected Scientific Papers of Paul A. Samuelson*, 3: 36.

[7] Paul A. Samuelson, *Foundations of Economic Analysis* (Cambridge, Mass.: Harvard University Press, 1947), 238.

[8] Ibid., 251.

[9] [9] See Samuelson, *Collected Scientific Papers*, 3:35.

[10] Ibid., 36.

[11] Ibid.

[12] Stanislaw Wellisz, On external diseconomies and the government-assisted invisible hand. *Economica,* n.s., 31 (November 1964): 345-362.

[13] Donald H. Regan, The problem of social cost revisited. *Journal of Law and Economics,* 15, no. 2 (October 1972): 427-437.

[14] Gerald E. Auten, Discussion, in *Theory and Measurement of Economic Externalities,* ed. Steven A. Y. Lin (New York: Academic Press, 1976), 38.

[15] Coase, Federal Communications Commission, 25.

[16] Stigler, *Theory of Price*, 113.

[17] Richard O. Zerbe, Jr., The problem of social cost: Fifteen years later, in *Theory and Measurement of Economic Externalities,* 33.

[18] Agnar Sandmo, Anomaly and stability in the theory of externalities. *Quarterly Journal of Economics,* 94, no. 4 (June 1980): 799.

[19] William J. Baumol, On taxation and the control of externalities. *American Economic Review,* 62, no. 3 (June 1972): 307-322.

[20] See the problem of social cost, 151-152.

[21] Baumol, On taxation, 307.

[22] Ibid., 309.

[23] See the problem of social cost, 152.

[24] Baumol, On taxation. 312.

[25] Ibid., 318.

Comment on Thomas W. Hazlett:

Assigning Property Rights to Radio Spectrum Users Why Did FCC License Auctions Take 67 Years?*

Professor Hazlett asks the question: Why did FCC license auctions take 67 years? About the only answer I can give is: Because that was the time it took. Hazlett seems to believe that once Leo Herzel and I had shown that it was more efficient to employ the pricing system for the allocation of the use of the radio frequency spectrum rather than relying on the FCC to make the allocation, all those without an interest in maintaining a zero price for use of the spectrum would be persuaded that pricing should be introduced. They did not. And I do not find it surprising. Having lived through World War I, World War II, the Great Depression, the emergence of communism in Russia and its spread (with the approval and active support of many intellectuals in the West), the triumph of Nazism in Germany (with the support of the great mass of the German people), the adoption of socialism in Britain, the horrors in countless countries all over the world in the post-war period (of which Bosnia is but a recent example), I find it difficult to ignore the role of stupidity in human affairs. Axel Oxentierna, a Chancellor of Sweden in the seventeenth century, said in a letter to his son: "You do not know, my son, with how little wisdom the world is governed." And it remains so. As Frank Knight has told us: Men are rational, also irrational. I have often wondered why economists, with these absurdities all around them, so easily adopt the

---

* *Journal of Law and Economics,* 1998, 41(S2), 577-580.

view that men act rationally. This may be because they study an economic system in which the discipline of the market ensures that, in a business setting, decisions are more or less rational. The employee of a corporation who buys something for $10 and sells it for $8 is not likely to do so for long. Someone who, in a family setting, does much the same thing, may make his wife and children miserable throughout his life. A politician who wastes his country's resources on a grand scale may have a successful career.

I have not made a serious study of the allocation of the use of the radio frequency spectrum since the early 1960s. I must therefore confine myself to Hazlett's remarks on the early history of this question, and particularly what he says about my 1959 article on the Federal Communications Commission. Unfortunately he misunderstands some of my remarks and this has the effect of magnifying our disagreements and of obscuring what I was attempting to say. Hazlett quotes the following statement from my article: "It is difficult to avoid the conclusion that the widespread opposition to the use of the pricing system for the allocation of frequencies can be explained only by the fact that the possibility of using it has never been seriously faced." From this, he draws the conclusion that it is my view that "public interest licensing was instituted due to an analytical omission" (which he terms the "error theory"). This is an incorrect conclusion. Nowhere do I discuss the political manoeuvering that led to the passage of the 1927 act. I had no "error theory." The widespread opposition of which I wrote referred to the views expressed to me at the time or that I found in books and journal articles, mainly written by academics who had no economic interest in the preservation of the existing system. The views of Dallas Smythe that I discuss in my article were representative of those then held.

Later in his paper, Hazlett returns to the "error theory" which he says has been "critiqued in its reading of the original development of radio law. While Coase based his historical reading on that rendered by the U.S. Supreme Court in the NBC case (1943) a 'revisionist' analysis has suggested that priority-in-use property rights allowed an orderly development of radio broadcasting...the licensing scheme adopted under the 1927 Radio Act was not the result of naiveté concerning property rights but was intended to *overrule* the orderly property rights regime then developing." Leaving aside the fact that I had no "error theory," and that the statement that I based my historical reading on the opinion in the NBC case is also untrue, I see no essential difference between Hazlett's view of what happened before the 1927 act and what I say in my FCC article: "There can be little doubt that, left to themselves, the courts would have solved the problems of the radio industry in much the same way they had solved similar problems in other industries. In the early discussion of radio law an attempt was made to bring the problem within the main corpus of existing law. ... And when the problem came before the courts, there seems to have been little difficulty in reaching a decision. No doubt, in time, statutes prescribing some special regulation would also have been required. But this line of development was stopped by the passage of the 1927 act, which established a complete regulatory system." I would not however wish to say that there was no naiveté about property rights among those who supported this legislation and I would not personally describe the process as "orderly."

It must be very difficult for people today to realise the character of the reaction in the 1950s to the proposal to use the pricing system to allocate use of the spectrum. In my FCC article, I discussed Dallas Smythe's views. I will give two other examples. In 1959, before my article was published, the FCC decided to hold hearings on the future of broadcasting and I was asked to testify. You can imagine what I proposed. When I concluded, the questioning was opened by Commissioner Philip S. Cross. His first question was: "Are you spoofing us? Is this all a big joke?" I was completely taken aback but I managed to reply: "Is it a joke to believe in the American economic system?" Later Commissioner Cross said that mine was "the most unique program yet presented."

The next example was more worrying to me. After the publication of my FCC article, I was invited by some of the economists at the Rand Corporation to come to Santa Monica and to help to prepare a report on Problems of Radio Frequency Allocation. This I did together with two economists at the Rand Corporation, Bill Meckling and Jora Minasian. A draft report was prepared which advocated a market solution. This draft report was circulated within Rand. The comments on it were highly critical and as a result, the report was suppressed. Here is an example that illustrates the character of the comments that were made:

> This is a remarkable document, both for its content and its methodology. Until I read it, I would not have believed it possible that a remark made by the Imperial Russian Delegate at the London Radiotelegraph Conference of 1912 could be combined with Spencerian economics to provide a solution for a politico-technological problem arising in the latter half of the twentieth century.
>
> Time has somehow left the authors behind. On the domestic scene, they ignore the social, cultural, and political values which have come to inhere in mass communications, in particular, broadcasting, as well as fifty years of administrative law developments. On the international level, it would appear that it has been kept from them that everywhere but in the United States, communications are almost totally a state function and monopoly, a condition which preceded socialism everywhere but which has been strengthened by the ascendancy on a wide scale of political socialism, or some variants there of, in many countries of the world, and by the resurgence of nationalism everywhere. I know of no country on the face of the globe—except for a few corrupt Latin American dictatorships—where the "sale" of the spectrum could even be seriously proposed.

The covering note sending the comments to the higher authorities at Rand expressed sorrow at having "to pass on such vigorously critical reviews." It suggested that, "Rand would suffer less if we were to cut our losses by not producing [a report] than to make further investment in it." The final paragraphs of the note were:

> If some form of manuscript must go forward, I would urge that a greatly shortened monograph be produced ... and written for an economic journal where readers are accustomed to ponder new models rather than to *evaluate* them as *policy* ideas. If the

present report is boiled down for publication in a journal, I am not sure what it can add to the original journal article by Coase, but that would be a matter for the journal referees to decide.

You will notice that neither ***** nor I have raised other types of considerations which bear on Rand's "public relations" in Government quarters and in the Congress. These would exist even if the report did a fine job of showing clearly what is wrong with the present system and gave a balanced evaluation of the advantages and costs of several alternative solutions. In that case, our vulnerability would be far less to the fire and counterfire of CBS, FCC, Justice, and most of all—Congress. But as the report is presently designed, I am afraid that to issue it ... is asking for trouble in the Washington—Big Business maelstrom because we haven't in the first place measured up to the intellectual requirements of the problem selected for study.

I trust that neither you nor the authors will take these criticisms as personal disrespect for the authors' talents, which indeed are high. I am sorry that at least a year ago at a many-hour meeting with some of the authors, I and Dan Ellsberg, among others, failed to persuade them off the path they have so doggedly trod.

Jora Minasian, who was present at the meeting referred to in the last paragraph, tells me that Daniel Ellsberg stated that by definition, the spectrum was a public good and consequently a market solution was not appropriate and that the project represented a waste of Rand's resources. These were not the only examples of the opposition to my ideas that I could cite but I hope they will suffice to show that there was widespread opposition at that time to the proposal to use pricing to allocate use of the radio frequency spectrum.

Series II

The Market for Ideas

Ning Wang

The second series of papers, "The Market for Goods and the Market for Ideas" (1974) and "Advertising and Free Speech" (1977a), focuses on the market for ideas. Here as elsewhere Coase was motivated by a puzzle, as he put it, "a mass of contradictions" (1977a). Economists and the public at large often welcome and deem beneficial government regulation in the market for goods, but they fiercely object to government regulation in the market for ideas. In "The Market for Goods and the Market for Ideas," Coase asked why people hold such conflicting views regarding government regulation in the two markets, particularly when the market for ideas is more susceptible to market failure and economic justifications for regulation there are ostensibly much stronger. In "Advertising and Free Speech," Coase examined a further puzzle within the market for ideas. While free speech in the United States of America is emphasized as a universal right, deemed essential for the working of a democratic society, and protected by the First Amendment, advertising is often viewed warily. Careful readers will note that Coase held a subtle and nuanced view toward government regulation. He observed "that regulation makes things worse or, at the best, makes very little difference, seems to be the usual finding of studies which have been made in areas ranging from agriculture to zoning, with many examples in between" (1977a), but he still believed that "we cannot rule out regulation in any market as being undesirable on an *a priori* basis" (1977a).

The Market for Goods and the Market for Ideas*

The normal treatment of governmental regulation of markets makes a sharp distinction between the ordinary market for goods and services and the activities covered by the First Amendment—speech, writing, and the exercise of religious beliefs —which I call, for brevity, "the market for ideas." The phrase, "the market for ideas," does not describe the boundaries of the area to which the First Amendment has been applied very exactly. Indeed, these boundaries do not seem to have been very clearly drawn. But there can be little doubt that the market for ideas, the expression of opinion in speech and writing and similar activities, is at the center of the activities protected by the First Amendment, and it is with these activities that discussion of the First Amendment has been largely concerned.

The arguments that I will be considering long antedate the passage of the First Amendment (which obviously incorporated views already held) and there is some danger for economists, although not necessarily for American lawyers, in confining our discussion to the First Amendment rather than considering the general problem of which it is a part. The danger is that our discussion will tend to concentrate on American court opinions, and particularly those of the Supreme Court, and that, as a result, we will be led to adopt the approach to the regulation of markets found congenial by the courts rather than one developed by economists, a procedure which

---

* *The American Economic Review,* 1974, 64 (2), 384-391.

already has gone a long way to ruin public utility economics and has done much harm to economic discussion of monopoly problems generally. This approach is confining in another way, since, by concentrating on issues within the context of the American Constitution, it is made more difficult to draw on the experience and thought of the rest of the world.

What is the general view that I will be examining? It is that, in the market for goods, government regulation is desirable whereas, in the market for ideas, government regulation is undesirable and should be strictly limited. In the market for goods, the government is commonly regarded as competent to regulate and properly motivated. Consumers lack the ability to make the appropriate choices. Producers often exercise monopolistic power and, in any case, without some form of government intervention, would not act in a way which promotes the public interest. In the market for ideas, the position is very different. The government, if it attempted to regulate, would be inefficient and its motives would, in general, be bad, so that, even if it were successful in achieving what it wanted to accomplish, the results would be undesirable. Consumers, on the other hand, if left free, exercise a fine discrimination in choosing between the alternative views placed before them, while producers, whether economically powerful or weak, who are found to be so unscrupulous in their behavior in other markets, can be trusted to act in the public interest, whether they publish or work for the *New York Times,* the *Chicago Tribune* or the Columbia Broadcasting System. Politicians, whose actions sometimes pain us, are in their utterances beyond reproach. It is an odd feature of this attitude that commercial advertising, which is often merely an expression of opinion and might, therefore, be thought to be protected by the First Amendment, is considered to be part of the market for goods. The result is that government action is regarded as desirable to regulate (or even suppress) the expression of an opinion in an advertisement which, if expressed in a book or article, would be completely beyond the reach of government regulation.

This ambivalence toward the role of government in the market for goods and the market for ideas has not usually been attacked except by those on the extreme right or left, The Western world, by and large, accepts the distinction and the policy recommendations that go with it. The peculiarity of the situation has not, however, gone unnoticed, and I would like to draw your attention to a powerful article by Aaron Director. Director quotes a very strong statement by Justice William O. Douglas in a Supreme Court opinion, a statement which is no doubt intended as an interpretation of the First Amendment, but which obviously embodies a point of view not dependent on constitutional considerations. Justice Douglas said: "Free speech, free press, free exercise of religion are placed separate and apart; they are above and beyond the police power; they are not subject to regulation in the manner of factories, slums, apartment houses, production of oil and the like." *(Beauharnis v. Illinois)* Director remarks of the attachment to free speech that it is "the only area where *laissez-faire* is still respectable."

Why should this be so? In part, this may be due to the fact that belief in a free market in ideas does not have the same roots as belief in the value of free trade in goods. To quote Director again: "The free market as a desirable method of organizing the intellectual life of the community was urged long before it was advocated as a desirable method of organizing its economic life. The advantage of free exchange of ideas was recognized before that of the voluntary exchange of goods and services in competitive markets." In recent years, particularly, I think in America (that is, North America), this view of the peculiar status of the market for ideas has been nourished by a commitment to democracy as exemplified in the political institutions of the United States, for whose efficient working a market in ideas not subject to government regulation is considered essential. This opens a large subject on which I will avoid comment. Suffice it to say that, in practice, the results actually achieved by this particular political system suggest that there is a good deal of "market failure."

Because of the view that a free market in ideas is necessary to the maintenance of democratic institutions and, I believe, for other reasons also, intellectuals have shown a tendency to exalt the market for ideas and to depreciate the market for goods. Such an attitude seems to me unjustified. As Director said: "The bulk of mankind will for the foreseeable future have to devote a considerable fraction of their active lives to economic activity. For these people, freedom of choice as owners of resources in choosing within available and continually changing opportunities, areas of employment, investment, and consumption is fully as important as freedom of discussion and participation in government." I have no doubt that this is right. For most people in most countries (and perhaps in all countries), the provision of food, clothing, and shelter is a good deal more important than the provision of the "right ideas," even if it is assumed that we know what they are.

But leave aside the question of the relative importance of the two markets; the difference in view about the role of government in these two markets is really quite extraordinary and demands an explanation. It is not enough merely to say that the government should be excluded from a sphere of activity because it is vital to the functioning of our society. Even in markets which are mainly of concern to the lower orders, it would not seem desirable to reduce the efficiency with which they work. The paradox is that government intervention which is so harmful in the one sphere becomes beneficial in the other. The paradox is made even more striking when we note that at the present time it is usually those who press most strongly for an extension of government regulation in other markets who are most anxious for a vigorous enforcement of the First Amendment prohibitions on government regulation in the market for ideas.

What is the explanation for the paradox? Director's gentle nature does not allow him to do more than hint at it: "A superficial explanation for the preference for free speech among intellectuals runs in terms of vertical interests. Everyone tends to magnify the importance of his own occupation and to minimize that of his neighbor. Intellectuals are engaged in the pursuit of truth, while others are merely engaged in earning a livelihood. One follows a profession, usually a learned one, while the other follows a trade or a business." I would put the point more bluntly. The market for ideas is the market in which the intellectual conducts his trade. The explanation of the paradox is self-interest and self-esteem. Self-esteem leads the intellectuals to magnify the importance of their own market. That others should be regulated seems natural, particularly as many of the intellectuals see themselves as doing the regulating. But self-interest combines with self-esteem to ensure that, while others are regulated, regulation should not apply to them. And so it is possible to live with these contradictory views about the role of government in these two markets. It is the conclusion that matters. It may not be a nice explanation, but I can think of no other for this strange situation.

That this is the main explanation for the dominance of the view that the market for ideas is sacrosanct is certainly supported if we examine the actions of the press. The press is, of course, the most stalwart defender of the doctrine of freedom of the press, an act of public service to the performance of which it has been led, as it were, by an invisible hand. If we examine the actions and views of the press, they are consistent in only one respect: They are always consistent with the self-interest of the press. Consider their argument that the press should not be forced to reveal the sources of its published material. This is termed a defense of the public's right to know—which is interpreted to mean that the public has no right to know the source of material published by the press. To desire to know the source of a story is not idle curiosity. It is difficult to know how much credence to give to information or to check on its accuracy if one is ignorant of the source. The academic tradition, in which one discloses to the greatest extent possible the sources on which one relies and thus exposes them to the scrutiny of one's colleagues, seems to me to be sound and an essential element in the search for truth. Of course, the counterargument of the press is not without validity. It is argued that some people would not express their opinions honestly if it became known that they really held these opinions. But this argument applies equally to all expressions of views, whether in government, business, or private life, where confidentiality is necessary for frankness. However, this consideration has commonly not deterred the press from revealing such confidences when it was in their interest to do so. Of course, it would also impede the flow of information to reveal the sources of the material published in cases in which the transmission of the information involved a breach of trust or even the stealing of documents. To accept material in such circumstances is not consistent with the high moral standards and scrupulous observance of the law which the press expects of others. It is hard for me to believe that the main thing wrong with the Watergate affair was that it was not organized by the *New York Times*. I would not wish to argue that there are not conflicting considerations in all these cases which are difficult to evaluate. My point is that the press does not find them difficult to evaluate.

Consider another example which is in many ways more striking: The attitude of the press to government regulation of broadcasting. Broadcasting is an important source of news and information; it comes within the purview of the First Amendment. Yet the program content of a broadcasting station is subject to government regulation. One might have thought that the press, devoted to the strict enforcement of the First Amendment, would have been constantly attacking this abridgment of the right of free speech and expression. But, in fact, they have not. In the forty-five years which have passed since the formation of the Federal Radio Commission (now transformed into the Federal Communications Commission), very few doubts about the policy have been expressed in the press. The press, which is so anxious to remain unshackled by government regulation, has never exerted itself to secure a similar freedom for the broadcasting industry.

Lest you think that I manifest a hostility to the American press, I would like to point out that the British press has acted in a similar fashion. In this case the contrast between actions and proclaimed beliefs is even stronger since what was established in Britain was a government- controlled monopoly of a source of news and information. It might have been thought that this affront to the doctrine of freedom of the press would have appalled the British press. It did not. They supported the broadcasting monopoly, mainly, as far as I can see, because they saw the alternative to the British Broadcasting Corporation (BBC) as commercial broadcasting and, therefore, as involving increased competition for advertising revenue. But if the press did not want competition for advertising revenue, they also did not want increased competition in the supply of news. And so they did their best to throttle the BBC, at least as a purveyor of news and information. When the monopoly was originally established (when it was still the British Broadcasting Company), the BBC was prohibited from broadcasting news and information unless obtained from certain named news agencies. No news could be broadcast before 7 p.m. and broadcasts likely to affect adversely the sale of newspapers faced other restrictions as well. Gradually, over the years, these restrictions were relaxed as a result of negotiations between the press and the BBC. But it was not until after the outbreak of World War II that the BBC broadcast a regular news bulletin before 6 p.m.[1]

But, it may be argued, the fact that businessmen are mainly influenced by pecuniary considerations is no great discovery. What else would one expect from the money-grubbers of the newspaper world? Furthermore, it may be objected, because a doctrine is propagated by those who benefit from it does not mean that the doctrine is unsound. After all, have not free speech and a free press also been advocated by high-minded scholars whose beliefs are determined by what is true rather than by more sordid considerations? There has surely never been a more high-minded scholar than John Milton. As his *Areopagitica* "for the liberty of unlicensed printing" is probably the most celebrated defense of the doctrine of freedom of the press ever written, it seemed to me that it would be worthwhile to examine the nature of his argument for a free press. Milton's work has another advantage for my purpose. Written in 1644, that is, long before 1776, we can see the character of the argument before there was any general understanding of how competitive markets worked and before the emergence of modern views on democracy.

It would be idle for me to pretend that I could act as a guide to Milton's thought. I know too little of seventeenth century England and there is much in Milton's pamphlet the meaning of which I cannot discern. Yet, there are passages which leap across the centuries and for whose interpretation no scholarship is needed.

As one would expect, Milton asserts the primacy of the market for ideas: "Give me the liberty to know, to utter, and to argue freely according to conscience, above all liberties" (p.44). It is different from the market for goods and should not be treated in the same way: "Truth and understanding are not such wares as to be monopolised and traded in by tickets and statutes and standards. We must not think to make a staple commodity of all the knowledge in the land, to mark and license it like our broadcloth and our wool-packs" (p.29). The licensing of printed material is an affront to learned men and to learning: "When a man writes to the world, he summons up all his reason and deliberation to assist him; he searches, mediates, is industrious, and likely consults and confers with his judicious friends; after all which done he takes himself to be informed in what he writes, as well as any that writ before him. If in this the most consummate act of his fidelity and ripeness no years, no industry, no former proof of his abilities can bring him to that state of maturity as not to be still mistrusted and suspected, unless he carry his considerate diligence, all his midnight watchings ... to the hasty view of an unleisured licenser, perhaps much his younger, perhaps far his inferior in judgment, perhaps one who never knew the labour of book-writing, and, if he be not repulsed or slighted, must appear in print like a puny with his guardian and his censor's hand on the back of his title to be his bail and surety, that he is no idiot or seducer, it cannot be but a dishonour and derogation to the author, to the book, to the privilege and dignity of learning" (p.27). Licensing is also an affront to the common people: "Nor is it to the common people less than a reproach; for if we be so jealous over them, as that we dare not trust them with an English pamphlet, what do we but censure them for a giddy, vicious, and ungrounded people, in such a sick and weak state of faith and discretion, as to be able to take nothing down but through the pipe of a licenser" (p.30). In the market for ideas, the right choices are made: "Let truth and falsehood grapple; who ever knew truth put to the worse in a free and open encounter" (p.45). Those who undertake the job of licensing will be incompetent. A licenser should be, according to Milton, "studious, learned, and judicious." But this is not what we are likely to get: "We may easily foresee what kind of licensers we are to expect hereafter: either ignorant, imperious, and remiss, or basely pecuniary" (p.25). The licensers are more likely to suppress truth than falsehood: "If it come to prohibiting, there is aught more likely to be prohibited than truth itself; whose first appearance to our eyes bleared and dimmed with prejudice and custom is more unsightly and unplausible than many errors" (p.47). Nor does Milton fail to tell us that the licensing scheme against which he was writing came about as a result of industry pressure: "And how it got the upper hand ... there was in it the fraud of some old patentees and monopolisers in the trade of book-selling" (p.50).

In the formation of Milton's views, selfinterest may perhaps have played a part, but there can be little doubt that his argument embodies a good deal of intellectual pride of the kind to which Director refers. The writer is a learned man, diligent and trustworthy. The licenser would be ignorant, incompetent, and basely motivated, perhaps "younger" and "inferior in judgment." The common man always chooses truth as against falsehood. The picture is a little too one-sided to be wholly convincing. And if it has been convincing to the intellectual community (and apparently it often has), it is surely because people are easily persuaded that what is good for them is good for the country.

I do not believe that this distinction between the market for goods and the market for ideas is valid. There is no fundamental difference between these two markets and, in deciding on public policy with regard to them, we need to take into account the same considerations. In all markets, producers have some reasons for being honest and some for being dishonest; consumers have some information but are not fully informed or even able to digest the information they have; regulators commonly wish to do a good job, and though often incompetent and subject to the influence of special interests, they act like this because, like all of us, they are human beings whose strongest motives are not the highest.

When I say that the same considerations should be taken into account, I do not mean that public policy should be the same in all markets. The special characteristics of each market lead to the same factors having different weights, and the appropriate social arrangements will vary accordingly. It may not be sensible to have the same legal arrangements governing the supply of soap, housing, automobiles, oil, and books. My argument is that we should use the same *approach* for all markets when deciding on public policy. In fact, if we do this and use for the market for ideas the same approach which has commended itself to economists for the market for goods, it is apparent that the case for government intervention in the market for ideas is much stronger than it is, in general, in the market for goods. For example, economists usually call for government intervention, which may include direct government regulation, when the market does not operate properly—when, that is, there exist what are commonly referred to as neighborhood or spillover effects, or, to use that unfortunate word, "externalities." If we try to imagine the property rights system that would be required and the transactions that would have to be carried out to assure that anyone who propagated an idea or a proposal for reform received the value of the good it produced or had to pay compensation for the harm that resulted, it is easy to see that in practice there is likely to be a good deal of "market failure." Situations of this kind usually lead economists to call for extensive government intervention.

Or consider the question of consumer ignorance which is commonly thought to be a justification for government intervention. It is hard to believe that the general public is in a better position to evaluate competing views on economic and social policy than to choose between different kinds of food. Yet there is support for regulation in the one case but not in the other. Or consider the question of preventing fraud, for which government intervention is commonly advocated. It would be difficult to deny that newspaper articles and the speeches of politicians contain a large number of false and misleading statements—indeed, sometimes they seem to consist of little else. Government action to control false and misleading advertising is considered highly desirable. Yet a proposal to set up a Federal Press Commission or a Federal Political Commission modeled on the Federal Trade Commission would be dismissed out of hand.

The strong support enjoyed by the First Amendment should not hide from us that there is, in fact, a good deal of government intervention in the market for ideas. I have mentioned broadcasting. But there is also the case of education, which, although it plays a crucial role in the market for ideas, is subject to considerable regulation. One might have thought that those who were so anxious to obstruct government regulation of books and other printed material would also find such regulation in the field of education obnoxious. But, of course, there is a difference. Government regulation of education commonly accompanies government financing and other measures (such as compulsory school attendance) which increase the demand for the services of intellectuals and, therefore, their incomes.[2] So self-interest, which, in general, would lead to support for a free market in ideas, suggests a different attitude in education.

Nor do I doubt that detailed study would reveal other cases in which groups of practitioners in the market for ideas have supported government regulation and the restriction of competition when it would increase their incomes, just as we find similar behavior in the market for goods. But interest in monopolizing is likely to be less in the market for ideas. A general policy of regulation, by restricting the market, would have the effect of reducing the demand for the services of intellectuals. But more important, perhaps, is that the public is commonly more interested in the struggle between truth and falsehood than it is in the truth itself. Demand for the services of the writer and speechmaker depends, to a considerable extent, on the existence of controversy—and for controversy to exist, it is necessary that truth should not stand triumphant and alone.

Whatever one may think of the motives which have led to the general acceptance of the present position, there remains the question of which policies would be, in fact, the most appropriate. This requires us to come to some conclusion about how the government will perform whatever functions are assigned to it. I do not believe that we will be able to form a judgment in which we can have any confidence unless we abandon the present ambivalence about the performance of government in the two markets and adopt a more consistent view. We have to decide whether the government is as incompetent as is generally assumed in the market for ideas, in which case we would want to decrease government intervention in the market for goods, or whether it is as efficient as it is generally assumed to be in the market for goods, in which case we would want to increase government regulation in the market for ideas. Of course, one could adopt an intermediate position—a government neither as incompetent and base as assumed in the one market nor as efficient and virtuous as assumed in the other. In this case, we ought to reduce the amount of government regulation in the market for goods and might want to increase government intervention in the market for ideas. I look forward to learning which of these alternative views will be espoused by my colleagues in the economics profession.

Notes

[1] For a discussion of the attitude of the press to the monopoly of British broadcasting, see Coase, pp. 103-110 and 192-193.
[2] See E. G. West, p. 101.

References

R. H. Coase, *British Broadcasting, A Study in Monopoly*, Cambridge, Mass. 1950.

A. Director, The parity of the economic market place, *Journal of Law and Economics*, Oct. 1964.

J. Milton, *Areopagitica, A Speech for the Liberty of Unlicensed Printing*, with introduction and notes by H. B. Cotterill, New York 1959.

E. G. West, The political economy of American Public School Legislation, *Journal of Law and Economics*, Oct. 1967.

Beauharnis v. Illinois, 343 U.S. 250, 286, 1952.

Advertising and Free Speech[*]

I. Free Speech

In a paper which I presented to the American Economic Association at their meeting in December, 1973, I outlined my approach, as an economist, to the problems of freedom of speech and registered my astonishment at current attitudes.[1] The argument of that paper did not command universal assent and as some, at least, of the objections involved a misunderstanding of my position, it seemed to me that I should begin this paper by re-stating my argument, in a way which, I hope, will make my position clearer.

Belief in free speech is embodied in the First Amendment: "Congress shall make no law ... abridging the freedom of speech or of the press ..." The clear purpose of the First Amendment is to limit severely the power of the government to regulate what has been termed the market for ideas—broadly speaking, what is written or spoken. In words that have often been quoted, and with approval, Justice Holmes described the fundamental belief which finds its expression in the First Amendment. It is that, "The ultimate good desired is better reached by free trade in ideas—that the best test of truth is the power of the thought to get itself accepted in the competition of the market."[2] A statement such as this displays an extreme faith in the efficiency of competitive markets and a profound distrust of

---

[*] *Journal of Legal Studies*, 1977, 6(1), 1-34.

government regulation. The First Amendment prohibitions on government action have received, and continue to receive, the strongest support from the intellectual community.

This same intellectual community has, of course, in general been very anxious that the government should extensively regulate activities not covered by the First Amendment and rarely a day passes without new proposals for further regulation. This striking difference in the policies espoused when dealing with speech or written material, which I will refer to for shortness as the market for ideas, and those which are thought appropriate for the ordinary market for goods and services is clearly something which calls for an explanation. It is not easy to find.

In the market for ideas, consumers are assumed to be able to choose appropriately between what they are offered without serious difficulty. As Milton said (and this has been repeated many times since), "Let truth and falsehood grapple; who ever knew Truth put to the worse in a free and open encounter?"[3] But in the market for goods, we do not seem to believe that consumers are able to make such a fine discrimination and it is deemed necessary to regulate producers with regard to what they tell consumers, how goods are to be labelled and described, and so on, lest consumers make the wrong choices. It is perhaps merely an extension of this assumption about consumer behavior in the two markets that whereas in the market for goods, producers are thought to be unscrupulous in their dealings, in the market for ideas fraud is not treated as a serious problem—which is at least consistent, since in a market in which consumers effortlessly detect false claims, what motive could there be for politicians, journalists or authors to attempt to make false or misleading statements?

But perhaps even more extraordinary is the difference in the view held about the government and its competence and motivation. I assume that support for the First Amendment prohibitions on government action—and the support is widespread—is based on beliefs about what the effects would be if the government intervened in the market for ideas. It seems to be believed that the government would be inefficient and wrongly motivated, that it would suppress ideas that should be put into circulation and would encourage those to circulate which we would be better without. How different is the government assumed to be when we come to economic regulation. In this area government is considered to be competent in action and pure in motivation so that it is desirable that it should engage in the regulation, in the minutest detail, of the goods and services which people buy, the terms on which they buy, the prices which they can pay, from whom they should be allowed to buy, and so on. Since we are concerned with the activities in these two different markets of the same government, why is it that it is regarded as incompetent and untrustworthy in the one market and efficient and reliable in the other?

So far as I know, no answer has ever been given—which, I hasten to add, may in part be due to the fact that the question is not normally raised. This does not mean that no justification is ever given for this difference in the role assigned to government in the two markets. But it has a very curious quality. It is held that things spiritual are more important than things material, that the mind is more important than the body. This is what I have termed the assumption of the primacy of the marketplace for ideas. Milton believed this:

Truth and understanding are not such wares as to be monopolised and traded in by tickets and statutes and standards. We must not think to make a staple commodity of all the knowledge in the land, to mark and license it like our broadcloth and our woolpacks .... Give me the liberty to know, to utter, and to argue freely according to conscience, above all liberties.[4]

John Stuart Mill adopted a similar position. He explains that,

The so-called doctrine of Free Trade ... rests on grounds different from ... the principle of individual liberty. ... Restrictions on trade, or on production for purposes of trade, are indeed restraints; and all restraint, *quâ* restraint, is an evil: but the restraints in question affect only that part of conduct which society is competent to restrain, and are wrong solely because they do not really produce the results which it is desired to produce by them. As the principle of individual liberty is not involved in the doctrine of Free Trade, so neither is it in most of the questions which arise respecting the limits of that doctrine; as, for example, what amount of public control is admissible for the prevention of fraud by adulteration; how far sanitary precautions, or arrangements to protect workpeople employed in dangerous occupations, should be enforced on employers.[5]

Aaron Director showed the fallacy of the belief in the primacy of the market for ideas:

For the bulk of mankind ... freedom of choice as owners of resources in choosing within available and continually changing opportunities, areas of employment, investment, and consumption is fully as important as freedom of discussion and participation in government.[6]

And, as is to be expected, Adam Smith, always sensible and shrewd, makes the same point when discussing the laws of settlement which impeded the mobility of labor, but which, he said, had not been denounced in the same way as had general warrants, which directly affected only the intellectual community.

Though men of reflection... have sometimes complained of the law of settlements as a public grievance; yet it has never been the object of any general popular clamour, such as that against general warrants, an abusive practice undoubtedly, but such a one as was not likely to occasion any general oppression. There is scarce a poor man in England of forty years of age...who has not in some part of his life felt himself most cruelly oppressed by this ill-contrived law of settlements.[7]

There is simply no reason to suppose that for the great mass of people the market for ideas is more important than the market for goods.

But even if the market for ideas were more important, it does not follow that the two markets should be treated differently. Support for the First Amendment is dependent on the view that government intervention in a particular market would be bad. Why not, then, be consistent and apply this view of government intervention more widely? If we want the First Amendment to be strictly observed, and believe therefore that limitations should be placed on the activities of the government in the marketplace of ideas because of the greater importance of that marketplace for the working of our society, why deny the same advantages to those whose welfare depends on the lesser market, the market for goods? As things stand, it seems as though it is desired to make the markets which cater to ordinary people less responsive to their needs. Certainly most intellectuals in the Western world, when comparing countries which abolish both the market for goods and the market for ideas with those which abolish the market for ideas but retain a modicum of freedom in the market for goods, seem to prefer those which eliminate both markets—which assigns a negative value to an efficient market for goods.

The present attitude toward the market for goods and the market for ideas is a mass of contradictions. Consumers and the government (as well as producers) are assumed to act in one way in one market and in another way in the other market. There does not seem to be any justification for this assumption. There may be implicit in this attitude a preference for an inefficient market for goods, though it embodies a belief which most intellectuals would reject, were it made explicit.

My discussion up to this point has proceeded on the basis that the assumption underlying the support for the First Amendment is correct, namely, that markets operate better if government intervention is strictly limited. But now let us suppose that the assumptions underlying the case for economic regulation are correct, that the government is competent to regulate and is so motivated as to do so properly, with the result that the regulation enables the market to work better. If we make such assumptions, it is immediately apparent that the case for government intervention is very much stronger in the market for ideas than it is in the market for goods. The market for ideas is one in which property rights are difficult to define or to enforce, and in which, according to the argument normally employed by economists, the market is bound to work badly, and in which, therefore, government action of one sort or another is desirable. And yet despite the fact it is in this market, in which, according to the view I describe, its potentialities for good seem so great, that government action is to be prohibited. The inconsistency in the policies recommended for the two markets remains.

II. Regulation

Economic regulation is the establishment of the legal framework within which economic activity is carried out. The term "regulation" in the United States is often confined to the work of the regulatory commissions; but regulation is also the result of legislative and judicial actions, and it seems ill-advised not to take these into consideration. The First Amendment does not, of course, prevent the passage of any laws relating to "speech or the press" but only those which "abridge" their freedom. Since any law will be likely to affect the relative profitability of different activities, encouraging some and discouraging others, and since it is inconceivable that no laws will be passed which affect speech or the press, the courts inevitably face a difficult task in deciding when a law "abridges" freedom of speech or of the press.

The modern theory of regulation tends to stress that regulation comes about as the result of the desire of producers to restrict competition and that in consequence regulation leads to a worsening in the economic situation. To the extent that this is true, it would be better to have less regulation. There is a great deal of evidence to support this position. In fact, that regulation makes things worse or, at the best, makes very little difference, seems to be the usual finding of studies which have been made in areas ranging from agriculture to zoning, with many examples in between.

Most of the studies relate to the activities of regulatory commissions, but there can be no doubt that many statutory provisions have similar results. One example very relevant in assessing the likely consequences of regulating advertising is the regulation of whiskey labelling. The control of whiskey labelling by the Federal Alcohol Administration was supposed to prevent fraud and promote competition. In fact, a recent study concludes that the kind of labelling regulations that were made led to deception and restricted competition. The authors of the study conclude by asking a general question: "Will implementation of ... proposals for additional consumer-protection legislation necessarily lead to a rise in consumer's welfare?"[8] I would add that since people do not consume the same mix of products and services, so-called consumer organizations are likely to promote the interests of particular groups of consumers and will thus bring much the same kind of harm as do the activities of producer organizations. Thus, lower utility prices may benefit those who are already consuming but may deny a supply to those who are not; pollution controls may provide additional recreational facilities, at the cost of higher prices for electricity, oil or chemicals, perhaps largely paid for by those who do not enjoy the recreation.

But whether as a result of pressure from producers or consumers, it is clear that regulation will often be inimical to the interests of the community as a whole. There seems to be some inclination to argue that all regulation would have this consequence. But I believe this would be wrong. No one emphasized more strongly than Adam Smith that the regulations of commerce are a result of the political pressure of those who stand to benefit from them. But his treatment is more comprehensive (in this as in other respects) than that of most contemporary economists:

> The interest of the dealers ... in any particular branch of trade or manufactures, is always in some respects different from, and even opposite to, that of the public. To widen the market and to narrow the competition, is always the interest of the dealers. To widen the market may frequently be agreeable enough to the interest of the public; but to narrow the competition must always be against it. ... The proposal of any new law or regulation of commerce which comes from this order, ought always to be

listened to with great precaution, and ought never to be adopted till after having been long and carefully examined, not only with the most scrupulous, but with the most suspicious attention.[9]

As Adam Smith indicates, producers are certainly interested in narrowing the competition but they also have an interest in widening the market. Producers, that is, have an interest in the passage of laws which lower the costs of carrying out transactions and in removing restrictions on trade. And this means that they have an interest in bringing about the kind of regulation which would improve the working of the economic system. So we cannot assume that all regulation will make things worse although proposals for regulation made by any given group of producers should no doubt be examined "with the most suspicious attention." One problem is that proposals for a change in the legal framework are likely to have a mixed character, simultaneously widening the market in one respect and narrowing the competition in another. And, of course, we should always have regard to how the regulation will be applied in practice, and this will depend on the circumstances of each case.

I have been puzzled as to why the studies of regulation show, I think without exception, that regulation either makes little difference or makes things worse. Somewhere one would have expected to find a regulation which did more good than harm. It may be that we are misled because our studies have concentrated so heavily on the regulatory agencies, which are often merely the political arm of a cartel, and act accordingly. I have come to the tentative conclusion that an important reason may be that the government at the present time is so large that it has reached the stage of negative marginal productivity, which means that any additional function it takes on will probably result in more harm than good. It does appear that the governmental machine is now out of control. If a federal program were established to give financial assistance to boy scouts to enable them to help old ladies cross busy intersections, we could be sure that not all the money would go to boy scouts, that some of those they helped would be neither old, nor ladies, that part of the program would be devoted to preventing old ladies from crossing busy intersections and that many of them would be killed because they would now cross at places where, unsupervised, they were at least permitted to cross.

When I put forward my view that the market for goods and the market for ideas should be treated in the same way, it was assumed by some that what I had in mind was that the market for ideas should be subject to government regulation. That was certainly true in an article which appeared in *Time*.[10] The belief that I was advocating regulation of the press seems to have been clinched by a remark I made to a reporter that "buying harmful ideas is just as bad as buying harmful drugs." Since it was assumed that harmful drugs must be regulated, it seemed to follow that I wanted the same thing in the market for ideas. My supposed conclusion was answered by arguing that harmful ideas were difficult to discover but that this was not so for drugs: "It is relatively easy to get an objective consensus on, say the toxic effects of thalidomide." In fact, it was not easy to foresee what the effects of thalidomide would be before it had been used, and a study of the new drug regulation in the United States (made in part because of the thalidomide experience) indicates that the main effect has been to decrease the supply of new drugs without any reduction in the proportion of inefficacious drugs among the smaller number that are now introduced.[11] So it is fairly clear that we would be better off without this new drug regulation. Experience with regulation in the market for goods suggests not the desirability of regulation in the market for ideas but the dangers of introducing regulation, anywhere.

However, this should not conceal from us that there is in fact regulation of the market for ideas. I gave education and broadcasting as examples in my paper to the American Economic Association. But an even more interesting example, since it directly affects freedom of speech and of the press, is the control exercised by the courts over what can be said or written in connection with the conduct of a trial. This has mainly attracted attention because of the conflict with the doctrine of freedom of the press resulting from the courts' attempting to control what can be reported in the press. But the procedures followed by the courts have a much more direct and more interesting relation to the problem we are discussing. In a court, it is of the utmost important that the truth be discovered. Whatever lawyers say when talking at large about freedom of speech, when it comes to their own affairs, they display great anxiety when truth and falsehood are grappling in a free and open encounter about the possibility that truth may be put to the worst. The result is the most highly regulated marketplace for ideas that it is possible to imagine. Who can speak, when they can speak, what they can speak about, the order in which people can speak, who is allowed to question them, what questions can be asked and much more are all determined by the regulations of the courts.[12] It is apparent that lawyers believe that, in their own business, it is only through a highly controlled marketplace for ideas—the absence, that is, of free speech as it is generally understood—that truth can be established. Whether all these regulations really do enable us to determine the truth with greater certainty, as against increasing the incomes of lawyers, I do not pretend to know. But I would be willing to accept that some of these regulations do have the effect of making it more likely that we will discover the truth. If this is so, it suggests that there may, on occasion, be advantages in a regulated marketplace for ideas.

What this comes down to is that we cannot rule out regulation in any market as being undesirable on an *a priori* basis. But the studies to which I have referred suggest that caution should be exercised in instituting new regulation since in practice the results of the regulation may be very different than those which the advocates of the regulation claim that it would bring. One of the problems at the present time is that the government is so overextended that any additional function which government undertakes, of whatever kind, is liable to do more harm than good. But this does not mean that we would be better off if all regulation were abandoned. This would, after all, be the equivalent of abolishing the legal system. Nor does it mean that in that happy but perhaps unattainable world in which we have vastly less regulation than at present, we would not have some regulation of the market for ideas, including perhaps some that does not now exist.

III. Advertising

Advertising, the dissemination of messages about the goods and services which people consume, is clearly part of the market for ideas. Intellectuals have not, in general, welcomed this other occupant of their domain. And the feeling of antipathy has been shared by economists, who, until comparatively recently, have tended to deplore rather than to analyse the effects of advertising. In recent years advertising has been studied more rigorously, and this has been accompanied by, or perhaps we should say has resulted in, a more sympathetic attitude to advertising. However, this work, though enlightening, is by no means decisive when we deal with the question of how advertising should be treated under the First Amendment.

Advertising may provide information or may change people's tastes. Normally, firms incur advertising expenditures because of the additional profit which results from the increased demand to which the information or the change in tastes leads. Advertising may also on occasion have as its motive to affect the attitudes of workers, making them, for example, more willing to work for the firm concerned. And it may also be used to influence public policy in a direction favorable to the firm's operations, presumably by affecting the behavior of people acting in the political system. Economists have always tended to look kindly on informative advertising, although since the information given is selective, it is admitted that on occasion it may lead people to make worse choices than they would without it. Recent work has shown that the informative content of most advertising must be large, as is shown by the fact that, for example, new products are advertised more heavily than old ones. Persuasive advertising, which conveys no information about the properties of the goods and services being advertised but achieves its effect through an emotional appeal, is commonly disapproved of by economists. It is not clear why. Any advertisement which induces people to consume a product conveys information, since the act of consumption gives more information about the properties of a product or service than could be done by the advertisement itself. Persuasive advertising is thus also informative. Advertising of new products,

I suspect, normally informs the consumer not through the facts and figures in the advertisement itself (the facts presented may indeed be as much an appeal to the emotions as the figures which are so commonly found in advertisements) but achieves this end through inducing the consumer to try the product and thus informing him in the most direct way.

Advertisements may also change people's tastes. No one doubts that tastes can change, although it is possible to describe what is commonly meant by a change in tastes without using the word. Given that an individual's tastes will usually be determined by a large number of factors other than advertising, e.g., by family influences, religion, education, genetic factors, and by the particular experiences which befall every individual, it is not to be expected that the effect of advertising on taste will normally be great, particularly as much advertising is not designed to change tastes and presumably does not. But this does not mean that the effect of advertising on taste is negligible, even if its only consequence is to speed up a change in taste which is occurring for some other reason.

Most economists seem to have thought that advertising which brings about a change in tastes is necessarily bad—either because advertising tends to corrupt our tastes or because, if it does not do this but merely produces a new set of demands no better than the old, advertising expenditures clearly represent a waste of resources. The possibility that advertising might serve, even in a small degree, to elevate tastes never seems to be considered. Yet, once we decide to take changes in tastes into account in assessing the worth of advertising (and I think we should) we need to decide whether the new tastes are better or worse than the old ones. Professor Phillip Nelson, who emphasizes, no doubt correctly, the informative aspects of advertising, tells us that he finds

> the hypothesis that advertising changes tastes intellectually unsatisfactory. We economists have no theory of taste changes, so this approach leads to no behavioral predictions. The intuitions of one group of economists are matched against the intuitions of other economists with no clear resolution.[13]

I would have thought that the belief that advertising had some effect on tastes, perhaps minor but not zero, was shared by everyone who is willing to agree that tastes can change. No doubt Professor Nelson is correct when he says that we do not have a theory of tastes. But ignorance about a subject seems an inadequate reason for not studying it.

The right way to think about this question is, in my view, that advocated by the greatest Chicago economist, Frank H. Knight. He points out that we have "a tendency to regard the growth of wants as unfortunate and the manufacture of new ones as an evil; what have not advertising and salesmanship to answer for at the hands of Veblen, for example!"[14] Knight's own attitude to wants is very different:

Wants ... not only are unstable, changeable in response to all sorts of influences, but it is their essential nature to change and grow; it is an inherent inner necessity in them. The chief thing which the common-sense individual actually wants is not satisfactions for the wants which he has, but more, and better wants.[15]

Knight rejects the idea that, "One taste or judgment is as good as another, that the fact of preference is ultimately all there is to the question of wants." On the contrary:

The consideration of wants by the person who is comparing them for the guidance of his conduct and hence, of course, for the scientific student thus inevitably gravitates into a *criticism of standards*, which seems to be a very different thing from the comparison of given magnitudes. The individual who is acting deliberately is not merely and perhaps not mainly trying to satisfy given desires; there is always really present and operative, though in the background of consciousness, the idea of and *desire for a new want* to be striven for when the present objective is out of the way. Wants and the activity which they motivate constantly look forward to new and "higher," more evolved and enlightened wants and these function as ends and motives of action beyond the objective to which desire is momentarily directed. The "object," in the narrow sense of the present want is provisional; it is as much a means to a new want as end to the old one, and all intelligently conscious activity is directed forward, onward, upward, indefinitely. Life is not fundamentally a striving for ends, for satisfactions, but rather for bases for further striving; desire is more fundamental to conduct than is achievement, or perhaps better, the true achievement is the refinement and elevation of the plane of desire, the cultivation of taste. And let us reiterate that all this is true *to the person acting*, not simply to the outsider, philosophizing after the event.[16]

What this means is that we have to judge an activity such as advertising, which influences tastes, by deciding whether it tends to produce good men and a good society, or, at any rate, better men and a better society. It is not easy to gauge the effect of advertising on taste, in part because it is obviously not great, but judging by the emphasis in advertisements on convenience, cleanliness and beauty, such effect as it has is presumably generally in the right direction. The effect on society which has attracted most attention, at any rate among economists, is its influence on competition. It used to be thought by many that advertising promoted monopoly but it is now becoming apparent as a result of recent studies that advertising tends to make the economic system more competitive. An extremely interesting study, and one which has had important repercussions on the formation of policy, is that by Professor Lee Benham on the effect of advertising on the prices of eyeglasses. Professor Benham compared the prices of eyeglasses in states which prohibited advertising relating to eyeglasses and eye examinations with the prices in states which allowed such advertising. The conclusion was clear: prices were lower in those states which allowed advertising. This study suggests that advertising tends to make the system more competitive, and this is consistent with other evidence.[17]

Of course, the conclusion that overall, advertising tends to improve the performance of the economic system or that it leads to an improvement in our tastes, does not determine whether advertising ought or ought not to be regulated. Few people, I suppose, would wish to abolish advertising altogether. Even though most advertising elevates taste to some degree, there is presumably some which corrupts it and though most advertising conveys information which makes the system more competitive, there is also no doubt some which, either because the information is misleading or fraudulent, worsens the performance of the economic system. Regulation, if it merely eliminated those advertisements which make things worse while retaining those that made things better (or even reducing their quantity slightly) would clearly be desirable.

We can form some idea as to whether regulation of advertising is likely to lead to an overall improvement by considering the work of the Federal Trade Commission regarding deceptive practices. Professor Richard Posner has made such a study and shows that many of the cases in which the Federal Trade Commission took action did not involve serious deception or even did not involve deception at all. For example, they objected to certain information not being supplied even in cases in which it was fairly clear that it was information the consumers did not want. And in other cases, the advertising was objected to even though it would be perfectly well understood by consumers. Professor Posner points out that it is unbelievable that an appreciable number of consumers would be (or even were intended to be) fooled in such cases as those in which the Federal Trade Commission ordered:

> A seller of dime store jewelry to disclose that its "turquoise" rings do not contain real turquoises, a toy manufacturer to disclose that its toy does not fire projectiles that actually explode, a maker of "First Prize" bobby pins to change the name lest a consumer think that purchase would make him eligible to enter a contest, and a manufacturer of shaving cream to cease representing that his product can shave sandpaper without first soaking the sandpaper for several hours.[18]

The Federal Trade Commission also took action in cases when there were adequate alternative legal remedies. There were, of course, cases of fraud in which action by the Federal Trade Commission was appropriate—but these represented in all the periods sampled a very small proportion of the total number of cases. Professor Posner summed the position for the fiscal year 1963 (and the results for the other periods sampled were not dissimilar) in the following words:

> ...The FTC bought little consumer protection in exchange for the more than $4 million it expended in the area of fraudulent and unfair marketing practices, and the millions more that it forced the private sector to expend in litigation and compliance. Besides wasting money on red herrings, it inflicted additional social costs of unknown magnitude by impeding the free marketing of cheap substitute products, including foreign products of all kinds, fiber substitutes for animal furs, costume jewelry, and inexpensive scents; by proscribing truthful designations; by harassing discount sellers; by obstructing a fair market test for products of debatable efficacy; and by imposing on sellers the costs of furnishing additional information and on buyers the costs of absorbing that information.[19]

The results of this study of the regulation of deceptive practices is much the same as other studies of regulation: there is no reason to suppose that whatever good was accomplished was sufficient to offset the harm that the regulation brought with it.

IV. The First Amendment, Advertising and Legal Opinion

Lawyers, like most other groups in western intellectual society, strongly believe in the doctrine of free speech, which, in the United States, is enshrined in the First Amendment. They have not been in agreement as to its reach nor as to those special reasons which make it important to preserve the kind of freedom protected by the First Amendment above all others. It is sometimes said that freedom of speech and of the press are essential for the proper working of a democratic society. No doubt they are. But this hardly gets to the heart of the matter. Surely such freedoms would be valuable in a nondemocratic society. Were the United States ruled by a king and an aristocracy, the value of freedom in the market for ideas would not disappear and might very well be increased. It is not without significance that Milton's *Areopagitica*, so much quoted by those who advocate free speech, was published in 1644, long before modern notions of democracy came into existence. We are, I believe, forced to reject the idea that belief in freedom in the market for ideas is dependent on a belief in democracy, or self-government, to use Meiklejohn's word. Indeed, as the range of activities grow to which the courts have extended the protection of the First Amendment, it becomes increasingly implausible to tie First Amendment rights to the working of the political system. Nude dancing is now covered, or uncovered, by the First Amendment and it would be difficult to argue that this activity, so dependent on the existence of adequate heating, is vital to the working of a democratic system. If we are to justify these rights, we must rely on values inherent in a system in which individuals are able to choose what they do (in this case, to speak, write or engage in similar activities) without direct government regulation.

I mentioned earlier the paradox that, while freedom from government regulation is considered essential in the areas of speech and writing, this is not true in the market for goods and services. So far as I know, no satisfactory reason has ever been given as why the market for ideas should be beyond the reach of government intervention. Thomas I. Emerson, in his book, attempted to justify this privileged position but I need not conceal that I consider his attempt to be unsuccessful.[20] He first points out correctly that, "No really adequate or comprehensive theory of the First Amendment has been enunciated, much less agreed upon." He then attempts to fill the gap. According to Emerson, the "fundamental purpose of the First Amendment" is "to guarantee the maintenance of an effective system of free expression."[21] This emphasis on "free expression" requires him to make a distinction between "expression" and "action." He argues that,

> in order to achieve its desired goals, a society or the state is entitled to exercise control over action—whether by prohibiting or compelling it—on an entirely different and vastly more extensive basis. But expression occupies a specially protected position. In

this sector of human conduct, the social right of suppression or compulsion is at its lowest point, in most respects nonexistent.[22]

Emerson's distinction between "expression" and "action" is roughly the distinction between the market for ideas and the market for goods. Maintenance of free expression is justified because (1) it assures individual self-fulfilment, (2) it enables us to attain the truth, (3) it secures the participation of members of the society in social, including political, decision-making, and (4) it maintains the balance between stability and change.[23] It seems to me that the arguments which Emerson uses to support freedom in the market for ideas are equally applicable in the market for goods.

Emerson lays great stress on freedom of expression as leading to self-fulfillment. No doubt it does. But freedom to choose one's occupation, one's home, the school one (and one's children) attends, what is studied at school, the kind of medical attention one receives, how one's savings are to be invested, the equipment one uses or the food one eats are surely equally necessary for self-fulfillment—and for most people are considerably more important than much of what is protected by the First Amendment. A similar point can be made about the other advantages which Emerson finds in freedom of expression. If freedom in the market for ideas enables us to discover and choose the truth, why would not freedom in the market for goods enable us to discover what is available and to choose more wisely what we purchase? Emerson speaks about participation in decision-making in political affairs. But why should people not be free to participate directly in economic affairs by competing in the market? As for the accommodation to change, there is surely no more delicate mechanism for adjusting to changing conditions than the market.

Why is it that intellectuals who, one might think, would be made uncomfortable by such inconsistency seem to be unaware that there is any inconsistency in their views, or that their justification for the special position accorded freedom of expression is little more than phrase-making "full of sound and fury, signifying nothing?" Aaron Director has given the answer to the question.[24] It is self-interest. The market for ideas is the market in which the intellectuals operate. They understand the value of freedom where their own activities are concerned. "Freedom of expression" is freedom for them. The market for goods is however, the market in which the money-making businessman operates. Regulation in this case is directed at the activities of another group and is, no doubt, made more attractive because intellectuals see themselves as doing the regulating. Furthermore, although, in general, intellectuals gain from freedom from direct government regulation in the market for ideas, since it generates controversy and therefore increases the demand for their services, in at least one area (and there are undoubtedly others) which one would normally consider as part of the market for ideas, education, such regulation has been welcomed, no doubt because it is seen to be accompanied by government financial support.

Advertising is in a curious position. On the one hand, it takes the form of speech or writing and one would expect therefore to find it protected by the First Amendment. It involves "expression" rather than "action," and, one would think, should obtain the same protection using Emerson's approach as other parts of the market for ideas. But, of course, advertising is connected with the market for goods, the domain of the businessman, which is treated as "action." Emerson himself has no doubt that advertising should not be brought within the protection of the First Amendment: "Communications in connection with commercial transactions generally relate to a separate sector of social activity involving the system of property rights rather than free expression."[25] But the question is not as clear-cut as this and it is to be expected that a good deal will be revealed about the criteria which the courts use in deciding whether an activity is protected by the First Amendment by examining how they handle the boundary case of advertising. How the courts have, in fact, treated this problem is the subject of the next section.

V. Advertising and the First Amendment: The Cases

The view that commercial advertising is not included in the First Amendment prohibitions is normally traced to the case of *Valentine v. Chrestensen* decided in 1942.[26] The Supreme Court's opinion, as we shall see, does not illuminate the subject, but the facts of that case and the arguments made in the progress of the case through the courts resulted in most of the important questions being presented. Consideration of this case suggests to me that the questions posed but left unanswered by the Supreme Court could not be suppressed forever and the disintegration of the Supreme Court's ruling in that case, which we can now see to be occurring, appears as an almost inevitable development.

The facts are simple. Mr. Chrestensen had acquired a Navy submarine which he exhibited, charging an admission fee. The submarine was moored at a pier in New York City. He had printed a handbill advertising the exhibition. On attempting to distribute the handbill in the city streets, he was told by the Police Commissioner that this was illegal since the Sanitary Code prohibited the distribution in the streets of commercial and business advertising matter. Mr. Chrestensen was, however, told that handbills solely devoted to "information or a public protest" could be distributed. He then had printed a double-faced handbill, on one side of which was printed the original advertisement (in a slightly modified form) and on the other side a protest against the action of the city in not allowing him to use a city pier. This was a genuine grievance, since the city's refusal had resulted in Mr. Chrestensen having to moor his submarine at a state pier, which was less accessible to the public. The police, however, prohibited the distribution of the double-faced handbill. As a result Mr. Chrestensen took action in the courts and the case finally went to the Supreme Court. The Court held that while "the streets are proper places for the exercise of the freedom of communicating information and disseminating opinion" and that this is a privilege that government "may not unduly burden or proscribe ... we are equally clear that the Constitution imposes no such restraint on government as respects purely commercial advertising." Mr. Chrestensen, of course, argued that he was engaged in "the dissemination of matter proper for public information, none the less so because there was inextricably attached to the medium of such dissemination commercial advertising matter." To this, the Supreme Court gave not so much a reply as a rebuff:

> It is enough ... that the stipulated facts justify the conclusion that the affixing of the protest against official conduct to the advertising circular was with the intent, and for the purpose, of evading the prohibition of the ordinance. If that evasion were successful, every merchant who desires to broadcast advertising leaflets in the streets need only append a civic appeal, or a moral platitude, to achieve immunity from the law's command.[27]

In the United States Circuit Court of Appeals, Mr. Chrestensen was successful in obtaining a decision to the effect that the police action infringed the First Amendment but this was accompanied by a very detailed dissenting opinion. And before the Supreme Court, the New York City Committee of the American Civil Liberties Union, among others, filed an Amicus Curiae brief. So the issues were fully ventilated. The majority opinion in the United States Circuit Court of Appeals was mainly concerned with the argument presented on behalf of the Police Commissioner, that the handbill, although on one side it contained material protected by the First Amendment, was "primarily" commercial. This, it was argued, was determined by the extent to which the material could be considered commercial and by the motive of the advertiser, whether, that is, he was actuated by pecuniary gain. But, said the majority, acceptance of such a point would result in the police becoming the arbiters of "the quantum of advertising as against protest and of the purpose of the citizen in speaking and writing." If the police weigh "purpose and intent, as well as the effect of the literary product", this "will pretty surely result in prohibiting freedom of expression in ways and to an extent quite unconnected with city sanitation". The majority commented:

> Plaintiff's handbill furnishes a good example of the uncertainty, not to speak of unreality, of the suggested distinctions. Sheer number of words favors the protest as

against all the rest of the handbill, whether it be considered advertising or mere factual information concerning the submarine. Spacing and display give at least equal place to the protest. But if intent and purpose must be measured, how can we say the plaintiff's motives are only or primarily financial? Is he just engaged in an advertising plot, or does he really believe in his wrongs? We know how opposition to oppression, real or fancied, grows upon a person, and we suspect that by now plaintiff regards himself as a crusader against injustice. If so, he is in the democratic tradition and within the protection of the Bill of Rights.

It will be observed that the majority do not here deal with the question of whether commercial advertising is protected by the First Amendment. They therefore added:

To avoid misunderstanding, perhaps we should say that, while absolute prohibition of commercial handbills seems to us of doubtful validity, yet we need decide no more here than that at least it cannot extend to a combined protest and advertisement not shown to be a mere subterfuge.[28]

The long dissenting opinion argued that the main fallacy in the majority opinion arose out of its assumption that it was dealing with a noncommercial handbill "which contains some related and incidental commercial or business advertising." One side of the handbill certainly contained a protest, which was protected, but there was no reason why this had to be printed on the same piece of paper as the advertisement. "It is as if the suit related to a handbill advertising an automobile for sale which also included an attack on Nazism or a protest against the tax on cigarettes." The question, to the dissenting judge, was: "Is that separable handbill ...wholly commercial?" On this, the judge had no doubt:

...The dominant purpose of most men, when engaged in business, is to seek customers and make profits. ... Chrestensen being a business man, we are more than justified in concluding that, as his sole purpose in connection with his original handbill was unquestionably commercial, his purpose in trying to distribute the second handbill ... was the same. We know that his business is that of showing his submarine for profit ... we know that he does not display his submarine for educational or propaganda purposes. Why, then, should we refuse to recognize that the handbill [in question] was commercial?

He found little difficulty in holding that the motive was pecuniary.

Suppose that a department store, whose owners were recognized as not being in business for their health, were to attempt to distribute ... a handbill saying nothing but this: "We have on display at our store many copies of beautiful early American furniture." If the store owners sought an injunction to restrain the city from preventing the distribution on the streets of such an advertisement, a court surely would not grant the injunction because the handbill itself contained nothing which disclosed a commercial intention. It would not say that, as the advertisement was silent as to sales, it must be assumed that there was little or no profit motive behind it, but merely a desire to educate. The judicial vision is not so feeble that it cannot look beyond the contents of such a paper.[29]

The dissenting judge then turns to the majority's clear indication that it would have found the ordinance unconstitutional, even if the handbill had been wholly commercial:

... the majority finds it difficult to see why (a) if ... a business man may not constitutionally be prevented from circularizing, in public places, a protest against official action affecting his business, he must not also (b) be similarly protected in distributing business circulars wholly designed to procure public patronage for profit.

Such a distinction seems to him easy to make:

> The historical events which yielded the constitutional protection of free speech and free expression do not by any means compel or even suggest the conclusion that there is an equally important constitutional right to distribute commercial handbills—for the purpose of profit-making—so imperative that the city's police power, must similarly be reduced (from prevention to punishment after the fact) when pieces of paper, devised for business purposes, may litter its streets to the injury of public health or safety. ... Such men as Thomas Paine, John Milton and Thomas Jefferson were not fighting for the right to peddle commercial advertising. ... As ours is a profit economy, no business man need apologize for seeking personal gain by all legitimate means. But the constitutional limitations on legislation affecting such pursuits are not as specific and exacting as those imposed on legislation interfering with free speech. To prevent the peddling of business handbills on the street still leaves the businessman at liberty to use other modes of advertising, as in newspapers, for instance.[30]

In the briefs submitted to the Supreme Court, the two parties largely relied on the opposing judicial opinions. The lawyers for the Police Commissioner argued that the addition to the handbill was a mere subterfuge. The concept of freedom of the press required them to make a distinction between commercial advertisements and opinion or protest literature:

> Commercial advertisements do not serve to aid the public in the discovery of "political and economic truth"; they serve only to make known to the public what the advertiser seeks to sell. Their motive is not "public education"; it is by definition always one of personal profit. ... To deny the City the power to remedy a patent evil by the only effective means of doing so is ... to exalt the business interests of the few above the welfare of the many.[31]

The brief submitted on behalf of Mr. Chrestensen argued that there was no constitutional justification for the distinction between commercial or noncommercial advertising:

> The alleged distinction between so-called property rights and so-called personal rights is a superficial play on words. Property rights are not limited to inanimate matter, as land and chattels. The most sacred rights of merchant, mechanic, and farmer, of master and servant, are, when analyzed, personal rights of individuals and most of them relate to their interest in securing for themselves some form of property.

The brief had earlier pointed out that newspapers were commercial enterprises, operated to make a profit.[32]

The amicus brief of the New York City Committee of the American Civil Liberties Union was more thorough-going in its support of Mr. Chrestensen's position. It claimed that,

> It is impossible to make a philosophically sound distinction between commercial and non-commercial handbills. ... If lines are to be drawn we submit that the basis of the distinction should be, not whether the matter distributed attracts attention to an article of commerce, but whether it is itself such an article or is a means of conveying information and opinion. For while the First Amendment is not designed to protect the sale of merchandise, we believe it covers all dissemination of "information and opinion" ... Information and opinion can relate to articles of commerce as well as to political or philosophical concepts.

They also pointed out that although Mr. Chrestensen aimed to make money exhibiting the submarine, the exhibit

> clearly had an educational and informative value. ... If the distribution of a leaflet

advertising this exhibit can be banned ... then, with equal logic, a leaflet could be banned which announced the holding of a lecture on some literary or artistic subject at which an admission fee was to be charged. For in such case it would be reasonable to suppose that the management of the lecture expected to make money out of it.

They also pointed out that the use of handbills was a means of advertising for small businessmen who could not afford radio or newspaper advertising.[33]

There are a series of questions involved in a case such as this. Is advertising, which is invariably either speech or writing or its equivalent, covered by the First Amendment? If the touchstone for protection under the First Amendment were that the message had to be spoken or written, there would be no problem: all advertising would be covered by the First Amendment. But if it is decided that advertising (or some advertising) is not covered by the First Amendment, it becomes necessary to distinguish between the uncovered messages and those other messages that are covered by the doctrine of freedom of speech. An advertising message is one designed to increase the sales or decrease the costs of providing some other service. Defined in this way, a speech by a lawyer, whether on a legal topic or not, made in order that potential clients should become aware of him or an article written by a professor in order to attract attention to himself and enable him to obtain a better position, or even the provision of a television program (say on public television) as a result of sponsorship by a firm would also be advertising. Economically, they are advertising and would be analyzed by an economist as such. But presumably the examination of motives which such a distinction would require would in general make it an impossible basis on which to found a legal distinction. Presumably the only advertising which potentially could be excluded from the protection of the First Amendment would be that which directly affected the sales of the product or service, or its costs. But this immediately raises the question of whether such advertising would be covered by the First Amendment when the business wishes to affect its sales or costs by obtaining a change in the law or in the regulations of some regulatory agency, or is directed to altering the attitude of workers by, for example, decreasing their willingness to strike, or by increasing the votes cast for a candidate thought to support a law favorable to the business. If such advertising messages are protected, this would leave unprotected only messages which directly affected sales. But in such a category, would advertising designed to sell a newspaper, a book, an educational program or a religious emblem be protected by the First Amendment not because the advertising as such was covered but because what was being sold was covered? Or would the advertising be covered if the product was sold by a not-for-profit organization? If advertising for such products and by such organizations were protected by the First Amendment, this would only leave without protection advertising by profit-making organizations which directly affected sales of products not covered by the First Amendment. But even in such cases, would the motive of the buyer rather than the seller be relevant? It is possible to buy something which itself seems to have no relationship at all to the concerns of the First Amendment, but whose purchase is clearly to further some end which is normally protected by the First Amendment. Take, for example, Mr. Chrestensen's submarine. Surely someone might wish to inspect the submarine in order to be able to come to a better opinion on defense expenditures and defense policy—a newspaper article which described the submarine and which was read with the same aim in view would clearly be protected. If the purpose for which the product is demanded is relevant, it becomes very difficult to put any bounds on the products the advertising of which could be brought within the protection of the First Amendment, since at one time or another almost any product will be necessary for facilitating the creation or spread of ideas. Unless the courts adopt the position either that *all* advertising or that *no* advertising is within the protection of the First Amendment, they face an almost insuperable task in deciding where to draw the line. At the same time, it is hardly possible for the courts to hold that no advertising is protected by the First Amendment. An erosion of the ruling in *Valentine v. Chrestensen* ultimately could hardly be avoided. And so it was to prove. But is there any resting place before reaching the point at which all advertising is covered by the First Amendment? That we have to discover.

The first questioning of the ruling in *Valentine v. Chrestensen* in the Supreme Court came in *Cammarano v. United States*.[34] The question involved in this case was whether the owners of a wholesale beer business could deduct from income for income tax purposes sums spent for advertisements which were designed to persuade voters to vote against a proposal which would have placed the retail trade in wine and beer in Washington exclusively in the hands of the State and which would have adversely affected and might indeed have destroyed their business. It was argued that the inability to deduct the full expenses for these advertisements raised a constitutional issue under the First Amendment, but no great stress was laid on this argument and *Valentine v. Chrestensen* does not seem to have been mentioned in any of the briefs. In any event, the Supreme Court rejected the view that the tax procedures violated the First Amendment. Justice Douglas, however, in a concurring opinion, took advantage of the opportunity to repudiate the Court's opinion in *Valentine v. Chrestensen*, of which he had himself been a member. The ruling, he said, "was casual, almost offhand." And it had not "survived reflection." Justice Douglas argued that the First Amendment is not "confined to discourse of a particular kind." It has been considered "essential to the exposition and exchange of political ideas, to the expression of philosophical attitudes, to the flowering of the letters," but "it has not been restricted to them." Protests against actions which would produce monetary loss come within the protection of the First Amendment, for example, picketing.

> A protest against government action that affects a business occupies as high a place. The profit motive should make no difference, for that is an element inherent in the very conception of a press under our system of free enterprise. Those who make their living through exercise of First Amendment rights are no less entitled to its protection than those whose advocacy or promotion is not hitched to a profit motive.

As a result, Justice Douglas found it "difficult to draw a line between that group and those who in other lines of endeavor advertise their wares by different means." In effect, what Justice Douglas seemed to be saying was that in his view, all advertising is protected by the First Amendment.[35] This is the position which the majority in the United States Court of Appeals seemed to hold when they tried *Valentine v. Chrestensen* and it was certainly the view expressed by the New York City Committee of the American Civil Liberties Union in their amicus brief.

In *New York Times v. Sullivan*[36], a police commissioner in Alabama sued the *New York Times* (and others) for statements appearing in a paid advertisement which he alleged to be libellous. He won his case in the Alabama courts but lost in the Supreme Court, in part, because, unless it could be shown that there was "actual malice," the making of false statements about public officials was protected by the First Amendment. The lawyers for the police commissioner had argued that the First Amendment did not apply to a "commercial" advertisement, relying on *Valentine v. Chrestensen*. This argument was rejected since the advertisement "communicated information, expressed opinion, recited grievances, protested claimed abuses, and sought financial support on behalf of a movement whose existence and objectives are matters of the highest public interest and concern."[37] The fact that the *Times* "was paid for publishing the advertisement" was considered as "immaterial." This presumably established that "non-commercial" advertising, or at least some categories of it, is protected by the First Amendment and also that the question of whether the publication was undertaken for a profit was irrelevant. This ruling also makes clear that the constitutional protection afforded to "non-commercial" advertisements applies even though what it says is false. The opinion quotes with approval an earlier statement of the Supreme Court, to the effect that the constitutional protection does not turn upon "the truth, popularity, or social utility of the ideas and beliefs which are offered." It even states that "a false statement may be deemed to make a valuable contribution to public debate, since it brings about," quoting Mill "the clearer perception and livelier impression of truth, produced by its collision with error" thus exhibiting great confidence in the ability of people to distinguish truth from falsehood.[38] Justice Black in a concurring opinion states that an "unconditional right to say what one pleases about public affairs is ... the minimum guarantee of the First Amendment" and regrets that the Court stopped short of saving this. Justice Goldberg expressed the view that the theory of the Constitution was that

> every citizen may speak his mind and every newspaper express its view on matters of public concern and may not be barred from speaking or publishing because those in control of government think that what is said or written is unwise, unfair, false, or malicious, which comes to the same thing as saying that on "matters of public concern," people should be allowed to speak or write things which are unwise, unfair, false or malicious.[39]

The next important case was *Pittsburgh Press Co. v. Pittsburgh Commission on Human Relations* decided in the Supreme Court in 1973. An ordinance of the Pittsburgh Commission on Human Relations was interpreted to mean that, a few exceptions apart, newspapers could not have sex-designated columns in "help wanted" advertisements. The issue was whether an ordinance which told a newspaper how it should arrange its advertisement pages infringed the First Amendment. Five justices decided it did not; four that it did. The majority relied on the ruling in the *Chrestensen* case. The advertisements were described as "classic examples of commercial speech,"[40] thus distinguishing the case from *New York Times v. Sullivan*. The argument that "commercial speech" should be given a higher level of protection than had been suggested by *Chrestensen*, that "the exchange of information is as important in the commercial realm as in any other," was found "unpersuasive" by the majority: "Discrimination in employment is not only commercial activity, it is *illegal* commercial activity..." The majority ended their opinion by emphasizing that their decision did not give the government authority

> to forbid Pittsburgh Press to publish and distribute advertisements commenting on the Ordinance, the enforcement practices of the Commission, or the propriety of sex

preferences in employment. Nor, **a fortiori**, does our decision authorize any restriction whatever, whether of content or layout, on stories or commentary originated by Pittsburgh Press, its columnists, or its contributors. On the contrary, we reaffirm unequivocally the protection afforded to editorial judgment and to the free expression of views on these and other issues, however controversial. We hold only that the Commission's modified order, narrowly drawn to prohibit placement in sex-designated columns of advertisements for nonexempt job opportunities, does not infringe the First Amendment rights of Pittsburgh Press.[41]

The other four Justices were not convinced. Mr. Chief Justice Burger, in his dissent, said that the decision

launches the courts on what I perceive to be a treacherous path of defining what layout and organizational decisions newspapers are "sufficiently associated" with the "commercial" parts of the papers as to be constitutionally unprotected and therefore subject to governmental regulation. ... The First Amendment freedom of press includes the right of a newspaper to arrange the content of its paper, whether it be news items, editorials, or advertising, as it sees fit.

Justice Douglas repeated his view that commercial materials also have First Amendment protection. Mr. Justice Stewart said the question is whether the government

can tell a newspaper in advance what it can print and what it cannot. ... The Court today holds that a government agency can force a newspaper publisher to print his classified advertising pages in a certain way in order to carry out governmental policy. After this decision, I see no reason why government cannot force a newspaper publisher to conform in the same way in order to achieve other goals thought socially desirable. And if government can dictate the layout of a newspaper's classified advertising pages today, what is there to prevent it from dictating the layout of the news pages tomorrow?[42]

The next case, *Bigelow v. Virginia*[43], decided in 1975, was to shatter whatever reliance may have been placed on the earlier cases but if it extended the protection afforded to advertisements, it also made the boundaries more indefinite. Bigelow was editor of a newspaper which carried an advertisement for an abortion service in New York. A Virginia law made it a misdemeanor to "encourage or prompt the procuring of abortion" by means, among other things, of an advertisement. Bigelow was convicted and his conviction was upheld by the Virginia Supreme Court, which largely relied on *Valentine v. Chrestensen*. The case against Bigelow, in the light of the earlier cases, was clearly strong: the business which advertised was a profit-making organization; the advertisement involved a commercial transaction, not a discussion of public policy; the market in medical services is commonly, and extensively, regulated by the government. The decision in the Virginia courts was, however, reversed, but in an opinion whose exact meaning is difficult to discern. The comment made by Justice Rehnquist, in a dissenting opinion (with which Justice White concurred), seems well taken:

> The Court's opinion does not confront head on the question which this case poses, but makes contact with it only in a series of verbal sideswipes. The result is the fashioning of a doctrine which appears designed to obtain reversal of this judgment, but at the same time to save harmless from the effects of that doctrine the many prior cases of this Court which are inconsistent with it.[44]

That part of the majority opinion which deals with the application of the First Amendment to Bigelow's advertisement is as follows:

> The legitimacy of appellant's First Amendment claim in the present case is demonstrated by the important differences between the advertisement presently at

issue and those involved in *Chrestensen* and in *Pittsburgh Press*. The advertisement published in appellant's newspaper did more than simply propose a commercial transaction. It contained factual material of clear "public interest." Portions of its message, most prominently the lines, "Abortions are now legal in New York. There are no residency requirements," involve the exercise of the freedom of communicating information and disseminating opinion.

Viewed in its entirety, the advertisement conveyed information of potential interest and value to a diverse audience—not only to readers possibly in need of the services offered, but also to those with a general curiosity about, or genuine interest in, the subject matter or the law of another State and its development, and to readers seeking reform in Virginia. The mere existence of the Women's Pavilion in New York City, with the possibility of its being typical of other organizations there, and the availability of the services offered, were not unnewsworthy. Also, the activity [abortion] advertised pertained to constitutional interests...

Moreover, the placement services advertised ...were legally provided in New York at that time.

We conclude, therefore, that the Virginia courts erred in their assumptions that advertising, as such, was entitled to no First Amendment protection and that appellant Bigelow had no legitimate First Amendment interest. We need not decide in this case the precise extent to which the First Amendment permits regulation of advertising that is related to activities the State may legitimately regulate or even prohibit.

... To the extent that commercial activity is subject to regulation, the relationship of speech to that activity may be one factor, among others, to be considered in weighing the First Amendment interest against the governmental interest alleged. Advertising is not thereby stripped of all First Amendment protection. The relationship of speech to the marketplace of products or of services does not make it valueless in the marketplace of ideas.

...The diverse motives, means, and messages of advertising may make speech "commercial" in widely varying degrees. We need not decide here the extent to which constitutional protection is afforded commercial advertising under all circumstances and in the face of all kinds of regulation.[45]

Justice Rehnquist comments that if the advertisement was protected by the First Amendment,

> the subject of the advertisement ought to make no difference. It will not do to say, as the Court does, that this advertisement conveyed information about the "subject matter of the law of another State and its development" to those "seeking reform in Virginia" and that it related to abortion, as if these factors somehow put it on a different footing from other commercial advertising. This was a proposal to furnish services on a commercial basis, and since we have always refused to distinguish for First Amendment purposes on the basis of content, it is no different from an advertisement for a bucket shop operation or a Ponzi scheme which has its headquarters in New York. If Virginia may not regulate advertising of commercial abortion agencies because of the interest of those seeking to reform Virginia's abortion laws, it is difficult to see why it is not likewise precluded from regulating advertising for an out-of-state bucket shop on the ground that such information might be of interest to those interested in repealing Virginia's "blue sky" laws...
>
> Assuming *arguendo* that this advertisement is something more than a normal commercial proposal, I am unable to see why Virginia does not have a legitimate public interest in its regulation. The Court apparently concedes ... and our cases have long held, that the States have a strong interest in the prevention of commercial advertising in the health field—both in order to maintain high ethical standards in the medical profession and to protect from unscrupulous practices.[46]

Justice Rehnquist considers the advertisement "commercial advertising" and holds that such "commercial advertising" does not enjoy constitutional protection.

It seems clear that much of our economic regulation is concerned with the provision of information to consumers and, if it is to be effective, also requires advertising to be regulated. Justice Rehnquist would presumably hold that there would be no constitutional bar to such regulation. We may regret both the original regulation and the regulation of advertising to which it leads but Justice Rehnquist's position, unlike that of the majority, is at least understandable. However, if the various statements about regulation made in the majority opinion come to be treated as of secondary importance, and emphasis is placed on their statement that "the advertisement conveyed information of potential interest and value to a diverse audience" and this is regarded as enough to afford First Amendment protection, then, given modern economists' findings about the informational value of advertising, we may expect to find in future a much greater range of commercial advertising brought within the scope of the First Amendment.

The regulations of the Federal Trade Commission which have as their aim the preventing of "false and misleading" advertising would seem to impinge directly on activities of a kind which normally would seem to come within the protection of the First Amendment. The determination by a government agency that a statement is false is completely alien to the doctrine of free speech and of freedom of the press.

The rationale of the First Amendment is that only if an idea is subject to competition in the marketplace can it be discovered (through acceptance or rejection) whether it is false or not. The viewpoint which underlies the giving of authority to the Federal Trade Commission to determine by an administrative procedure whether a statement is false or not has a very different character. It substitutes a government decree for the working of an uncontrolled marketplace. The contrast between the philosophy which supports the First Amendment and that which gives such authority to the Federal Trade Commission is even more striking when it has to decide not whether a statement is false but whether it is misleading. This means that the Commission has to inquire into the way in which information will be used before deciding whether it will allow it to be disseminated, the very kind of activity which the First Amendment is supposed to discourage the government from undertaking. And when in the performance of its task the Federal Trade Commission has to judge between conflicting scientific views (as may also be true when it is investigating alleged "false" advertising), the actions of the Commission, as Professor Posner remarks, are inconsistent with the spirit of the First Amendment. Nor does an investigation of the actual performance of the Commission, such as that undertaken by Professor Posner, allay our anxieties. And to judge from a recent staff memorandum of the Federal Trade Commission (issued December 4, 1974), which argues that the Commission has the power to regulate at least some kinds of corporate image advertising, that is, advertising not directly related to the sale of the firm's products or services, some within the Commission claim that it has powers which go far beyond what we would ordinarily think of as regulation of advertising.[47] Similarly, the recent decision of the Federal Trade Commission to proceed against firms, not because their advertising is "false" but because it incorporates claims without there being a reasonable basis for them, will involve a government determination of what is a reasonable basis for holding an opinion, something on which normally there will be no possible basis on which people could agree, as well as an enquiry into the beliefs of those making the claim. It will involve the very kind of governmental action which it is the purpose of the First Amendment to prevent.[48]

We may see what the present situation is by considering some of the cases. Two cases, dealing with the dissemination of the same information (or misinformation) carried out in two different ways, in one of which it was decided that the Federal Trade Commission could regulate but not in the other, illustrate the way in which the American legal system handles the problem and the paradox to which it leads. In the first case, *Perma-Maid Co. v. Federal Trade Commission*, decided in June 1941 by the Circuit Court of Appeals, it was held that it was legal for the Commission to prohibit a firm manufacturing stainless steel utensils from representing "that food prepared or kept in aluminum utensils was detrimental to health," and that the preparation of food in aluminum utensils "caused formation of poisons and that the consumption of such food would cause ulcers, cancers, cancerous growths and other ailments, afflictions and diseases." [49] The Commission had concluded that these representations were both false and misleading, that aluminum cooking and storage utensils were quite satisfactory and did not produce poisons or cause diseases. The special interest of the case from our standpoint comes from the fact that the representations to which the Commission objected were found in pamphlets and circulars which were not written was published by Perma-Maid but were merely distributed by them, presumably because the information (or misinformation) contained in them would increase the demand for their products, in much the same way as a baby food manufacturer might distribute a book on the joys of motherhood. However, the Commission was not content to leave the matter there. It also proceeded against the author of the pamphlets and the firm which published and sold them in *Scientific Mfg. Co. v. Federal Trade Commission*.[50] The pamphlets were written by a chemist, Force, who wished "to propagate his own unorthodox ideas and theories." Neither Force nor the company of which he was president and which published the pamphlets had any interest in the manufacture or sale of cooking utensils. The Commission found the statements in the pamphlets "false, misleading and disparaging" and held that the pamphlets were an "instrumentality by means of which uninformed or unscrupulous manufacturers, distributors, dealers and salesmen may deceive or mislead members of the purchasing public and induce them to purchase utensils made from materials other than aluminum."[51] The Commission therefore ordered Force and his company to cease and desist from distributing the pamphlets. The Circuit Court of Appeals held (in October 1941) that, according to their reading of the Federal Trade Commission Act, the Federal Trade Commission did not have the authority to enjoin the distribution of the pamphlets because Force and his company were not "engaged or materially interested in the cooking utensil trade." But they also indicated that the Federal Trade Commission was barred from preventing the distribution of the pamphlets by the First Amendment:

Surely Congress did not intend to authorize the Federal Trade Commission to foreclose expression of honest opinion in the course of one's business of voicing opinion. The same opinion ...[may become] enjoinable by [the Federal Trade Commission] if ... it is utilized in the trade to mislead or deceive the public or to harm a competitor.[52]

The result is paradoxical in the extreme. If "false and misleading" information is disseminated by a firm with a clear economic interest in deceiving or misleading consumers, and about whose statements on the subject, therefore, consumers are likely to be most suspicious and least likely to be deceived, the distribution of the "false and misleading" information can be prevented. However, someone without any economic interest is disseminating "false and misleading" information and whose statements therefore consumers are more likely to believe is allowed to distribute the misinformation.

The regulations of professional associations, such as those of doctors, lawyers, pharmacists and opticians (which have often been given the force of law by making conformity to them a condition for state licensing to practice) commonly prohibit advertising by members of the association. So far as I know, the early cases which challenged these regulations did not lay great stress on the First Amendment. This is, however, in process of change.

In 1975, in the United States District Court, Virginia, as a result of a case brought against the State Board of Pharmacy, it was held unconstitutional, under the First Amendment, to prohibit price advertising by pharmacists.[53] The argument against the law was that the advertising was informational, that to prohibit price advertising made it more difficult for consumers to discover where drugs could be purchased at least cost and that this caused greatest hardship to the elderly and poor. It was further argued that "the First Amendment assures its freedoms to the auditor and reader as stoutly as it does the speaker and writer." The State Board of Pharmacy relied on the ruling in the *Chrestensen* case that commercial speech or writing is not protected by the First Amendment. The court rejected this argument: "The right-to-know is the foundation of the First Amendment. ... Consumers are denied this right by the Virginia statute." They also argued that the "belief that price advertising will inflate the market for the drugs is wholly untenable, since the medicine is controlled by prescriptions of physicians and so the sale of the drugs is not even at the druggists' will."[54] This is an awkward and potentially very dangerous qualification. It suggests that advertising would only be protected by the First Amendment when it did not lead to behavior regarded as undesirable by the government. In this case, advertising is desirable because government regulation has made sure that drugs are only demanded in circumstances in which they ought to be used and the lower prices benefit the elderly and poor.

This case was followed by another quite similar case in California, *Terry v. California State Board of Pharmacy*.[55] Shirley Terry was a recipient of public assistance who would have to take drugs for the rest of her life. The issue before the court was narrowly circumscribed. The injunction sought only applied to price advertising. "The plaintiffs are not asserting a right to receive information concerning the quality, effectiveness or capabilities of the drugs, information which tends more directly to promote the product ... the narrow issue before this court is whether low-income consumers of prescription drugs are entitled under the First Amendment to receive information consisting of the retail price at which pharmacies sell prescription drugs."[56] Relying on recent Supreme Court decisions, such as *Pittsburgh Press* and *New York Times v. Sullivan*, the court notes that commercial speech has been given some First Amendment protection. The advertising in this case could be distinguished from advertising "designed to promote the sale of a product," to which the doctrine of *Chrestensen* applied.

While [price] information is commercial in that it consists of data upon which a consumer may base a decision to purchase, it is not promotional in the same sense as the advertising of cigarettes or submarine tours. Prescription drugs may only be purchased when medically necessary. The consumer does not freely choose to buy the product; he is directed to do so by his physician. The information sought here will make it more likely that plaintiffs will be able to purchase these health essential items. The promotional advertising of cigarettes and submarine tours seeks to generate new demand for goods by consumers who had expressed no previous interest in the products. By touting the virtues of the product, the advertising is intended to create a commercial transaction that would not otherwise occur.

In the present case, if commercial transactions are created,

The health needs of the society are served, since a physician has already determined that the prescription drug ... is medically necessary to the well-being of the consumer-patient. Further, the advertising sought here is limited to price and does not extend to promotional gimmicks extolling the product and generating artificial demand.[57]

The reasons urged for supporting the prohibition on price advertising were four in number: (1) that it would "generate artifical demand for prescription drugs," (2) that it would mislead consumers, (3) that it would facilitate the forging of prescriptions, and (4) that it "would tend to lower the standards of the profession of pharmacy." The first reason, the court answered by pointing out that the prescription was subject to the control of the physician. The court also said that the posting of prices need not be deceptive and that the prohibition of price advertising was a "very indirect method of combating forgery." As for price advertising lowering the professional standards of pharmacists, the court said that such advertising "will not compel any pharmacist to lower the level of his professional practice."[58] No attention was given to the possibility that greater price competition might reduce the willingness, indeed ability, of the pharmacists to supply services such as advice on the proper use of drugs or the interaction of drugs taken on prescriptions from different doctors (to use examples given by the court), the argument being essentially the same as the so-called "service argument" for resale price maintenance. It was the court's view that the state's interests were only minimally advanced by prohibiting price advertising and the injunction requested by the plaintiff was therefore granted.

It is apparent that the development of the argument in both the Virginia and California cases is very similar. The decision in both cases was that the rationale of the First Amendment included a "right-to-know" and that therefore a prohibition on price advertising was unconstitutional. But the way in which this conclusion was reached is disquieting. While recognising the informational value of advertising in the case of price advertising, the opinions seemed to deny a similar informational value to advertising when it related to the "quality, effectiveness or capabilities" of drugs. However, once the informational value of price advertising is recognized, it seems difficult to deny all value to the advertising of other qualities of the drug or to pretend that all increases in demand brought about by advertising are "artificial," an adjective which seems to be used to denote "undesirable." It would seem probable that these decisions do not define the outer bounds of the applicability of the First Amendment to advertising but merely mark a stage in a gradual expansion of the kinds of commercial speech which will be brought within the protection of the First Amendment by the courts.

VI. Concluding Remarks

It is not easy to describe the present position of legal opinion on advertising and free speech. Only a poet can capture the essence of chaos. Nor is it easy to foresee how things will develop. Lacking any rationale for the First Amendment, with the courts depending on time-honored slogans to sustain conclusions, there is no obvious resting-place, from the moment the slogans cease to work their magic. At the present time, the courts are tending to bring a greater proportion of advertising within the protection of the First Amendment. And cases now proceeding through the courts, such as the litigation concerning what egg producers can say about the relationship between the consumption of high-cholesterol foods and heart disease, and by food concerns, on what can be said about margarine in advertisements, will undoubtedly continue the process.[59] Where will it end?

To express an opinion on such a question is obviously perilous but will be attempted as the basis for discussion. Strange though the workings of the legal system may be, they are not devoid of sense. I have argued, in my "Problem of Social Cost,"[60] that rights to perform certain action should be assigned in such a way as to maximize the total wealth (broadly defined) of the society. The same is true when we come to what are termed personal rights or civil liberties, the kind of activity covered by the First Amendment. Some legal writers have sought to treat First Amendment rights as being, in some sense, absolute and have objected to what is termed the "balancing" by the courts of these rights against others. But such "balancing" is inevitable if judges must direct their attention to the general welfare. Freedom to speak and write is bound to be restricted when exercise of these freedoms prevents the carrying out of other activities which people value. Thus it is reasonable that First Amendment freedoms should be curtailed when they impair the enjoyment of life (privacy), inflict great damage on others (slander and libel), are disturbing (loudness), destroy incentives to carry out useful work (copyright), create dangers for society (sedition and national security), or are offensive and corrupting (obscenity). The determination of the boundaries to which a doctrine can be applied is not likely to come about in a very conscious or even consistent way. But it is through recognition of the fact that rights should be assigned to those to whom they are most valuable that such boundaries come to be set.

As we have seen from our discussion of the cases, it is only in recent years that there has been any serious consideration of the relation of advertising to freedom of speech and of writing. Now that the value of advertising in providing information has been accepted, it seems improbable that it will long be thought that this is true only for price advertising. And the action of the Federal Trade Commission in treating prohibitions by professional associations of advertising by their members as anticompetitive will bring greater awareness of the informational role of advertising. Similarly, the many studies of the failures of governmental regulatory agencies which have been made in recent years, are bound to make the courts somewhat reluctant to expand and more willing to take advantage of opportunities to contract the regulation of advertising. Where will it end? It seems likely that the law will be interpreted to allow the Federal Trade Commission to continue to regulate false and deceptive advertising, but with greater freedom for what can be said in advertising than now exists, and with somewhat diminished powers for the various government agencies which regulate advertising.

Addendum

In the concluding paragraphs of my paper, I indicated the direction in which I thought the courts would probably move. A recent Supreme Court decision has confirmed the correctness of my general conclusion.

The case, discussed earlier, which involved the power of the Virginia State Board of Pharmacy to regulate the advertising of drug prices, was taken to the Supreme Court.[61] In an opinion which avoided those contortions which would have been necessitated by pretending that its earlier decisions were correct, the Supreme Court embraced, with little qualification, the doctrine that commercial speech was covered by the First Amendment. They note "in past decisions the Court has given some indication that commercial speech is unprotected" but this was the result of a "simplistic approach." With *Bigelow* "the notion of unprotected 'commercial speech' all but passed from the scene." In holding that commercial speech is protected by the First Amendment, they explain that they are not saying "that it can never be regulated in any way."

What is at issue is whether a State may completely suppress the dissemination of concededly truthful information about entirely lawful activity, fearful of that information's effect upon its disseminators and its recipients. Reserving other questions, we conclude that the answer to this one is in the negative.[62]

Now that it has been decided that commercial speech is covered by the First Amendment, consideration of the limits of its application, the inevitable "balancing," can proceed in a sensible manner, a process in which the studies by economists of the effects of advertising may be expected to play a useful role.

Notes

[1] R. H. Coase, The market for goods and the market for ideas, 64 *American Economic Review*, pt. 2, at 384 (Papers & Proceedings, May 1974).
[2] *Abrams v. United States*, 250 U.S. 616, 630 (1919).
[3] John Milton, *Areopagitica: A Speech for the Liberty of Unlicensed Printing* 6 (H. B. Cotterill ed. 1959).
[4] Id. at 29, 44.
[5] John Stuart Mill, *On Liberty, in Utilitarianism, Liberty, and Representative Government*, 150-151 (Everyman ed. 1951).
[6] Aaron Director, The parity of the economic market place, 7 *Journal of Law and Economiçs.* 1, 6 (1964).
[7] Adam Smith, *The Wealth of Nations,* 141 (Edwin Cannan ed. 1937).
[8] Raymond Urban & Richard Mancke, Federal regulation of whiskey labelling: From the repeal of prohibition to the present. 15 *Journal of Law and Economics.* 411, 426 (1972).
[9] Adam Smith, supra note 7, at 250.
[10] *Ideas v. Goods, Time,* January 14, 1974, at 28.
[11] Sam Peltzman, An evaluation of consumer protection legislation: The 1962 Drug Amendments, 81 *Journal of Political Economy.* 1049, 1076-1086 (1973).
[12] For a discussion of this subject, see John Henry Wigmore, *Evidence in Trials at Common Law,* at Book I (1940).
[13] Phillip Nelson, *The Economic Consequences of Advertising,* 48 J. Bus. 213 (1975).
[14] Frank Hyneman Knight, *The Ethics of Competition and Other Essays,* 22 (1935).
[15] Id.
[16] Id. at 22-23.
[17] Lee Benham, The effect of advertising on the price of eyeglasses. 15 *Journal of Law and Economics.* 337 (1972).
[18] Richard A. Posner, Regulation of advertising by the FTC 18-19 (*American Enterprise Institute Evaluative Studies,* no. 11, Nov., 1973).
[19] Id. at 21.
[20] Thomas I. Emerson, *Toward a General Theory of the First Amendment* (1966).
[21] Id. at vii-viii.
[22] Id. at 6.

[23] Id. at 3-15.
[24] Supra note 6, at 6.
[25] Supra note 20, at 105n.
[26] *Valentine v. Christensen,* 316 U.S. 52 (1942) rev'd 122 F.2d 511 (2d Cir. 1942).
[27] Id. at 54-55.
[28] 122 F.2d 511, 515-516.
[29] 122 F.2d 517, 519, 521.
[30] Id. at 522, 524.
[31] Brief for Petitioner at 16, 24-25.
[32] Brief for Respondent at 14.
[33] Brief of N.Y.C. Comm. of the A.C.L.U. as Amicus Curiae, at 2, 3, 5.
[34] *Cammarano v. United States,* 358 U.S. 498 (1959).
[35] Id. at 514.
[36] *New York Times v. Sullivan,* 376 U.S. 254, 266 (1964).
[37] Id. at 226.
[38] Id. at 271, 279 n.19.
[39] Id. at 297, 299 (Black & Goldberg, JJ. concurring).
[40] *Pittsburgh Press v. Pittsburgh Comm'n on Human Relations,* 413 U.S. 376, 385 (1973).
[41] Id. at 391.
[42] Quotations from dissents will be found in 413 U.S. 393-395, 400, 403-404.
[43] *Bigelow v. Virginia,* 421 U.S. 809 (1975).
[44] Id. at 829-830.
[45] Id. at 821-822, 825-826.
[46] Id. at 831-832.
[47] Federal Trade Commission, Statement of proposed enforcement policy regarding corporate image advertising (December 4, 1974).
[48] See Gerald J. Thain, advertising regulation: The contemporary FTC approach, *Fordham Urban Law Journal.* 349, 376-381 (1973).
[49] *Perma-Maid Co. v. Federal Trade Commission,* 121 F.2d 282, 284 (6th Cir. 1941).
[50] *Scientific Mfg. Co. v. Fed. Trade Comm'n,* 124 F.2d 640 (3d Cir. 1941).
[51] Id. at 641-642.
[52] Id. at 644-645.
[53] *Virginia Citizens Consumer Council, Inc. v. State Bd. of Pharmacy,* 373 F. Supp. 683 (1974), aff'd, 425 U.S. 748 (1976).
[54] Id. at 685, 687.
[55] *Shirley Terry v. California State Bd. of Pharmacy,* 395 F. Supp. 94 (E.D. Va. 1975), aff'd, 96 S. Ct. 2617 (1976).
[56] Id. at 99.
[57] Id. at 102.
[58] Id. at 105-106.

[59] *Fed. Trade Comm'n v. Nat'l Comm'n* on Egg Nutrition, 517 F.2d 485 (1975), cert. denied, 96 S. Ct. 2623 (1976); and *Anderson, Clayton & Co. v. Washington State Dep't* of Agriculture, 402 F. Supp. 1253 (W.D. Wash. 1975).

[60] R. H. Coase, The problem of social cost, 3 *Journal of Law and Economics.* 1 (1960).

[61] *Va. State Bd. of Pharmacy v. Virginia Citizens Consumer Council,* 425 U.S. 748 (1976). 1830, 1831 (1976).

[62] Id. at 773.

Series III

Empirical Study

Ning Wang

The third series consists of two empirical papers. "Payola in Radio and Television Broadcasting" is an exemplary case study of the impact of changes in the law on the working of the economy. Payola refers to undisclosed payments made to obtain inclusion of materials in broadcast programs. Coase discovered that payola was a common business practice that had long existed in the music industry and migrated into the radio and broadcasting industry in the 1930s before it was criminalized in 1960 by the United States government. Payola was a pricing mechanism and a source of income for DJs and station owners, an advertising payment for record companies, a rival for music publishers, and in the eyes of some congressmen and government agents a "corrupted" and "deceptive" channel of "bad music." The legislation against payola, pushed by many forces with differing intentions, affected multiple margins. Many of these, not surprisingly, served some special business interests instead of the public interest, and at the expense of small players.

"Blackmail" is the only article Coase (1988b) wrote that falls squarely into the economic analysis of law. He examined the so-called "paradox of blackmail" in legal literature: Although it may be lawful to do something, it becomes unlawful to demand money for refraining from doing it. Coase approached blackmail as an economist and reframed the question, "When is it right and when wrong to pay someone not to do something?" Extending the powerful economic analysis developed in "The Problem of Social Cost," "Blackmail" provides an economic rationale for the law against blackmail: Blackmail contains a common feature shared by all other criminal activities in that they all damage, or threaten to damage, property. In his analysis, Coase also brought out the law's economic impact. The laws concerning blackmail, like other branches of criminal law, serve a vital economic function, to protect and preserve property in society and enhance its efficient employment.

Coase conducted empirical work in the form of case study, a method that has long been discredited among modern economists, who, thanks to growing computing power and financial resources, place their wager instead on statistical analysis of aggregated data and more recently on research designs that utilize random controlled trials and quasi-experiments to deliver credible results (e.g., Angrist and Pischke, 2010). Eschewing formal methods, Coase deployed basic economic reasoning to analyze and illuminate the problem at hand. His prosaic writing is detailed, meticulous, and perceptive. For present-day scholars in empirical law and economics, who are constantly worried about missing data and identification strategies, Coase's empirical work, with a total absence of technical sophistication, might seem homespun and outdated. It is up to them to show, however, what added values and further insights econometrics can bring to Coase's case study. In the meantime, we have to admit that there simply is no golden path to truth, highway or low way. That something close to a golden path is in our possession is a fatal deceit. Pluralism in methods is our best bet.

Coase's disparaging remarks made in the early 1960s, "if you torture data enough, nature will always confess," must have antagonized many data analysts. Yet, two decades later Edward Leamer (1983) admitted in plain words in *American Economic Review* that "hardly anyone takes anyone else's data analyses seriously". A recent retrospective view comes to corroborate Coase's suspicion of the abuse of statistics, "much of the applied econometrics of the 1970s and early 1980s lacked credibility" (Angrist and Pischke, 2010). We have to leave it to scholars in the future to decide whether randomized controlled trials will fare better.[1]

Leaving aside the technical issues, we can better appreciate a striking feature of Coase's approach to empirical work. Most economists take their models as a laboratory to test out ideas in an ideal situation. Empirical work is carried out to identify what factors cause a certain event; this search for causality is detached from, and often done without, asking why and how the causes actually work, and how significant they are relative to collaborating background factors. In both cases, there is little pressure to get hands dirty and grasp the iceberg of detailed mechanisms and processes beneath the tip of causal factors. In contrary, Coase insisted on the real world economy as the only legitimate laboratory for economists to see what works and what does not. He disparaged the common practice that "when economists find that they are unable to analyze what is happening in the real world, they invent an imaginary world which they are capable of handling" (1988c). Nonetheless, Coase's direct approach and case study method is costly in time, impossible to standardize, and hard to emulate. We hope this volume can help to bring down the cost of learning and doing Coasean law and economics and thus expand its market share.

---

[1] For an early cautionary assessment, see Deaton and Cartwright (2017). The authors warn us that, "Which method is most likely to yield a good causal inference depends on what we are trying to discover as well as on what is already known. When little prior knowledge is available, no method is likely to yield well-supported conclusions."

Payola in Radio and Television Broadcasting[*]

I. Introduction

Payola in radio and television broadcasting may be defined as undisclosed payments (or other inducements) which are given to bring about the inclusion of material in broadcast programs.[1] The making of such payments has become a crime as a result of amendments to the Communications Act in 1960[2], and is now prohibited by regulations of the Federal Communications Commission (FCC)[3]. The aim of this paper is (1) to discover why these payments came to be made, (2) to consider whether the results of allowing such payments should be regarded as beneficial or harmful, and, in the light of this, (3) to evaluate the worth of the 1960 amendments to the Communications Act and of the FCC's regulations.

---

[*] *Journal of Law and Economics*, 1979, 22(2), 269-328. I am greatly indebted to Mrs. Clara Ann Bowler who, as research assistant, showed considerable enterprise in unearthing information on payola from a wide variety of sources. I am also grateful for financial assistance to the Law and Economics Program of the University of Chicago Law School and the Foundation for Research in Economics and Education. I have to thank officials of both the Federal Communications Commission and the Federal Trade Commission for their help in providing me with information. They are not, of course, responsible in any way for the use which I have made of this information. It is pleasant to recall that I started to write this paper at Stanford University in 1977 while a Senior Research Fellow at the Hoover Institution. In revising this paper, I have greatly benefited from comments made by participants at seminars at UCLA and the Hoover Institution and by written comments by Professors Edmund W. Kitch, John H. Langbein, H. Douglas Laycock, Bernard D. Meltzer, and Geoffrey R. Stone of the University of Chicago Law School and by Professor Earl A. Thompson of UCLA.

To understand why payola became so common in the broadcasting industry it should be realised that payola became a feature of the broadcasting industry not in the late 1950s, when the practice received considerable publicity in the press and was investigated by a congressional committee, but in the 1930s and that it entered the broadcasting industry simply as a continuation of business practices which were normal in the popular music industry. Section II gives an account of the history of payola (or its equivalent) in the popular music industry. This shows not only why such payments were made but also why it was to be expected that payola would ultimately make its appearance in the broadcasting industry. Nor should it be supposed that the 1960 amendments to the Communications Act represented the first attempt to regulate payola. As is demonstrated in Section III, numerous attempts had been made over a long period before 1960 to do this. The main proponents of such regulation were the music publishers and their arguments in support of their position make clear the effects such regulation was expected to produce. The 1960 amendments were, however, brought about by a combination of events which took place in the 1950s. These events are described in Section IV. An account is given in Sections V and VI of the resulting change in the law and of its implementation by the FCC. In Section VII, I consider, in the light of the historical materials in the earlier sections, what effects the 1960 amendments are likely to produce and I attempt to assess whether the situation brought about by the change in the law represents, on balance, an improvement in the situation.

II. Payola in the Popular Music Industry

Payola in connection with radio programs seems first to have been noticed in the press in the late 1930s. It was then reported that dance band leaders and performers were given gifts by music publishers to induce them to include certain songs in their programs.[4] This was the period of the "big bands" and their performances in hotels and ballrooms were regularly broadcast by radio stations. The popularity of a song and therefore the sales of sheet music as well as performance royalties (and therefore the profits of the firm that published the song) depended, so it was thought, on its "exposure" by the "big bands" and it was therefore understandable that music publishers should endeavour to get them to play their pieces. Given the inefficiency of barter, direct money payments were no doubt often made. Another arrangement said to be common was for a dance band leader to be given a financial interest in the publishing house or in the copyright of a song.[5]

Such payola was merely a continuation of practices which had long existed in the music industry. About a hundred years before payola became a feature of the radio broadcasting industry, it has been recorded of the London music publishing house, Novello, that members of the Novello family used to sing songs published by the firm with a view to increasing the sales of the firm's sheet music:

The sisters, Cecilia, Clara, and Sabrina Novello, either as singers or as teachers,... assisted directly and indirectly to further the love for music ... and to augment the fortunes of the house, by bringing its publications into notice. This valuable form of help, highly appreciated by Alfred Novello [the head of the firm], together with his own exertions as a vocalist, mitigated the cost of advertisement, which in those days was burdened with a heavy duty, and was oppressed by a capricious mode of estimating the amount.[6]

The Novello firm also organized choral concerts and the motive was no doubt in part to increase the demand for music published by Novello since it is not to be expected that music published by the sponsoring firm would be neglected. For example, we are told that in 1867, "Madame Arabella Goddard played at the Monday Popular Concert, for the first time in public, Book Eight of Mendelssohn's 'Lieder ohne Worte,' a few days before its publication by the firm."[7] There is no mention of musicians being paid to perform music at concerts not organized by the Novello firm although on occasion this may have been done. According to the head of the Boosey music publishing firm, this was certainly the practice of British music publishers late in the nineteenth century:

> In the old days the leading singers ... received a royalty for a term of years upon all new songs introduced by them ... There was a special reason for giving the leading singers royalties because if a leading soprano, contralto, tenor or baritone introduced a new song at the ballad concerts, all the smaller singers, according to their voices, would take up the ballads made popular by the star artists. After a while, however, a certain W. H. Hutchinson appeared on the horizon, and he saw at once, being publisher and composer, that he could never get his songs advertised through concerts under the big ballad concert system. He therefore approached all the smaller singers, and paid them so much a time for so many concerts, provided they sang one of the songs that he was pushing ... I was the first of the leading publishers to understand immediately that this new system was going to deal a severe blow to our old system, so, although we still paid the big singers royalties, I set to work at once subsidizing the small singers in the same way that Hutchinson did.[8]

Similar practices were also common in the United States. Books relating to the history of popular music in America are filled with accounts of the activities of song-pluggers, whose exploits often outshine those of the performers. Such books are not normally scholarly publications and lack detailed references to sources, and, indeed, are probably not accurate in all their particulars. But the general picture they paint is clear. Isaac Goldberg has described the efforts made in the 1880s and 1890s to switch the allegiance of a performer from one music publisher to another. "Pay his board bill ... Buy him a suit of clothes ... Promise her a glittering stone ... Present him with a trunk ... Subsidize his act with a weekly pourboire. The performer heard but one refrain: 'Sing our song!' "[9] Edward B. Marks, a leading American music publisher, has written of this same period as follows:

The best songs came from the gutter in those days. Indeed, when I began publishing in 1894, there was no surer way of starting a song off to popularity than to get it sung as loudly as possible in the city's lowest dives ... When a number was introduced from the stage of one of the more pretentious beer halls, that was a plug! And a plug ... is any public performance which is calculated to boost a song ... In the nineties, a young music publisher had to know his way about the night spots. It was important to get his wares before the bibulous public; so he had to spend a large part of his time making the rounds for plugs, and more plugs ... Sixty joints a week I used to make. Joe Stern, my partner, covered about forty. What's more, we did it every week.[10]

Later, he remarked that the "train of association whereby 'Annie Rooney' eventually appeared on the piano in a small town banker's house would have shocked many a fine community."[11]

Isaac Goldberg says this of the song-plugger: "The Plugger ... is the publisher's lobbyist wherever music is played. He it is who, by all the arts of persuasion, intrigue, bribery, mayhem, malfeasance, cajolery, entreaty, threat, insinuation, persistence and whatever else he has, sees to it that his employer's music shall be heard."[12] Services mentioned as being provided to performers by music publishers include free copies of sheet music[13], orchestral arrangements[14], and rehearsal rooms[15]. In addition, gifts and money were given to performers as an inducement to sing particular songs. It is reported of the Shapiro-Bernstein firm that from its inception (in the 1890s), it "instituted a policy of getting stage stars to sing their songs by means of tactful, though not always inexpensive, bribes. Lottie Gilson, for example, was once presented a diamond ring valued at $500."[16] And we are told that (also in the early 1890s) a composer-publisher, Charles K. Harris, was "able to place his song (*After the Ball*) in Charles Hoyt's fabulous extravaganza *A Trip to Chinatown* by the simple expedient of paying the singing star, J. Aldrich Libbey, $500 in cash and a percentage of the song's royalties."[17]

Isaac Goldberg tells us that in the middle 1890s, an attempt was made to eliminate such payments. The music publishers "banded together and agreed to give up the practice of buying singers to plug their works." However, the agreement was not successful. "Publishers began to make secret arrangements with headliners; the duplicity was discovered, and the lid blew off."[18] By the early 1900s, such song-plugging arrangements seem to have been commonplace. "To get a musical comedy star or vaudeville headliner to use a song was ... the surest way a plugger knew to launch a song successfully and keep it alive for years ... Before long, performers were beginning to get a regular weekly stipend from a publisher."[19] Of Al Jolson in the 1910s, the same author says that he made "more song hits than any other single performer of his generation. Along Tin Pan Alley, it became a truism that to get Jolson to sing a song was to have a big hit on your hands. Publishers used cajolery, flattery, the intercession of Jolson's closest friends to get him to sing their numbers. When these failed, bribery was called upon. One publisher gave him the gift of a race horse; others got him a cut in a song's royalties; still others listed him as collaborating lyricist or composer." [20] Al Jolson provides but a spectacular example of a common practice. The position as it existed in 1912 was described in *Variety*:

> A few seasons ago the vaudeville singer selected the song wanted, and blithely asked the publisher for a weekly salary to sing it. Not all did but the great majority. The publisher paid the price, as other competitors stood ready to bid ... They "put on" a number one week, and "took off" the next, using someone else's song instead. To hold singers, publishers advanced the "plugging scale" somewhat. Then another kind of money-paying publisher appeared. He offered to make the "production," plunged heavily on gowns for "woman singles," supplied "special drops," did almost everything possible. The "act-making" publisher says he doesn't pay money, but that statement is accepted doubtfully.[21]

In May, 1916, the practice of publishers making payments to performers was again noted in *Variety* when it was reported that some music publishers were threatening legal action against performers who had taken money to sing the publishers' songs but who, after receiving payment in advance, had failed to do so (or had not done so to the extent agreed). This report makes clear both that paying performers was an accepted part of the music publishers' business and that no serious doubts were entertained about its legality. The report adds that, "there is a large possibility of [the publishers] combining their complaints for individual and collective protection."[22]

Whatever arrangements may subsequently have been made to check on the compliance of performers with the terms of their agreements, it is certain, that the practice of paying performers continued. Of course, its character changed. As Isaac Goldberg said in 1930: "Plugging methods have simply followed the transformation of the mechanical agencies for publicity. Once it was Libbey's face and figure that shone from the sheets on the piano racks. Now it is Rudy Vallee's. Nor is it an accident that Libbey was a singer, while Vallee is a band-leader. We have become band-minded. The big names ... are no longer ... purely singers ... They are Paul Whiteman, Ted Lewis, Ben Bernie, Vincent Lopez, Paul Ash. For plugging certain numbers these leaders collect 'cut in' on payments and royalties, even as did the Libbeys of 1893. There is little philanthropy in Tin Pan Alley. If you scratch my back, I must scratch yours or your palm."[23] It is therefore hardly surprising to learn that, when the "big bands" became an important part of radio programming, payola entered the broadcasting industry. It was a normal business practice in the popular music industry in the United States.[24]

III. Early Attempts to Regulate Payola

Although payments to performers by music publishers, in one form or another, continued right through the 1930s, it should not be concluded that there were no attempts to stop the practice. An unsuccessful attempt by music publishers in the 1890s to make an agreement to ban payola was noted in the previous section.[25] A more serious attempt was made late in 1916. Earlier in that year, a report in *Variety* seemed to suggest that the music publishers were trying to establish some general scheme for checking whether performers carried out the terms of their agreements.[26] But when the collective action came, it had a very different character. It aimed to abolish what we now call payola, but was, at that time, called the "payment system."

The first move had a somewhat unusual character. In October, 1916, it was reported in *Variety* that the head of a "5-and-10-cent store syndicate" was attempting to bring the music publishers together "to eliminate the existing evils of the business, the principal one being the payment system". Under his plan, publishers would promise to "discontinue paying professional singers for 'popularizing' their numbers." A committee "composed of outside men would decide whether the publisher was guilty of a violation of the rules." If found guilty, "the 5-and-10-cent stores would discontinue sale of the violator's products." Although "several of the larger firms had tentatively agreed to combine under such arrangements," many were clearly unwilling to do so. They were suspicious of the motives of the organizer. "It is gossip among the music men that the syndicates always advocated the payment of moneys to professional singers, they claiming a better service was assured and the songs popularized more quickly and a demand for copies simultaneously created. Just why the syndicate people should become suddenly interested in organizing the publishers seemed a problem to the veterans of the trade and they began looking around for the friendly reason." Some publishers seem to have thought that the scheme might enable the store syndicates to secure "complete control of the selling end of all popular music." In any case, it would be "quite as simple for the publishers themselves to reorganize independently of the syndicates and after forming an association, appeal to the syndicates for their cooperation."

It was clear that the scheme of the 5-and-10-cent storeman would not succeed. But the report in *Variety* concluded that some such arrangement was needed since the "'payment system' is slowly but surely tearing large chunks into [the publishers'] reserve bank rolls." But nothing would be done "until some disinterested party takes the initiative," since "everyone is suspicious of his competitor." But there was hope.

"It is understood another attempt will be made by an outsider to bring the publishers together."[27]

This account is disingenuous. The outsider was none other than John J. O'Connor, business manager of *Variety,* and he actively set about organizing an association of music publishers. He secured the cooperation of vaudeville theater operators (or certain of them) and persuaded music publishers to join. He became the first chairman of the association and Edward B. Marks, whose exploits as a song-plugger we have already noticed,[28] became its first president. The name given to the association was the Music Publishers' Protective Association (MPPA).[29] Preliminary moves to establish the association were reported in *Variety* late in 1916.[30] By May, 1917, the MPPA was formed, the headline to the report in *Variety* giving this news being, "Song Payments End This Week." In the same issue of *Variety,* there was an advertisement which gave the aims of the MPPA:

> The primary and main object of this association just formed shall be to promote and foster clean and free competition among music publishers by eradicating the evil custom of paying tribute or gratuities to singers or musicians employed in theatres, cabarets and other places to induce them to sing or render music, which custom has worked to the detriment of the theatre management and the public through the rendition of music, not because of its merits, but because those singing or rendering it received gratuities in some form for so doing. Such practices have tended to discourage and retard the work of music writers, whose labors have not had a free field for competition.[31]

During 1917, *Variety* reported with enthusiasm on the success of the MPPA. Immediately after its formation, *Variety* reported: "The payment system to singers automatically became a thing of the past this week when the publishers notified their clients that in future all dealings would necessarily have to be conducted without the cash propositions. As far as could be ascertained, there has not been a single instance where the singer has not agreed to do all in his power to cooperate with the publishers, the majority recognizing the future good to be attained by the abolition of payments."[32] At the end of 1917, an article in *Variety* summed up what had been accomplished. The MPPA had "wiped out the most insidious curse ... the 'payment system' ... the [MPPA] has not only lived, but has strengthened itself beyond the fondest dreams of its organizers."[33]

These accounts which appeared in *Variety* about the success of the MPPA were inaccurate. Isaac Goldberg, after stating that the MPPA "ostensibly put a stop to the payment system," adds: "It is optimistic to believe that the practice has been eliminated."[34] Hazel Meyer says this of the formation of the MPPA: "Within twenty-four hours, the overt payola to vaudeville performers stopped. Within another twenty-four hours, payola was underground."[35] David Ewen says this: "It did not take long for now one publisher, now another, to devise devious ways of influencing performers to use their songs. The most effective way, and the hardest to pin down as a violation of the rules, was to give a star a share in the song's royalties ... The fact that the performer thus profited from the future success of the song made him more partial to including it in an act or show."[36] Even Edward B. Marks, who was president of the MPPA and was no doubt inclined to magnify its accomplishments, states: "We got rid of the flagrant evil of paying acts, but the sub rosa practice never entirely ceased."[37] It is abundantly clear, not only from these opinions, but from other evidence, that "the payment system" or what we would now call "payola" continued after the formation of the MPPA.

This outcome would not have surprised most music publishers since there seems to have been considerable scepticism about the possibility of abolishing the "payment system" when the idea of an association was first broached.[38] But if this was so, why did all the important music publishers join the MPPA? Some (but certainly not all) undoubtedly thought they would be better off if this restraint on competition were instituted. This would also be true of those few popular music publishers who did not use the "payment system" to promote their own properties or who were not adept in using it. Edward B. Marks may have been one of those. He said this of the "payment system": "Stern and I stood out against the thing, because we sensed that it would ruin the houses that spent the most money. It took will power to stay out of the procession, just a little more than I had. One day I authorized our professional manager ... to go ahead and see to it that our numbers got a few breaks. In two days he came back disappointed. 'Boss,' he said, 'I can't give your money away. Every team worth a damn is signed to sing for other publishers.'"[39] It was apparently shortly after this experience that Marks agreed to become MPPA's first president.

But even those who would benefit from the abolition of the "payment system" might well have hesitated to join if they thought their competitors would not abide by the rules, as many no doubt did. It seems that O'Connor's success in securing the cooperation of some of the vaudeville theatre operators was decisive in inducing the hesitant (or hostile) to join. It is said that O'Connor was able to enlist their aid by taking an executive of the Keith-Albee-Orpheum circuit to a show in which the same song ("I Didn't Raise My Boy to Be a Soldier," an antiwar song of the day) was used in a whole series of acts: the melody served as background music for the opening animal act, accompanied a dramatic sketch, was sung first by a duo and later by a quartet, was used in a "pepped-up" version to introduce the comic, while the melody was again used to accompany (in waltz time) the acrobatic troup which closed the show. It was a song-plugger's triumph.[40] Whether or not this incident really took place, it is clear that, even though there may not have been great hostility to the "payment system" among vaudeville theatre operators (it would obviously lower the amounts that had to be paid to artists), there was some concern that the use of vaudeville theatres for song-plugging might affect the popularity of the shows.[41] What the manager of the Keith-Albee-Orpheum circuit apparently did was to refuse to allow music to be performed unless the publisher of the music was a member of the MPPA.[42] At first, three prominent firms, Feist (publisher of "I Didn't Raise My Boy to Be a Soldier"), Remick, and Harms, declined to join the MPPA, but after the announcement of the ban on the music of publishers not members of the MPPA they did so.[43]

The reasons why the music publishers joined the MPPA seem fairly clear. But why did O'Connor undertake the task of organizing the association? Was it an example of that philanthropy which is apparently so rare in the popular music industry? According to Hazel Meyer, it was not. She states that O'Connor drew the attention of the management of *Variety* to the negative relationship between payola and *Variety's* advertising revenues and was then given authority to act as that "disinterested party" who, according to *Variety,* was needed to bring the publishers together.[44] The view that the "payment system" might have been dampening *Variety's* advertising revenues is not illogical. Paying a singer to popularize a song is a form of promotional expenditure and therefore competitive with other promotional activities, including paying for an advertisement for the song in a trade periodical. But whatever O'Connor's motives may have been, the results achieved by the MPPA must have been a disappointment. What seems to have happened is that at first the "payment system" simply became, in Edward B. Marks's words, "sub rosa," but, as time went by, the need for concealment was less acutely felt. The MPPA, by its rules, had authority to fine members who used the "payment system," but we are told that these rules were "unenforced and ineffective."[45]

An opportunity to correct the situation came with the establishment of the National Recovery Administration (NRA) in June, 1933.[46] The act creating the NRA empowered members of an industry to draw up a code which, once approved by the NRA-code authorities and signed by the president, became binding on the whole industry. The first draft of such a code for the music publishing industry was submitted to the NRA on September 1, 1933.[47] The initiative in formulating this code was taken by the MPPA, and its chairman, Mr. John G. Paine, was the driving force in the negotiations.[48] The popular music publishers (that is, the members of the MPPA) made it clear that Section 8 of the code, which consisted of "Trade Practice Rules," and was largely designed to prohibit "payola," was for them the most important part of the code. In the official case history of the music publishers' code, it is stated that "representatives of [the popular music publishers] ... said, from time to time, that they were willing to agree to any other provisions in the Code that the Government desired if they might be granted these Trade Practice Rules."[49] The standard music publishers (broadly speaking, those who published classical music) expressed no interest in the Trade Practice Rules, and the task of justifying these provisions was assumed by the popular music publishers.

In the hearing on the proposed code in July, 1934, Mr. Paine explained that

the MPPA was organized 17 years ago in an endeavor to put a stop to ... unfair trade practices which are in the nature of bribes paid to orchestra leaders, radio performers and to other artists who appear in public, to induce those artists to perform the copyrighted composition of one publisher in competition or in opposition to their selecting ... the composition of another publisher.... These practices run into enormous sums of money annually and are extremely costly to the industry. We have tried as an association, to put a stop to them. We cannot very readily do that because we cannot control the whole industry but only the members of the Association, and that is one of the reasons we have felt the need of the code because by having it, we would be able to control these activities and practices in connection with the entire industry... [The code] is protective ... of the small publisher who does not have the money, does not have the capital, to go out and buy this talent....We feel [that] the exploitation should be ... solely on the merit of the musical composition which is offered. If I go to Mr. Rudy Vallee ... with my musical composition I think he should decide whether he will include that in his repertoire solely on the merit of my ... composition and not because I happen to be a wealthy publisher and can pay him a substantial sum of money to put mine in to the exclusion of somebody else's whose musical merit might be even greater than mine. We feel that the competition should be solely on the basis of the merit of the composition and not on any extraneous inducements.[50]

Other provisions in the code were justified by Mr. Paine on the ground that they were necessary to prevent evasion. For example, the prohibition on the supply of special arrangements was needed because, in practice, it would merely be a means of evading the ban on payola:

> We go to an orchestra leader and we say:"... We would like very much to have you use this musical composition." He looks it over and says he is not particularly interested in that musical composition, that it does not quite fit his particular band ... and then we say to him ".... You make a special arrangement ... and we will pay you whatever that cost is ..." That is just a subterfuge for paying directly to the orchestra leader because in ... practically all instances, the orchestra has its own arranger who arranges the music for the particular and peculiar instrumentation of that orchestra, and that arranger is on a salary.[51]

The effect of the code, according to Mr. Paine, would be to prevent public performance being "dominated completely and absolutely by those publishers that have substantial bankrolls to the utter exclusion of those publishers who may have meritorious compositions, good writers, and yet no money for exploitation."[52] What the NRA code did was to impose on the music publishing industry the regulations which the MPPA had attempted unsuccessfully to introduce in 1917. Section 8 of the music publishers' code is reproduced in Appendix A. There was also a section in the radio broadcasting code which prohibited payola and this will also be found in Appendix A. According to a representative of the National Association of Broadcasters this provision was inserted in the radio broadcasting code at the request of the music publishers.[53] The chairman of the Code Authority for the Music Publishing Industry was Mr. Paine, who was also chairman of the MPPA. Although the original draft of the music publishers' code had been submitted on September 1, 1933, owing to bureaucratic delays the code was not finally approved until March 4, 1935, to become effective March 18, 1935. However, on May 27, 1935, the Supreme Court declared the act establishing the NRA unconstitutional; as a result the NRA code for the music publishing industry was only in operation for about two months.[54]

In a letter dated June 18, 1935, sent to an NRA official, Mr. Paine stated that the Supreme Court decision had removed "the most valuable aid to the [music publishing] industry which we have had ever in our history ... Should some method be devised which would again give to our industry a code effective upon the whole industry, which would be aimed only at eliminating the practices set out in Article 8 of the Code ... we feel that the savings will be so beneficial to our industry that we can undoubtedly solve most of the commercial problems which lie before us."[55]

The method which Mr. Paine had in mind to ensure that the industry continued to abide by the Trade Practice Rules of the NRA code was soon to be revealed. About four months after the NRA act had been declared unconstitutional, on September 20, 1935, the MPPA submitted to the Federal Trade Commission (FTC) Trade Practice Rules for the music publishing industry. In a memorandum sent to the Trade Practices Board of the FTC by a staff member it was noted that the rules proposed "were taken practically verbatim from the [NRA] Code of Fair Competition for the Music Publishing Industry." This approach to the FTC by the MPPA was quite proper. The FTC could approve rules of fair trade practices for an industry, once it has determined that to grant the industry's request would not sanction practices contrary to law or be in some way inimical to the public interest. Such rules are divided into two groups. The FTC took the position that group I rules were legally binding and took appropriate action to enforce them. Group II rules were advisory. Their observance was considered desirable but their nonobservance was not per se a violation of the law. However, if it was determined that nonobservance would result in unfair competition or unfair deceptive acts or practices, the FTC might take the same action as it would for group I violations.[56]

This application of the MPPA was to have a difficult passage.[57] While there was some support for the proposed rules within the FTC, reservations were expressed about the legality of the provisions and their desirability. Lengthy negotiations followed with Mr. Paine and his legal counsel, Joseph V. McKee (a former mayor of New York City). The character of the obstacles to FTC approval may be gathered from a memorandum sent by the Trade Practices Board to the Commission in June, 1937. The memorandum first describes the situation of the popular music industry: "The products of the industry consist of popular songs, orchestrations and musical compositions. To induce members of the public to buy it is necessary to afford them the means of hearing the tune of the musical composition, for it is only when they are attracted by the tune that they are induced to buy. Thus in promoting the sale of their products the members of the industry constantly strive to have their songs and musical compositions accepted by those providing public entertainment and played or performed over the radio, in theaters or by orchestras or singers in hotels, restaurants and other places of public amusement." It then explains that the "practice has grown up of publishers paying so-called bribes or making gifts of money, articles or favors to orchestra leaders, singers and other artists to play or sing their songs ... It is the purpose of the proposed trade practice conference to provide rules prohibiting it." It notes that "the employers of such musicians, singers or artists, for the most part at least, have no objection to such professional employees receiving such payments or gifts. It is proposed, however, to prohibit the practice when indulged in either with or without such employer's consent. Except for this the practice has much similarity to commercial bribery. Our ordinary commercial bribery rule is limited to cases where the bribe is paid without the knowledge or consent of the employer."[58]

The drafting problem as seen by the staff of the Trade Practices Board is then described but hardly resolved:

The [MPPA] desires that the rules prohibit the practice "with or without" the knowledge or consent of the employer and moreover, that they be placed in Group I as compulsory. Otherwise, it is claimed, the rules would mean little and would be ineffectual and not worthwhile. Under the circumstances therefore the rules will have to be phrased so as to prohibit practices which are contrary to law and no more. In our study of the proposed rules thus far we have not been fully convinced that they prohibit only that which is illegal. On the other hand, however, we are likewise not yet fully convinced of the impossibility of making such rules eligible for Group I, although thus far we have not been able to devise appropriate language which would, in our judgment, bring the rules wholly within the law and at the same time meet the situation which the applicant desires, namely, complete and compulsory prohibition of such "song plugging" practices. While strict legal construction ... of the rules [submitted by the MPPA] would seem to bring them within the Group I category, proof of a case thereunder would appear to be next to impossible.[59]

The memorandum next alludes to the antitrust suit pending against the American Society of Composers, Authors, and Publishers (ASCAP), of which the popular music publishers were, of course, members. The existence of this suit seemed to some in the FTC enough to bar approval of the rules even though the Department of Justice had stated in a letter that the "proposed rules ... do not affect the issues in the antitrust suit."[60]

The memorandum also referred to a charge by an independent music publisher—one, that is, not affiliated with a motion picture company—that the proposed rules would inflict great harm on such independent publishers. He said that many independent publishers "signed the petition unwillingly because of threats that their songs would be boycotted by orchestra leaders and artists under the control of the dominant music publishers." The harm this publisher had in mind was recounted in the memorandum:

> Through using the songs and orchestrations of their own publishing subsidiaries in their motion pictures and their large chains of theaters throughout the country, such affiliated publishers, who are competitors of the independents, have means for exploiting their songs and orchestrations in public performances without the necessity of resorting to "song plugging" ... The independent publisher claims that not having such motion picture outlets, it is necessary for him to induce orchestras and singers in hotels, restaurants and in other non-controlled places of entertainment to play his music in order that the public may hear his tunes and thus become interested in buying his sheet music. It should be remembered that it is only when the buying public are

attracted by the tune that they can be induced to buy. And the tune can, of course, only be imparted audibly. The opponents, therefore, claim that if these rules should deprive the independent publishers of the privilege of paying orchestra leaders or other artists to sing, play or perform their compositions, their means of bringing their tunes to the attention of the public would be cut off and the business would be monopolized by the motion picture corporations and their subsidiaries who have control of the use of songs and music in motion pictures and in motion picture theaters throughout the country.

The chief examiner of the FTC reported that it "appears from the record so far made, that at least some of the independent publishers under duress or threat of injury to their business agreed to the Proposed Trade Practice Conference rules as submitted to the Commission by the Industry" and that it was the opinion of his investigating attorney that the proposed rules "would mean the elimination of the independent publisher."[61]

The position was further complicated by the fact that the MPPA announced in the press that it had already put the trade practice rules into effect and in terms which gave the impression that this had been sanctioned by the FTC. "The applicant's committee has expressed fear that unless the Commission grants the conference promptly, violations of the rules will increase because members of the industry are beginning to realize that the rules, although put into effect by the association, have not as yet been sanctioned or approved by the Commission and therefore may not be enforceable."[62]

The Trade Practice Board's conclusion was as follows: "...we do not believe the trade practice conference matter should be postponed to await conclusion of further investigation ... if, under all the circumstances, the Commission... feels that a trade practice conference is not feasible or desirable, the application should be denied forthwith... On the other hand, we do not see how material harm could come from holding a conference and allowing all sides to be heard in an effort to thrash out the whole matter."[63] Given the divergent views within the FTC, it is hardly surprising that the commission, on July 13, 1937, denied the application for a conference. However, following representations from the industry and modification of their proposed rules, the FTC rescinded this decision on July 30, 1937 and agreed to hold a trade practice conference.[64]

After this conference, held on October 4, 1937, the FTC received a letter from the Southern Music Publishing Company, New York City, which said that the conference proceedings "represented only an expression of the wishes and desires of the motion picture owned publishers and a few long established independent houses." The rules were, however, tentatively approved by the FTC and an oral hearing was set for January 4, 1938.[65] In the meantime, the commission had received a letter from Mr. Albert Bader, President, Independent Music Publishers, U.S.A., claiming that the proposed rules were "concocted under the influence of the ASCAP and the MPPA, the representative organizations of the Music Publishers Monopoly."[66]

The Trade Practice Board recommended approval of the rules. The chief counsel of the FTC, however, noted the pending antitrust suit and the charges of monopoly against members of the MPPA. He concluded: "I believe that the approval of the Trade Practice Rules should be considered as the grant of a privilege and that in no event should it be extended unless the sponsors come before the Commission with absolutely clean hands and unquestioned honesty of purpose and intent." He therefore recommended that approval of the rules be denied, leaving it open to the MPPA to make a new application "as soon as all pending charges against the members of this industry have been disposed of."[67] On May 25, 1938, the FTC rejected the proposed trade practice rules for the music publishing industry.[68]

One more attempt was to be made in the 1930s to eliminate payola. In 1939, the song-pluggers formed a union, affiliated with the American Federation of Labor, the Music Publishers' Contact Employees Union. From the reports, in November, 1939, about the contract to be signed between the union and the music publishers, we learn that one of its main provisions was intended to prevent payola. *Billboard* had this to say: "Basic element in the contract (and likewise in the original formation of the union) is the abolition of the evil of bribery for song plugs, contact men feeling that the situation was growing to a point where a publisher's checkbook would finally obviate the necessity of maintaining a plugging staff." The contract provided for a fine for any publisher found guilty by an arbitration board of resorting to payola, plus the posting of a $1,000 bond to be retained by the union if the publisher repeated the offense.[69] The account in *Variety* gave more detail about the practices which would subject a publisher to such penalties: "The unfair practice clause ... bars publishers from giving or offering any form of gratuity or reward for a plug, including cut-ins, or the making of special arrangements or extractions but prevents them from having their employees attending band leaders' command performances or special nights, unless the consent of the union has been obtained."[70]

There would have been little difficulty in the music publishers and the union coming to an agreement to restrict payola. The publishers wanted to impose these regulations on the industry; the song-plugger employees of the publishers would see the abolition of payola as leading to an increased demand for their services. The American Federation of Musicians (AFM), some of whose members received the payola, did not welcome this development. Although indicating that they would cooperate, they were, in fact, reluctant to help the new union. The president of the New York local of the AFM is reported to have said that if payola is to be abolished, "the music men must do it for themselves." And *Billboard* added: "AFM officials are ... known to regard the bribery angle as not in their province and they do not care to deter a leader from picking up a little extra money in this way."[71]

There is no reason to suppose that the Music Publishers' Contact Employees Union was able to stop payola. It was reported in *Variety* in 1944 that the contact men's salaries had risen so high that they were making payments to broadcasters and performers out of their own pockets.[72] And in 1945, payola was apparently so widespread that some publishers threatened to make open payments for broadcasting plugs for their songs.[73] It is clear that the union had not been able to stop payola. Up to the end of World War II, all attempts to stop payola seem to have failed.

IV. The Situation in the 1950s

Until the end of World War II, payola, although it affected the radio programs broadcast, did not normally involve directly either the radio stations or their employees. It consisted of payments by music publishers to performers. By the 1950s, its character had changed radically. The predominant form of payola became payments by record companies (who were often also music publishers) to disc jockeys. Whether because of a change in tastes in music, a change in the composition of the potential audience of radio stations following the advent of television, an improvement in the quality of recordings, or more probably a combination of all these factors (and others), "big band" radio programs disappeared and there emerged as an important form of programming on radio stations the disc jockey who played recordings, interspersed with comments and commercials. At first, record companies (or some of them) had resisted such programming, no doubt believing that listening to records on the radio would reduce the demand for records to be played at home.[74] But it soon became apparent that the playing of a record by a disc jockey increased the sales of that record and the desire of record companies to have their records played on disc jockey programs led naturally to payola. In the trade press throughout the 1950s there are repeated references to record companies making gifts or money payments to disc jockeys to play their records.[75] However, it was not until late in 1959 that payola came under congressional scrutiny.

In the meantime, the broadcasting industry was the subject of several congressional investigations. At first, it was corruption within the FCC itself which attracted attention. Commissioner Mack was alleged to have been given money to obtain his support for the award of a television channel to a particular applicant (who was in fact successful). This resulted in the resignation and later indictment of the commissioner.[76] It was a continuation of this concern about improper relations between the FCC and the industry that in 1960 led to the resignation of the chairman of the FCC, Commissioner Doerfer, following his acceptance of hospitality from a broadcast-station operator.[77] Attention, however, soon shifted from corruption within the FCC to corruption within the broadcasting industry itself and to the need to give the FCC additional powers to regulate the industry.

In 1958, Senator Smathers introduced a bill which provided that no one engaged in music publishing or the manufacture and distribution of musical records could hold a license to operate a broadcasting station. This bill seems to have been an outcome of the rivalry between two organizations controlling musical copyrights, the American Society of Composers, Authors, and Publishers (ASCAP) and Broadcast Music, Inc. (BMI). Broadcasting stations and the networks (who also owned recording companies) were stockholders in BMI. It was alleged that broadcasting organizations favoured the playing by disc jockeys of records in which they had an interest. It is easy to see that this practice would have affinities with payola. However, in the course of the enquiry, there were many references to payola, one witness stating that it was paid to disc jockeys to induce them to play BMI songs.[78] But these payments to disc jockeys do not seem to have occasioned any great concern at that time. Senator Pastore likened the practice to paying "a headwaiter $5 to get a desirable table."[79] The bill never passed.

It was part of the case against BMI, with Mr. Vance Packard as the principal proponent, that the disc jockeys had filled their programs with "whining guitarists, musical notes put to a switchblade beat, obscene lyrics about hugging, squeezing and rocking all night long," which they substituted for the music of such composers as Cole Porter, Richard Rodgers, and Irving Berlin (who were members of ASCAP). It was clear to Mr. Packard that "something more than artistic judgment or poll results was going into the decision to feature rock and roll, or rhythm and blues" and in support of this statement he referred to an article which appeared *in Billboard* in 1951 which stated that "the 'payola' situation is worst among the rhythm and blues spinners." According to Mr. Packard, the "rock and roll surge" really got going when RCA-Victor made a contract with a "pallid, sullen young man named Elvis Presley."[80] Although no legislation resulted from these hearings, the idea that the demand for "rock and roll" music was created by the broadcasters through playing records of such music on disc jockey programs and that this was in some way connected with payola was to remain a factor influencing congressional attitudes.

The next congressional enquiry arose out of charges in 1958 that the popular television quiz shows, which had been presented as honest contests, had in fact been rigged, that the contestants were groomed before the programs, knew the questions that were to be put to them and how they should answer and that the contestant who would win was arranged in advance. The contests were the subject of a New York grand jury investigation. After completion of this investigation, the testimony given to the grand jury was made available to the Subcommittee on Legislative Oversight of the House of Representatives, which then held its own hearings. The proceedings of the subcommittee left no doubt that the charges were true. But payola did not make its appearance until the proceedings were nearing their end.

It was then disclosed that the owner of a department store, Mr. Hess of Allentown, Pennsylvania, had paid $10,000 so that an employee, Mr. Hoffer, would be a contestant on the most popular of the quiz programs, the "$64,000 Question." It had been expected by Mr. Hess that the contestant, in the course of being introduced, would be asked where he was employed and in fact this happened. The transaction offended the moral sensibilities of some congressmen as the following extracts from the hearings show:

Mr. Rogers: Did you feel what you were doing was wrong, Mr. Hess?

Mr. Hess: I thought it was a terrific promotion for the store.

....

Mr. Flynt: So basically as far as you were concerned the whole idea of getting Mr. Hoffer on there was to plug your store. We will say it was deceitful, at the very least.

Mr. Hess: I thought it was a good promotion.

Mr. Flynt: Yes, but you were not trying to promote an honest quiz show. You were trying to plug your store.

Mr. Hess: I didn't know whether he could answer the questions or not.[81]

Following a statement by Mr. Hess that he had appeared on a TV show with Kate Smith for a payment, he explained, under questioning by Mr. Lishman, counsel to the subcommittee, that such payments were common:

Mr. Lishman: Do you think this was a common practice in order to get these plugs that a person would have to pay?

Mr. Hess: It was not "was"; it is a common practice.

Mr. Lishman: It is. Isn't it a fact that the sponsor buys the time and unbeknownst to the sponsor ostensibly somebody gets a free ride by paying some side money to a producer. Is that the case?

Mr. Hess: This is considered a business today. There are plenty of people ...

Mr. Lishman: It is considered a business?

Mr. Hess: Yes.

Mr. Lishman: Wouldn't this closely approach commercial bribery, in your opinion?

Mr. Hess: Commercial what?

Mr. Lishman: Commercial bribery.

Mr. Hess: No, sir. This is a recognized business. There are certain people in New York that do just nothing but plug words.

...

Mr. Lishman: Are these people commonly known as "schlukmeisters" that you are referring to? Schlukmeisters, masters of making a sharp bargain on the side? Is that what they are known as in the trade? You say it is a business. I am trying to find the business name for them.

Mr. Hess: These people are in the business like everybody else and it is a recognized thing with them.

Mr. Lishman: Don't you think it is a fraud on the sponsor who pays the big sum of money to get the program format established and buys the time of the network and then someone comes along and for a comparatively small amount of money gets a free ride on the sponsor's program?

Mr. Hess: I think it is a terrific thing for a little business to be able to get on some of those big network shows.[82]

Mr. Hess also pointed out that his store also made payments to newspaper columnists. He mentioned the names of Jack O'Brien, Bob Considine, and Mr. John Hall Levine, public relations manager at the Hess store, gave more particulars of these transactions. He provided the subcommittee with a list of TV shows on which a mention of the Hess store or its activities had been obtained by a payment of money in the 1950s. They included the Steve Allen "Tonight" show and "Name That Tune."[83] In his testimony, he added the Dave Garroway "Today" show and the "Garry Moore Show."[84] He also mentioned that in a television film with the locale in New York City, one of their trucks had been spotted.[85] Mr. Levine also added the names of Hal Boyle and Earl Wilson to the names of newspaper columnists mentioned by Mr. Hess. When Congressman Bennett started to question Mr. Levine about the columnists, the chairman (Mr. Oren Harris) intervened to say "that gets into the newspaper business" and Mr. Bennett said "I withdraw the question about the newspapers because I guess that is out of our field."[86] In statements issued after this testimony, Earl Wilson denied that he had received money from Hess while Jack O'Brien denied that he had mentioned the Hess store. Other columnists (Bob Considine, Stanley Delaplane, and Hal Boyle), who had mentioned the store in their columns, explained that the payments they received were for "personal appearances" or "travel expenses." But the question of payments to newspaper columnists seems to have attracted very little attention compared to that accorded payments to disc jockeys.[87]

The members of the subcommittee showed great interest in the way in which Mr. Hess made his payments.[88] Who actually received the $10,000 paid (in cash) to secure Mr. Hoffer's appearance on the "$64,000 Question" was never revealed. And Mr. Schwartz who, it was said, was handed the money by an employee of the Hess store, claimed that his testimony might "tend to defame, degrade or incriminate some person" and his testimony was in consequence taken in executive session and was not published.[89] Mr. Hess, mindful no doubt of the presence at the hearings of a representative of the district attorney of New York, showed considerable circumspection in his answers on this subject. What is apparent, however, is that this particular transaction was very unusual. Normally the payment was made by check and to a public relations firm. How the public relations firm obtained these "mentions" for the Hess store, whether by payment or in some other way, was not disclosed.

The heads of two of the networks were questioned about Mr. Hess's transactions. Mr. Kintner, President of the National Broadcasting Company (NBC), said that the showing of some fashions from the Hess store on the "Today" show, probably arose because the show wants to have interesting people on it and "apparently some public relations firm told the Hess Department Store that they could get some interesting person on 'Today'."[90] This, he thought, was not objectionable. Asked about the practice of producers or employees of NBC being paid to insert plugs into programs, Mr. Kintner said that it was not "general," was "reprehensible" and would lead to dismissal if discovered. However, he added a qualification: "You understand the operation of all these types of shows, for example—and this is just a theoretical example—if Miami wants the 'Today' show to come to Florida, in order to boom for tourists, the program, itself, may be paid some of the costs of transportation, but it does not go to the individuals or staff, and it is part of the budget of the show. I would not consider the example I gave as reprehensible."[91] Mr. Stanton, President of the Columbia Broadcasting System (CBS), said that the practices disclosed by Mr. Hess's testimony were "deplorable." But he did not "quarrel with the idea that personalities and institutions retain agents, public relations people, to try to get as much public attention as possible. The place where I draw the line is the passing of money from the act or from the personality to the person who writes the column or does the show or plans the display window, or whatever that might be."[92]

At the end of the hearings into the television quiz programs, there were introduced into the record a letter and memorandum from Mr. Burton Lane (composer of the musical score for "Finian's Rainbow" and a number of popular songs) in his capacity as president of the American Guild of Authors and Composers. The letter stated in part that the "practices of audience deception in broadcasting which have been revealed in the testimony adduced before your committee, is by no means limited to quiz programs. It has a counterpart in the promotion of music, and in music products. There is no doubt that commercial bribery has become a prime factor in determining what music is played on many broadcast programs and what musical records the public is surreptitiously induced to buy."[93] The memorandum gave examples of payola, mainly taken from the trade press. According to *Variety*, it was Burton Lane's letter which led to the payola enquiry.[94] Whether this is true or not, the great payola enquiry followed.

The hearings on "payola and other deceptive practices"[95] opened with a statement by the chairman of the subcommittee, Representative Oren Harris, in which he referred to the Hess testimony and to Burton Lane's letter. He continued: "Since that time, the subcommittee has been flooded with complaints ... about ... the selection of material sent over the airwaves [being] influenced by undisclosed economic inducements. When this happens, we are told, the public interest suffers in many ways. The quality of broadcast programs declines when the choice of program materials is made, not in the public interest, but in the interest of those who are willing to pay to obtain exposure of their records. The public is misled as to the popularity of the records played. Moreover, these practices constitute unfair competition with honest businessmen who refuse to engage in them. They tend to drive out of business small firms who lack the means to survive this unfair competition."[96] Mr. Harris said that the subcommittee had not "prejudged any of these matters,"[97] although this was not evident from the questioning which followed.

The first witness was Mr. Norman Prescott, who had been a disc jockey with WBZ, Boston, and who had accepted from record distributors, over approximately a three-year period, payments totaling about $10,000. He had been reluctant to testify (apparently because he did not wish to incriminate others) but had agreed to cooperate with the subcommittee, according to its counsel, after they confronted him "at every turn" with "documentary proof " collected by the subcommittee's investigators. Mr.

Prescott explained that he left WBZ in July, 1959, because, among other things, he was "disgusted with the payola conditions in the industry; and I walked away from it for that reason." There is some conflict about this in the testimony—the manager of WBZ said that Mr. Prescott was fired. Mr. Prescott testified that he considered payola to be bribery and explained that it comes about because "it is impossible to play the big percentage of the output of the manufacturers. That is why payola is functioning today and will continue to function if something is not done about it." Payola led to the playing of "rock and roll" records:

Mr. Bennett: Well, do you think without payola that a lot of this so-called junk music, rock and roll stuff, which appeals to the teenagers would not be played, or do you think that kind of thing would be played anyway, regardless of the payola?
Mr. Prescott: Never get on the air.
Mr. Bennett: Do you think payola is responsible for it?
Mr. Prescott: Yes; it keeps it on the air, because it fills pockets.[98]

The effect of Mr. Prescott's testimony was to suggest that payola was widespread, that it was immoral, that it prevented the broadcasting of "good music," and that it should be stopped by new legislation. Mr. Harris complimented Mr. Prescott on his "frank and forthright" testimony. "Even though you were at first, understandingly so, reluctant to provide information or talk about it to the investigators or our staff, after you got into it and found out what the situation was, you have been very helpful, explaining for the record just how this business operates from the standpoint of an experienced man."[99]

Later witnesses, record manufacturers and distributors who made the payments and the disc jockeys who received them, denied, when pressed by members of the subcommittee, that the payments were wrong or improper. Indeed they usually denied that these payments were "payola," in the sense that the disc jockeys agreed to play records in return for the payments. The payments were made for taking charge of record hops (dances at which the records were played), for consultation, for advice, for listening to records, or were gifts. The congressmen, as was to be expected in men of their experience, expressed scepticism or outright disbelief at these explanations. Nor need we doubt that whatever the ostensible reason for these payments, the aim was to increase the likelihood that the records of the suppliers would be played. But the fact that the transactions might be held to constitute commercial bribery in New York State, where many of the transactions took place, doubtless made many witnesses reluctant to be completely candid about them.

The remainder of the hearings were largely devoted to the affairs of Dick Clark, who was responsible for an ABC network television show on which he played records while teenagers danced and also another show on which the performers sang the songs they had recorded. Until late in 1959, when, under pressure from ABC, Mr. Clark disposed of most of his outside interests, he had been an owner or part owner of several music-publishing and record-manufacturing corporations and also of a record-pressing corporation. It was implied that Mr. Clark received payola in an indirect form, that individuals or firms who had their music published by or recorded by or pressed by one of the corporations in which he had an interest were more likely to have their records played or music performed on his programs. Mr. Clark denied that he had ever agreed to play records or select songs in return for business given to his corporations or that he had ever taken payola. The closest Mr. Clark ever came to an admission that his outside interests may have influenced him in his choice of records was the following: "The truth, gentlemen, is that I did not consciously favor such records. Maybe I did so without realizing it." The questioning by members of the subcommittee and its counsel was unable to shake Mr. Clark's contention that he had not accepted payola in any form.[100]

Nonetheless, the testimony made it clear that the acceptance of payola by disc jockeys was widespread, a conclusion confirmed by information uncovered by the FTC. The FTC started its investigations late in 1959 after receiving "a letter of complaint ... dated about November 2, from a record manufacturer who offered to supply some names, dates, and places."[101] The publicity given to payola by the congressional committee also brought complaints "from the public ... in unprecedented volume."[102] The investigations of the FTC revealed the pervasive character of payola and the many forms that it assumed. In his testimony to the subcommittee, Mr. Earl W. Kintner, Chairman of the FTC, said that the investigations had revealed 255 disc jockeys or other employees of broadcast licensees and 7 broadcast licensees as having received payola. Payola took the form of cash payments (which might be on a regular weekly or monthly basis), royalties on the sales of records, a share in a record company, advertisements in the disc jockeys' hit sheets, the reimbursement of recording stars' fees for appearances on the disc jockeys' programs or at record hops which they organized, expensive gifts, and mortgage loans on disc jockeys' homes. The FTC also investigated what had come to be known as "plugola," the kind of activity in which Mr. Hess had been involved and found that there were firms which regularly engaged in securing such "plugs" on broadcast programs. That such "plugola" was extremely common was made evident by published reports about performers who received payments or gifts for mentioning certain products in the course of their programs.[103] The FTC seems to have taken no legal action to deal with "plugola", no doubt because the change in the law in 1960 made the FCC the agency primarily responsible for regulating these activities. The FTC issued many complaints against record manufacturers and distributors and, in most cases, these firms entered into a consent decree whereby they agreed not to give "without requiring full public disclosure" money or other material consideration to anyone to select and broadcast records in which they had "a financial interest of any nature" or to influence the employee of a broadcasting station or anyone else to do so.[104] The basis for this action by the FTC seems to have been that the "concealment of such payments is a deceptive act within the meaning of Section 5 of the Federal Trade Commission Act since listeners are misled into believing that the recordings played are selected strictly on their merits or public popularity."[105] These payments were also likened to "push money" (paid to the employees of retail stores to "push" certain products) and constituted unfair competition since the records of those who paid payola would be played more frequently than "those who made no such contribution or refused to pay tribute."[106]

The congressmen on the subcommittee were consistently hostile to payola. It was "bribery," "immoral," "wrong," "reprehensible," and so forth. Records were played because of undisclosed economic inducements rather than because it was in the public interest. These feelings were undoubtedly enhanced by the press accounts of a convention of disc jockeys held in Miami Beach, Florida in June, 1959, at which the record manufacturers and distributors seem to have attended to the disc jockeys' every need with a lack of restraint which recalled Rome under the emperors.[107] And in the background of the questioning was a hostility to "rock and roll" (the music played by many disc jockeys), defined as "raucous discord" by Congressman Moss, who argued that "good music did not require the payment of payola."[108] As has been said, in these hearings there was "an assumption that rock was 'bad' music ... and that it could only have been forced on the public by illegal business activities."[109] The upshot of these deliberations was that the subcommittee recommended, among other things, amendments to the Communications Act which would make payola a crime in the broadcasting industry. These amendments became law on September 13, 1960.

V. The 1960 Amendments to the Communications Act

Up to September, 1960, the only authority which the FCC had to regulate payola came from Section 317 of the Communications Act of 1934. It read as follows: "All matter broadcast by any radio station for which service, money, or any other valuable consideration is directly or indirectly paid, or promised to or charged or accepted by, the station so broadcasting, from any person, shall, at the time the same is so broadcast, be announced as paid for or furnished, as the case may be, by such person." This section, which was taken, substantially unchanged, from the Radio Act of 1927, had apparently been based on a section of the Postal Appropriations Act of 1912 under which editorial and other published material appearing in newspapers receiving second-class mailing privileges had to be clearly marked "advertisement" if money or other valuable consideration had been paid in return for publication.[110]

Until 1959, the administration of Section 317 does not appear to have created any great difficulty for the FCC.[111] However, the situation revealed by the congressional enquiries presented the FCC with a new problem. Section 317 referred to the disclosure of payments or other valuable consideration made to the station. But payola in the 1950s did not, generally speaking, involve payments to stations; rather they were made to disc jockeys. It was presumably this fact that led to the FTC being the administrative agency which took action to stop payola rather than the FCC. However, in December, 1959, as a result of the publicity given to payola, the FCC sent an enquiry to all broadcast licensees and the answers received led the FCC to conclude that broadcast stations were not complying with Section 317. In March, 1960, the FCC issued a public notice in which it explained what, in its view, compliance with Section 317 implied. The playing of free records should be accompanied by an announcement indicating that the station had received consideration for playing them and stating from whom the consideration had been received. All mentions of, or the playing of records to be featured at outside activities, such as "record hops" where a profit would be derived or where broadcast exposure is provided in exchange for payment of a performer's fee or the donation of records, prizes, or the use of a hall should be accompanied by an announcement. This would identify those who benefited financially from the activity "as well as other parties providing consideration in any form whatsoever in exchange for ... broadcast exposure." Announcements were also required when transportation, accommodation, and other expenses were paid for in "remote" pickups as an inducement to broadcast material about "a place, product, service or event." This was required because otherwise "the public may reasonably believe that the licensee considered the place, event, etc., to be of sufficient news or entertainment value so as to justify extraordinary expenditures in order to provide broadcast coverage when, in fact, consideration offered by a party or parties other than the licensee or commercial sponsor of the program was responsible, to a degree, for the decision to broadcast the particular program material."[112] The commission rejected the argument that no announcement is called for because these are normal business practices and the press are regularly given such favors, since special requirements have been imposed on broadcasting stations. The commission also explained that "plugola" and "sneaky commercials" violated Section 317.[113]

The FCC's interpretation of Section 317 brought protests from the broadcasting industry, protests which became part of the discussion of the amendments to the Communications Act which were then being considered in Congress. There was general agreement that change in the law was required to deal with payola. Late in 1959, the attorney general sent a report to the president on "Deceptive Practices in Broadcasting Media." The attorney general argued that when a broadcast license is awarded the broadcaster "enters into an agreement with the government to serve the public interest in return for the valuable privilege he is granted."[114] In particular, programming should not be determined by "naked commercial selfishness."[115] A disc jockey receiving payola "does not disclose that he is being paid to play the record and creates the impression that it is being broadcast because of its merit."[116] Given his view that the government could impose extensive regulation in return for the license, it is not surprising that the attorney general concluded that the FCC and the FTC "appear to have authority adequate under existing law to eradicate most, if not all, of the deceptive and corrupt practices in broadcasting which have been disclosed—particularly if the agencies are accorded the full cooperation of the broadcasting industry."[117]

However, since the FCC's authority was limited to the actions of stations and did not extend to employees, "Legislation should be enacted which would make it a criminal offense for employees of stations to accept payola for material which is broadcast without making arrangements with the broadcaster for an appropriate sponsorship announcement."[118]

The problem was to devise a wording (and interpretation) of the new law which would secure "the full cooperation of the broadcasting industry". In testimony to the subcommittee, it was argued on behalf of the industry that the FCC's interpretation of Section 317 was too restrictive. After this testimony, the staff of the subcommittee submitted draft amendments to the Communications Act to representatives of the industry, including the National Association of Broadcasters and the networks ABC, CBS, and NBC. There followed several meetings with the staff of the subcommittee, at which representatives of the FCC were present. Later, the conclusions of the broadcasting industry, about how the Communications Act should be amended, were sent to Representative Oren Harris, who was both chairman of the subcommittee and of the main committee on Interstate and Foreign Commerce. These conclusions set out not only what the law should be but also a series of illustrations on how the law should be interpreted.[119]

The sections in the act relating to payola substantially followed the proposals of the broadcasting industry. To the old Section 317 was added a proviso: "*Provided* that 'service or other valuable consideration' shall not include any service or property furnished without charge or at a nominal charge for use on, or in connection with, a broadcast unless it is so furnished in consideration for an identification in a broadcast of any person, product, service, trademark, or brand name beyond an identification which is reasonably related to the use of such service or property on the broadcast."[120] The effect of this proviso was to allow broadcasting stations to accept products or services without charge for use in broadcasting without any announcement being required provided that its use was reasonably related to the program. The illustrations, which were reproduced in the report of the committee recommending that the amendments be passed, and which therefore became part of the legislative history, indicate what this proviso was intended to accomplish.[121] For example, if a Coca-Cola distributor furnished a Coca-Cola dispenser for use in a drugstore scene, no announcement was required. And, of course, it was made clear that the playing of free records would no longer require an announcement (unless more were supplied than were needed for broadcast purposes), thus reversing the previous legal position, at any rate as the FCC believed it to have been. (The complete list of illustrations will be found in Appendix B.)

Other parts were added to Section 317. In the case of "any political program or any program involving the discussion of any controversial issue," subsection (a)(2) provided that the FCC could require an announcement if films, records or other materials or services were provided free or at a nominal charge "as an inducement to the broadcast of such program." It should be noted, however, that "news releases" furnished to stations by government, business, labor unions, or similar organizations or by private persons did not require any announcement even though "editorial comment therefrom is used on a program" (illustration 11). By subsection (d), the FCC was empowered to waive any requirement of the section if this would serve "the public interest, convenience, or necessity."

A new section, 508, was added to deal with payments which were made not to the stations but to employees of the station or program producer. It was provided that the station's employee who received payments to include material in programs and also the person who made them had to inform the station about them, and, in the case of payments to a program producer's employee, disclosure had to be made to the employer, or to the person for whom the program was being produced or to the licensee of the station over which the program was to be broadcast. A supplier of a program had to disclose any information about such payments of which he had information to the person to whom it was supplied for broadcasting. In Section 317, an obligation was placed on the station to make an appropriate announcement when there were such payments and also to "exercise reasonable diligence" to obtain this information. The proviso to Section 317 also applied to Section 508. Violation of Section 508 could result in a fine of $10,000, imprisonment for one year, or both.

VI. Implementation of the 1960 Amendments to the Communications Act

With the passage of the amendments to the Communications Act, implementation of the law prohibiting payola became the responsibility of the FCC. The FTC stopped issuing complaints against record manufacturers and distributors and dismissed several complaints which were still outstanding (these appear to have been cases in which the FTC complaint had been contested). The basis for these dismissals was that the public interest was now fully protected by the amendments to the Communications Act and that continued prosecution by the FTC would be "an unnecessary expenditure of time, effort and funds."[122] Some firms which had earlier entered into consent decrees attempted to have them set aside but, although Commissioner Elman thought this should be done, mainly because not to do so would mean that only those firms which had cooperated with the FTC would be subject to decrees, the rest of the commission decided to let their earlier orders stand.[123]

The FCC, in its enforcement of the new law, had been given illustrations by the House Committee on Interstate and Foreign Commerce, worked out in cooperation with industry representatives, indicating how the amendments should be interpreted. In short, the aim was to prevent "extreme types" of payola while avoiding "some of the hardships" which would have resulted from the FCC's interpretation of the old sponsor identification provision as set out in its public notice of March 16, 1960.[124] These congressional illustrations made it clear that payments in cash or in kind to bring about the inclusion of material in programs required that an announcement be made but that, when it came to the provision of free material without any agreement for identification beyond its use on the program, the law was to be liberally interpreted. In particular, the provision of free records for playing on a program did not require an announcement (illustration 1). We have seen that the supply of a Coca-Cola machine for use in a drugstore scene did not require an announcement (illustration 11). Similarly, the supply of an identifiable automobile to be driven by a detective to chase the villain did not require an announcement (illustration 17). In the same way, the supply of a refrigerator for a kitchen scene did not require an announcement (illustration 15), but this would be required if the actress made a reference to the brand (illustration 22). However, if the refrigerator is furnished as a prize on a give-away show and the brand name, cubic capacity, and the particulars are mentioned, no announcement was required because "the costly or special nature of the prizes is an important feature of this type of program" (illustration 23a). Again, if an aircraft manufacturer furnished free transportation to the cast of a show and the arrival of the cast is shown on the program (the name of the manufacturer being identifiable on the fuselage), no announcement was required, although it would be if an extra close-up of the insignia was shown (illustration 24). (The full list of illustrations will be found in Appendix B.)

The FCC was soon to add two more illustrations of its own. The networks and the National Association of Broadcasters submitted to the FCC in December, 1960, new illustrations relating to automobiles and hotels. These were accepted by the FCC with some minor changes in wording and became illustrations 28 and 29. The effect was to broaden the previous exemptions. FCC illustration 28 amended illustration 17 to allow the supply of automobiles "for other business purposes in connection with the production of the programs, such as transporting the cast, crews, equipment and supplies from location to location or transporting executive personnel to business meetings in connection with the production of the programs." Similarly, congressional illustration 14 had allowed a hotel to originate programs on its premises without an announcement. FCC illustration 29 allowed a hotel also to provide room and board for "cast, production and technical staff" and to provide other services such as electrical and cable connections without an announcement being required.

The other illustrations of the FCC (30 to 36) did not significantly change the position from what it had been before the 1960 amendments. Illustration 33 made clear that the regulations against payola applied to political broadcasts and required that "the true identity of the person or persons by whom and in whose behalf payment was made" should be disclosed.[125] In illustration 35, the FCC reaffirmed its earlier opinion (made in connection with the supply of a film of the Senate Kohler hearings by the National Association of Manufacturers) that an announcement of the name of the supplier of a film was required. (The full list of the FCC's illustrations will be found in Appendix C.)

The waiver from the payola regulations which the FCC granted for feature films produced initially for theater showing should also be noted. The early negotiations about the interpretation of the 1960 amendments had been carried out with representatives of the broadcasting industry. The film industry does not appear to have become aware of the possible effect of these amendments on its operations until later, and it was not until the final debate in the Senate that serious questions were raised about their impact on the industry. It was then stated that these amendments could be interpreted in such a way as to make illegal many of the normal business arrangements of the film industry.[126] Shortly after the new law came into effect, the FCC held a conference with representatives of the film industry.[127] Following this, in October, 1960, the Alliance of Television Film Producers filed a petition with the FCC asking for a ruling that the old law applied to all films produced before the date of the new law and for the issue of a waiver for films produced after that date. That the amendments did not apply to films produced before September 13, 1960, when the new law came into effect, was readily conceded by the FCC. The problem that remained concerned films produced after this date. The FCC proposed to issue a regulation stating that all such films would "in the absence of an adequate showing to the contrary, be presumed to have been intended for television exhibition"[128] and therefore subject to its regulations on payola. The FCC's view, which it buttressed with facts it had gathered about the film industry, was that "one of the purposes behind the production of virtually all 'feature' films produced today is eventual television exposure."[129]

The film industry argued that FCC regulations concerning payola should not be applied to films produced for theater distribution, even though they might be broadcast in future years. They claimed that the film industry was commonly supplied with "props" such as automobiles for use in films or for other corporate purposes without payment and that to require "credit lines" would greatly reduce the value of such films for second-run syndication, since sponsors making products competitive with those mentioned in the "credits" would not use the films. This would reduce the number of films available for broadcast purposes and/or would lower the quality of those produced.[130]

Although the FCC continued to claim that it had the right to regulate feature films, it did not adopt the subsection under which all films would be presumed to be "intended for television exhibition," and it also decided to waive the requirements of the new Section 317 for feature films produced initially for theatrical exhibition. To justify this action, the FCC stated that its "prior experience with respect to the administration and enforcement of Section 317, of course, contains nothing which would indicate that the theatrical motion picture industry has engaged in practices which were felt to be contrary to the public interest as it relates to broadcasting." This is understandable since the previous law did not call for the FCC to look into the practices of the motion picture industry. The FCC continued: "Lacking any such indications in our own experience, we next turn to the ... proceedings before the Special House Subcommittee on Legislative Oversight. A thorough overview of the proceedings ... similarly fails to indicate the existence of practices in the motion picture industry similar to those which had been found to exist in the broadcasting industry." This again is hardly surprising since the subcommittee was largely concerned with the broadcasting industry and particularly with the activities of disc jockeys. After acting in a manner which recalls Nelson placing a telescope to his blind eye, the FCC is able to conclude that "we are aware of no public interest considerations which dictate the immediate adoption of a rule similar to that proposed ... before we adopt a rule which might have some disruptive and dislocating economic effects and which might inhibit program production ... we believe that we should have evidence indicative of a need for such a rule."[131]

There is something paradoxical about the contrast between the considerable efforts made by the film industry to avoid being subject to the new law and the opinion of the FCC that there did not appear to be any practices in the industry which would justify the enforcement of the anti-payola provisions. There can be no doubt that if these feature films had been produced to be shown first on television, the business arrangements involved in their production would have required special announcements. Perhaps what the FCC had in mind was that the film industry did not appear to engage in the cruder forms of payola, such as were disclosed in the 1959 congressional enquiry. But, as the Begelman affair indicates, the film industry is not without employees capable of engaging in them.[132] It is hard to believe that the business arrangements in making feature films are not essentially the same as those found in making films for the broadcasting industry (and which have been held to require regulation).

The House Committee on Interstate and Foreign Commerce explained that the 1960 amendments only dealt with payments in cash or their equivalent. They did not cover indirect benefits which accrued to licensees and their employees, and which might affect the selection of program material, such as stock ownership or other interests in the production of programs or program material. However, the committee added that "disclosure of such benefits may be required by the commission under its general rulemaking powers."[133] In 1961, the FCC published proposed rules covering indirect benefits (with examples).[134] All comments filed with the commission opposed the proposed rules. Some argued that the FCC lacked the authority to make such rules. The FCC issued a new notice setting out proposed new rules in 1970. The FCC maintained that the selection of program material, such as the records to be played on a radio program should be made "on its merits i.e., not on the basis of what will further the non-broadcast financial interests of the licensee or someone else involved in the selection process."[135] To make this possible, persons having such a financial interest should be insulated from the selection process and if this could not be done, steps should be taken to ensure that such financial interests were not a factor influencing the selection of program material. To the extent that this was done, no announcement would be required. However, if such insulation was not possible, and where such financial interests were, or might be, a factor influencing the selection of program material, an announcement should be made except where the financial interest was "readily apparent." The FCC, in a series of examples, dealt with the practical problems that would be faced by licensees and others in conforming to such rules. Up to the present time, the FCC has not issued rules relating to indirect benefits.

According to the House Committee on Interstate and Foreign Commerce, reporting on the 1960 amendments, their main purpose was to stop the "extreme types" of payola and in particular the cash payments (and other favors) given to disc jockeys by record producers and distributors.[136] What has been the effect of the change in the law? Those writers on the record industry who deal with the subject state that payola has continued.[137] Reports in the press tell the same story.[138] The FCC's own investigations confirm the essential accuracy of these accounts. In 1964, the FCC announced that it had received "allegations from many sources indicating the continued existence of 'payola,' 'plugola' and other related practices by broadcast licensees,"[139] and, as a consequence, the FCC, starting in 1966, conducted non-public hearings on the subject. These hearings left little doubt that payola had not been stopped by the change in the law.[140]

Starting in 1973, the Department of Justice (assisted by the Internal Revenue Service and the FCC), as well as four grand juries, investigated payola in the record industry for two years, as a result of which they concluded that payola had been received by radio station employees in sixteen cities. Sixteen individuals and six corporations were indicted by grand juries in Newark, Philadelphia, and Los Angeles for "violating the federal statute banning under-the-table payoffs for playing records, as well as for travelling between states to commit bribery, for mail and wire fraud, for filing false income tax returns and for perjury." In addition, a fourth grand jury, in New York City, indicted a former president of the CBS/Record Group and a former director of artist relations for CBS Records, for income tax evasion. Both had earlier been fired by CBS after allegations that they had engaged in payola.[141] In April, 1976, four executives of the Brunswick Record Company were fined and given prison terms, after a trial in which radio station music directors (who had been granted immunity), gave testimony that they had received cash payments from representatives of the company. The lawyers for the executives had argued that "cash payments were a way of life in the record industry and part of the promotion end of the business," to which the judge replied, "If this is true, then the record business is a dirty business indeed."[142] It should be noted that although these cases are usually referred to in the press as "payola" cases and the headline in the *New York Times* said that the Brunswick executives were sentenced "for payola," the charge in such cases, whether because of plea bargaining or for some other reason, is usually income tax evasion, perjury, or some similar offense, rather than infringing the Communications Act. In the case of the Brunswick executives, they were found guilty of a conspiracy to sell records for cash and not report the income and defrauding recording artists and song writers of their royalties. In December, 1976, the FCC announced that it had received "new information and new complaints from the public" and it resumed its proceedings on payola.[143] The proceedings have not yet terminated.

So far as I know, no action has ever been taken by the FCC to prosecute any licensees or their employees, using the 1960 amendments to the Communications Act. Even in the investigations of the Department of Justice in 1973-1975 the FCC seems to have played a minor role. The chief of the FCC's Complaints and Compliance Division has indicated that he lacks the resources for a full-scale investigation of payola.[144] However, in its regulation of individual licensees, the FCC does take into account any information which it uncovers about payola and imposes administrative sanctions when the licensee has not exercised "reasonable diligence" in preventing payola.[145] This has given the individual licensee an incentive to set up procedures which make the giving of payola more difficult. A common way in which this has been done is for the program director of the station to prepare play-lists from which disc jockeys are required to choose the records which they play on their programs.[146] Although, no doubt, payola is on occasion received by the man who prepares the play-list, the procedure must discourage the making of such payments and has almost certainly had the effect of reducing the number of transactions involving payola and, very probably, the total amount paid.

Other evidence points in the same direction. There is now said to be greater reliance by record companies on the promotion man (the equivalent in the record industry of the song-plugger) to do what is necessary to obtain "exposure" for their records. "With the diminuation of direct payola, the industry representative or promo man was restored to a position of importance ... In part, this restored the majors to a place of competitive advantage over the [independents] since many of the smaller companies, having relied heavily upon payola, did not have a promotional apparatus of any magnitude."[147] Promotion includes advertisements in trade papers, mailings, personal appearances by recording stars, visits to radio stations, the supply of records, as well as other activities which build "goodwill" and which, if not payola, border on it.

Although payola continues, there can be little doubt that its incidence has been reduced since 1960. The fact that there have been no prosecutions by the FCC does not mean that the 1960 amendments to the Communications Act have been without effect.

VII. The Rationale of the 1960 Amendments

The payola enquiry by the House subcommittee which preceded the enactment of the 1960 amendments to the Communications Act was conducted as if everything that really mattered had already been discovered. The underlying purpose seems to have been to obtain confessions of guilt from the witnesses and to demonstrate the high moral standards of the congressmen. No attempt was made to understand the phenomenon under consideration, to enquire what would happen if the proposed legislation was passed, or to consider, if payola had adverse consequences, whether there were alternative ways of dealing with it. In the circumstances it is hardly surprising that widely held misconceptions about payola were perpetuated by the enquiry.

In spite of the fact that payola is commonly referred to as commercial bribery,[148] most cases of payola do not involve commercial bribery as that term is generally understood. A person is guilty of commercial bribery, according to the New York Penal Law, "when he confers, or agrees to confer, any benefit upon any employee, agent or fiduciary without the consent of the latter's employer or principal, with intent to influence his conduct in relation to his employer's or principal's affairs."[149] The victim of commercial bribery is the employer, whose employees are induced to perform acts inimical to his interest. It is obvious that payola would not constitute commercial bribery if the employer was aware that it was being given and did not object to its acceptance or even encouraged it. As was said by a judge in New York: "It would seem that there could be no violation of the [commercial bribery] statute if the principal or employer had knowledge and either approved or condoned the act of his employee or agent."[150]

What is apparent from the history of payola is that it has not been the employers who objected to the acceptance of payola by their employees. Nor can there be much doubt that in most cases they were aware of what was going on. It was the music publishers who wished to put a stop to the payments made to dance band leaders and singers rather than the hotels and dance halls in which they performed or the radio stations on which their programs were broadcast. When payola was banned in the NRA code for the broadcasting industry, this provision was inserted, not at the behest of the broadcasters, but of the music publishers. And later, when the music publishers wanted the FTC to approve a code of fair practice which would make payola illegal, the Fair Practice Board of the FTC noted that "the employers of such musicians, singers or artists, for the most part at least, have no objection to such professional employees receiving such payments or gifts."[151] Still later, in the 1950s, when payola was directed to disc jockeys, it was apparently a letter from Burton Lane, representing the American Guild of Authors and Composers, which led to the payola enquiry and it was a record company's complaint which set into motion the FTC's investigation of the payments which record companies made to disc jockeys.

While all this was happening, the operators of radio stations remained passive.

The inference that I draw from this conduct is that most of them did not consider the acceptance of payola by disc jockeys as particularly harmful to their interests. This inference is strengthened if we have regard to the actions of the FCC, which since the change in the law in 1960, has used fines and other administrative sanctions, to make sure that broadcast licenses show "reasonable diligence" in combatting payola. This is something which one would have supposed that they would do without FCC prodding if payola really harmed them.

The lack of any serious effort on the part of the broadcasting industry in the 1950s to prevent payola suggests that there was a broad congruence of interest between the operators of radio stations and the disc jockeys. This was undoubtedly true. And the reason for this becomes clear if we compare the results of a system without payola with one in which payola is received by disc jockeys. Assume that the operator of a radio station (no doubt in the person of the music director or some similar officer) chooses the records to be played and there is no payola (although the records are supplied free). He would select records so as to attract as large an audience as possible, which would enable him to maximize the revenue obtained from the sale of commercial time. He may also be concerned about the composition of the audience but this complication will be ignored for the time being. Now assume that the choice of records to be played is made by the disc jockey, who receives payola. That such payments are made does not necessarily imply that there has been a change in the records played from what it would have been without payola. Suppose, for example, that the disc jockey wished to play the same records as those the station operator would have chosen. The disc jockey would not be denied an income from payola. Record companies would be willing to pay the disc jockey to play these records since there would presumably be other records which could be substituted for them without any great loss of audience and for which payola could be obtained. The ability of disc jockeys to obtain payola would lower the salary for which they would be prepared to work for radio stations and would therefore increase station profits. But disc jockeys would receive a reward for the extra work in which they engaged to obtain payola and so their earnings would also rise. Payola would benefit both the operators of radio stations and the disc jockeys.

Although it is unlikely that the records selected would remain exactly the same in the new situation, the claim of some disc jockeys that their acceptance of payola had not affected their choice of records is not perhaps as far from the truth as might at first appear. To induce a disc jockey to play a particular record, a record company would be willing to pay up to the increase in profits which would result from playing the record. But a disc jockey would not simply play those records for which he was offered the greatest payola. Like the radio station operator, he would also want to have a large audience since a fall in the rating of his show would lead both to a reduction in his salary and to a reduction in the amount which record companies would offer as payola for playing any given record. In assessing his gain from playing a record, a disc jockey would have to deduct from the payola he would receive from playing a less popular record both the fall in his salary and the loss of payola received from playing other records. This calculation would make a disc jockey reluctant to play less popular records. But even if there were some loss in revenue from commercials the station operator would not suffer since this would be offset by the reduction in the disc jockey's salary. Station profits would rise or, at the least, remain the same.

The harmony between the interests of the broadcast licensee and the disc jockey is probably even greater than this analysis would indicate. It has been assumed that since a station operator (not receiving payola) would wish to maximize the size of the audience, to entrust the selection of records to a disc jockey (receiving payola) could not increase but could only reduce the station's audience. But this would not necessarily happen. It seems probable that disc jockeys, who are not part of management, would be able to see more representatives of the record companies, would be closer to their audience, would be more aware of trends in popular music, and would also know better which records were suitable for their own particular programs. As a consequence, a transfer of the choice of records to the disc jockey need not entail a reduction in audience and may indeed lead to an increase.

Payola is also likely to have some effect on the character of programming. Since record programs will become more profitable with payola, there may be a tendency for such programs to displace non-record programs. There may also be a change in the character of the record programs themselves. Up to now it has been assumed that the revenue from commercials depended solely on the size of the audience. But it is obvious that the composition of the audience may also be of importance since advertisers prefer an audience more heavily weighted with persons likely to buy their products. The addition of payola as a source of income for the disc jockey (and, indirectly, for the station) would almost certainly mean that the records played would be such as to attract an audience which included more record buyers than if the aim of the program was simply to gather an audience for commercials for clothing, cosmetics, cameras, or whatever was advertised in the commercials. Such a change in audience would, of course, only come about if the gain from the additional payola offset the loss in revenue from the sale of commercial time. All in all, it is easy to see why the operators of radio stations were not in the forefront of those opposing payola and therefore why it is hard to regard payola as constituting commercial bribery.

But the view that payola was commercial bribery was not the sole basis for objecting to it. It was also argued that it fosters deception. As the attorney general said in his report to the president: "A disc jockey who receives such a payment does not disclose that he is being paid to play the record and creates the impression that it is being broadcast because of its merit."[152] The FTC adopted a similar point of view except that the phrase it used was "merits or public popularity."[153] This deception, according to the attorney general and the FTC, comes about because listeners assume (in the absence of any disclosure that the disc jockey is receiving money from record companies) that a disc jockey has picked what he considered to be the best of the current records and they are therefore led to buy these records without checking or hearing others. The result is a disappointment for the purchasers, who become tired of playing the record sooner than they (although not necessarily their families) had hoped. Or they may discover that a record which they had been led to believe would be extremely popular is not and this may adversely affect the enjoyment they derive from playing the record. That this may happen is not open to dispute. But it seems improbable that such deception would occur on a large scale. Purchasers not only hear the disc jockey—they also hear the record before buying. And a disc jockey who receives payola would not wish to disappoint his listeners often since otherwise they would cease to take his recommendations seriously and his income would fall.

It has been suggested to me that even though a disc jockey receiving payola would tend to play records which would appeal to his particular audience, deception would still exist in that, if there were disclosure of the fact that the disc jockey was being paid by record companies, the attitude of his listeners would be adversely affected and this would result in them being less willing to purchase the records played on his programs. As it is generally agreed that hearing a record is the most powerful factor bringing about its purchase, presumably this disclosure of payola would lead to a decline in the sales of records (as well as less pleasure from the programs). Whether listeners would be happier with disclosure is another matter. The prevalence of self-deception suggests that there are many truths that we prefer not to know. Unfortunately, those conducting the congressional inquiry thought it unnecessary to investigate what listeners thought the motives of the disc jockeys were or how they felt about them or what their record-buying habits really were, and so it is difficult to come to any conclusion on these questions. One may, however, doubt whether the disclosure of the existence of payola would make much difference since disc jockeys are skilled in handling commercials, an art in which sincerity (or the appearance of sincerity) is generally considered important.

The puzzle to be explained is why the stations did not make a direct charge for playing records and thus eliminate, at least to a large extent, the opportunities for payola. The sales staff of a station are expert in the pricing and selling of commercial time, and it would be surprising if they could not carry out this function more efficiently than most disc jockeys. There would appear to be three possible explanations for this failure to make a direct charge. First, payola is more difficult to trace and may therefore be omitted from an income tax return with less risk than a salary. Consequently, the amount by which the station could reduce the disc jockey's salary would be more than the amount of the payola (since income tax would be paid on his salary). Second, the amount which the stations could charge for playing records would be reduced to the extent that disclosure of these payments diminished the sales of records, a factor which obviously would not affect the payola received by disc jockeys. I am, however, inclined to lay more stress on a third explanation, namely that the obstacle to direct charges was the form of announcement which the FCC would have required the stations to make. I base this on the FCC's ruling in 1960 on the announcements required in connection with the broadcast use of "free records" and on the response to this of the stations, who regarded the FCC's requirements as completely unacceptable. They complained that the announcements which had to accompany the playing of each record turned a large part of the program into a commercial and imposed a great hardship on the listening public.[154] It is easy to see that such policies on the part of the FCC would discourage the stations from attempting to introduce a charge for broadcasting records. The FCC never seems to have thought that a charge for broadcasting records was desirable and was therefore never led to search for a form of announcement which would have been acceptable to the stations but which would let listeners know that payments were made by record companies.

The objection to payola by the attorney general and the FTC should be differentiated from much that was said by congressmen in the payola enquiry. Echoing what the music publishers had said about the choice of songs in the period before World War II, the congressmen argued that the records should be chosen because of their "merit" or because they served "the public interest." The attorney general and the FTC argued that since the disc jockey did not disclose that he had accepted payola he created the false impression that the records broadcast were chosen on their merit. Their objection would be removed if there were disclosure of the payments. The congressmen's objection would apply whether or not the payments were disclosed. However, it is an objection of little practical importance. The alternative in the United States to a system involving payola is not one in which the choice of program depends on merit but one in which program content is determined by its success in assembling the right kind of audience for the commercials. The main effect on the programs of the abolition of payola would be to displace record programs which were attractive to record buyers by record programs which appealed to buyers of other goods and services. It seems difficult to argue that such programs would have more "merit" (considered as record programs). What undoubtedly caused the congressmen (and others) to think in this way was their belief that the records actually played (mainly rock and roll and similar music) lacked merit, were corrupting, and would not be played in the absence of payola. The music may have been corrupting, but the congressmen seem to have thought that the choice of "immoral" music was due to "immoral" business practices. But payola has always been a feature of the popular music industry. In times past, when the public enjoyed songs with music (and lyrics) very different from those of today, it was these songs which were promoted by payments to performers. What has been promoted by payola has always depended on what the public would buy (sheet music earlier and records more recently) after they had heard the music. And this has depended on the tastes of the period. But the congressmen were not wholly wrong. Although there has to be a receptivity to a type of music if it is to be successfully promoted, without promotional activity (which includes payola), the movement towards a new type of music would undoubtedly be slower (because the opportunity of hearing it would be less). So the abolition of payola, if it would not necessarily have stopped or reversed the trend towards rock and roll music, would have slowed it down and would therefore have resulted, at least for a period, in more "good music" being broadcast. Another factor would work in the same direction. Payola, by leading to the playing of records which appealed to record buyers rather than to consumers of the goods advertised in the commercials, would result in the audience containing relatively more teenagers who are more likely than other age groups to enjoy rock and roll music.

The FCC, in justifying the "sponsor identification" rule (under which payola is prohibited), has adopted a point of view similar to that of the FTC: "...the public is entitled to know by whom it is persuaded."[155] In its notice about indirect benefits, the FCC added that "the public is no less entitled to know of the existence of such benefits and motivations as in the other kind of case where the inducement is created by payments or the furnishing of programs without charge."[156] Concealment of the fact that program material was broadcast because of a payment or other consideration constituted "deception."[157] Of course there is usually no problem. A soap, automobile, drug, or cosmetics concern, which has paid for the expenses of a program will normally want everyone to know that it sponsored the program. But even if there is concealment, what prompted a supplier to provide program material may not matter to the radio and television audience. A consumer's ability to choose wisely between what is offered to him may not depend on knowing the "benefits and motivations" which prompted its supply. Of course, it was the FCC's contention that knowledge of whether a disc jockey received a payment from record companies helps the audience to appraise the worth of the disc jockey's opinions—and this may be true. But there are other programs in which knowing who paid for it or the motivations of the supplier can influence even more the response to the program. For example, in the case of news programs and commentaries, knowledge of the source of finance and the political and religious doctrines and affiliations of the speaker is likely to influence the degree of confidence one has in the accuracy of the news and the responsibility of the comment. However, in this case full disclosure is not required. There need be no announcement when "news releases are furnished to a station by Government, business, labor and civic organizations, and private persons, with respect to their activities, and editorial comment therefrom is used on a program" (House committee illustration 11). It is not easy to reconcile this exemption in an area in which the case for disclosure is strong with the FCC's view of what the anti-payola provisions are intended to accomplish, or with the attitude taken towards the acceptance of payola by disc jockeys.

On the other hand, it would not seem important in choosing between programs or in one's enjoyment of them to know how the salaries of the performers are determined. Among the House committee's illustrations of cases to which the anti-payola provisions did not apply was the following: "A well-known performer appears as a guest artist on a program at union scale because the performer likes the show, although the performer normally commands a much higher fee" (illustration 20). Philanthropy being rare in the entertainments industry, it is easy to imagine the circumstances which would lead a performer to like a show and to be willing to work at less than his normal fee. These include boosting the sales of his records, increasing the likelihood of obtaining concert engagements or roles in films and so on. A similar question has arisen in relation to performers whose normal fee is not much higher than the union rate. The FCC has held that it violates the anti-payola provisions for a performer, paid the union rate, to arrange for a recording company or other business to reimburse the producer for part or all of his fee, even though it is announced at the end of the program that "promotional assistance" has been received from that recording company or business. Similarly, it is a violation for a group to make a similar arrangement under which the producer is reimbursed for the difference between the union rate for a single performer and that for a group. Again, it is a violation for a performer to reimburse the producer for special expenses involved in his act. For example, it would violate the anti-payola provisions for a performer "to reimburse the producer for the fees paid by the latter to musicians, not normally provided in the program, who accompanied the performer."[158] Payola, in effect, exists whenever an attempt is made to circumvent union restrictions on methods of payment. The result is to allow well-known performers to take into account the other benefits which flow from appearing on a broadcast program but to restrict or deny this possibility to less well-known performers. The aim of this regulation, if we believe the FCC, is to prevent the public from being deceived.

If we have regard not to what congressmen and government agencies have said about the purpose of the anti-payola provisions but to the business interests which, over the years, have sought to curb payola, it becomes easier to discern what these provisions were expected to accomplish. Up to World War II, there is no doubt about the businesses that wanted payola to be abolished. The music publishers tried to secure this on many occasions and for those of them still alive in 1960, the amendments to the Communications Act would have represented the final passage into law of the anti-payola provisions of the NRA codes. After the war, when payola was paid by record companies to disc jockeys, it was the suppliers of "good music" (the music, that is, of composers such as Oscar Hammerstein, Richard Rodgers, Irving Berlin, and Burton Lane) who objected to payola. This hostility to payola came to the fore in 1958 and 1959 and was, it seems clear, in large part a response to the changes which took place in the 1950s in the kind of music purchased.

In the 1950s, particularly from 1955 on, "rock and roll" music became extremely popular. Many new record companies were formed, mainly concentrating on the new music. The effect on the market shares of existing companies was dramatic. In the years 1948 through 1955, four companies (Capitol, Columbia, Decca, and RCA-Victor) had, on an average, 78 per cent of the records which were ever on *Billboard's* top ten Hit Parade, and the figure was never less than 71 per cent (in 1953). In 1956, the share of the hit records of these four companies was 66 per cent, in 1957, 40 per cent, in 1958, 36 per cent, and in 1959, 34 per cent.[159] These changes in the popularity of different kinds of music also affected the relative positions of the two major royalty collecting agencies, ASCAP and BMI. BMI was heavily concentrated in country and western music and rhythm and blues while ASCAP was more evenly spread over all types of music. During the period 1948 through 1955, 68 per cent of the tunes which were number 1 on *Billboard's* top hits were controlled by ASCAP, and ASCAF's share was never less than 50 per cent (in 1951). In 1956, its share was 23 per cent, in 1957 and 1958, 25 per cent and in 1959, 31 per cent.[160]

In the circumstances, it is hardly surprising to find that the suppliers of "good music" came to the conclusion that something was wrong with the economic organization of the popular music industry. In the 1958 hearings, it was argued that the networks and broadcasting stations, as a result of their ownership of BMI, had encouraged the playing of BMI-controlled pieces on disc jockey programs and that this was the main reason why "good music" had been displaced by "bad music." But it was also claimed that disc jockeys had been induced to play BMI records by means of payola. In the 1959 hearings, no reference was made to BMI and the growth in the popularity of rock and roll music was ascribed solely to payola.

That payola in the late 1950s was used in the main to promote the playing of rock and roll and similar music is true. Indeed, as early as 1951, it had been reported in *Billboard* that "by universal agreement in the music trade, the payola situation is at its worst among the rhythm and blues spinners."[161] There can be no doubt that the new companies, which entered the business in the 1950s and succeeded in securing such an important share of the record market, relied on payola to obtain "exposure" for their records. In an article in *Variety* in January, 1958, dealing with the inroads which the "indies" [independents] had made into the markets of the major record companies, there is a barely disguised reference to the part played by payola in the operations of the independents:

Another aspect of the indie breakthrough is its free-wheeling operation. Working without the problems of a fixed overhead and a "loose" bookkeeping system, the indies have been able to knock the majors out of the box in key areas. Working with hustling freelance distributor setups, the indies have been able to kick off their product in the areas that serve as a springboard for nationwide prominence. It's on the local level, particularly, that the indies have been outscoring the majors with giveaway deals and "special" considerations for dee jays but this is all the start they ask. And, as has been evidenced by the mopup during the past year, it's all they need.

Since it's open season in the disk business all year round, more small labels than ever before have been able to climb on the national hit lists. Some of the labels weren't even around the year before. The market became wide open for such left field diskery entries as Keen, Phillips International, Cameo, Imperial, Chess, Aladdin, Roulette Sun, Speciality, Gone, Ember, Checker, Ebb, Lance, Paris, Class, Vee-Jay and Argo.[162]

To sell music on a large scale it is necessary that people hear it. Payola is one way of inducing people to play it so that it can be heard. From a business point of view, the ban on payola is therefore simply a restraint on one kind of promotional or advertising expense. Before World War II, when it was the music publishers who wished to see payola abolished, their aim was to eliminate one dimension of competition and thereby to increase their total profits. What they wanted was similar to the more general bans on advertising which have been instituted by various professional associations. After World War II, when opposition to payola came from those segments of the popular music industry which were hurt by the rise of the new music and the associated development of new record companies, the aim of the business interests which sought to curb payola seems to have been not so much to secure a general benefit for the industry as to hobble their competitors.[163]

Mr. Paine, in justifying the anti-payola provisions of the NRA code, said that it would protect the small publisher,[164] and Congressman Oren Harris, in his introductory remarks to the payola enquiry, said that "we are told" that payola tends "to drive out of business small firms who lack the means to survive this unfair competition."[165] Such statements convey a completely false impression. Although the music publishers' attempts to regulate payola do not seem to have been designed to harm the small publisher, it was, in fact, small firms which protested to the FTC in the 1930s about the harm they would suffer if payola was banned.[166] In the period after World War II, all record companies seem to have given payola to disc jockeys, but, as we have seen, the smaller companies thrived on it. These companies lacked the name-stars and the strong marketing organization of the major companies, and payola enabled them to launch their new records in a local market and, if success there was achieved, to expand their sales by making similar efforts in other markets. There is no reason to suppose that a ban on payola would, in general, have helped the small music publishers or has helped the small record companies.

Since the 1960 amendments to the Communications Act impose a restraint on a particular kind of advertising expenditure, it is to be expected that it would lead firms to increase other forms of promotional activity, trade press advertising, mailings, visits by salesmen, personal appearances by performers and, in general, all other forms of "plugging." And this appears to have happened. We have seen that shortly after payola became illegal, there was apparently an increased activity by the promotion departments of record companies.[167] An article in *Fortune*, published in April, 1979, by Peter W. Bernstein, indicates that this heightened activity has continued. It notes that record companies are "vastly increasing promotion expenses, while the most powerful form of advertising—radio play—remains free." At the same time the smaller companies have lost ground: ... small record companies, and small divisions of big companies have been making deals with, or selling out to, their big competitors—principally because the majors have built up distribution systems so powerful that smaller companies using wholesale middlemen have lost their ability to compete in the retail marketplace ... Six major companies—CBS, Capitol, MCA, Polygram, RCA, and Warner Communications—now control more than 85% of the U.S. market.[168] This growth in concentration was probably largely a result of the larger companies adjusting to the new taste in music but the 1960 amendments, which made payola illegal, undoubtedly helped in the process.

It is consistent with the view that a ban on payola would lead to an increase in other promotional activities that, in the past, support for curbing payola has come from those likely to benefit from this diversion of advertising expenditures: *Variety* early in the century and the song-pluggers at the time their union was formed. What the song-pluggers then said that they feared was that the "publisher's check book would finally obviate the necessity of maintaining a plugging staff."[169] This makes clear one of the disadvantages of the ban since, leaving aside its anti-competitive aspects, advertising is diverted from a form which, apart from the expenses involved in giving payola, does not use resources to a form that does. By leading to the employment of more resources in promotional activity, the ban on payola has a tendency to reduce the national product elsewhere.

Of course, firms will only expand their other promotional activities up to the point where they yield sufficient additional net income to cover their cost, and it could be that the increase in the amount spent on these promotional activities would be less than the amount previously paid as payola. In this case industry profits would rise by the amount by which the payola previously paid exceeded the increase in expenditures on other promotional activities. This was presumably the belief of the music publishers before World War II. But the rise in profits inherent in this situation would have other effects. In the case of the record companies, such an increase in profits would lead to an increase in the supply of new records. Previously, record companies would have been deterred from expanding their output of new titles because they thought that the probable additional receipts would not warrant increasing the additional cost. But in the new situation, the probable net income from producing a record would have risen. The effect would be for the output of new titles to expand. And this would lead to a decrease in the probable receipts from any given new title. When these probable receipts have fallen sufficiently to make it no longer worthwhile to incur the costs of producing additional records, the expansion in output would cease. If the records in the additional supply induced by the ban on payola were on average essentially the same as those already produced in terms of the pleasure given to their audience, it seems clear that the expansion in the output of records would entail a waste of resources.

What has been described as happening after the ban on payola is the normal result of a situation in which no price is exacted for the receipt of a valuable service.[170] Indeed, in the early days, what we now call payola was termed the "payment system", or, as economists would say, the pricing system. When a pricing system is not used and something of value is provided for nothing, people are willing to incur costs up to its worth in order to secure the benefits of that service. One reason, among others, for pricing a service is to avoid this unnecessary use of resources. Normally we consider such pricing as natural without considering the advantages it brings. If locating stores on a particular street or in a particular section of a town enables those stores to achieve greater sales, we expect that the rent charged will reflect this. In the same way, if the playing of a record by a radio station increases the sales of that record, it is both natural and desirable that there should be a charge for this. If this is not done by the station and payola is not allowed, it is inevitable that more resources will be employed in the production and distribution of records, without any gain to consumers, with the result that the real income of the community will tend to decline. In addition, the prohibition of payola may result in worse record programs, will tend to lessen competition, and will involve additional expenditures for regulation. The gain which the ban is thought to bring is to make the purchasing decisions of record buyers more efficient by eliminating "deception." It seems improbable to me that this problematical gain will offset the undoubted losses which flow from the ban on payola. But no attempt was made, before the 1960 amendments were adopted, to estimate the gains and losses which would flow from the change in the law and an assessment of its effects must remain very imprecise. Futhermore, no attempt was made to discover whether it might be possible to devise a form of announcement which would alert listeners to the fact that payments were made by record companies whose records were played (so that "deception" could be prevented) without the clutter of announcements to which broadcasters objected when the FCC wanted the stations to make announcements when free records were used. If this could be done, it would be possible to prevent the deception without bringing about those other disadvantages which result from the present regulations of the FCC.

It is not enough to outlaw payments simply because they can be described as "improper." Some attempt should be made to discover why such payments are made and what would in fact happen in the world as it exists if they were made illegal.

Notes

[1] The term "payola" is generally said to have been introduced by the trade periodical *Variety* and its popularity resulted from its use in that periodical. In *Webster's Third New International Dictionary*, payola is defined as "an undercover or indirect payment for a commercial favor" (as to a disc jockey for plugging a song).

[2] See P.L. 86-752, 74 Stat. 895-897.

[3] See Applicability of Sponsorship Identification Rules (Public Notice), 40 Fed. Reg. 41936 (1975).

[4]   See Variety, Feb. 9, 1938, at 1; and Id. Feb. 23, 1938, at 1.
[5]   See Variety, Feb. 23, 1938, at 1 & 48.
[6]   See Joseph Bennett, *A Short History of Cheap Music* 31 (1887) (at University of Chicago Library).
[7]   Id. at 111.
[8]   See William Boosey, *Fifty Years of Music* 26-27 (1931).
[9]   Isaac Goldberg, *Tin Pan Alley* 112 (1930).
[10] Edward B. Marks, *They All Sang* 3-4 (1934).
[11] Id. at 18.
[12] Isaac Goldberg, *supra* note 9, at 203.
[13] Edward B. Marks, *supra* note 10, at 209.
[14] David Ewen, *The Life and Death of Tin Pan Alley* 59 (1964).
[15] Id. at xii.
[16] Id. at 66.
[17] Id. at 17.
[18] Isaac Goldberg, *supra* note 9, at 206.
[19] David Ewen, *supra* note 14, at 133.
[20] Id. at 117.
[21] *Variety*, Dec. 20, 1912, at 32.
[22] *Variety*, May 26, 1916, at 5.
[23] Isaac Goldberg, *supra* note 9, at 210.
[24] It was at the same time, and for the same reason, that payola entered broadcasting in Britain. "Plugging had existed in the music market long before the appearance of broadcasting, and special payments to singers and musical directors by publishers and writers had long been a recognized means of ensuring public performance of new works. Faced with a broadcasting monopoly, the only means of directly influencing the content of music programmes was for the publisher or song writer to pay dance band leaders for playing selected items. Those who were unable to make such payments were simply left out. To satisfy the large number of complaints about plugging, the BBC prohibited dance band leaders from using announcing microphones." Alan Peacock & Ronald Weir, *The Composer in the Market Place* 65-66 (1975). They add in a footnote: "Whilst plugging has always involved special payments, it was also, until about 1930, regarded as a legitimate form of advertisement in the music trade..." Id. at 2.
[25] See pp. 273 *supra*.
[26] See pp. 273-274 *supra*.
[27] *Variety*, Oct. 6, 1916, at 3.
[28] See pp. 272 *supra*.
[29] For accounts of the formation of the Music Publishers' Protective Association, see Edward B. Marks, *supra* note 10, at 134-135, David Ewen, *supra* note 14, at 135, and Hazel Meyer, The Gold in Tin Pan Alley 158-62 (1958).
[30] *Variety*, Nov. 3, 1916, at 5; Id., Nov. 24, 1916, at 5.
[31] *Variety*, May 4, 1917, at 4.
[32] *Variety*, May 11, 1917, at 11.

[33] *Variety*, Dec. 28, 1917, at 8.
[34] Isaac Goldberg, *supra* note 9, at 206-207.
[35] Hazel Meyer, *supra* note 29, at 162.
[36] David Ewen, *supra* note 14, at 135-136.
[37] Edward B. Marks, *supra* note 10, at 135.
[38] When Edward B. Marks was first approached, he states that, "At first, I demurred" Edward B. Marks, *supra* note 10, at 134. See also the statements in *Variety*, Dec. 28, 1917, at 8.
[39] Edward B. Marks, *supra* note 10, at 134.
[40] See Hazel Meyer, *supra* note 29, at 160-161. This tale is repeated in David Ewen, *supra* note 14, at 135.
[41] Compare Hazel Meyer, *supra* note 29, at 158. In Variety, Dec. 3, 1915, at 5, the general booking manager for the Loew Circuit was reported as objecting to an agent who was directing his acts what songs to sing. The music publisher involved was Leo Feist. The agent denied that he had required his acts to sing Feist songs but "stated he felt under obligation to the Feist firm for furnishing the small time with such a large number of new tunes."
[42] See Hazel Meyer, *supra* note 29, at 161.
[43] Id. at 162.
[44] Id. at 155, 158.
[45] Sidney Shemel & M. William Krasilovsky, *This Business of Music* 97 (rev. ed. 1971).
[46] 48 Stat. 195 (1933).
[47] See P. A. Markland, Case History of the Code of Fair Competition for the Music Publishing Industry, Code No. 552, Oct. 12, 1935, at 5f, contained in Approved Code Histories, Division of Review, Records of the National Recovery Administration (Record Group 9, National Archives, Washington D.C.).
[48] See the Report of H. Brewster Hobson, Asst. Deputy Administrator, June 22, 1935, at 2, contained in Appendix I of Case History of the Code of Fair Competition for the Music Publishing Industry, *supra* note 47.
[49] Id. at 11.
[50] Testimony of John C. Paine, Chairman, Board of the Music Publishers Protective Ass'n in The Music Publishing Industry: Hearings on a Code of Fair Practices and Competition before the National Industrial Recovery Administration 158-161 (July 26, 1934), contained in Vol. III, Code of Fair Competition for Music Publishing Industry, Transcripts of Hearings, 1933-1935, Records of the National Recovery Administration (Record Group 9, National Archives, Washington D.C.).
[51] Id. at 162.
[52] Id. at 164.
[53] Letter from Oswald F. Schuette, Nat'l Ass'n of Broadcasters, to Dr. Lindsay Rogers, Deputy Administrator, National Recovery Administration, Dec. 15, 1933, contained in Music Publishing Industry, Code No. 552, Consolidated Approved Code Industry File, Records of the National Recovery Administration (Record Group 9, National Archives, Washington D.C.).
[54] Report of H. Brewster Hobson, *supra* note 48, at 2.

[55] Letter from John C. Paine to H. Brewster Hobson, June 18, 1935, contained in Consolidated Approved Code Industry File, *supra* note 53.

[56] See Federal Trade Commission, Control of Unfair Practices through Trade Practice Conference Procedure of the Federal Trade Commission (TNEC Monograph No. 34, 1941).

[57] The following account of the attempt to secure the FTC's approval for a Code of Fair Competition for the Music Publishing Industry is based on memoranda and various other material made available to me by the Federal Trade Commission. These materials have been collected as U.S. Federal Trade Commission, Materials on the Popular Music Industry used in Preparation of R. H. Coase's Payola in Radio and Television Broadcasting (available at University of Chicago Law School Library). The pagination on the following notes refers to the bound volume of materials at the University of Chicago Law School Library.

[58] Id. at 242-244.

[59] Id. at 244.

[60] Id.

[61] Id. at 245-246.

[62] Id. at 245-248.

[63] Id. at 248.

[64] Id. at 254, 262.

[65] Id. at 289, 276.

[66] Id. at 312.

[67] Id. at 332.

[68] Id. at 325.

[69] *Billboard*, Nov. 25, 1939, at 15.

[70] *Variety*, Nov. 22, 1939, at 39. "Cut-ins" refer to the practice of making a band leader or performer a part-composer of a song and therefore giving him a share in the copyright royalties.

[71] *Billboard*, Nov. 25, 1939, at 15.

[72] *Variety*, Aug. 2, 1944, at 31.

[73] *Variety*, Nov. 21, 1945, at 49.

[74] At the Hearings on a Code of Fair Practices and Competition for the Radio Broadcasting Industry, Vol. 1, at 149 (Sept. 27, 1933), RCA-Victor made a request, which was supported by Mr. H. A. Huebner of the American and Brunswick Record Corporation, to put a provision in the code which would make it a violation "to broadcast records without prior written consent of the manufacturer of such records." Later Mr. Huebner indicated that he would support a provision to ban "all use of records for broadcasting," Id., at 157. The hearings are contained in Transcript of Hearings, 1933-1935, Records of the National Recovery Administration (Record Group 9, National Archives, Washington, D.C.).

[75] See, for example, the articles mentioned in Investigation of Television Quiz Shows: Hearings before a Subcomm. of the House Comm, on Interstate & Foreign Commerce, 86th, 1st Sess. at 1142-1147 (1959) [hereinafter cited as Investigation of Television Quiz Shows]; and Meyer, *supra* note 29, at 154-185.

[76] See Investigation of Regulatory Commissions and Agencies: Hearings before a Subcomm. of the House Comm, in Interstate & Foreign Commerce, 85th Cong., 2nd Sess., pt. 4 (Feb.-March, 1958).

Mack was indicted, but criminal charges were dropped in August 1961. New York Times, Aug. 31, 1961, at 41, col. 1.

[77] For the circumstances surrounding Doerfer's resignation, see *Broadcasting*, March 14, 1960, at 31-40.

[78] Amendment to Communications Act of 1934: Hearings before the Subcomm. on Communications of the Senate Committee on Interstate & Foreign Commerce, 85th Cong., 2nd Sess. at 208.

[79] Id. at 209.

[80] Id. at 138. Mr. Vance Packard's testimony is at 106-141.

[81] Investigation of Television Quiz Shows, *supra* note 75, at 964, 970.

[82] Id. at 959.

[83] Id. at 1008.

[84] Id. at 1007, 1009.

[85] Id. at 1010.

[86] Id. at 1012.

[87] See the *New York Times*, Nov. 5, 1959, at 28; Id. Nov. 6, 1959, at 16; Id. Nov. 13, 1959, at 12; and *Time*, Nov. 16, 1959, at 65.

[88] Investigation of Television Quiz Shows, *supra* note 75, at 967.

[89] Id. at 1024.

[90] Id. at 1045.

[91] Id. at 1046.

[92] Id. at 1106.

[93] Id. at 1142.

[94] *Variety*, Nov. 11, 1959, at 1.

[95] Responsibilities of Broadcasting Licensees and Station Personnel: Hearings before a Subcomm. of the House Comm. on Interstate & Foreign Commerce on Payola and Other Deceptive Practices in the Broadcasting Field, 86th Cong., 2d Sess. (1960).

[96] Id. at 1.

[97] Id. at 2.

[98] Id. at 39.

[99] Id. at 42. Mr. Norman Prescott's testimony is found in Id. at 3-45. The testimony of Mr. Paul O'Friel, general manager of WBZ, denying that Mr. Prescott left WBZ voluntarily is found in Id. at 1548-1549.

[100] Id. at 1182. Mr. Clark's testimony will be found in Id. at 1168-1233.

[101] Id. at 658.

[102] 1960 FTC Annual Report 52.

[103] Mr. Kintner's testimony is in Responsibilities of Broadcasting Licensees, *supra* note 95, at 640-666. For a published report about the prevalence of "plugola," see *Time*, Nov. 23, 1959, at 63-66.

[104] *Supra* note 102, at 52-53.

[105] *Supra* note 95, at 641.

[106] *Supra* note 102, at 52.

[107] See *Time*, June 9, 1959, at 50.

[108] Responsibilities of Broadcasting Licensees, *supra* note 95, at 869.

[109] Charles Belz, *The Story of Rock* 109 (1969).

[110] See the discussion at 67 Cong. Rec. 5488.

[111] Only two policy statements seem to have been issued by the FCC before 1960: one related to how a sponsor should be identified and the other to "teaser" announcements. 40 FCC 2 (1950);40 Id., 60(1959). Only one incident seems to have called for extensive FCC action. When the National Association of Manufacturers supplied broadcast stations with a film of the Senate Hearings on the Kohler labor dispute, the FCC intervened to require that an announcement be made stating that the film had been made available by the association. KSTP, Inc., 17 Radio Reg. (P. & F.) 553 (1958); Storer Broadcasting Co., Id. at 556a; Westinghouse Broadcasting Co., Id. at 556d.

[112] 40 FCC 73 (1960).

[113] Id. at 69-75.

[114] U.S. Dep't of Justice, Report to the President by the Attorney General on Deceptive Practices in Broadcasting Media iii (1959).

[115] Id. at iv.

[116] Id. at 9.

[117] Id. at v.

[118] Id. at 52.

[119] Communications Act Amendments: Hearings before a Subcomm. of the House Comm, on Interstate & Foreign Commerce, 86th Cong., 2d Sess. 157-163 (1960).

[120] H.R. Report No. 1800, 86th Cong., 2d Sess. at 20 (1960).

[121] Id. at 1-26.

[122] See, for example, Chess Record Corp., 59 FTC 361 (1961). Other cases will be found at 58 FTC 1016 (1961); and in 59 FTC 166, 209, 230, 302 (1961).

[123] See Bernard Lowe Enterprises *et al.,* 59 FTC 1485 (1961). However, in at least one case (involving the Radio Corporation of America), an earlier order was set aside, 62 FTC 1291 (1963).

[124] See pp. 296-297 *supra*.

[125] This requirement was to cause some difficulty for the FCC. See 52 FCC 2d 701 (1975).

[126] 106 Cong. Rec. 176 25-26 (Aug. 25, 1960).

[127] See 34 FCC 829, 832 (1963).

[128] Id. at 833, 834.

[129] Id. at 838-839.

[130] Id. at 833.

[131] Id. at 841-842.

[132] In February 1978, David Begelman resigned as president of Columbia Pictures Industries Inc. amid allegations of a cover-up within the company involving forgery charges. The Begelman affair brought on investigations of financial practices throughout the film industry. See the *New York Times*, Feb. 7, 1978, at 1, col. 2; and *New York. Times Index* 1978, at 221.

[133] See H.R. Report No. 1800, *supra* note 120, at 19-20.

[134] 40 FCC 119 (1961).

[135] 35 Broadcast Announcement of Financial Interest, Fed. Reg. 7983 (released May 18, 1970).

[136] H.R. Report No. 1800, *supra* note 120 at 19.
[137] See Arnold Passman, *The Dee Jays*, 242-243 & 258-259 (1971); R. Serge Denisoff, *Solid Gold: The Popular Record Industry* 232, 260, & 273-279 (1975); Paul Hirsch, *The Structure of the Popular Music Industry* 54 (Survey Res. Center, Inst, for Soc. Res., Univ. of Michigan, n.d., c. 1967); and Steve Chappie & Reebee Garofalo, *Rock 'n' Roll Is Here to Pay* 183 (1977).
[138] See Jack Anderson, New Disc Jockey Payola Uncovered, *Washington Post*, March 31, 1972; and Disc Jockey Play-for-Drugs Outlined, *Washington Post*, April 21, 1972; The Specter of Payola' 73, *Newsweek*, June 11, 1973, at 74, 79.
[139] See "Payola" "Plugola" and Other Related Practices (FCC 64-1101) 29 Fed. Reg. 16220 (released Nov. 27, 1964).
[140] I was given permission by the FCC to read most of the transcript of the non-public hearings (Docket No. 16648) at the Washington office of the FCC.
[141] See *Broadcasting*, June 30, 1975, at 27-29.
[142] See the *New York Times*, April 13, 1976, at 66; and *Broadcasting*, Feb. 23, 1976, at 53-54, and April 19, 1976, at 47.
[143] FCC Notice (released Dec. 30, 1976).
[144] See *Broadcasting*, June 30, 1975, at 27.
[145] Id.
[146] See R. Serge Denisoff. *supra* note 137, at 234; Paul Hirsch, *supra* note 137, at 63; Charles Belz, *supra* note 109, at 116.
[147] R. Serge Denisoff, *supra* note 137, at 233.
[148] See, for example, the Attorney General's Report to the President, *supra* note 114, at 39-40.
[149] New York Penal Law, § 180 at 326 (McKinney).
[150] June Fabrics v. Teri Sue Fashions, 194 Misc. 267, 270, 81 N.Y.S. 877 (1948).
[151] See pp. 282 *supra*.
[152] *Supra* note 114, at 9.
[153] FTC Notice (released Dec. 6, 1959).
[154] See FCC File 13454, Original Vol. 3 (National Archives, Washington, D.C.).
[155] 40 FCC 105 (1961).
[156] 40 FCC 119 (1961).
[157] 25 Fed. Reg. 2406 (1960).
[158] 23 FCC 2d 588-589 (1970).
[159] See Richard A. Peterson & David G. Berger, Cycles in Symbol Production: The Case of Popular Music, 40 *American Sociological Review*. 158, 160 (1975).
[160] I am grateful to Professor Richard A. Peterson, Vanderbilt University, who provided me with these figures.
[161] *Billboard*, Jan. 13, 1951, at 1, col. 4.
[162] *Variety*, Jan. 8, 1958, at 215.
[163] See pp. 314 *supra*. Richard A. Peterson & David G. Berger state that "[in] an effort to curb the influence of the new independents, and protect their investment in the crooners they had promoted

into stardom, the older established Tin Pan Alley-oriented companies 'exposed' the payola practices of these new entrepreneurs in 1958." Three Eras in the Manufacture of Popular Music Lyrics in The Sounds of Social Change 295-296 (edited by R. Serge Denisoff & Richard A. Peterson, 1972). This statement is in part based on confidential sources and cannot therefore be checked. But it is not inconsistent with what can be learnt from published sources.

[164] See pp. 280 *supra*.
[165] See pp. 292 *supra*.
[166] See pp. 283, 284, 285 *supra*.
[167] See pp. 306 *supra*.
[168] Peter W. Bernstein, The Record Business: Rocking to the Big-Money Beat, *Fortune*, April 23, 1979, at 59, 61.
[169] See pp. 285 *supra*.
[170] Susan Rose-Ackerman adopts a somewhat similar position in *Corruption: A Study in Political Economy* (1978). See pp. 204-205.

Appendix A
NRA Code of Fair Competition for the Music Publishing Industry No. 552

Article VIII: Trade Practice Rules

1. No member of the Industry shall pay or give, directly or indirectly, or in any other manner present to any performer, singer, musician, or orchestra leader, employed by or otherwise performing under contract for another, or to their agents or representatives, any sum of money, gift, rebate, royalty, favor, or any other thing or act of value, when the purpose is to induce such person to sing, play, perform, or to have sung, played, or performed, any works published, copyrighted, owned, and/or controlled by such member of the Industry.

2. No member of the Industry shall furnish without charge to any performer, singer, musician, orchestra leader, or other professional person, any copies other than regular professional copies of musical compositions published by such member or regularly published orchestrations of such musical compositions; it being intended

that no member of the Industry shall furnish special arrangements of such professional copies or such orchestrations to any performer, singer, musician, orchestra leader, or other professional person, or to any one designated by, or representing, or associated with such persons, nor pay such persons for the making of any such arrangements. If, however, any member of the Industry permits such persons to make a special arrangement, then no member of the Industry shall extract parts or otherwise copy such special arrangement thus made, either in whole or in part, nor pay for such extractions or copying; but nothing contained herein shall be deemed to limit the transposition of any musical work from one key to another.

3. No member of the Industry shall: (a) purchase tickets, or pay for any advertisement in the program, for any benefit, performance, dance, or similar function, if the purchase is in effect a gift to, or a favor for, any performer; (b) pay for any advertisement in a catalogue of a mail-order house; (c) pay for any advertisement in a dealer's and/or distributor's catalogue or house-organ; (d) insert advertising in any trade paper, or other like periodical, if the advertisement is intended to puff, flatter, compliment, or exploit any performer, singer, or orchestra leader.

4. No member of the Industry shall pay, present, or otherwise give any money, service, favor, or thing or act of value, to any owner, lessee, manager, employee, or other person in control of or interested in, any talking machine company, radio broadcasting company or station, electrical transcription company, motion picture company, or any place of public entertainment, for the privilege of performing, recording or reproducing, or having performed, recorded or reproduced, in such places, any works published, copyrighted, owned and/or controlled by such member of the Industry. Any member of the Industry may engage the facilities of a broadcasting studio or hire any theatre or other place of public entertainment for the purpose of having performed therein any of the musical compositions published, copyrighted, owned and/or controlled by such member, provided however, that a public announcement is made at such performance that the performance is at the expense of

such member and for the purpose of exploiting the said musical compositions of such member.

5. No member of the Industry shall pay, or contract to pay any compensation, of any nature whatsoever, either as royalties or otherwise, to any performer, singer, actor, musician or orchestra leader, or any agent or representative thereof, either directly or indirectly, in connection with the publication in printed form of any song or other musical composition, unless such person shall be the bona fide composer, arranger, or writer of the words and/or music of such song or musical composition.

6. No member of the Industry shall give, permit to be given, or offer to give, anything of value for the purpose of influencing or rewarding the action of any employee, agent, or representative of another in relation to the business of the employer of such employee, the principal of such agent or the represented party, without the knowledge of such employer, principal or party. This provision shall not be construed to prohibit free and general distribution of articles commonly used for advertising except so far as such articles are actually used for commercial bribery as hereinabove defined.

7. No member of the Industry shall give away, directly or indirectly, or through any subsidiary or associated company, or through any person employed by such member, copies of music or other musical material except for the bona fide purposes of "sampling," either to the trade or to professional performers. All such copies of music and musical material given away under the provisions of this Article must be plainly marked in some appropriate manner to indicate that they are not for resale. Each member of the Industry shall keep in some appropriate manner an accurate account of the merchandise thus given away.

8. No member of the Industry shall publish advertising (whether printed, radio, display, or any other nature), which is misleading or inaccurate in any material particular, nor shall any member of the Industry in any way misrepresent any services, policies, values, credit terms, products, or the nature or form of the business conducted.

9. No member of the Industry shall publish or sell any book of songs, pamphlet, song sheet, or other compilation of songs, or the lyrics of songs, without the special written permission of the several copyright owners whose works appear in such compilation.

10. No member of the Industry shall pay, furnish, bestow, or in any other manner, directly or indirectly, present to any customer, teacher, or any person, firm, or corporation whatsoever, or to their agents, or any one representing them, any sum of money, gift, bonus, refund, rebate, royalty, service, or any other thing or act of value in excess of published rates and discounts, as a bribe, secret rebate, or other inducement to acquire any business or custom from such person, firm, or corporation.

11. No member of the Industry shall pay transportation charges in any form whatsoever upon any musical works sold, consigned, or otherwise designated for shipment to a purchaser or prospective purchaser, except in instances where musical works are sold for cash or where delivery is to be made within the recognized local delivery limits of the city within which such member is situated.

12. No member of the Industry shall wilfully induce or attempt to induce the breach of existing contracts between competitors and their customers or sources of supply, either foreign or domestic, or otherwise interfere with or obstruct the performance of any such contractual duties or services, with the purpose and effect of hampering, injuring, or embarrassing competitors in their business.

NRA Code of Fair Competition for the Broadcasting Industry

Article VII: Trade Practices

4. General Provisions: No broadcaster or network shall accept or knowingly permit any performer, singer, musician, or orchestra leader regularly employed by such broadcaster or network to accept any money, gift, bonus, refund, rebate, royalty service, favor, or any other thing or act of value from any music publisher, composer,

author, copyright owner, or the agents or assignees of any such persons for performing or having performed any musical or other composition for any broadcaster or network when the purpose is to induce such persons to sing, play, or perform, or to have sung, played, or performed any such works.

Appendix B
Interpretative Illustrations of the House Committee on Interstate and Foreign Commerce from
H.R. Rep. No. 1800, 86th Cong., 2d Sess. 20-26 (1960)

A. Free Records

1. A record distributor furnishes copies of records to a broadcast station or a disc jockey for broadcast purposes. No announcement is required unless the supplier furnished more copies of a particular recording than are needed for broadcast purposes. Thus, should the record supplier furnish 50 or 100 copies of the same release, with an agreement by the station, express or implied, that the record will be used on a broadcast, an announcement would be required because consideration beyond the matter used on the broadcast was received.

2. An announcement would be required for the same reason if the payment to the station or disc jockey were in the form of cash or other property, including stock.

3. Several distributors supply a new station, or a station which has changed its program format (e.g., from "rock and roll" to "popular" music), with a substantial number of different releases. No announcement is required under Section 317 where the records are furnished for broadcast purposes only; nor should the public interest require an announcement in these circumstances. The station would have received the same material over a period of time had it previously been on the air or followed this program format.

4. Records are furnished to a station or disc jockey in consideration for the special plugging of the record supplier or performing talent beyond an identification reasonably related to the use of the record on the program. If the disc jockey were to state "This is my favorite new record, and sure to become a hit; so don' t overlook it", and it is understood that some such statement will be made in return for the record and this is not the type of statement which would have been made absent such an understanding, and the supplying of the record free of charge, an announcement would be required since it does not appear that in those circumstances the identification is reasonably related to the use of the record on that program. On the other hand, if a disc jockey, in playing a record, states "Listen to this latest release of performer 'X' a new singing sensation," and such matter is customarily interpolated in the disc jockey's program format and would be included whether or not the particular record had been purchased by the station or furnished to it free of charge, it would appear that the identification by the disc jockey is reasonably related to the use of the record on that particular program and there would be no announcement required.

B. Where payment in any form other than the matter used on or in connection with the broadcast is made to the station or to anyone engaged in the selection of program matter

5. A department store owner pays an employee of a producer to cause to be mentioned on a program the name of the department store. An announcement is required.

6. An airline pays a station to insert in a program a mention of the airline. An announcement is required.

7. A perfume manufacturer gives five dozen bottles to the producer of a giveaway show, some of which are to be identified and awarded to winners on the show, the remainder to be retained by the producer. An announcement is required since those bottles of perfume retained by the producer constitute payment for the identification.

8. An automobile dealer furnishes a station with a new car, not for broadcast use, in return for broadcast mentions. An announcement is required; the car constituting payment for the mentions.

9. A Cadillac is given to an announcer for his own use in return for a mention on the air of a product of the donor. An announcement is required since there has been a payment for a broadcast mention.

C. Where service or property is furnished free for use on or in connection with a program, but where there is neither payment in consideration for broadcast exposure of the service or property, nor an agreement for identification of such service or property beyond its mere use on the program

10. Free books or theater tickets are furnished to a book or dramatic critic of a station. The books or plays are reviewed on the air. No announcement is required. On the other hand, if 40 tickets are given to the station with the understanding, express or implied, that the play would be reviewed on the air, an announcement would be required because there has been a payment beyond the furnishing of a property or service for use on or in connection with a broadcast.

11. News releases are furnished to a station by Government, business, labor and civic organizations, and private persons, with respect to their activities, and editorial comment therefrom is used on a program. No announcement is required.

12. A Government department furnishes air transportation to radio newscasters so they may accompany a foreign dignitary on his travels throughout the country. No announcement is required.

13. A municipality provides street signs and disposal containers for use as props on a program. No announcement is required.

14. A hotel permits a program to originate on its premises. No announcement is required. If, however, in return for the use of the premises, the producer agrees to mention the hotel in a manner not reasonably related to the use made of the hotel on that particular program, an announcement would be required.

15. A refrigerator is furnished for use as part of the backdrop in a kitchen scene of a dramatic show. No announcement is required.

16. A Coca-Cola distributor furnishes a Coca-Cola dispenser for use as a prop in a drugstore scene. No announcement is required.

17. An automobile manufacturer furnishes his identifiable current model car for use in a mystery program, and it is used by a detective to chase a villain. No announcement is required. If it is understood, however, that the producer may keep the car for his personal use, an announcement would be required. Similarly, an announcement would be required if the car is loaned in exchange for a mention on the program beyond that reasonably related to its use, such as the villain saying: "If you hadn't had that speedy Chrysler, you never would have caught me."

18. A private zoo furnishes animals for use on a children's program. No announcement is required.

19. A university makes one of its professors available to give lectures in an educational program series. No announcement is required.

20. A well-known performer appears as a guest artist on a program at union scale because the performer likes the show, although the performer normally commands a much higher fee. No announcement is required.

21. An athletic event promoter permits broadcast coverage of the event. No announcement is required in absence of other payment by the promoter or agreement to identify in a manner not reasonably related to the broadcast of the event.

D. Where service or property is furnished free for use on or in connection with a program, with the agreement, express or implied, that there will be an identification beyond mere use of the service or property on the program

22. A refrigerator is furnished by X with the understanding that it will be used in a kitchen scene on a dramatic show and that the brand name will be mentioned. During the course of the program the actress says: "Donald, go get the meat from my new X refrigerator." An announcement is required because the identification by brand name is not reasonably related to the particular use of such refrigerator in this dramatic program.

23. (a) A refrigerator is furnished by X for use as a prize on a giveaway show, with the understanding that a brand identification will be made at the time of the award. In the presentation, the master of ceremonies briefly mentions the brand name of the refrigerator, its cubic content, and such other features as serve to indicate the magnitude of the prize. No announcement is required because such identification is reasonably related to the use of the refrigerator on a giveaway show in which the costly or special nature of the prizes is an important feature of this type of program.

(b) In addition to the identification given in (a) above, the master of ceremonies says: "All you ladies sitting there at home should have one of these refrigerators in your kitchen." or says: "Ladies, you ought to go out and get one of these refrigerators." An announcement is required because each of these statements is a sales "pitch" not reasonably related to the giving away of the refrigerator on this type of program.

The significance of the distinction between the identification in (a) and that in (b) is, that in (a) it is no more than the natural identification which a broadcaster would give to a refrigerator as a prize if he had purchased the refrigerator himself and had no understanding whatever with the manufacturer as to any identification. That is to say, in situation (a), had the broadcaster purchased the refrigerator he would have felt it necessary, in view of the nature of the show, adequately to describe the magnitude of the prize which was being given to the winner. On the other hand, the broadcaster would not, where he had purchased the refrigerator, have made the type of identification in situation (b), thus providing a free sales "pitch" for the manufacturer.

24. (a) An airplane manufacturer furnishes free transportation to a cast on its new jet model to a remote site, and the arrival of the cast at the site is shown as part of the program. The name of the manufacturer is identifiable on the fuselage of the plane in the shots taken. No announcement is required because in this instance such identification is reasonably related to the use of the service on the program.

(b) Same situation as in (a), except that after the cameraman has made the foregoing shots he takes an extra closeup of the identification insignia. An announcement is required because the closeup is not reasonably related to the use of the service on the program.

25. (a) A station produces a public service documentary showing development of irrigation projects. Brand X tractors are furnished for use on the program. The tractors are shown in a manner not resulting in identification of the brand of tractors except as may be recognized from the shape or appearance of the tractors. No announcement is required since the identification is reasonably related to the use of the tractors on the program.

(b) Same situation as in (a), except that the brand name of the tractor is visible as it appears normally on the tractor. No announcement is required for the same reason.

(c) Same situation as in (b), except that a closeup showing the brand name in a manner not required in the nature of the program is included in the program, or an actor states: "This is the best tractor on the market." An announcement is required as this identification is beyond that which is reasonably related to the use of the tractor on the program.

26. (a) A bus company prepares a scenic travel film which it furnishes free to broadcast stations. No mention is made in the film of the company or its buses. No announcement is required because there is no payment other than the matter furnished for broadcast and there is no mention of the bus company.

(b) Same situation as in (a), except that a bus, clearly identifiable as that of the bus company which supplied the film, is shown fleetingly in highway views in a manner reasonably related to that travel program. No announcement is required.

(c) Same situation as in (a), except that the bus, clearly identifiable as that of the bus company which supplied the film, is shown to an extent disproportionate to the subject matter of the film. An announcement is required, because in this case by the use of the film the broadcaster has impliedly agreed to broadcast an identification beyond that reasonably related to the subject matter of the film.

27. (a) A manufacturer furnishes a grand piano for use on a concert program. The manufacturer insists that enlarged insignia of its brand name be affixed over normal insignia on the piano. An announcement is required if an enlarged brand name is shown.

(b) Conversely, if the piano furnished has normal insignia and during the course of the televised concert the broadcast includes occasional closeups of the pianist's hands, no announcement is required even though all or part of the insignia appears in these closeups. Here the identification of the brand name is reasonably related to the use of the piano by the pianist on the program. However, if undue attention is given the insignia rather than the pianist's hands, an announcement would be required.

Appendix C
Interpretatve Illustrations of the Federal Communications Commission from
40 FCC 141, 149-151

28. (a) An automobile manufacturer or dealer furnishes to a producer of television programs a number of automobiles with the understanding that the producer will use them, or some of them, in some of his programs which call for the use of automobiles; and that the automobiles may be used for other business purposes in connection with the production of the programs, such as transporting the cast, crew, equipment and supplies from location to location or transporting executive personnel to business meetings in connection with the production of the programs. There is no understanding that there will be any identification on the television programs beyond an identification which is reasonably related to the use of the automobiles on the programs. No other consideration is involved. Under such uses, no announcement is required.

29. (a) A hotel permits a program to originate from its premises and furnishes hotel services, such as room and board, for cast, production and technical staff, and also furnishes other elements for use in connection with the programs to be broadcast, such as electricity and cable connections, free of charge, and with no other consideration. There is no understanding that there will be an identification of the hotel on the program beyond that reasonably related to the use made of the hotel on the program.

No announcement is required.

(b) If the hotel pays money or furnishes free or at a nominal charge any services or items which are not for use on or in connection with the program (e.g., furnishing free or at a nominal charge room and board for the producer for any period of time not related to the production of the program at the hotel site), an announcement is required.

E. Effective Date

30. Does Section 317 as amended on September 13, 1960 apply to programs or portions of programs produced or recorded prior to September 13, 1960?

No, unless valuable consideration was provided to a broadcast station (rather than to a producer or other person) for the program or the inclusion of any program matter therein and the program was broadcast after said date.

F. Nature of the Announcement

31. A station broadcasts spot announcements which solicit mail orders from listeners. The sponsor is merely referred to in the announcements and in the mail order address as "Flower Seeds" or "Real Estate" or "Record Man." Such a reference to the sponsor of the announcements is insufficient to constitute compliance with the Commission's sponsorship identification rules because it is limited to a description of the product or service being advertised. The announcement requirement contemplates the explicit identification of the name of the manufacturer or seller of goods, or the generally known trade or brand name of the goods sold ...

32. A station broadcasts "Teaser" announcements utilizing catch words, slogans, symbols, etc., designed to arouse the curiosity of the public by telling it that something is coming soon. The sponsor of the announcements is not named therein, nor is any generally known trade or brand name given, but it is the intention of the station and the advertiser to inaugurate at a later date a series of conventional spot announcements at the conclusion of the "Teaser" campaign. Announcements of this type do not comply with the Commission's sponsorship identification rules. All commercial matter must contain an explicit identification of the advertiser or the generally known trade or

brand name of the goods being advertised ...

33. A station carries an announcement (or program) on behalf of a candidate for public office or on behalf of the proponents or opponents of a bond issue (or any other public controversial issue). At the conclusion thereof, the station broadcasts a "Disclaimer" or states that "the preceding was a paid political announcement." Such announcements per se do not demonstrate compliance with the sponsorship identification rules. The rules do not provide that either of the above-mentioned types of announcements must be made, but they do provide in such situations that an identification be broadcast which will fully and fairly disclose the true identity of the person or persons by whom or in whose behalf payment was made. If payment is made by an agent, and the station has knowledge thereof, the announcement shall identify the person in whose behalf such agent is acting. If the sponsor is a corporation, committee, association or other group, the required announcement shall contain the name of such group; moreover, the station broadcasting any matter on behalf of such group shall require that a list of the chief officers, members of the executive committee or members of the board of directors of the sponsoring organization be made available upon demand for public inspection at the studios or general offices ... of the station ...

34. Must the required sponsorship announcement on television broadcasts be made by visual means in order for it to be an "appropriate announcement" within the meaning of the Commission's Rule?

Not necessarily. The Commission's Rule does not contain any provision stating whether aural or visual or both types of announcements are required. The purpose of the Rule is to provide a full and fair disclosure of the facts of sponsorship, and responsibility for determining whether a visual or aural announcement is appropriate lies with the licensee ...

G. Controversial Issues

35. (a) A trade association furnishes a television station with kinescope recordings of a Senate committee hearing on labor relations. The subject of the kinescope is a strike being conducted by a labor union. The station broadcasts the kinescope on

a "sustaining" basis but does not announce the supplier of the film. The failure to make an appropriate announcement as to the party supplying the film is a violation of the Commission's sponsorship identification rules dealing with the presentation of program matter involving controversial issues of public importance. Moreover, the Commission requires that a licensee exercise due diligence in ascertaining the identity of the supplier of such program matter. An alert licensee should be on notice that expensive kinescope prints dealing with controversial issues are being paid for by someone and must make inquiry to determine the source of the films in order to make the required announcement ... A station which has ascertained the source of kinescopes is under an additional obligation to supply such information to any other station to which it furnishes the program.

(b) Same situation as above, except that the time for the program is sold to a sponsor (not the supplier of the film) and contains proper identification of the advertiser purchasing the program time. An additional announcement as to the supplier of the films is still required, for the reasons set forth above.

(c) Same situation as in (a) or (b), above, except that only *excerpts* from the film are used by a station in its news programs. An announcement as to the source of the films is required ...

36. A church group plans to film the proceedings of its national convention and distribute film clips "dealing with numerous matters of profound importance to members of (its) faith" in order to "disseminate to the American people information concerning its objectives and programs." The group requests a general waiver under Section 317(d) of the Communications Act so that it need not "waste" any of the short periods of broadcast time donated to it by making sponsorship identification announcements. In the below-cited case, the Commission did not grant such a waiver because of the absence of information indicating that the subject matter of the clips was not controversial and because the alleged "loss" of a few seconds of air time was not of decisional significance vis-a-vis Congressional and Commission policy relating to issues of public importance.

Blackmail

An economist venturing to speak on a legal question must tread delicately. He finds himself dealing with institutions the detailed workings of which are largely unknown to him. He encounters a literature in which the doctrines, concepts, and vocabulary are completely unfamiliar. An economist wishing to understand how the legal system operates inevitably faces formidable obstacles, at any rate if he is without legal training, as most economists are. And yet, having said this, any economist interested in understanding the real economic world rather than those imaginary worlds the analysis of which fills the pages of the economic journals, cannot ignore the influence of the legal system on the working of the economic system. Here I am not mainly thinking of the law relating to regulation, antitrust, and taxation where, even if the exact effect of the law may not be easy to discover, that it has an important influence is not likely to be overlooked. What I have in mind is that more general relationship between the legal and economic systems which I discussed in "The Problem of Social Cost."[1] Economists commonly assume that what is traded on the market is a physical entity, an ounce of gold, a ton of coal. But, as lawyers know, what are traded on the market are bundles of rights, rights to perform certain actions. Trade, the dominant activity in the economic system, its amount and character, consequently depend on what rights and duties individuals and organizations are deemed to possess—and these are established by the legal system. An economist, as I see it, cannot avoid taking the legal system into account. It is a burden we have to bear. Economists cannot be expected to pronounce on the detailed arrangements of the legal system, but we may be able to contribute something to our understanding of how the legal system affects the economic system and thus to the development of those general principles which should govern the delimitation of rights.

In "The Problem of Social Cost" I thought I was able to contribute something to the analysis of the law of nuisance. Today I turn to the problem of blackmail. I am emboldened to do this because of the lack of any consensus among lawyers about the nature of blackmail or about how it should be handled. Professor A. H. Campbell, writing in 1939 in the *Law Quarterly Review* on "The Anomalies of Blackmail," starts his article by saying: "The law of blackmail has something in common with the blackmailer: It allows its student no peace of mind."[2] And Professor James Lindgren, writing in 1984 in the *Columbia Law Review,* starts his article, "Unraveling the Paradox of Blackmail" by saying: "Most crimes do not need theories to explain why the behavior is criminal. The wrongdoing is self-evident. But blackmail is unique among major crimes: No one has yet figured out why it ought to be illegal."[3]

Whether an economist can contribute to what is clearly a difficult legal question is problematical, but I will try. And I am the more willing to do so because the question of blackmail came up at a very early stage when I was developing the ideas which were later to appear in "The Problem of Social Cost." I was then at the Center for Advanced Study in the Behavioral Sciences at Stanford, and that year another fellow at the Center was David Cavers of the Harvard Law School. When I discussed my ideas with him he pointed out, correctly, that if someone had a right to commit a nuisance, he might threaten to create that nuisance simply to extract money from those who would be harmed by it, in return of course for agreeing not to do so. In effect, Cavers felt that what I was advocating would lead to blackmail or something analogous to it. Some economists made the same point after I used this approach in my article on the Federal Communications Commission.[4] This led me to include some passages in "The Problem of Social Cost" which were intended to deal with this objection. I explained, using the example of the cattle raiser and the crop farmer, that if the cattle raiser was liable for the damage brought about by his cattle, the crop farmer might plant crops which otherwise would not be profitable because the resulting crop damage would be such that the cattle raiser, to avoid having to pay for the damage, would be willing to pay the crop farmer not to plant these crops. However, if the situation were reversed and the cattle raiser were not liable for the damage brought about by his cattle, he might increase the size of his herd above what it would otherwise be, thereby increasing crop damage, in order to induce the crop farmer to pay him for agreeing to reduce the size of the herd. My purpose in pointing this out was to show that actions which were undertaken solely for the purpose of being paid not to engage in them, actions which could be called blackmail, would arise whatever the rule of liability or, if you like, the system of rights. I did this not to initiate a discussion of blackmail, but rather to avoid having to do so. In any case, had I wanted to discuss the subject of blackmail, a regime of zero transaction costs would have provided a poor setting in which to do so.

Of course, it would not be necessary actually to plant the crops or increase the herd before agreeing not to do so. All that need be done would be to threaten to take such actions—and for most people payment for not carrying out a *threat* is the essence of blackmail. Of course, it is reasonable to suppose that someone wishing to obtain money for agreeing not to engage in an activity would normally not engage in it before negotiating, but would threaten to do so since this would be less costly. And when money or some other advantage is to be extracted for not revealing unsavory information about someone (the case most people have in mind when they speak of blackmail), the only way to proceed is to threaten, since, once the information has been disclosed, no blackmail is possible. Although I did not examine blackmail in "The Problem of Social Cost," my attitude to the problem raised by Cavers and others was clearly complacent. I pointed out that such activities or threats were a preliminary to an agreement and did not affect the long-run equilibrium. I accepted the fact that bluff and threats were a normal part of business bargaining, and I spoke of the terms of the agreement depending on the shrewdness of the parties. Later, Harold Demsetz pointed out that if there are many cattle raisers and crop farmers and there is competition among them, since refraining from this blackmailing behavior costs nothing, the amount that would have to be paid to obtain an agreement not to engage in it would tend towards zero.[5] Blackmail incidental to a business relationship did not appear normally to be a serious problem. In any case, since bargaining is an inevitable feature of an exchange economy, there is not a great deal that can be done about it. This complacent attitude tends to be reinforced for an economist by the belief that there are no losers in an exchange—it is beneficial to both parties. But is this also true of a transaction in which the object is to suppress information, as is the case in many blackmailing transactions?

No doubt there are economists who think that it is. An illustration of this point of view can be found in a work of fiction written by two economists, both of whom were professors at the University of Virginia and one of whom still is. I am referring to the book, *The Fatal Equilibrium,* written by Professors Breit and Elzinga, using the pseudonym Marshall Jevons.[6] In that book, a young economist is being considered for promotion to a tenured position at Harvard. He discovers that one of the members of the promotion and tenure committee is a fraud. Speaking to his fiancée, the young economist, Dennis Gossen, says: "The culprit has as much as confessed it to me, although not in so many words, and has promised to support my promotion if I'll keep quiet."[7] His fiancée replies: "Dennis, that sounds like blackmail."[8] Dennis, however, does not agree. He responds: "I wouldn't call it blackmail. It's like gains from trade in a way. Support my promotion and keep your reputation. I keep quiet and you help me get tenure."[9] His fiancée is not reassured and most people would share her feeling. Unlike the agreements made as a result of business negotiations, the attempt to obtain money or some other advantage for not disclosing unsavory information about someone is disliked by most people. Why is this so?

Ordinary people have a fairly clear idea of what blackmail involves and do not like it. As an example which fits very well the ordinary person's view of blackmail I have chosen a case of which there is a full account in the Old Bailey Trial Series. Mr. Bechhofer Roberts, the editor, in his foreword, has this to say:

Blackmail is by many people considered the foulest of crimes—far cruller than most murders, because of its cold-blooded premeditation and repeated torture of the victim; incomparably more offensive to the public conscience than the vast majority of other offences which the law seeks to punish—but there is on record one case of blackmail, perhaps the only one, which is redeemed to some extent from baseness by the circumstances in which it arose, by the personalities of its participants, and by certain elements of high comedy which accompanied its development.[10]

This was "The Mr. A Case." I remember reading about it as a schoolboy, since it attracted a great deal of attention in the British newspapers.

In 1919, in the morning of Christmas night, in the St. James and Albany Hotel, in Paris, a bedroom door was opened and an Englishman entered who discovered Mrs. Robinson in bed with Mr. A, whose real name I need hardly say was not Robinson. It was, after all, the season of goodwill. There is a conflict in the testimony about what happened next. According to the Englishman, Mrs. Robinson jumped out of bed and attacked him, saying "My brute of a husband." According to Mrs. Robinson, the words she uttered were addressed to Mr. A and were "I must get back tonight before that brute reaches my husband." Mr. A was not present at the trial to straighten out the contradiction. That Mrs. Robinson should so testify was understandable given that the Englishman who entered the bedroom was not Mr. Robinson but a Mr. Newton whose occupations are given by Mr. Bechhofer Roberts as "confidence-trickster, blackmailer, cardsharper, forger," [11] an impressive list on any resumé. Whatever was really said in that bedroom in Paris, Mr. A seems to have believed that Newton was Mrs. Robinson's husband.

At this point I should disclose that Mr. A was Prince Sir Hari Singh, the heir presumptive to his uncle, the Maharajah of Kashmir, the pseudonym Mr. A being used at the trial at the request of the India Office. After the intrusion of this unexpected visitor, Prince Hari Singh apparently sought the advice of his aide-de-camp, Captain Arthur, who, according to Mr. Bechhofer Roberts, had been recommended for this position by the India Office and whose views were therefore to be taken seriously. Captain Arthur seems to have warned the Prince that Robinson would sue for divorce in England naming him as co-respondent and that heavy damages could be exacted. This of itself would not have disturbed the Prince. The vast majority of the inhabitants of Kashmir were polygamists who presumably would not have found his conduct shocking. And the Prince's wealth was such that he could pay any sum an English court was likely to award (without noticing it). But Captain Arthur apparently also told the Prince that the scandal which would accompany such divorce proceedings would lead the India Office to veto his accession to his uncle's throne. The Prince then drew up two cheques for £150,000 or £300,000 in total (equivalent in real terms to five or six million dollars today). Captain Arthur left for London with the cheques, his mission being to pay Mr. Robinson not to sue for divorce. On arrival in London, however, Captain Arthur went to see Hobbs, a man specialising in the shady side of the law. Hobbs opened a banking account in the name of Robinson, paid in one cheque, furnished the bank with a specimen signature, and proceeded to draw out the whole of the £150,000 with cheques signed "C. Robinson." The second cheque was not cashed since the Prince's solicitors in London, on learning of the matter, insisted on payment being stopped. You will by now have guessed that what I have been describing was an ingenious blackmailing scheme devised by Captain Arthur. The Prince was not the first, and will not be the last, to regret that he trusted a government department's recommendation. Hobbs paid about £40,000 each to Newton and to Captain Arthur. But what of Mr. and Mrs. Robinson? Hobbs told Robinson that Mr. A was willing to pay £20,000 to stop divorce proceedings. Robinson balked at first, but finally agreed to accept £25,000, out of which Hobbs, who knew how a lawyer ought to behave, took £4,000 as his professional fee. He gave Robinson banknotes totalling £21,000 (worth perhaps forty thousand dollars today). Robinson testified that he handed the banknotes to his wife. According to his counsel, Robinson did this "to protect his wife from any temptation to lead an immoral life in the future," [12] although one would have thought the effect would have been the exact opposite. Newton proceeded to India with the second cheque (the Prince's solicitors having been told falsely that it had been destroyed) with a view to obtaining more money, but the Prince's Indian wife died and the Prince was obliged, for religious reasons, to go into seclusion. Newton returned empty-handed. The Prince took no further action.

That the scheme came to light was the result of a disagreement between Captain Arthur and Hobbs, from whom Arthur tried, without success, to get more money. Captain Arthur then imprudently told Robinson that it was not £25,000 but £150,000, that Mr. A had paid for the concealment of what the judge called "the defilement" of Robinson's wife, but the judge, Lord Darling, was noted for his witticisms. Robinson, on learning how he had been deceived, of course, was appalled by this dishonesty. He consulted his solicitors, and it was finally decided to claim £150,000 from the bank in which Hobbs had deposited the cheque for negligently paying to Hobbs what should have been paid to him. Although the jury decided that Mr. and Mrs. Robinson were not parties to the blackmailing scheme, this action failed, mainly because the judge held that Robinson was laying claim to the proceeds of a theft. However, the exposure of the blackmail at the trial resulted in Hobbs being tried and sentenced to a term of imprisonment. Captain Arthur, who was in France and could not be extradited to England, was tried in France (where the offense occurred) and found guilty. Newton, who had been paid £3,000 (equivalent to fifty or sixty thousand dollars today) by the bank to appear as a witness in the first trial, turned King's evidence in the trial of Hobbs, and thus avoided prosecution and made a profit out of the affair. He was a very talented confidence-trickster. Mr. Robinson, who was described by counsel as an "intermittent husband," no doubt resumed his previous relationship with his wife. Notwithstanding the jury's finding, it seems probable that the Robinsons were involved in the blackmailing scheme along with Hobbs, Newton, and Arthur, but even if they were, it is clear that they were completely outclassed. Mr. A, who by this time had come out of seclusion, succeeded in due course to his uncle's throne without any objection from the India Office. I have not told all the twists and turns of this strange tale, but this case embodies the main elements of what the ordinary person thinks of as blackmail. A person is trapped acting in a way which he believes would harm his reputation if disclosed. He pays a sum of money to prevent disclosure. The victim takes no action to bring the blackmailer to justice, because to do so would lead to that disclosure which he was anxious to avoid.

I have said that blackmail is not likely to arise out of business relationships. It is most likely to be found where there is a desire to conceal disreputable personal behaviour (or what is regarded as such). It is therefore somewhat unexpected that what are considered to be the leading cases on the law of blackmail in England are concerned with business relationships. I will start with the case of *The King v. Percy Ingram Denyer.*[13] This case is commonly referred to as *Rex v. Denyer* and I will just refer to it as *Denyer.*

The Motor Trade Association, composed of manufacturers, wholesalers, retailers, and users of what were termed "motor goods," was empowered by its by-laws to put on its "stop list" the name of anyone selling an automobile or associated products above or below the manufacturer's list price. For someone to be on the stop list meant that no member of the Association would trade with him. Mr. Read, who operated a garage in Devon, was visited at the end of 1925 by a representative of the Association, who posed as someone who had come from abroad and was going to buy a house and wanted a car. Mr. Read was induced by this man to sell a tire and to offer to sell an automobile below list price. In January 1926, Mr. Read received a letter, signed by Mr. Denyer, the stop list superintendent, saying that unless he paid £257 to the Association, he would be put on the stop list, a step which Mr. Read testified would put him out of business. Mr. Read took the letter to the police, and Mr. Denyer was indicted for blackmail. The offense was described in the Larceny Act, 1916, as follows: "Every person who ... utters, knowing the contents thereof, any letter or writing demanding of any person with menaces, and without any reasonable or probable cause, any property or valuable thing ... shall be guilty of felony and on conviction thereof liable to penal servitude for life."[14] Mr. Denyer was tried at Exeter, found guilty and he was sentenced to six days in prison, which must have been a relief, given that he could have received penal servitude for life. Note that the offense was not that the Association induced Mr. Read to sell below the list price, nor that they threatened to put Mr. Read on the stop list. The Association was registered as a trade union and it was legal for them to do these things. The offense was that Mr. Denyer demanded a sum of money for refraining from putting Mr. Read on the stop list. The case was taken to the Court of Criminal Appeal, and the verdict of the lower court was upheld. The Lord Chief Justice had this to say:

> It has been said again and again, that because this Trade Protection Association had the legal right to put the name of Mr. Read upon the stop list, it therefore had a legal right to demand money from him as the price of abstaining from putting his name upon the stop list. In the opinion of the Court, that proposition is not merely untrue; it is precisely the reverse of the truth. It is an excuse which might be offered by blackmailers to an indefinite extent. There is not the remotest nexus or relationship between a right to put the name of Mr. Read upon the stop list, and a right to demand from him £257 as the price of abstaining from that course.[15]

It will have been noticed that this case is similar to the "Mr. A Case" in that both Mr. A and Mr. Read were set up to commit an act on the basis of which the demand for money was made. But it would not have been possible to use the Lord Chief Justice's criteria in the "Mr. A Case." Mr. Robinson had a perfect right to bring divorce proceedings against his wife on the grounds of her adultery with Mr. A, and it was certainly legal for Mr. A to settle the case by a payment to Mr. Robinson. And yet there is no question in anyone's mind that the "Mr. A Case" involved blackmail. The English courts soon had an occasion to reexamine the question.

An automobile dealer, Hardie and Lane, had been led to sell an automobile below list price in the same way as had Mr. Read. Hardie and Lane were then offered the same proposition—stop list or fine— and they elected to pay the fine. An agreement was made under which the fine was to be paid in two installments. However, before the second installment was paid, *Denyer* was decided. Thereupon, Hardie and Lane refused to pay the second installment and sued for the return of the money that they had already paid. They won their case in the lower court based on the argument in *Denyer*, but in 1928 this decision was appealed. In the Court of Appeals, Hardie and Lane lost. The argument of *Denyer* was rejected.[16]

I will quote to you some passages from the opinion of Lord Justice Scrutton which will indicate why he disagreed with *Denyer*.

> I am quite unable to understand how it can be illegal to say "I could lawfully put you on the stop list, but if you will do something which is not illegal, and is less burdensome to you than the stop list, I will not exercise my power." ... A member of a club after dinner in a row damages some club property. He is told he is liable to expulsion, but that the committee will not enforce it if he makes good the damage. Are the committee conspirators who have obtained money, or money's worth, by threats, which can be recovered by the member? ... There is nothing illegal in agreeing to do a legal act, to avoid action which the other party may legally take ... A. has land facing a new house of B.'s. A. proposes to build on that land a house which will spoil the view from or light to B.'s house and depreciate the value of his property. B. implores A. not to build. A. says: "I will not build if you pay me £1,000, but I shall build if you do not." B. pays the money and A. does not build. Could it be seriously argued that B. could recover the money back as obtained by threats? A valued cook comes to her mistress and says: "Raise my wages by £20 a year or I shall give you notice." The mistress foreseeing, and much disturbed in mind by, the tragedy that the loss of the cook would involve, pays the money. Can she recover it as obtained by threats?[17]

Later, Lord Justice Scrutton dealt directly with the Lord Chief Justice's rejection of the proposition that because the Association had the right to put Mr. Read on the stop list it also had the right to demand money for not doing so. He said this:

The Lord Chief Justice says it is an excuse which might be offered by blackmailers to an indefinite extent. I cannot understand this. The blackmailer is demanding money in return for a promise to abstain from making public an accusation of crime. The very agreement is illegal.... A man has no right to suppress his knowledge of a felony. How can this be analogous to proposing not to do a thing which you have a legal right to do, if money is paid you, there being no public mischief in the agreement?[18]

It will have been noticed that while making some telling points Lord Justice Scrutton's response does not meet the problem of the "Mr. A Case," since he appears to assume that blackmail involves suppression of knowledge of a felony. Adultery, at least in England, is not a crime.

As a student taking the Bachelor of Commerce degree at the London School of Economics I took a law course in either 1929 or 1930 in which these cases, which had only recently been decided, were discussed. The purpose was to acquaint us with the law relating to trade associations, although our teachers did not fail to draw our attention to the interesting situation arising out of this conflict between the criminal and the civil sides of the court system, particularly as the Lord Chief Justice issued a statement after the case of *Hardie & Lane, Ltd. v. Chilton* had been decided in which he said that unless and until the decision in *Denyer* was reversed by the House of Lords, it will be binding for the purpose of the administration of the criminal law. Although these two cases were presented to us in connection with the law of trade associations, what appealed to the economist in me was the question: when is it right and when wrong to pay someone not to do something? I retained the memory of these cases over the years, and I often wondered how the conflict between these two decisions was ultimately resolved. But it was not until I went to the University of Chicago Law School in 1964, some 35 years after I had been taught about these cases, that I learned what had happened. This is what I found.

In 1937, a friendly action, *Thorne* v. *Motor Trade Ass'n*, presumably arranged by the Motor Trade Association, was taken to the House of Lords.[19] The question to be decided was whether the opinion of the Court of Criminal Appeal or that of the Court of Appeals was correct. I need not leave you in suspense. The opinion in *Denyer* was disapproved. The law lords particularly objected to the statement of the trial judge that "a person has no right to demand money, according to the Act of Parliament as a price of abstaining from inflicting unpleasant consequences upon a man."[20] As Lord Wright said:

> There are many possible circumstances under which a man may say to another that he will abstain from conduct unpleasant to the other only if he is paid a sum of money. Thus he may offer not to build on his plot of land if he is compensated for abstaining ... Or a man may offer to abstain from prosecuting for a common assault or infringement of his trade mark if he is paid compensation ...[21]

However, having disapproved of the basic proposition underlying the opinion in *Denyer*, they also expressed their disapproval of Lord Justice Scrutton's opinion that if one has a legal right to do something, one also has a legal right to demand money for abstaining from doing it. Lord Atkin said this:

> Scrutton L. J. appeared to indicate that if a man merely threatened to do that which he had a right to do the threat could not be a menace within the Act ... This seems to me to be plainly wrong, and I entirely agree with the criticism of this proposition made by the Lord Chief Justice in *Rex v. Denyer.* The ordinary blackmailer normally threatens to do what he has a perfect right to do-namely, communicate some compromising conduct to a person whose knowledge is likely to affect the person threatened. Often indeed he has not only the right but also the duty to make the disclosure, as of a felony, to the competent authorities. What he has to justify is not the threat, but the demand of money ... The only question is whether the demand would be without reasonable or probable cause. It is here that I am unable to agree with the decision in *Denyer's* case. It appears to me that if a man may lawfully, in the furtherance of business interests,

do acts which will seriously injure another in his business he may also lawfully, if he is still acting in furtherance of his business interests, offer that other to accept a sum of money as an alternative to doing the injurious acts. He must no doubt be acting not for the mere purpose of putting money in his pocket, but for some legitimate purpose other than the mere acquisition of money.[22]

Lord Wright continued:

There are many cases where a man who has a "right," in the sense of a liberty or capacity of doing an act which is not unlawful, but which is calculated seriously to injure another, will be liable to a charge of blackmail if he demands money from that other as the price of abstaining. Such instances indeed are very typical cases of blackmail ... Thus a man may be possessed of knowledge of discreditable incidents in the victim's life and may seek to extort money by threatening, if he is not paid, to disclose the knowledge to a wife or husband or employer, though the disclosure may not be libellous ... Again a legal liberty (that is something that a man may do with legal justification) may form the basis of blackmail. Thus a husband who has proof of his wife's adultery, may threaten the paramour that he will petition in the Divorce Court unless he is bought off. Though it is possible that the facts of such a case might show merely the legitimate compromise of a claim to damages, on the other hand, the facts might be such as to constitute extortion and blackmail of a serious type.[23]

And other law lords expressed themselves to the same effect.

All this brings us to what Professor Lindgren has termed the "paradox of blackmail"—that although it may be lawful to do something, it may be unlawful to demand money for refraining from doing it.[24] But when is it unlawful? The law lords leave this obscure. "The facts may show," said Lord Wright. But what facts, and how do they show it? The Motor Trade Association really presented them with a relatively easy case. Once it was agreed that Parliament had granted it the power, because it was a trade union, to put someone's name on a stop list, a procedure which could ruin a business (for I gather that the stop list at that time in England would be effective), it becomes hard to object to an action which merely reduced somewhat the profits of that business. As Lord Russell said:

> Having it in their power to place the plaintiffs on the Stop List, but being desirous of taking a more lenient course, they gave the plaintiffs the option of paying a fine. I am wholly unable to understand how it can be suggested that this was not an eminently reasonable thing to do.[25]

The problem is, as Dennis Gossen of *The Fatal Equilibrium* would have explained, there are always gains from trade, and blackmail involves a trade. It is in the interest of the blackmailer to make payment of the money more attractive than the alternative. In this limited sense, he also will want to be lenient. Dennis Gossen, I imagine, would have regarded the demand, "your money or your life" as the offer of a bargain. Of course, murder is a crime and there is no problem in characterising this particular offer as blackmail. But suppose the offer had been: "Your money or I will tell your wife." To be murdered might well seem a preferred alternative. And yet telling his wife would certainly not be a crime. However, demanding money for abstaining from telling her would very likely be blackmail and therefore a crime. Why? The law lords threw little light on this question. Lord Atkin admitted that the rules of the Association were capable of being abused.[26] Lord Wright said that the money demanded must be "reasonable and not extortionate."[27] And Lord Roche said:

> A demand of a sum extortionate in amount would, I think, clearly be evidence fit to be left to a jury in a civil case of an intent to injure as opposed to an intent to protect trade interests and in a criminal case of the fact that the sum was demanded without reasonable or probable cause ... It would, in my opinion, be both erroneous and mischievous to give colour to the opinion that because a demand of money [by the

Association] is not necessarily unlawful or a crime it cannot under any circumstances be either the one or the other.[28]

This is not really helpful. As you know, extortion is often used as a synonym for blackmail, and to say that there is no extortion unless the demand is extortionate does not aid us in identifying blackmail. One has the impression that the law lords failed to get a handle on the problem.

It is not, therefore, surprising to learn that when, in 1966, the Criminal Law Revision Committee came to examine the law relating to blackmail in the United Kingdom, it found the position very unsatisfactory.[29] The Committee in their report point out that though there is no offence called "blackmail," the name is commonly applied to "the group of offences of demanding property with menaces and similar conduct."[30] The law is, however, as they say, "obscure" and "very complicated."[31] Nonetheless, in practice things have not worked out too badly, "but this is due rather to restraint and common sense of prosecutors in limiting prosecutions to what is clearly recognizable as blackmail in the ordinary sense than to any merits in the law itself."[32] It seems that blackmail, like pornography, is difficult to define, but you know it when you see it.

Faced with the problem of defining blackmail, the Committee felt that it had to go back to "first principles." They say:

> In general terms it seems reasonably clear that the offence should include at least making an improper demand of a financial character accompanied by threats. Further, on any view it should apply to a threat to injure a person or to damage his property unless he pays something to which the person who makes the demand does not pretend to be entitled ... Equally there is no doubt that it should be blackmail for a person to demand something merely as the price of not revealing some discreditable conduct of which he happens to know.[33]

Having said this, the Committee noted that there were serious difficulties in applying these general propositions. When is a demand improper, and when is it permissible to make a threat to reinforce a demand? The Committee finally decided that the test of illegality in making a demand should be "whether the person in question honestly believes that he has the right to make the demand."[34] Similarly, when dealing with the threat, they argue "that the only satisfactory course would be to adopt a subjective test and to make criminal liability depend on whether the person who utters the threat believes in the propriety of doing so."[35]

As a result of the deliberations of this Committee, a section of the Theft Act, passed in 1968 in England, defined blackmail:

A person is guilty of blackmail if, with a view to gain for himself or another or with intent to cause loss to another, he makes any unwarranted demand with menaces; and for this purpose a demand with menaces is unwarranted unless the person making it does so in the belief—(a) that he has reasonable grounds for making the demand; and (b) that the use of the menaces is a proper means of reinforcing the demand.[36]

This, although more definite than the old law, clearly requires a good deal of interpretation. Nonetheless, there is no reason to suppose that this will lead to serious difficulties in the administration of the law. The old law was even more obscure and yet, as we have seen, there seems to have been few problems in its administration. There is in effect an unstated law of blackmail which cannot be discovered from the statutes, but which is based on the common sense of prosecutors, juries, and judges and which it might be possible to infer from a detailed study of the cases. Some economists, and perhaps some lawyers, would expect that such an investigation would show that the decisions in the cases were those that led to the value of production (in its widest sense) being maximised. Whether this would be the result of such an investigation I do not know. But what I will now do is to consider what I think the decisions would be if in fact they had this character.

Let us therefore return to the analysis of "The Problem of Social Cost" and examine an example, not the cattle raisers and crop farmers of that article, but one used by the judges in the Motor Trade Association cases. A threatens to build a house which will spoil the view from, and block the light to B's house. My understanding of the legal situation in England is that A would normally be entitled to build, even though it had these consequences. Suppose that, as in Lord Justice Scrutton's example, A demands £1,000 as the price of agreeing not to build and that B pays this. Is this blackmail? Suppose that A would not have built, whether B made this payment or not, because the cost of building a house on this site exceeded the price at which it could be sold. In these circumstances, the demand for £1,000 could be regarded as blackmail or something akin to it. It is a payment to A for agreeing not to do something which he has no interest in doing. The £1,000 does not represent what A would have lost by not building—the threat to build is made simply to extract money from B. Of course, if A would have gained £600 by building the house, only £400 of the £1,000 would represent a blackmailing demand. But if blackmail is paid, it is because the value to B of preserving his amenities is greater than the additional value that would be created by the construction of the house. The payment of blackmail leaves the allocation of resources unaffected and the value of production is maximised. The only effect is to transfer money from B to A. Since we cannot assume that *B* is more worthy than A, what is wrong with it?

When I referred to the problem of blackmail in "The Problem of Social Cost," it was simply to show that, however rights were defined, there would always be opportunities for this type of blackmail. I pointed this out in the section of the article in which it was assumed that transactions were costless and in which therefore no resources were absorbed in bargaining. In such a world, it is not clear what the objection would be to this type of blackmail. The position is, however, very different if we make the realistic assumption that transaction costs are positive. It is obviously undesirable that resources should be devoted to bargaining which produces a situation no better than it was previously.

Economists discuss exchange, but until recently have been very little interested in the process of exchange, and have certainly not devoted much attention to the problem of blackmail. Normally, when they notice something which appears to be wrong in the working of the economic system, they follow the prescriptions of Pigou and advocate government action, usually some form of taxation, but sometimes regulation. Pigou does not discuss blackmail as such, but his attitude to it can be inferred from his discussion, in *The Economics of Welfare,* of the situation in which "the relations between individual buyers and sellers are not rigidly fixed by a surrounding market," [37] a condition which is, of course, extremely common. Pigou then says that "it is plain that activities and resources devoted to manipulating the ratio of exchange may yield a positive private net product; but they cannot ... yield a positive social net product ..."[38] These activities are described by Pigou as "bargaining" and "deception." This is what he says of bargaining:

> Of bargaining proper there is little that need be said. It is obvious that intelligence and resources devoted to this purpose ... yield no net product to the community as a whole ... These activities are wasted. They contribute to private, but not to social, net product ... Where their clients, be they customers or workpeople, can be squeezed, employers tend to expend their energy in accomplishing this, rather than in improving the organisation of their factories. When they act thus, the social net product even of the earliest dose of resources devoted to bargaining may be, not merely zero, but negative. Whenever that happens, no tax that yields a revenue, though it may effect an improvement, can provide a complete remedy. For that absolute prohibition is required. But absolute prohibition of bargaining is hardly feasible except where prices and conditions of sale are imposed upon private industry by some organ of State authority.[39]

Pigou evidently feels that there is nothing more to be said on this subject. He therefore turns to "deception" and reaches a similar conclusion: "The social net product of any dose of resources invested in a deceptive activity is negative. Consequently, as with bargaining, no tax that yields a revenue, though it may effect an improvement, can provide a complete remedy, and absolute prohibition of the activity is required."[40]

"The Problem of Social Cost" was intended to influence the thinking, not of lawyers, but of economists and its main purpose was to demonstrate the inadequacies of the Pigovian approach and to put forward what the author hoped was something better. The Pigovian approach, as I have just said, sets up an ideal world and then by government action, usually some form of taxation or less commonly government regulation, endeavors to reproduce that ideal state in the real world. We can see what it leads to in the case we are discussing. Bargaining, which involves bluff, threats, and, to some degree, deception, should apparently be eliminated by a prohibitive tax imposed, I suppose, "per unit of bargaining" or "per unit of deceit," an operation which can be carried out on a blackboard but nowhere else. But since elimination is what is wanted, the right tax would be one which yielded no revenue, and Pigou apparently concludes that this is not a practical solution. He then states that "Absolute prohibition is required ... [but this] is hardly feasible except where prices and conditions of sale are imposed upon private industry by some organ of State authority."[41] As Pigou does not discuss the subject further, the significance of this statement is not evident. To me, it demonstrates the bankruptcy of the Pigovian approach, but this could hardly have been Pigou's purpose. Pigou's solution would require the State to fix the terms of every transaction, a procedure which would paralyse the working of the economic system. I argued in "The Problem of Social Cost" that in deciding on economic policy, we should not concern ourselves with the ideal (whatever that may be) but should start with the available alternatives and should endeavor to discover which among them produces, in total, the best result.

Furthermore, I argued that the available alternatives were not confined to the imposition of taxes or direct governmental regulation, as most economists seem to have thought, but included changes in the law governing the rights and duties of individuals and organizations. The definition of the rights that individuals and organizations are deemed to possess is important because, by setting the starting point, it determines what transactions have to be carried out to achieve any other constellation of rights, and therefore the costs of so doing. People will wish to negotiate to change the initial constellation whenever this would increase the value of production—but only after deducting the costs of the necessary transactions. And these costs depend on the initial legal position. It is therefore easy to see that the final outcome is affected by the law. I concluded in "The Problem of Social Cost" that the value of production would be maximised if rights were deemed to be possessed by those to whom they were most valuable, thus eliminating the need for any transactions.

In a blackmailing scheme, the person who will pay the most for the right to stop the action threatened is normally the person being blackmailed. If the right to stop this action is denied to others, that is, blackmail is made illegal, transaction costs are reduced, factors of production are released for other purposes and the value of production is increased. This is an approach which comes quite naturally to an economist and was certainly the way in which I first analysed the problem of blackmail.

Blackmail involves the expenditure of resources in the collection of information which, on payment of blackmail, will be suppressed. It would be better if this information were not collected and the resources were used to produce something of value. Professor Lindgren has objected to this rationale for making blackmail illegal on the ground that it does not explain why it is illegal to demand money for not revealing information accidentally acquired.[42] He gives as an example the case of a workman on a ladder who blackmailed a clergyman after observing him engaged in paying attention to a member of his flock which apparently went well beyond the call of duty.[43] While it is true that in such a case no resources were used to collect the information, resources would certainly be employed in the blackmailing transaction. Furthermore, it is difficult for me to believe that, were blackmail made legal, such accidental sightings would not occur more frequently.

Nonetheless, I believe that Professor Lindgren is right in sensing that this objection to blackmail, correct though it may be, does not explain why there is such general support for making blackmail not merely illegal, but a crime. After all, in public life we often observe great tolerance of, and indeed encouragement for, policies which waste resources on a grand scale. It is not because blackmail involves a misallocation of resources that the Criminal Law Revision Committee considers as "entirely justified" the "detestation with which blackmail is now commonly regarded."[44] In a passage I have already quoted Mr. Bechhofer Roberts says that "Blackmail is by many people considered the foulest of crimes—far crueller than most murders, because of its cold-blooded premeditation and repeated torture of the victim."[45] The Criminal Law Revision Committee comments that blackmail "can be an extremely cruel offence, causing endless misery."[46]

It is not difficult to understand why people feel this way. A blackmailer threatens to do something which will harm his victim unless he is paid a sum of money or receives some other benefit, and by emphasizing the unpleasant consequences for the victim of not meeting his demands (or even inventing them, as in the "Mr. A Case"), he endeavours to extract as much as he can from him. It may be objected that this is exactly what happens in business negotiations. And this is correct. But the situations are not identical. The demands made by a businessman are constrained by the competition of other businessmen, by the fact that the party threatened is likely to have a good idea of whether the threat has to be taken seriously and by the adverse effects on future business of being difficult in negotiating. None of this applies in the ordinary blackmail case. There is no competition. The victim *has* to deal with the blackmailer. The victim is also likely to be uncertain about the blackmailer's real intentions. And concern for future business will not moderate a blackmailer's demands. If this factor has any influence, it pays the blackmailer to be unreasonable and even to carry out his threat, since this would make future victims take his threats more seriously. And there are even more important differences. The blackmailer's actions generate fear and anxiety—blackmailing involves more than the employment of resources which leave the value of production unchanged—it causes real harm which reduces the value of production just as with Pigou's railway whose sparks cause fires in the adjoining woods. The position is, however, much worse for the blackmail victim than the owner of the woods. He cannot appeal to the law, since this would involve that disclosure of facts which he is anxious to avoid. But there is, I believe, another difference, even more important than the others. Business negotiations (which may also cause anxiety) either lead to a breakdown of the negotiations or they lead to a contract. There is, at any rate, an end. But in the ordinary blackmail case there is no end. The victim, once he succumbs to the blackmailer, remains in his grip for an indefinite period. It is moral murder. And, as the Criminal Law Revision Committee says: "It is certain that a great deal of it goes on which never comes to light."[47]

The problem is that all trade involves threatening not to do something unless certain demands are met. Furthermore, negotiations about the terms of trade are likely to involve the making of threats which it would be better if they were not made (and in this Pigou is right). But it is only certain threats in certain situations which cause harm on balance and in which the harm is sufficiently great as to make it desirable that those making them should be prosecuted and punished. I think it is clear what is wrong with blackmail. The problem is to know how to deal with it. The British solution seems to have been to pass a statute defining blackmail which makes no clear distinction between these cases but leaves it up to the prosecutors, juries, and judges to be sensible. Whether this is the best that can be done is a question for lawyers to decide. It would be a sad day if all the answers had to be provided by economists.

Notes

[1] Coase, The Problem of Social Cost, 3 *Journal of Law and Economics*. 1 (1960).
[2] Campbell, The Anomalies of Blackmail, 55 *Law Quarterly Review*. 382, 382 (1939).
[3] Lindgren, Unraveling the Paradox of Blackmail, 84 *Columbia Law Review*. 670, 670 (1984).
[4] Coase, The Federal Communications Commission, 2 *Journal of Law and Economics*. 1 (1959).
[5] Demsetz, When Does the Rule of Liability Matter? 1 *Journal of Legal Studies*. 13, 23-24 (1972).
[6] M. Jevons, The Fatal Equilibrium (1985).
[7] Id. at 102.
[8] Id.
[9] Id. at 102-103.
[10] The Mr. A Case 9 (C.E. Bechhofer Roberts ed., The Old Bailey Trial Series, No. 7, 1950).
[11] Id. at 27.
[12] Id. at 20.

[13] The King v. Denyer [1926] 2 K.B. 258.
[14] Id. at 261.
[15] Id. at 268.
[16] Hardie & Lane, Ltd. v. Chilton, [1928] 2 K.B. 306.
[17] Id. at 315-317.
[18] Id. at 322.
[19] Thorne v. Motor Trade Ass'n, 1937 App. Cas. 797.
[20] Id. at 812.
[21] Id. at 820.
[22] Id. at 806-807 (citations omitted).
[23] Id. at 822.
[24] See Lindgren, *supra* note 3, at 670-671.
[25] Thorne v. Motor Trade Ass'n, 1937 App. Cas. 797, 812.
[26] Id. at 808.
[27] Id. at 818.
[28] Id. at 824-825.
[29] Criminal Law Revision Committee, Eighth Report, Theft and Related Offences, 1966, Cmnd. No. 2977, at 54-61.
[30] Id. at 54.
[31] Id.
[32] Id.
[33] Id. at 56-57.
[34] Id. at 57.
[35] Id. at 59.
[36] Theft Act, 1968, ch. 60, § 21; see E. Griew, The Theft Acts 1968 & 1978, §§ 12-01 to -34 (1986).
[37] A.C. Pigou, *The Economics of Welfare* 200 (4th ed. 1932).
[38] Id.
[39] Id. at 201 (footnotes omitted).
[40] Id. at 203.
[41] Id. at 201 (footnote omitted).
[42] Lindgren, *supra* note 3, at 690, 695.
[43] Id. at 690.
[44] Criminal Law Revision Committee, *supra* note 29, at 61.
[45] The Mr. A Case, *supra* note 10, at 9.
[46] Criminal Law Revision Committee, supra note 29, at 61.
[47] Id.

Series IV

History of Law and Economics

Ning Wang

The fourth and last series of papers deals with the history of law and economics. "Law and Economics at Chicago" (1993) is the Henry C. Simons Memorial Lecture Coase presented in 1992 at the University of Chicago Law School. It gives his account of the early history of the inroads of economics into the law school and the gradual rise of law and economics, including the important role played by the new journals founded at the University of Chicago. "Law and Economics and A. W. Brian Simpson"(1996) is a rebuttal of an article by A.W. Brian Simpson (1996), "Coase vs. Pigou Reexamined." Here, Coase first observed that law and economics contains two separate lines of research, the economic analysis of law, spearheaded by Richard Posner and the study of the law's economic impact which he identified with himself. "Law and Economics: A Personal Journey" (2015) is an autobiographical essay, based on the 17th Annual Coase Lecture that Coase delivered in 2003 to celebrate the Centennial of the University of Chicago Law School. In it Coase discussed his long academic career intertwined with the rise of law and economics.

Law and Economics and A. W. Brian Simpson[*]

To understand a man ... one must know the subject matter of the discipline in which he is writing: It takes an economist to read an economist.

George J. Stigler[1]

The subject of law and economics when it started in the 1960s presented a difficult problem for the lawyers and economists who had an interest in it. Most lawyers were unfamiliar with the approach of economists and with the concepts they employ. Most economists knew little about the detailed working of the legal system and inevitably found the legal literature difficult to understand because of their unfamiliarity with its vocabulary and its doctrines. That this was the case is quite understandable—it is difficult for most people to be really proficient in more than one subject. Of course, there was Leonardo da Vinci—and there is Richard Posner—but no subject can flourish if it has to depend exclusively or even largely on such exceptionally well endowed individuals.

Law and economics consists of two parts which are quite separate although there is a considerable overlap. The first consists of using the economists' approach and concepts to analyze the working of the legal system, often called the economic analysis of law. At the time law and economics started, there had been general movement of economists into the other social sciences, sociology, political science and the like. However, I expressed the view (in 1975) that we should not expect

---

[*] *Journal of Legal Studies*, 1996, 25(1), 103-119.

economists "to continue indefinitely their triumphal advance" [2] into law and the other social sciences. I argued that once these other social scientists "have acquired the simple but valuable truths which economics has to offer," and this I considered to be the natural competitive response, "Economists ...will have lost their main advantage and will face competitors who know more about the subject matter than they do."[3] I do not know what has happened in the other social sciences but this is exactly what has happened in the study of law and economics in the 20 years that have elapsed since the writing of these words. The difficulties that were encountered when law and economics started that I mentioned in the previous paragraph have been overcome. In the economic analysis of law, lawyers now have the predominant role. They may work in collaboration with economists but in the main they have acquired enough economics to be able to conduct their analysis in a thoroughly professional way, indeed many of the lawyers now writing on the economic analysis of law have a Ph.D in economics.

The second part of law and economics is a study of the influence of the legal system on the working of the economic system. It is the part of law and economics in which I am most interested. Economists, at first, endeavoured to carry out their researches by a study of legal cases both to learn about the details of actual business practices (information largely absent in the economics literature), and to appraise the impact on them of the law. I (and no doubt others) have used the legal cases to illustrate the economic problem. By giving the problem concrete form, study of the cases served to focus our attention. Economists were of course hampered by their unfamiliarity with the terms employed by lawyers but even more by the way the problem was posed in the legal proceedings. However, this problem no longer hinders economic research to the same extent. Economists are now making extensive direct investigations of contractual arrangements, of relations between firms outside contract and of the activities carried out within firms and of how all of these are affected by the law. The study of legal cases now plays a minor role in this part of law and economics. Reliance on the information in legal cases is not likely to disappear completely but it is no longer a major source.

I now turn to "The Problem of Social Cost." I discussed in my Simons lecture of 1992 what my aim was in writing it:

> It is generally agreed that this article has had immense influence on legal scholarship, but this was no part of my intention. For me, "The Problem of Social Cost" was an essay in economics. It was aimed at economists. What I wanted to do was to improve our analysis of the working of the economic system. Law came into the article because in a regime of positive transaction costs, the character of the law becomes one of the main factors determining the performance of the economy. ... I had no intention of making a contribution to legal scholarship. I referred to legal cases because they afforded examples of real situations as against the imaginary ones normally used by economists in their analysis. ... I did something else. I pointed out that the judges in their opinions often seemed to show a better understanding of the economic problem than did many economists even though their views were not expressed in a very explicit fashion. I did this not to praise the judges but to shame economists.[4]

Notwithstanding the many references to my work in the literature on the economic analysis of law in the last 35 years, I have never attempted to contribute to it. Richard Posner has spoken of my insouciance about the economic analysis of law. But my unwillingness to take part in the discussions of this subject is a result of the factors mentioned in the first paragraph, my lack of knowledge of the detailed working of the legal system and my very superficial knowledge of the legal literature. I admit that this lack of knowledge is a deficiency. But it is surely a virtue not to write on a subject of which one is ignorant. I wish Professor Brian Simpson had shown a similar prudence. He writes about economics and economists from the point of view of an historian and a lawyer. It is not surprising to find that his article contains so many misunderstandings of my position and misstatements about me and my work.

Professor Simpson seems not to have read my various statements regarding my aim in writing "The Problem of Social Cost" and the perplexity he often expresses from time to time concerning my intentions is, in the circumstances, understandable. Had he realized what I had in mind I do not believe he would have found statements such as the following objectionable: "It would ... seem desirable that the courts should understand the economic consequences of their decisions and should, in so far as this is possible without creating too much uncertainty about the legal position itself, take these consequences into account when making their decisions. Even when it is possible to change the legal delimitation of rights through market transactions, it is obviously desirable to reduce the need for such transaction and thus reduce the employment of resources in carrying them out."[5] How far the legal system will be able to operate in such a way as to produce these desirable results is another matter. But in the common law countries (although, of course, economics being an international discipline I also thought of my analysis as applying to countries with other legal systems), I interpreted the statements by legal writers, such as Prosser, to mean that the economic consequences were taken into account, at any rate in nuisance cases, and the opinions in some of the cases that I quoted seemed to bear that out. As legal scholars, such as Judge Posner and others writing on the economic analysis of law, have adopted a similar view, this suggests that my interpretation of Prosser and the judges, ill-informed though it may have been, may well have been correct. But this is a question for lawyers to discuss, particularly those working on the economic analysis of law.

I now turn to a more important matter. Simpson says that the "first idea ... which runs through all Coase's writings, is deep skepticism as to the desirability of government intervention."[6] I very much doubt whether Simpson has read all my writings and it may be that his failure to do so explains why he makes this misleading statement about my views. I will give an account of their evolution. As a young man I was a Socialist. The first challenge to this belief came when, in 1931, 5 months before I took the final examinations for the B.Com. degree, I attended Arnold Plant's seminar at the London School of Economics (LSE). He introduced me to Adam Smith's invisible hand and to the advantages of a competitive system. He also pointed out that government schemes in the economic sphere were often ill-conceived and were introduced to placate special interests. I adopted many of Plant's positions but continued to regard myself as a Socialist. That this meant holding what could be considered, and were, inconsistent positions was not unusual at that time. Abba Lerner, a fellow student and a fine theorist, with whom I had a very friendly relation, also believed in the virtues of a competitive system but was even more attached to Socialism than I was. Calabresi has ascribed my introduction into economic analysis of the costs of using the pricing system (transaction costs) in my article "The Nature of the Firm" (1937) as coming about because of my Socialist beliefs at that time.[7] It is very difficult to know where one's ideas come from but for all I know he may well be right. I certainly did not get this idea from Arnold Plant and neither he nor Lionel Robbins ever showed any interest in "The Nature of the Firm." My socialist sympathies gradually fell away and this process was accentuated as a result of being assigned in 1935 at LSE the course on the Economics of Public Utilities. I soon found that very little was known about British public utilities and I set about making a series of historical studies of the water, gas, and electricity supply industries and of the post office and broadcasting.

These researches taught me much about the public utility industries and they certainly made me aware of the defects of government operation of these industries, whether municipal or through nationalisation. These researches were interrupted by the war, when I joined the civil service, at first, for a short period, in the Forestry Commission, then responsible for timber production, and for the rest of the war, in the Central Statistical Office, one of the Offices of the War Cabinet. This war-time experience did not significantly influence my views but I could not help noticing that, with the country in mortal danger and despite the leadership of Winston Churchill, government departments often seemed more concerned to defend their own interests than those of the country.

In 1951 I migrated to the United States. My book, *British Broadcasting*, had been published in 1950. I decided to continue my research into the broadcasting industry, drawing on the experience of Canada and the United States, as well as that of Britain.

In 1959, my article "The Federal Communications Commission" was published. In that article I argued, when discussing the establishment of property rights in the radio frequency spectrum, that although the delimitation of rights was an essential preliminary to market transactions, the way these rights would be used would be independent of the initial decision. What I said was thought to run counter to Pigou's analysis by a number of economists at the University of Chicago and was therefore, according to them, wrong. At a meeting in Chicago I was able to convince these economists that I was right and Pigou's analysis faulty. As a result I was asked to write the article that became "The Problem of Social Cost." In that article, among other things, I discuss the role of government regulation. The following quotations indicate my general position:

> Satisfactory views on policy can only come from a patient study of how, in practice, the market, firms and government handle the problem of harmful effects. ... It is my belief that economists, and policy makers generally, have tended to over-estimate the advantages which come from governmental regulation. But this belief, even if justified, does not do more than suggest that governmental regulation should be curtailed. It does not tell us where the boundary line should be drawn. This, it seems to me, has to come from a detailed investigation of the actual results of handling the problem in different ways.[8]

In 1964, I became editor of the *Journal of Law and Economics*. I used that position to encourage lawyers and economists to make these detailed investigations. When I wrote my 1960 article I thought I knew the effects of nationalisation, based on British experience, but I knew next to nothing about regulation in the United States. I hoped as a result of these studies to learn the circumstances in which governmental regulation improved the situation and those in which it did not. As I explained in a paper in 1974, this expectation was disappointed: "The main lesson to be drawn from these studies is clear: They all tend to suggest that the regulation is ineffective or that, when it has a noticeable impact, on balance the effect is bad, so that consumers obtain a worse product or a higher-priced product or both as a result of the regulation. Indeed this result is found so uniformly as to create a puzzle: One would expect to find, in all these studies, at least some government programs that do more good than harm."[9] What was the solution to this puzzle? I said that one explanation might be that the studies happen "to have involved cases in which there was a failure of government regulation and that further investigation will uncover many examples of success." [10] But I argued that although there may be something to this explanation, it was hardly likely to change the main conclusion. Another explanation would be that "the costs of government are always greater than they would be for the market transactions that would accomplish the same result" [11] but this explanation I rejected. I surmised that "the most probable reason we obtain these results is that the government is attempting to do too much" and "that it has reached the stage at which, for many of its activities, as economists would say, the marginal product is negative." [12] This means that the advice we should give at present that "all government activities should be curtailed," but "our experience with the present over-expanded government machine may not give us much indication of what tasks the government should undertake when the sphere of government has been reduced to a more appropriate size."[13]

My views on government intervention in the economy have changed over my life but they have always been driven by factual investigations. My studies in Britain led me to be doubtful about the benefits of nationalisation. When I came to the United States, I was generally supportive of government regulation (of which I knew very little apart from what was said in the textbooks) but my views were changed (or formed) by the studies made since then, many published in the *Journal of Law and Economics*. My present position is that which I expressed in 1974. It has been factually driven. But that it is possible to have too much of a thing does not mean that it is not desirable to have any. Our problem is to find out when state action does improve the situation. It is inaccurate to say that I have a "general skepticism about state action."

I need not say very much about Simpson's discussion of *Sturges v. Bridgman* since the information he gives additional to that in my account is of little interest to an economist except perhaps that Wigmore Street was a commercial street and Wimpole Street a residential street. I will make but one point. Simpson thinks no market transaction such as I described would have been possible since neither of the parties would have been willing to place their rights on the market. This would have been offensive. I do not believe this. I have no doubt that had Mr. Bridgman's income fallen by a million pounds if he was not able to use his mortars in the way he had been, that a bargain would have been struck allowing him to continue to do so. In any case, as the first sentence of "The Problem of Social Cost" indicates, the article was concerned with the actions of business firms. They will normally be attempting to maximise their profits and the etiquette governing the relations of neighbours would have little relevance for their behaviour.

However, Simpson's main criticism of my article relates to my treatment of Pigou. The heading of the section in which I discussed Pigou's views is "Pigou's Treatment in *The Economics of Welfare*" and it was with his views as expressed in that book (from which many of the economists of my generation derived their own treatment) that I was mainly concerned. Simpson enlarges the scope of the enquiry to include other works of Pigou and also includes some biographical material. I have no particular quarrel with what he says about Pigou, the person. He was a very strange man. I heard Pigou lecture on only one occasion, a very pedestrian performance as I remember it. Tales about Pigou abounded. I always assumed that some were invented, encouraged by the fact that it was impossible to dismiss a tale as improbable, given the known peculiarities of his behaviour. On the occasion of his London lecture I was told that there was a discussion about whether he could wear a gown as his trousers had holes in some awkward places and they needed to be covered. Whether this was true I don't know—with Pigou it was difficult to be sure. Simpson refers to his dislike for women and fondness for young men. This is correct. He was very pleased when Austin Robinson was made professor at Cambridge instead of his wife, Joan Robinson, although she was, without question, a much greater economist. What he liked about the decision was that it asserted the superiority of the male. As to Pigou's romantic attachments to young men, he seems to have displayed his feelings with a lack of discretion that irritated some of his Cambridge colleagues.[14]

None of this need impugn Pigou's economics except that it suggests a certain other-worldliness that would not be helpful in an economist. More to the point is what Hugh Dalton says. Dalton was a student of Pigou's, then joined the faculty of the London School of Economics, became a Labour Party politician and Chancellor of the Exchequer in the post-war Labour Government. This is his description of Pigou: "Pigou was a Man of the Temple of Truth, fixed in Cambridge. His system never greatly changed. He gave the impression of using one machine, most beautiful and powerful in its construction, to solve a series of problems, the solutions all tending, after he had settled down into middle age, to have a certain family likeness."[15] Pigou seems to have lacked any practical sense. Austin Robinson tells us that "Pigou was never, as an economist, quick to see intuitively the order of magnitude and the potential danger of economic forces, and he was never a person to whom colleagues turned instinctively for advice in the sphere of economic policy making."[16] In the introductory section to my book, *The Form, the Market and the Law,* I said that Pigou's examples "are really illustrative of his position rather than the basis for it," and I quote Austin Robinson as saying that Pigou was "seeking always realistic illustrations for quotation in his own work."[17] I added that "this indicated his manner of working."[18] In a footnote to this passage I said that I possess Pigou's copy of a book cited in *The Economics of Welfare* and that Pigou's markings and comments indicate his manner of working.[19] This was a reference back to the text and it implies that these markings etc. were what one would expect if Pigou was looking for examples for "quotation in his own work." They confirm Austin Robinson's statement. Simpson comments: "The context in which this is said suggests that these markings and annotations are not the product of a superior intellect, nor evidence of a sound manner of working."[20] This statement of Simpson's is an invention. I never suggested any such thing nor did I think it nor did the context suggest it. Pigou was an intelligent man. That I found his views on state action in the economic sphere to be wanting does not imply anything about Pigou's intellect. I share George Stigler's opinion: "Pigou's views of the competence of the state were, like his predecessor's views, a tolerably random selection of the immediately previous views, warmed by hope. ... Pigou did not differ from his less illustrious colleagues in the superficiality of his judgments on the economic competence of the state. ... He differed only in writing more pages of economic analysis of fully professional quality than almost any other economist of the twentieth century."[21]

I now turn to Simpson's discussion of the railway sparks example. This is what he says: "Coase says that Pigou's use of the example is presumably intended to show how it is possible for State action to improve on 'natural tendencies.' The passage quoted from Pigou comes from Pigou's book, but not from the section in which he deals with sparks. Coase's claim seems mistaken."[22] It is true that the passage quoted from Pigou comes from a different section of the book but it happens to be the section in which he sets out the aim of Part II, in which the sparks example appears. This is Pigou's summary of chapter 1 of Part II: "The general problem of this Part is to ascertain how far the free play of self-interest, acting under the existing legal system, tends to distribute the country's resources in the way most favourable to the production of a large national dividend, and how far it is feasible for State action to improve upon 'natural' tendencies."[23] In chapter 2 of this Part we find the sparks example: "It might happen, for example, *as will be explained more fully in a later chapter*, that costs are thrown upon people not directly concerned through, say, uncompensated damage done to surrounding woods by sparks from railway engines" (my italics).[24] This is an example of a divergence between private and social product since the operator of the railway will not take into account, in deciding on his actions, the damage to surrounding woods when he does not have to compensate their owners. In the later chapter (chapter 9) to which Pigou directs our attention, we read that when there are these divergences, self-interest will not "tend to make the national dividend a maximum; and consequently, certain acts of interference with normal economic processes may be expected, not to diminish, but to increase the dividend."[25] Simpson points out that "Pigou nowhere said that the state should do anything at all about uncompensated damage caused by sparks from railway locomotives." [26] In a literal sense this is true. What Pigou said is that there is a divergence between private and social product when there is uncompensated damage to surrounding woods by railway sparks and that when there are these divergencies (and he said this in the chapter to which we are directed in the same sentence that he talks about railway sparks) specific acts of interferences may be expected to increase the national dividend. I took it that Pigou wished compensation to be paid since the divergence arose because it was not. I then investigated the circumstances in which compensation would not be paid at the time Pigou wrote.

I found in *Halsbury's Laws of England* that under the common law, compensation would not normally be paid if the railway had statutory authority. Simpson says that "Although there is a doctrinal sense in which this is correct, it misled Coase."[27] Having read his historical account of the evolution of the legal doctrines about liability for damage by railway sparks (about which I had been ignorant) I accept completely his statement that in the nineteenth century, "There was no government decision to this effect, in the sense in which Coase uses this concept. Instead the doctrine was evolved by the judges, just like the common law itself." [28] However, I was not concerned in my article with the situation in the nineteenth century but with what it was at the time Pigou wrote. The Railway (Fires) Act of 1905 was in force at the time the first edition of *The Economics of Welfare* was published and the same Act as amended in 1923 for subsequent editions. In these acts some exceptions were made to the common law doctrine although in the main it was left intact. More exceptions could have been made or the common law doctrine could have been repudiated. This was not done. This is what I meant when I said that Pigou's example only existed at the time *The Economics of Welfare* was published "as a result of a deliberate choice of the legislature."[29]

Simpson has an exaggerated idea of the importance to me of whether Pigou correctly understood the legal situation that resulted in compensation not being paid for damage resulting from railway sparks. To me it was just another case of an economist giving an example without investigating why it could occur. His lack of knowledge of the legal position regarding railway sparks did not lead me to the conclusion that Pigou was a confused thinker, as Simpson claims. Had Pigou correctly described the legal position, I would have been interested, pleased and surprised. But it would not have affected my belief that Pigou's economic approach was flawed—and this is what mattered to me. Simpson's failure to understand my point of view could only have been compounded by a mistake he made. To the question "Why did Coase think that Pigou favoured stated intervention over engine sparks?" he gives the answer, "Coase reaches his conclusion by relying on a much later passage in Pigou's *The Economics of Welfare*, chapter 20 of Part II."[30] This is wrong. What I said in "The Problem of Social Cost" was: "In conjunction with what he says in chapter 9 of Part II, I take Pigou's policy recommendation to be, first, that there should be State action to correct this 'natural' situation, and second, that the railways should be forced to compensate those whose woods are burnt."[31] Simpson studied chapter 20. The chapter I referred to and from which I quoted was chapter 9.

Whether Simpson, had he studied the right chapter, would have revised his opinion of my argument seems to me doubtful. Simpson disputes my statement that "Pigou's basic position was that, when defects were found in the working of the economic system, the way to put things right is through some form of government action."[32] He maintains this despite the fact that Pigou says that his purpose in Part II is "to bring into clearer light some of the ways in which it now is, or eventually may become, feasible for governments to control the play of economic forces in such wise as to promote the economic welfare, and, through that, the total welfare of their citizens as a whole."[33] Simpson describes Pigou's position in these words:

> It is hardly an exaggeration to say that Pigou demonstrated that self-interest operating through the market is unlikely to lead to an optimal use of resources but that he had no developed idea as to what, if anything, should be done about this. ... By 1937, when he published his *Socialism versus Capitalism*, he had come to have grave doubts even

about the use of bounties and taxes in either a capitalist or a communist system. ... Ignorance of the facts militated against the use of these possible remedies. ... Pigou's view was thus much the same as that of Coase, though he was marginally less skeptical about the merits of state action.[34]

I am completely baffled by these statements and cannot understand how Simpson came to make them. How was it possible for someone to go through *Socialism versus Capitalism* to find the one passage (of approximately two pages) in which Pigou expressed the same thought that I had without reading the rest of the book?

Pigou in his final chapter of *Socialism versus Capitalism* starts by telling us that his discussion in the earlier chapters is "inadequate to determine our practical choice between capitalism and socialist central planning."[35] But now consider the passages with which Pigou concludes this chapter:

The fact, however that we are without the data and the instruments of thought necessary for assured judgment, does not entitle us to sit back with folded hands. For to sit so is itself to take a decision; to make the great refusal, to declare ourselves in advance opponents of any change. In human affairs it is rarely possible to demonstrate absolutely—even though our criteria of "good" be agreed—that one course of action is "better" than another. The data are always imperfect. Nevertheless, having equipped ourselves with the relevant knowledge and technique, we must use these imperfect data as best we may, and take the plunge, and *judge*. There is no other way.

In this field an economist has no special qualification. Indeed, as a more or less cloistered person, he is worse qualified than many others, who, maybe, have less knowledge of the relevant facts. A wide experience of men and of affairs and a strong "feel" for what, with the human instruments available, will or will not work, are needed here. These the present writer, like most academic persons, does not possess; and, unlike some academic persons, he is aware that he does not possess them. None the less, to conclude a book like this without some sort of confession of faith on the issues with which it deals would be open to misconception. Something, however crude and tentative, must be adventured.

If, then, it were in the writer's power to direct his country's destiny, he would accept, for the time being, the general structure of capitalism; but he would modify it gradually. He would use the weapon of graduated death duties and graduated income tax, not merely as instruments of revenue, but with the deliberate purpose of diminishing the glaring inequalities of fortune and opportunity which deface our present civilisation. He would take a leaf from the book of Soviet Russia and remember that the most important investment of all is investment in the health, intelligence and character of the people. To advocate "economy" in this field would, under his government, be a criminal offense. All industries affected with a public interest, or capable of wielding monopoly power, he would subject at least to public supervision and control. Some of them, certainly the manufacture of armaments, probably the coal industry, possibly the railways, he would nationalise, not, of course, on the pattern of the Post Office, but through public boards or commissions. The Bank of England he would make in name—what it is already in effect—a public institution; with instructions to use its power to mitigate, so far as may be, violent fluctuations in industry and employment. If all went well, further steps towards nationalisation of important industries would be taken by degrees. In controlling and developing these nationalised industries, the central government would inevitably need to "plan" an appropriate allocation for a large part of the country's annual investment in new capital. When these things had been accomplished, the writer would consider his period of office at an end, and would surrender the reins of government. In his political testament he would recommend his successor also to follow the path of gradualness—to mould and transform, not violently to uproot; but he would add, in large capitals, a final sentence, that gradualness implies action, and is not a polite name for standing still.[36]

In the earlier chapters of *Socialism versus Capitalism*, Pigou's sympathy with socialism is everywhere evident. A few examples will suffice. We are told that, "As regards the technical efficiency of particular industries it is impossible to say *in general terms* that the dominant capitalist form—the joint stock company—is superior or inferior to whatever socialized form would be the most likely alternative to it."[37] When he considers the problem of incentives, Pigou concludes that, "Socialism should be allotted *some* more marks than its rival."[38] In saying this, Pigou probably had in mind his statement made earlier in the same chapter that, "In Russia there can be no doubt that under the new régime tremendous enthusiasm for work on the part of manual wage-earners has been evoked. Mr. and Mrs. Webb give a vivid picture of the high spirit that these men, feeling themselves servants of their own State, not of private profit-makers, display."[39] Regarding investment, Pigou says this: "It may be, no doubt, that a central planning authority would make *less* provision for investment than would be made through the private action of individuals in a similarly placed capitalist society. But the Russian experiment suggests that it is *likely* to make *more* provision. There is certainly no ground for asserting *a priori* that in this field socialist central planning will produce situations less favourable to general well-being than capitalism would do."[40] I am at a loss to explain how it is, after reading the concluding section of *Socialism versus Capitalism* as well as the other statements from that book that I have reproduced, that Simpson could say that Pigou was only marginally less sceptical about the merits of State action than I am, particularly as it is his view that I have a deep scepticism regarding the desirability of State action. Of course the explanation may be that Simpson did not read *Socialism versus Capitalism*. But if so, how did he find the short passage to which he refers?

I now turn to the section of Simpson's article entitled "Pigou as Straw Man." It starts with the following sentence: "Since Pigou did not express or apparently hold the view attributed to him, the question arises as to what he is doing in the article at all."[41] Since Simpson does not tell us what the view was that I attributed to Pigou that he does not express or hold, we are left to guess. As I do not believe that I have attributed to Pigou any view that he did not hold, it is not easy for me to guess what Simpson had in mind. But as this sentence follows closely on his statement that Pigou is only "marginally less skeptical" than I am about the desirability of State action,

I assume that my supposed error relates to my statements about Pigou's view on this subject. What I said in *The Firm, the Market and the Law* was: "Pigou's basic position was that, when defects were found in the working of the economic system, the way to put things right was through some form of government action. This view is expressed with numerous qualifications, but it represents the central tendency in his thought."[42] In chapter 1 of Part II of *The Economics of Welfare*, Pigou says that his purpose is "to bring into clearer light some of the ways in which it now is, or eventually may become, feasible for governments to control the play of economic forces to promote the total welfare of their citizens as a whole."[43] In chapter 9, he says that when there is a divergence between private and social products, "certain specific acts of interference with normal economic processes may be expected, not to diminish, but to increase the dividend."[44] And in chapter 20 he states that when "the free play of self-interest will cause an amount of resources to be invested different from the amount that is required in the best interest of the national dividend, there is a *prima facie* case for public intervention."[45] I regard these statements as ample justification for my description of Pigou's basic position and I think what Pigou says in *Socialism versus Capitalism*, to which Simpson draws our attention, considerably strengthens my case.

I now come to the reason why Pigou's treatment appears in the article. It could not be left out. To economists of my generation, Pigou's way of looking at the problem of social cost was the way to analyze it. As Stigler has said, "The disharmonies between private and social interests produced by external economies and diseconomies became gospel to the economics profession. Economists accepted this gospel the way they accept supply and demand as the forces determining prices—instinctively and without misgivings."[46] Samuelson, for instance, describes Pigou's position without dissent as follows: "His doctrine holds that the equilibrium of a closed economy under competition is correct except where there are technological external economies or diseconomies. Under these conditions, since each individual's actions have effects on others which he does not take into account in making his decisions, there is a *prima facie* case for intervention."[47] Stigler's own account in *The Theory of Price* (1952 edition) is even more striking: "There can be real differences between the alternative product of a resource to society and to an industry or firm or, in Pigou's terminology, between the marginal social product and the marginal private product. ... Some of the disharmonies between private and social products are large and important, and they are dealt with by a variety of techniques such as taxes and subsidies, dissemination of information, and the police power, for example, zoning."[48] This exposition by Stigler is pure Pigou. Simpson speaks of Pigou as my target. This is wrong. My target (or targets) were the modern economists who had adopted Pigou's approach. In fact, I have had some success and many economists consider that I have provided them with an improved analytical system. One only needs to compare the treatment of this question in the 1952 edition of Stigler's *Theory of Price* with what he says in the 1966 edition. I sent a copy of "The Problem of Social Cost" to John Hicks, one of the great economic theorists of this century and a major contributor to the New Welfare Economics. In his reply Hicks said: "I do think you are doing a very interesting job in bringing these legal decisions into relation with economic theory; I wish there were more people doing this. You are of course clearly right on the main point. I suppose Pigou's trouble here, as elsewhere, was that he was not firmly clear what it was that he was maximizing."

The significance of my article for economic analysis and why Pigou's treatment was rightfully discussed in the article were unfortunately hidden from Simpson and he produces a somewhat bizarre explanation for Pigou's appearance in my article: "Coase, in the tradition of the political economists, adopts a rhetorical device, which is first of all to attribute a commitment to the merits of government intervention to Pigou, and then to present Pigou as a deeply confused thinker. The form of the argument then is this: If you believe X, then you are in bad company, for you believe something particularly associated with the thinking of Y, a deeply confused economist. The very fact that Y believed X becomes itself a reason for skepticism."[49] Simpson says in this passage that I write "in the tradition of the political economists." Recall what he says earlier in his article about them: "They tended to say much the same as each other, relying not on formal proofs or empirical studies, but on appeals to common sense and assertions of the supposedly obvious. ... The practice was to assert in rhetorical tones ... the validity of propositions so broad as to be quite incapable of falsification or demonstration. That this technique could be effective cannot be doubted; the most notable victims of the early political economists were the Irish peasants who died in the Great Famine."[50] Simpson employs here (and elsewhere in his article) a form of argument that it is impossible to answer. And I will not try.

All this is regrettable. I need not reiterate the argument in "The Problem of Social Cost" in which I criticise Pigou's approach and develop my own. Most economists seem to have understood my argument and it is no disgrace to a legal historian that he has not, although the patronising tone of his remarks seems inappropriate. But there is little point in debating the merits and demerits of "The Problem of Social Cost." The article has played its part in launching the subject of "law and economics". In judging the worth of an article, as I said in appraising some of Stigler's work, "What really matters is whether the contribution moves the subject forward, makes us aware of possibilities previously neglected, and opens up new and fruitful avenues of research."[51] Judged in this way, "The Problem of Social Cost" can be considered a success. Since its publication a vast amount of work has been carried out by lawyers and economists in developing the subject and although often influenced by "The Problem of Social Cost," what they have done has left that article far behind. It is now a relic, to be interpreted and, I am afraid, misinterpreted, by historians of thought. As regards law and economics, and particularly that part called "the economic analysis of law," there is now an immense literature written in the main, as I said at the beginning of this paper, by lawyers sufficiently knowledgeable in economics. In its range, quality, and interest, it constitutes a most impressive achievement. If Simpson wishes to consider whether an economic approach can be helpful in the analysis of law, this is where he should look. He would then realise that it is not enough to say, as he does at the end of his paper, that the courts should "confine their activities to the vigorous protection of rights."[52] It is the task of scholars to study in a systematic way what these rights should be and what legal doctrines and procedures are likely to bring us closer to this result.

Notes

[1] George J. Stigler, Does Economics Have a Useful Past? 1 *History of Political Economy*. 217, 219 (1969).
[2] R. H. Coase, Economics and contiguous disciplines, in *Essays on Economics and Economists*, 34, 44 (1994). This article was originally published in *The Organization and Retrieval of Economic Knowledge* (Mark Perlman ed. 1977).
[3] Id.at 45.
[4] R. H. Coase, Law and economics at Chicago, 36 *Journal of Law and Economics*. 239, 250-251 (1993).
[5] R. H. Coase, The problem of social cost, in *The Firm, the Market and the Law,* 95, 119 (1988). This article was originally published in 3 *Journal of Law and Economics*. 1 (1960).
[6] A. W. Brian Simpson, *Coase v. Pigou* Reexamined, in this issue, at 58.
[7] Guido Calabresi, The pointlessness of Pareto: Carrying Coase further, 100 *Yale Law Journal*. 1211, 1212(1991).
[8] Coase, *supra* note 5, at 118-119.
[9] R. H. Coase, Economists and public policy, in *Essays on Economics and Economists*, *supra* note 2, at 47, 61. This article was originally published in *Large Corporations in a Changing Society* (J. Fred Weston ed. 1975).
[10] Id. at 62.
[11] Id.
[12] Id.
[13] Id. at 63.
[14] See, for example, David Newsome, On the edge of paradise: A. C. Benson, the diarist, 202 (1980): "Pigou is a fool; these romantic attachments may do great good to the inspirer and the inspired, but they should be conducted with some seemliness and decorum." John Clapham, the economic historian, at 359, was also disturbed by "Pigou's fatuous worship of an undergrad. They are always together. The undergrad reads the lesson in the chapel, and Pigou, who *never* attends, appears in his place and the undergrads giggle."
[15] Hugh Dalton, Call Back Yesterday, 1887-1931, at 60 (1953).
[16] Austin Robinson, Arthur Cecil Pigou, in *International Encyclopedia of the Social Sciences,* 90, 94 (David L. Sills ed. 1968).
[17] Ronald H. Coase, The firm, the market and the law, in *The Firm, the Market and the Law, supra* note 5, at 1, 22.

[18] Id.
[19] Id. at 22-23 n.33.
[20] Simpson, in this issue, at 65.
[21] George J. Stigler, The economist and the state, in *The Economist as Preacher and Other Essays,* 119, 128 (1982). This article was originally published in 65 *American Economic Review.* 1 (1975).
[22] Simpson, in this issue, at 67.
[23] A. C. Pigou, *The Economics of Welfare*, at xii (4th ed. 1948).
[24] Id. at 134.
[25] Id. at 172.
[26] Simpson, in this issue, at 66-67.
[27] Id. at 76.
[28] Id. at 84.
[29] Coase, *supra* note 5, at 138.
[30] Simpson, in this issue, at 68.
[31] Coase, *supra* note 5, at 135-136.
[32] Coase, *supra* note 17, at 20.
[33] Pigou, *supra* note 23, at 129-130.
[34] Simpson, in this issue, at 72-73.
[35] A. C. Pigou, *Socialism versus Capitalism,* 135 (1937).
[36] Id. at 136-139
[37] Id. at 93.
[38] Id. at 101.
[39] Id. at 99-100
[40] Id. at 133-134
[41] Simpson, in this issue, at 74.
[42] Coase, *supra* note 17, at 20.
[43] Pigou, *supra* note 23, at 129-130.
[44] Id. at 172.
[45] Id. at 331.
[46] George J. Stigler, *Memoirs of an Unregulated Economist,* 75 (1988).
[47] Paul A. Samuelson, *Foundations of Economic Analysis,* 208 (1947).
[48] George J. Stigler, *The Theory of Price,* 104-105 (1952).
[49] Simpson, in this issue, at 75.
[50] Id. at 74.
[51] R. H. Coase, George J. Stigler, in *Essays on Economics and Economists, supra* note 2, at 199, 207.
[52] Simpson, in this issue, at 97.

Law and Economics At Chicago[*]

It is a double honor to have been invited to deliver the Simons lecture on the occasion of the celebration of the centennial of the University of Chicago. Although at my age a century seems a rather short period, we all know that the University of Chicago has not suffered from the usual human limitations. It emerged from the ground fully grown. It had neither an infancy nor an adolescence and wasted no time in working its way to the top. It started at the top. Economics at the University of Chicago was no exception. The first head of the economics department, J. L. Laughlin, himself a redoubtable authority on money, set about recruiting a formidable faculty, including Thorstein Veblen. When I went as a student to the London School of Economics in 1929, some thirty-seven years after the formation of the University of Chicago, its economics department was recognized to be one of the most powerful in the world. Foremost in our minds at the time, mainly as a result of the teaching of Lionel Robbins, was Frank Knight. He was regarded at the London School of Economics as one of the greatest of economists and his book, *Risk, Uncertainty, and Profit*, [1] was closely studied by all serious students of economics there. Then there was Jacob Viner, an economic theorist of great ability and erudition, whose work put him in the top rank of economists. Another member of the faculty was Henry Schultz, one of the pioneers of econometrics, whose empirical work on the derivation of

---

[*] *Journal of Law and Economics*, 1993, 36(1), 239-254. Presented as the Henry C. Simons Memorial Lecture on April 7, 1992, at the John M. Olin Centennial Conference in Law and Economics at the University of Chicago Law School.

statistical demand schedules was regarded as a major contribution to economics. Finally there was Paul Douglas, a strange man who thought it more important and interesting to be a United States senator than a professor at the University of Chicago. His empirical work on wages and the labor market, however, was very important and was much admired, by me among others. He became celebrated as the originator of the Cobb-Douglas production function. It is a measure of the strength of Chicago economics at that time that had there been a Nobel Prize in economics in the years before World War II, there is no doubt that all four of these men would have been recipients.

However, none of these men, with the possible exception of Knight, can be said to have contributed to the subject of my lecture, law and economics, the development of which is bound up with the University of Chicago and particularly with the Law School. To understand how this came about, we must turn to Henry Simons, in whose memory this series of lectures was instituted. Henry Simons was a protégé of Knight having been a junior colleague of his at the University of Iowa. He joined the economics department of the University of Chicago in 1927. Whereas I studied the writings of the four Chicago economists I have mentioned and was personally acquainted with all of them except Paul Douglas, I did not read Simons's writings with great care and never met him. What I know about Simons is largely based on what Aaron Director and George Stigler have said and on a study of his papers. Unlike the four Chicago economists, Knight, Viner, Schultz, and Douglas, Simons was not an international figure. His name was known to me and when his pamphlet, *A Positive Program for Laissez Faire,* was published in 1934, I bought a copy (its American price was twenty-five cents), and I read it. I still possess my copy, but its excellent condition attests that it was not something that I studied with great attention.

It is not difficult to understand why I was not attracted to Simons's pamphlet. It is, as Simons says, "a propagandist tract." It is written with passion and a sense of impending doom: "The future of our civilization hangs in balance."[2] An Englishman, comforting himself with the thought that somehow or other we manage to muddle through, could not be expected to share Simons's fears, and I did not. In any case, the pamphlet was more an essay in political philosophy than economics. And when it did touch on economics, or at any rate on those parts of economics in which I was interested, his views were such as to provoke serious reservations. He thought that the regulation of railroads and public utilities generally had been a dismal failure. And what was his solution for this problem? He argued that, "The state should face the necessity of actually taking over, owning, and managing directly, both the railroads and the utilities, and all other industries in which it is impossible to maintain effectively competitive conditions."[3] Carrying out Simons's proposals would have involved the nationalization of a large part of American industry, perhaps the greater part. It is a strange route to laissez-faire and brings to mind the proposals of Oskar Lange and Abba Lerner for market socialism. For other industries, those not candidates for nationalization, Simons said that, "There still remains a real alternative to socialization, namely, the establishment and preservation of competition as the regulative agency."[4] But how was this to be accomplished? He thought that the antitrust laws should be used to bring about a drastic restructuring of American industry. "The Federal Trade Commission must become perhaps the most powerful of our governmental agencies."[5] I can give the flavor of Simons's approach by describing some of his proposals regarding the corporation:

> There must be an outright dismantling of our gigantic corporations. ... Few of our gigantic corporations can be defended on the ground that their present size is necessary to reasonably full exploitation of production economies: their existence is to be explained in terms of opportunities for promoter profits, personal ambitions of industrial and financial "Napoleons," and advantages of monopoly power. We should look forward to a situation in which the size of ownership units in every industry is limited to the minimum size of operating plant requisite to efficient, but highly specialized production—and even more narrowly limited, if ever necessary to the maintenance of freedom of enterprise.[6]

What Simons had in mind is made clearer in a footnote: "It will be necessary to revise notions commonly accepted (especially by courts) as to the maximum size of firm compatible with effective competition. The general rule and ultimate objective should be that of fixing in each industry a maximum size of firm such that the results of perfect competition would be approximated even if all firms attained the maximum size. One may suggest, tentatively, that in major industries no ownership unit should produce or control more than 5 percent of the total output."[7]

Another example of Simons's position is furnished by his attitude to advertising and other promotional activities. "It is a commonplace that our vaunted efficiency in production is dissipated extravagantly in the wastes of merchandising. ... If present tendencies continue, we may soon reach a situation where most of our resources are utilized in persuading people to buy one thing rather than another, and only a minor fraction actually employed in creating things to be bought."[8] In making such statements and generally in dealing with industrial organization, Simons provides no empirical backing for his contentions, makes no serious investigation of what the effects of his proposals would be on the efficiency with which the economic system would operate, nor does he consider whether the Federal Trade Commission would be likely to do what he wanted or whether, even if it wanted to do so, it would be possible for it to acquire the information necessary to implement his proposals. Simons's approach is the very antithesis of that which was to become dominant as a result of the emergence of that new subject, law and economics. Stigler's description of Simons is eminently just: Simons was a utopian.[9]

In saying this I do not mean to denigrate the quality of Simons's mind. Thomas More was no mean figure. Aaron Director, Milton Friedman, and George Stigler have all acknowledged Simons's influence on their thought, and only a powerful mind could do this. Gordon Tullock has described how attendance at Simons's course changed the way he thought about economic problems and has told us that this was also the case with Warren Nutter. That Simons was able to influence in a fundamental way the views of these two talented but fiercely independent men is a tribute to the quality of his mind. Moreover, it also needs to be realized that, although Simons was a fine price theorist, his main interest was not in the economics of industrial organization but in macroeconomics, and particularly in monetary theory and policy, and here he was to have an extremely important influence on the development of the views held in Chicago. It would therefore be churlish to emphasize in this lecture the weaknesses of his views on industrial organization were it not that the subject of law and economics has been little concerned with the monetary system and is intimately related to the economics of industrial organization. What can, I think, be said with confidence is that Simons, who influenced Milton Friedman, and therefore the world, on money, played little or no part in the development of the ideas which make up the modern subject of law and economics.

And yet, having said that, there is no question that Simons played a crucial role in establishing the law and economics program at the Law School. He was the first economist to join the faculty of the Law School and since then the Law School has never been without an economist (and sometimes it has had more than one). Simons's accession to the Law School was not, however, the result of a strongly felt need by the law professors to have an economist as a colleague. It came about accidentally as a partial response to problems that had arisen in the economics department. When in 1934 the question of renewing Simons's contract came up in the economics department, there was strong opposition to his reappointment, particularly on the part of Paul Douglas. Simons had published little and was not a popular teacher. Simons, however, had a strong supporter in Knight, who did not hide his feelings. In the event, Simons was reappointed but later received a half-time appointment in the Law School, where he had some friends, and this must have mollified somewhat those people in the economics department who had opposed his reappointment. Appointed an assistant professor in 1927, he was not promoted to associate professor until 1942, and, as Stigler points out, "only with the backing of the Law School."[10] In 1945, some eighteen years after he was appointed to the faculty, Simons was granted tenure, at first in the Law School and later in the economics department.[11] In the Law School, where he seems to have been a more popular teacher than he was in the economics department, Simons taught price theory. Walter Blum believes that, although Simons had some friends in the Law School, the older faculty were either opposed or indifferent to his appointment. I do not know how far Simons discussed with his colleagues or included in his teaching the views to be found in *A Positive Program for Laissez Faire,* but if he did, the very looseness of his thinking would have been found congenial by the law professors, and it certainly would not have posed a threat to their way of thinking that the later sharper analysis of law and economics was to do. At any rate, Simons established the tradition that there should be an economist on the faculty of the University of Chicago Law School. But Simons was to take a step which was to help to make possible all that law and economics was to accomplish at Chicago. He played an important part in bringing Aaron Director to the Law School. Yet the tale is not simple. The distinguished scholar, and my old colleague, Friedrich Hayek, who, as some of you know, died quite recently in Germany at the age of ninety-two, was to play an equally important part—and in some respects more important part than Simons—in making it possible for Aaron Director to come to the University of Chicago Law School.

Aaron Director received his bachelor's degree from Yale in 1924. He then became Director of Workers Education for the Oregon State Federation of Labor and Head of Portland Labor College. In 1927 he came to the University of Chicago for graduate studies in economics and in 1930 was appointed an instructor in economics, having been in 1929 an instructor in labor economics at Northwestern while still pursuing his studies at Chicago. He became a research assistant of Paul Douglas and wrote with him *The Problem of Unemployment,* published in 1931. In 1935, Aaron Director went to work for the Treasury Department, and in 1937 to 1938 he visited the London School of Economics. Towards the end of his stay at the London School of Economics, Frank Knight wrote to Lionel Robbins and asked for his opinion of Director, apparently with a view to using what he said to secure a university position for Director. Robbins in his reply[12] spoke of Director's "charm, his urbanity and his most extensive culture" although preferring to dwell on "his judgment, his scholarship and his analytical ability." In a covering letter[13] Robbins referred to Director's "quite unique balance of qualities—a perfectly civilized man." In the event, Director went to Washington D.C., where he was employed in various government positions until 1946.

We now have to return to Simons to learn how the University of Chicago Law School was able to avail itself of what Robbins rightly called Director's "quite unique balance of qualities." In 1945, or perhaps a little earlier, Simons conceived the idea of establishing an "Institute of Political Economy." The aim would be to bring together a group of "traditional liberal" or "libertarian" economists, to arrange visits for "libertarian" professors from other institutions, and to provide support for their work.[14] Simons seems to have regarded formation of the institute as a last-ditch effort to keep alive ideas in danger of being lost, and his remarks often have a note of desperation. The institute "should not be mainly concerned with formal economic theory nor should it engage substantially in empirical research. It should focus on central, practical problems of American economic policy and governmental structure. It should afford a center to which economic liberals everywhere may look for intellectual leadership or support. It should seek to influence affairs mainly through influencing professional opinion and by preserving at least one place where some political economists of the future may be thoroughly and competently trained along traditional-liberal lines."[15] Simons goes on to explain why Chicago should be that one place. This is what he said: "Chicago economics still has some distinctively traditional-liberal connotations and some prestige. Here, more than elsewhere, the project would be that of sustaining or keeping alive something not yet lost or submerged—and something which here, too, will shortly be lost unless special measures are taken."[16] As this indicates, Simons thought the situation, even at Chicago, was precarious: "The outlook at Chicago, if better than elsewhere, is not very promising. Our divisional dean has no apprehension of economic liberalism and a distinct hostility toward it, and the same is true of most persons in the other social science departments. Among higher administrative officers, there is at best only indifference, or provisional toleration, toward such political economy. A few members of the Law School and School of Business are interested or sympathetic, as are other individual faculty members here and there. In the Department of Economics we are becoming a small minority."[17] Simons's gloomy forebodings proved to be completely unjustified. The year 1946 saw the appointment of Aaron Director in the Law School and of Milton Friedman in the Economics Department. Friedman, of course, has never thought that being a "small minority" was a handicap.

I must now introduce Friedrich Hayek into this story. Hayek had written during the war his famous book *The Road to Serfdom*,[18] which argued that socialism, of whatever kind, was bound to pose a grave threat to political and economic freedoms. When Hayek failed to secure a commercial publisher in America for this book because of its supposed limited appeal, on the recommendation of Aaron Director the University of Chicago Press agreed to publish it. You know what happened. *The Road to Serfdom* became a best-seller, selling over 200,000 copies; a condensation was published in *Reader's Digest;* and it was translated into sixteen languages. As a result of the interest in his work created by this success, Hayek was brought into contact with H. W. Luhnow of the Volker Fund of Kansas City. More than this I do not know, but it had the result that the Volker Fund came to support Hayek's activities. At the end of the war, Hayek worried that European civilization, with its ideas and values, was in danger of immediate disintegration. To counter this danger, Hayek was anxious that contacts should be established as soon as possible between scholars in all countries, belligerent and neutral, who believed in the values of a liberal society. Out of Hayek's efforts to foster such cooperation came the formation of the Mont Pelerin Society. But Hayek also played a crucial role in the events which would lead to the bringing into existence of the Law and Economics Program at the University of Chicago Law School.

I do not know the details of the tale I am about to tell, but the broad picture is, I think, correct. Simons, presumably knowing about Hayek's general aims and of his connection with Luhnow, sent to Hayek, in 1945, a copy of his proposal for the establishment of an institute of political economy. It included the suggestion that Aaron Director should be the head of the institute. The choice of Director for this position would have been welcomed enthusiastically by Hayek, who, quite apart from any gratitude he may have felt for his help in securing publication of *The Road to Serfdom,* would certainly have shared Robbins's extremely favorable view of Director formed during his stay at the London School of Economics. Probably on the suggestion of Hayek, an outline of a research project entitled "A Free Market Study" was prepared. This research project came to supersede Simons's proposal for an institute of political economy. It seems to have been assumed by Hayek that, as a matter of course, the research project would be undertaken by Director. From this point on Hayek became the central figure, negotiating with Robert Maynard Hutchins, chancellor of the University of Chicago, with Wilber Katz, dean of the Law School, with the Volker Fund, and with Aaron Director, concerning the carrying out of this project at the University of Chicago and about the terms on which Director would be appointed to conduct what Katz referred to as the "Hayek Research Project." In the end, it was agreed to appoint Director for five years as research associate with the rank of professor to conduct what was called in the memorandum[19] sent to the Volker Fund, "a study of a suitable legal and institutional framework of an effective competitive system." However, before the final arrangements were made, Simons died, and Katz asked that the terms of the Volker grant be modified to allow Director to do some teaching.[20]

Aaron Director has said that the research project "never amounted to very much," but that was not true of his teaching.[21] Both in and out of the classroom, Director was extremely effective as a teacher, and he had a profound influence on the views of some of his students and also on those of some of his colleagues at the University of Chicago both in law and economics. At first Director taught the course on "Economic Analysis and Public Policy," essentially a price theory course, but later he was invited by Edward Levi to collaborate with him in teaching the antitrust course. After an attempt at joint teaching, it was decided to divide the teaching into four days for Levi and one for Director. What happened has been described by some of those who took the course. Wesley Liebeler has said this: "For four days each week Ed Levi would develop the law and would use the traditional techniques of legal reasoning to relate the cases to each other and create a synthesis of the kind ... lawyers ... are familiar with to explain and rationalize the cases. It was some accomplishment. ... For four days Ed would do this, and for one day each week Aaron Director would tell us that everything that Levi had told us the preceding four days was nonsense. He used economic analysis to show us that the legal analysis simply would not stand up."[22] Robert Bork has commented: "One of the pleasures of that course was to watch Ed agonizing as these cases he had always believed in and worked on were systematically turned into incoherent statements. Ed fought brilliantly for years before he finally gave way."[23] From then on, the superiority of the economic analysis of the law, at least in the area of antitrust, came to be firmly held at the University of Chicago Law School. This belief was strengthened by the establishment of the Antitrust Project, which brought, among others, John McGee, Robert Bork, and Ward Bowman to the Law School to conduct research on antitrust problems. Their work and that of other students of Director, for he himself published little, brought his ideas and approach to the attention of the academic world outside Chicago. But the Antitrust Project did more than this. It was out of the Antitrust Project that the law and economics program evolved.

I joined the University of Chicago Law School in 1964 (at first in a joint appointment with the Business School), and soon afterward Director retired, and I became responsible for the law and economics program. My situation was very different from that faced by Director when he came to the Law School. Director created the Law and Economics program. I inherited it. By then, as a result of Director's teaching, the economic analysis of law was no longer an idea but a fact. The *Journal of Law and Economics* existed. There were law and economic fellowships with the whole program financed by the Volker Fund. Furthermore, and this was extremely important, there were now law professors who took an active part in the program, at first Kenneth Dam and Edmund Kitch, later to be joined by Richard Posner. There was however an additional element which led to a change in the emphasis of the program, the publication in volume 3 of the *Journal of Law and Economics* of "The Problem of Social Cost."[24] 1 will therefore say something about how I came to write this article and about its influence on the subject of law and economics. It is difficult to be objective when speaking of one's own work, but I will try.

At the London School of Economics, I had been responsible for the course on the economics of public utilities, and this led me to study, among other industries, the organization and finance of broadcasting in Britain. This resulted in the publication in 1950 of a book, *British Broadcasting: A Study in Monopoly*. In 1951 I migrated to the United States, and, once there, I began a general study of what I termed the "political economy of radio and television." In 1958 I spent a year at the Center for Advanced Study in the Behavioral Sciences at Stanford. I used my time there to investigate the work of the Federal Communications Commission (FCC), particularly its policies in allocating the use of the radio frequency spectrum. The article which resulted was published in volume 2 of the *Journal of Law and Economics*.[25] In one section of that article I suggested that use of the radio frequency spectrum should be determined, not as a result of administrative decisions, but by the pricing mechanism. It is sometimes said that I introduced the idea of using prices to allocate the spectrum. But this is untrue. The first time this was proposed, at any rate in print, was by a student author, Leo Herzel, in an article in the *University of Chicago Law Review* in 1951.[26] When I first read this article I thought, and it was quite natural to think this, that Leo Herzel had been influenced by Aaron Director and Milton Friedman. But this also is untrue. While he was an undergraduate, Herzel had become very interested in the debate over whether a rational, efficient system for allocating resources would be possible under socialism. As a result, he read Abba Lerner's *The Economics of Control* soon after it was published in 1944.[27] This debate, particularly Lerner's detailed proposal for market socialism in *The Economics of Control,* was the inspiration behind his views. The difference between Lerner's scheme and that of Herzel is that, as he notes in his article, unlike the situation in a socialist system, the broadcasters under his proposal would operate "in their own economic interest ... to increase profits" and would not have to follow abstract rules.[28] I, of course, understood and agreed with the logic of the argument of Lerner and Herzel. Abba Lerner had been a fellow student and colleague at the London School of Economics and our relationship was very friendly. I was well acquainted with his views, and I knew their strength. But on reading Herzel's article I did not immediately jump to the conclusion that a market with pricing would be superior to regulation by the FCC. It was necessary to take into account the existence of transaction costs. However, my investigations while at the Center at Stanford led me to believe that the problem of establishing a system of property rights which could be the subject of trading was not as difficult as one might have supposed, and they certainly made it abundantly clear to me that the Federal Communications Commission conducted its affairs in an extremely imperfect way. The question of whether pricing should be used to allocate the use of the radio frequency spectrum was, however, clinched for me by the reply to Leo Herzel's article which appeared in a subsequent number of the *University of Chicago Law Review,* written by Dallas Smythe, who had been chief economist of the Federal Communications Commission.[29] His objections were so incredibly feeble (I refer to them in my article) that I concluded that, if this was the best that could brought against his proposal, Leo Herzel was clearly right.

However, it is my belief that what was important for economics in my article on "The Federal Communications Commission" was not the proposal to institute pricing, important though this may be as a policy issue when considering the radio frequency spectrum, but that I went on to discuss the rights that would be, or should be, acquired by the successful bidder, something which economists rarely, if ever, did when they advocated the pricing of resources. This discussion of the rationale of property rights, with its attack on A. C. Pigou, was, however, thought to be erroneous by the economists at Chicago. I was even urged to omit this section from the FCC article. But I refused, arguing that, even if my argument was an error, it was a very interesting error. Their objections centered on what George Stigler was later to term the "Coase Theorem." Invited to give a workshop at Chicago, I said I would do so if there would also be an opportunity for me to discuss my error with them. Stigler in his autobiography gives a lively and very Stiglerian description of what happened. I met one evening at Aaron Director's home with Milton Friedman, George Stigler, Arnold

Harberger, John McGee, Reuben Kessel, and others, and after a long discussion, it was agreed that I had not committed an error.[30] I was then asked to write up my argument for publication in the *Journal of Law and Economics*. This I did, entitling the article "The Problem of Social Cost," a title adapted from Frank Knight's article, "Fallacies in the Interpretation of Social Cost."[31] Knight also criticized Pigou, but more important from my point of view was that my argument could be seen as a natural extension of Knight's insight that the institution of property rights would ensure that the excessive investment which Pigou thought private enterprise would make in industries subject to decreasing return would not in fact happen. In "The Problem of Social Cost" I exposed a similar error of Pigou's, due again to the fact that he had not realized that his problem arose because of the failure to institute property rights. In "The Problem of Social Cost" I set out my argument at greater length, more precisely, and I applied it to a wider range of economic problems than I had in the FCC article. Had it not been that these Chicago economists thought that I had made a mistake in the article on "The Federal Communications Commission," it is probable that "The Problem of Social Cost" would never have been written.

Recently as part of the preparation for this lecture I read the article on "The Federal Communications Commission," and I must say that the section to which objections were raised seems to me so simple and so clear that it is difficult to understand why it was not immediately accepted. I suppose this lack of comprehension represents another example, about which Thomas Kuhn has told us, of the difficulty which scientists find in changing their analytical system, or, as he puts it, in moving from one paradigm to another.[32] It is generally agreed that this article has had an immense influence on legal scholarship, but this was no part of my intention. For me, "The Problem of Social Cost" was an essay in economics. It was aimed at economists. What I wanted to do was to improve our analysis of the working of the economic system. Law came into the article because, in a regime of positive transaction costs, the character of the law becomes one of the main factors determining the performance of the economy. If transaction costs were zero (as is assumed in standard economic theory) we can imagine people contracting around the law whenever the value of production would be increased by a change in the legal position. But in a regime of positive transaction costs, such contracting would not occur whenever transaction costs were greater than the gain that such a redistribution of rights would bring. As a consequence the rights which individuals possess will commonly be those established by the law, which in these circumstances can be said to control the economy. As I have said, in "The Problem of Social Cost" I had no intention of making a contribution to legal scholarship. I referred to legal cases because they afforded examples of real situations as against the imaginary ones normally used by economists in their analysis. It was undoubtedly an economist who invented the widget. But in "The Problem of Social Cost" I did something else. I pointed out that the judges in their opinions often seemed to show a better understanding of the economic problem than did many economists even though their views were not always expressed in a very explicit fashion. I did this not to praise the judges but to shame economists. Richard Posner, who had been set on the right road through his contact with Aaron Director at Stanford and who then moved to Chicago, picked up what I had said about the judges and ran with it. I have never attempted to follow him. For one thing, he runs much faster than I do. He also runs in a somewhat different direction. My interest is primarily in the economic system, whereas his main interest is in the legal system, although the interrelationships between these two social systems leads to a considerable overlapping of interest. In the development of the economic analysis of the law or, as I would prefer to put it, of the legal system, Posner has clearly played the major role.

I now turn to the influence of the *Journal of Law and Economics*, which in my view, has been a major factor in establishing "law and economics" as a separate field of study. The decision to establish such a journal was made in the mid-1950s by the authorities at the University of Chicago Law School, that is to say, Edward Levi, and the first issue came out in October 1958—at any rate, that is the date on the first issue. The aim of the *Journal* was said to be the examination of public policy issues of interest to lawyers and economists. Aaron Director suggested that it should be called the

*Journal of La*w "or" *Economics,* but, fortunately, "honest Aaron" did not get his way. The early issues of the *Journal* contained articles of considerable interest to me. There was, for example, John McGee's article, "Predatory Price Cutting: The Standard Oil (New Jersey) Case";[33] there were two articles on water rights by J. W. Milliman[34] and by Edgar S. Bagley;[35] there was Lester Telser's article "Why Should Manufacturers Want Fair Trade";[36] Marshall Colberg's "Minimum Wage Effects on Florida's Economic Development";[37] James Crutchfield's article on fishery regulation;[38] and of course, that celebrated article by George Stigler and Claire Friedland, "What Can Regulators Regulate? The Case of Electricity";[39] and there were others of a like nature. This was law and economics as I conceived it. It did not lessen my admiration for the *Journal* that these early issues included four of my articles, on the FCC, on social cost, on competition in the British postal service, and on the allocation to government departments in the United States of use of the radio frequency spectrum, particularly as these were articles that it would have been difficult if not impossible to publish in any of the existing journals. Consequently, when I was approached to fill Aaron Director's place on his retirement, what I found most attractive about coming to Chicago was the opportunity it gave me of editing the *Journal.* Indeed, it is probable that without the *Journal* I would not have come to Chicago. I knew nothing of the original aim of the *Journal.* What I wanted to do was to encourage the type of research which I had advocated in "The Problem of Social Cost," and I used my editorship of the *Journal* as a means of bringing this about.

"The Problem of Social Cost" demonstrated that in a regime of zero transaction costs (the assumption of standard economic theory) negotiations would always lead to a solution which maximized wealth. Consequently, the kind of government action that economists thought to be required was completely unnecessary given the assumptions of their analytical system. But, of course, all that this did was to show the emptiness of the Pigovian analytical system. Once the assumption of zero transaction costs is abandoned and the fact that carrying out market transactions is a costly process is incorporated in the theory, it follows that alternative ways of coordinating the employment of resources, even through costly and in various ways imperfect, could not be dismissed out of hand as inferior to reliance on the market. What would be best depended on the relative costs of these alternative ways of coordinating the employment of resources, and about this we knew very little. As I said in "The Problem of Social Cost":

> Satisfactory views on policy can only come from a patient study of how, in practice, the market, firms and governments handle the problem of harmful effects. Economists need to study the work of the broker in bringing parties together, the effectiveness of restrictive covenants, the problems of the large-scale development company, the operation of governmental zoning and other regulating agencies. It is my belief that economists, and policy makers generally, have tended to overestimate the advantages which come from government regulation. But this belief, even if justified, does not do more than suggest that government regulation should be curtailed. It does not tell us where the boundary line should be drawn. This ... has to come from a detailed investigation of the actual results of handling the problem in different ways.[40]

The main aim of my editorship of the *Journal* was to encourage economists and lawyers to undertake such investigations. It was done by supporting faculty research, by granting fellowships to those willing to conduct these investigations, by making available financial assistance, and above all by offering the opportunity for publication. At the same time improvements in the theory were made by Harold Demsetz, Steve Cheung, Oliver Williamson, and others. As time went by, more and more articles were submitted without any encouragement from me. I even began to see articles in the *American Economic Review* that I would like to have published in the *Journal of Law and Economics,* an occurrence which both pleased and displeased me. This change in the direction of research was helped forward by the formation by George Stigler of the Center for the Study of the Economy and the State in the Business School from which flowed a series of studies of the effects of government regulation. In the editorship of the *Journal of Law and Economics* I was joined by William Landes, and later the editorship of the *Journal* was enlarged to include Dennis Carlton and Frank Easterbrook and, finally, Sam Peltzman. Opportunities for publication were further enlarged by the establishment in 1972 of the *Journal of Legal Studies,* edited by Richard Posner and later by Richard Epstein. Meanwhile, greater opportunity for publication has also been afforded by the establishment elsewhere of journals devoted to the subject of law and economics such as the *Journal of Law, Economics and Organization* at Yale.

The Law and Economics Program at Chicago now operates in a very different environment from that of the early 1960s. Law and economics is now professionally recognized as a separate discipline or subdiscipline. Excellent work and in quantity is going forward in law schools all over the United States. This new situation has been marked by the formation of the American Law and Economics Association. The task of establishing the subject has been accomplished. Legal scholarship also moves forward in a new spirit. Ernest Rutherford said that science is either physics or stamp collecting, by which he meant, I take it, that it is either engaged in analysis or in operating a filing system. Much, and perhaps most, legal scholarship has been stamp collecting. Law and economics, however, is likely to change all that and, in fact, has begun to do so.

I am very much aware that, in concentrating in this lecture on law and economics at Chicago, I have neglected other significant contributions to the subject made elsewhere such as those by Guido Calabresi at Yale, by Donald Turner at Harvard, and by others. But it can hardly be denied that in the emergence of the subject of law and economics, Chicago has played a very significant part and one of which the University can be proud. How the Law and Economics Program of the University of Chicago Law School will fare in the next century I leave to the Simons lecturer of 2092.

Notes

[1] Frank Knight, *Risk, Uncertainty, and Profit* (1921; reprinted 1957).
[2] Henry C. Simons, *A Positive Program for Laissez Faire: Some Proposals for a Liberal Economic Policy*, 1 (1934).
[3] Id. at 11-12.
[4] Id. at 12.
[5] Id. at 19.
[6] Id. at 19-21
[7] Id. at 38.
[8] Id. at 31-32.
[9] George J. Stigler, *The Economist as Preacher and Other Essays,* 170 (1982).
[10] Id. at 167.
[11] George J. Stigler, *Memoirs of an Unregulated Economist*, 187-190 (1988).
[12] Lionel Robbins, reply on file in the Dean's Office, University of Chicago Law School.
[13] Id.
[14] Henry C. Simons, Memorandum I on a proposed Institute of Political Economy, 2 (Henry C. Simons Papers, U. Chi. Law School Archives, undated).
[15] Id. at 12.
[16] Id. at 5.
[17] Id. at 5-6.
[18] Friedrich Hayek, *The Road to Serfdom* (1944).
[19] Memorandum on file in the Dean's Office, University of Chicago Law School.
[20] Edmund W. Kitch, ed., The fire of truth: A remembrance of law and economics at Chicago, 1932-1970, 26 J. Law & Econ. 180-181 (1983). This article is a transcript of a panel discussion edited by Kitch, who was also a panel participant. Kitch also provided a foreword, afterword, and footnotes.
[21] Id. at 181.
[22] Id. at 183.
[23] Id. at 184.
[24] R. H. Coase, The problem of social cost, 3 *Journal of Law and Economics.* 1 (1960).
[25] R. H. Coase, The Federal Communications Commission, 2 *Journal of Law and Economics.* 1 (1959).
[26] Leo Herzel, "Public interest" and the market in color television regulation, 18 *University of Chicago Law Review.* 802-816 (1951).
[27] Abba P. Lerner, *The Economics of Control: Principles of Welfare Economics* (1944).
[28] Herzel, *supra* note 26, at 813.
[29] Dallas W. Smythe, Facing facts about the broadcast business, 20 *University of Chicago Law Review.* 96 (1952).
[30] Stigler, *supra* note 11, at 75-80.
[31] Coase, The problem of social cost, *supra* note 22; Frank H. Knight, Fallacies in the interpretation of social cost, 38 *Quarterly Journal of Economics.* 582 (1924), reprinted in *Readings in Price Theory*,

selected by a committee of the American Economic Association (George J. Stigler & Kenneth E. Boulding eds. 1952) and published by Richard D. Irwin, Inc.

[32]   Thomas S. Kuhn, *The Structure of Scientific Revolutions* (2d ed. 1970).

[33]   John McGee, Predatory price cutting: The Standard Oil (New Jersey) Case, 1 *Journal of Law and Economics*. 137 (1958).

[34]   J. W. Milliman, Water law and private decision-making: A critique, 2 *Journal of Law and Economics*. 41 (1959).

[35]   Edgar S. Bagley, Water Rights Law and public policies relating to ground water "mining" in the Southwestern States, 4 *Journal of Law and Economics*. 144 (1961).

[36]   Lester Telser, Why should manufacturers want fair trade? 3 *Journal of Law and Economics*. 86 (1960).

[37]   Marshall Colberg, Minimum wage effects on Florida's economic development, 3 *Journal of Law and Economics*. 106 (1960).

[38]   James A. Crutchfield, an economic evaluation of alternative methods of fishery regulation, 4 *Journal of Law and Economics*. 131 (1961).

[39]   George Stigler & Claire Friedland, What can regulators regulate? The case of electricity, 5 *Journal of Law and Economics*. 1 (1962).

[40]   Coase, *supra* note 24, at 18-19.

Law and Economics: A Personal Journey*

I am very happy, for more reasons than one, to be able to participate in the centennial celebrations of the Law School. Nonetheless, it is a strange experience for me to be giving a Coase lecture. After all, any lecture I give is a Coase lecture. The situation is made more awkward since the ostensible purpose of this lecture series, at least in part, is to honor Ronald Coase. We are told to honor our mother and father but there is no commandment to honor ourselves. Indeed, for most of us, it would be unnecessary. As Adam Smith said, we do not normally think of anyone as being deficient in self-love. The situation is made even more awkward for me since the subject on which I have decided to speak is "Law and Economics," and I can hardly avoid giving a good deal of attention to my own contributions to the subject and how I came to make them. I'm afraid all this reminds me of Mr. Toad in *The Wind in the Willows*. So, when the Dean asked me to give this lecture, the thought of Mr. Toad led me to hesitate. But when the Dean asks you to do something, in the end there is little one can do except tremble and obey. So here I am.

Dean Levmore also told me that what I should do is to acquaint the students, particularly the first-year students, with the problems of one of the subjects taught at the Law School. I naturally chose "Law and Economics." I have crafted this

---

* *Man and the Economy*, 2014, 1(1),69-78. This lecture was first delivered on April 1, 2003 at the University of Chicago Law School. Professor Coase made a few minor changes on August 15, 2003. Even though the video of the lecture has been available online for some time, the text, to our knowledge, has never been published. Now, with the permission of the Coase Society which owns the copyright, we make it available to a wider audience.

lecture to interest the students at the Law School. Indeed, much that I have to say is autobiographical in character since what I did as a student and young instructor, and even later, illustrates the part that students play in the development of a subject. Others may listen in but this is not a public lecture. I regard my audience to be the students. My lecture is intended to interest, instruct and encourage the students. The autobiographical character of my lecture has another advantage. It enables me to describe the curious chain of events that led to the emergence of that new subject, law and economics, and which has affected its development.

In giving my view on "Law and Economics," you should remember that I am not a lawyer and that I am a Professor of Economics, not a Professor of Law and Economics. Such knowledge of law as I possess comes from some courses I took as an undergraduate at the London School of Economics studying for a Bachelor of Commerce degree in the years 1929 to 1931. As part of the curriculum I took courses in commercial and industrial law. I cannot remember all the courses I took but they included the law of contracts, the law of employer and employee (then called the law of master and servant), the law relating to trade associations, workman's compensation and others I cannot now remember. I greatly enjoyed these courses with their discussion of cases and I read the Law Reports and followed the precedents back to discover that the original cases on which the doctrines were based were completely different from those to which it was subsequently applied. The Law Courts are situated in the Strand, a few hundred yards from the London School of Economics, and I went there to follow the proceedings and to admire the quick wit and acting ability of the barristers. We were also made acquainted with some of the important American cases. I remember reading an article by Goodhart on the Palsgraf case, in which a railway guard, helping a passenger to board a train, knocked a package from his arms. The package contained fireworks of which the guard was ignorant. There was an explosion and the concussion knocked over some scales some distance away which injured a woman who then sued the railway. The decision in the American courts was the opposite of that come to in the British courts, in a somewhat similar case, *Smith v.*

London and Southwestern Railway. I greatly enjoyed these discussions. In preparing for this lecture, I looked at the book reprinting Goodhart's article. While turning the pages, I notice a reference in a footnote to *Rylands v. Fletcher*. It was like seeing the name of an old friend with whom you had once had a special relationship, but the nature of which you had completely forgotten.

The fact of the matter is that I enjoyed the law courses more than any of the others I took. This is understandable given the nature of the others. Take accounting. We were told about the different but acceptable ways in which depreciation or the cost of materials taken from stock could be calculated or the value of goodwill determined (this was extremely flexible). It never seems to have bothered these accountants that these different procedures all resulted in different profit figures. It was a perfect course for an Enron accountant. I also took psychology, including industrial psychology, in which were told about a study at the Hawthorne plant of the Western Electric Company in Chicago. This studied the motivation of workers and the need to be considerate of their feelings. I also took a course in statistics which was very useful and others, such as business administration, the contents of which I cannot now remember. At this stage it was the law courses that most interested me and, I suppose, had nothing intervened, that there is good chance that I would have ended up as a lawyer. But something did intervene. And here my tale illustrates the importance for a student of being at a place where not only the faculty is good but which also has a good student body. In my case, what intervened was the appointment at the London School of Economics of Arnold Plant as Professor of Commerce in 1930. Plant had previously been Professor of Commerce at the University of Cape Town, South Africa.

I attended Plant's seminar at the end of my second year at LSE, about five months before I completed the course work for the B.Com. It was a revelation. He told us how the pricing system controlled production, of the importance of property rights, about the working of a competitive system, and also that government regulation was commonly designed to protect special interests. This was heady stuff and all news to me, being at that time a socialist and never having taken a course in economics while at LSE. But Plant was no theorist and his views, serviceable and robust though they were, were not very precise. I discussed Plant's views with my friend and fellow student Ronald Fowler and also with economics specialists at LSE, among whom I remember Abba Lerner, Victor Edelberg and Vera Smith (who became Vera Lutz on marrying Friedrich Lutz of Princeton). As I had not taken any courses in economics it was these discussions with fellow students in 1932 plus the reading they led me to, that made me an economist. However, at this stage it still seemed more likely that I would become a lawyer rather than an economist. As it happened, I had passed the examinations of the University of London for the subjects taken in the first year at the University while still at school, high school as it would be called here. As a result, since three years residence at the University were required before a degree could be granted, I had to continue in residence at LSE for another year before obtaining my degree. I decided to spend the additional year studying industrial law. However, no doubt as result of Plant's influence, I was granted by the University of London a Sir Ernest Cassel Travelling Scholarship for the next year. I had been interested in the question of why industries were organized in different ways and I decided to go to the United States to study this question, working under Plant's supervision, the requirement of residence at LSE being somewhat loosely interpreted.

I could have chosen any country. That I chose to go to the United States, was, I feel sure, due to the fact that most of the literature on business administration and industrial organization was American. That I am able to give you an account of what I did there is due to the fact that I corresponded with Ronald Fowler, my friend and fellow student, and he had kept many of my letters as well as drafts of his replies. My aim while I was in America was to find an explanation for why industries were organized in such different ways—the problem of vertical and lateral integration as I put it. I also took with me another problem. Plant was opposed to government schemes for coordinating production—the pricing system would do all the coordination necessary. Yet, in his lectures on business administration, he spoke of management as coordinating the work of the various factors of production used in the firm. How could one reconcile these different approaches? Why didn't the pricing system make the firm unnecessary? Here in my investigations I benefited from having taken a Bachelor of Commerce rather than an economics degree. With all its faults we did get acquainted with what went on in business in the real world. The result was that when I went to America, I did not spend most of my time visiting economists in American universities. Indeed, in one of my letters to Fowler, I refer to the views of academics as "bilge." What I did was to visit factories and businesses and discuss with businessmen the problems that vexed me. I could do this because of my B.Com training. By the summer of 1932, I got the answer to my question—Why were some operations coordinated within the firm by management while others came about as a result of market transactions. The pricing mechanism or use of the market was not free. You had to find the other partner to an exchange, negotiate with him, draw up contracts, monitor the performance and so on. This was costly. It was the comparison of these costs, transaction costs as they have come to be called, with the costs of carrying out the same operations within the firm that determined which would be chosen. This was all very simple but it had not been seen before, largely because the existence of firms had been taken for granted. This explicit introduction of the concept of transaction costs was to play an important part in the analysis of the working of the economic system and was also to play an important part in "Law and Economics." But this was to come many years later.

When I returned from America, I was appointed an assistant lecturer at the Dundee School of Economics and Commerce, no doubt as a result of Arnold Plant's recommendation. I started work in Dundee in October 1932. In a letter to Fowler I describe the contents of my first lecture in a course on the organization of the business unit. It was the argument of "The Nature of the Firm." I comment in my letter to Fowler, "As it was a new approach (I think) to this subject, I was quite pleased with myself. One thing I can say is that I made it all up myself." As I said in my Stockholm lecture, "I was then 21 and the sun never ceased to shine."

In 1934 while still at Dundee I completed the first draft of "The Nature of the Firm," revised it in 1936, after I had joined the economics department at LSE, and it was published in *Economica* in 1937. How it was received by my elders and betters is I think extremely instructive. On the day the article was published, on the way to lunch, the two professors of commerce, one of whom was Plant, congratulated me on the article but never referred to it again. The professor of banking, whose name I suppress, said somewhat sarcastically that it smelled of the lamp, by which he meant that it was an academic exercise without real significance. Lionel Robbins, the head of the economics department, of which I was a member, never referred to the article ever and neither did Hayek, although my relations with both of them were quite cordial. My elders simply did not see the significance of the article, nor did it get any support in the wider academic community. There were some footnote references to "The Nature of the Firm," but the ideas in it were not picked up. The only support I got was from my contemporaries, particularly from Ronald Fowler and from Duncan Black, who had been the fellow assistant lecturer with me in Dundee. If this tale has any general significance it is that new ideas are most likely to come from the young, who are also the group most likely to recognize the significance of those ideas. Professors like Plant may get you going and provide the essential support in the early stages but once you get going it is the interchange with your contemporaries that really matters. It is the interchange in a student body that is the cauldron of discovery.

I now turn to "The Problem of Social Cost," where the tale is completely different but the lesson to be drawn from it is much the same. When I was appointed an assistant lecturer at the London School of Economics in 1935, my teaching duties included giving a course on the Economics of Public Utilities. I soon found that very little was known about the subject in Britain and I began a series of historical studies of water, gas, electricity, the Post Office and broadcasting to find out what the facts were. In 1950, my book *British Broadcasting: A Study in Monopoly* was published. In it I explained how it was that broadcasting became a public monopoly in Britain and I questioned the reasons advanced to justify it. I visited the United States in 1948 to find out how a commercial broadcasting system operated. Then in 1951 I migrated to the United States and started a research project that I called "The Political Economy of Broadcasting," based on experience in Britain, the United States and Canada. The study was never completed but I wrote a paper "The Federal Communications Commission," which in a curious way was to lead to the modern subject of Law and Economics. However, this only came about because of a student note in the *University of Chicago Law Review*. This student note therefore played a crucial part in the events leading to the emergence of "Law and Economics" as a separate subject.

It is sometimes said that I originated the idea of using prices to determine use of the radio frequency spectrum. This is wrong. The idea was first put forward by Leo Herzel, a student at the University of Chicago Law School, in a student note in the *Law Review* in 1950, dealing with the choice by the FCC of the color television system to be used in the United States. He said: "A much more controversial alternative would be to abandon regulation by government fiat altogether and to substitute the market… The FCC would lease channels for a stated period to the highest bidder." I read this article, but at first I was not convinced. There was, after all, the problem of defining the property rights and making sure that these rights were respected. But then there appeared a reply to Leo Herzel's article by Dallas Smythe who had been chief economist of the FCC. His arguments were so weak that I concluded that Leo Herzel was right and I adopted his proposal when I wrote my article on "The Federal Communications Commission." And where did Leo Herzel get his idea from? It came from Abba Lerner's book *The Economics of Control* that Leo Herzel read in 1944 or 1945. Abba Lerner was of course one of the group of students at the London School of Economics from whom I learned my economics and in the preface to the book he acknowledges the influence, among others, of Arnold Plant. However, Abba Lerner was a socialist who thought that a socialist system could be run in such a way as to reproduce the optimum results as described in economic theory, in the main, by imitating the market, but not always. I remember that he went to Mexico to persuade Trotsky that all would be well in a communist state if, among other things, prices were set equal to marginal costs.

Convinced that use of the radio frequency spectrum could be determined by the price mechanism in the same way as other goods and services, I wrote an article on "The Federal Communications Commission" in 1958 to 1959, while at the Center for Advanced Study of the Behavioral Sciences at Stanford. In the case of radio, the signal of one station interfering with and worsening the reception of others was a real problem and this led me to examine the usual approach of economists at that time to this kind of problem, that developed by the English economist, Pigou. He spoke of the difference between private and social products, and he wished to restrain the activity of those harming others. He proposed doing this by means of taxes, but the same result could be achieved in other ways. I objected to the Pigovian approach. We were dealing with a reciprocal problem. Suppression of the harm that one producer creates inevitably inflicts harm on him. The problem is to stop the greater harm. I illustrated the nature of the problem by examining the English legal case of *Sturges v. Bridgman*. In this case, the working of a confectioner's machinery disturbed a doctor who occupied neighboring premises. The doctor won his case in the courts. I pointed out that although the machinery no doubt caused harm to the doctor, restricting the methods of production that could be employed by the confectioner harmed him. I illustrated the situation with some hypothetical figures. I said that the doctor would be willing to waive his right if the confectioner would compensate him for the additional costs he would incur in carrying out his consulting elsewhere. I assumed this to be $200. The confectioner would pay the doctor up to the additional cost imposed on him by the change in his methods of production (which I assumed to be $100). With these figures the doctor would not accept less than $200 and the confectioner would not pay more than $100 for the doctor to waive his right. But consider the position if the confectioner had won the case. The confectioner would be willing to waive his right for a payment greater than $100, the doctor would be willing to pay up to $200 to induce the confectioner to do this. The result is that the confectioner would waive his right. What this showed was that the legal decision did not affect the way resources were used. As I put it "the delimitation of rights is an essential prelude to market transactions but the ultimate result (which maximizes the value of production) is independent of the legal decision."

While I was writing the FCC paper, Abba Lerner visited the Center for Advanced Study in the Behavioral Sciences at Stanford. He enquired what I was doing. I told him about my argument that the way in which resources was used was independent of the legal decision on ownership of rights. He got the point in a minute and agreed with it. David Laidler says in his article on Abba Lerner in the *International Encyclopedic of Social Sciences* that Lerner was impressed by my argument and applied it in areas in which he was interested.

That Lerner and I were so easily able to agree was understandable. It was due to what James Buchanan in his book *Cost and Choice* calls "the London tradition," a view of the concept of "opportunity cost" based on Wicksteed's *Commonsense of Political Economy* that Lionel Robbins recommended that we all read at LSE. Buchanan quoted a passage from an article of mine that appeared in 1938 as giving a particularly clear statement of the LSE position.

> The cost of doing anything consists of the receipts which could have been obtained if that particular decision had not been taken. When someone says that a particular course of action is "not worth the cost," this merely means that he prefers some other course—the receipts of the individual, whether monetary or nonmonetary does not matter, will be greater if he does not do it. This particular concept of costs would seem to be the only one which is of use in the solution of business problems, since it concentrates attention on the alternative courses of action which are open to the businessman. Costs will only be covered if he chooses, out of the various courses of action which seem open to him, that one which maximizes his profits. To cover costs and to maximize profit are essentially two ways of expressing the same phenomenon.

It is easy to see why, holding this view, I analyzed the case of *Sturges v. Bridgman* in the way I did. It also illustrates the importance of being at a school at which you learn useful ideas.

However, though the economics department at the University of Chicago is among the best in the world, economists in that department did not see the situation in the same way that I did. They objected to my analysis in the passage dealing with the case of *Sturges v. Bridgman* and indeed wanted me to delete it from my article on the FCC. However, I held my ground and the passage remained in the article as published.

I never really understood what the objection to my argument was. I think, but I cannot be sure of this, that these Chicago economists thought that if you possessed a right to do something, your costs would be lower than if you did not possess the right and had to purchase it. In this case, you had to make a payment that would be unnecessary if you possessed the right. What they ignored, if my surmise is correct, is that if you did not use these rights, you could sell them, so that using them yourself cost you what they would fetch in the market. The cost was the same whether you possessed the right or not. This result is of course dependent on ignoring transaction costs but this is usual in price theory.

Some months after my FCC paper was published, with the error in it, I was invited by Stigler to give a paper at the Industrial Organization Workshop. I accepted on condition that I could have a discussion of my error. A meeting was arranged which took place at Aaron Director's home with about 20 Chicago economists present: Aaron Director, George Stigler, Milton Friedman and others. I have only the haziest idea of what happened. The discussion was hot and heavy and lasted about two hours, with Milton Friedman the most active. In the end it was agreed that I was right. The effect on the participants, or at any rate most of them, and certainly on George Stigler, was dramatic. Steven Cheung in his piece on me in the *New Palgrave Dictionary of Economics*, says that, according to McGee, who was present, "As the debaters left Aaron Director's house in a state of shock they murmured to one another that they had witnessed intellectual history." I did not share this feeling. I could not understand why a statement the equivalent of $2 + 2 = 4$ should be treated as on a par with $E = MC^2$. As I've said, I have no clear recollection of the discussion. What I do seem to remember as a turning point was when Harberger said, "If you cannot show that the marginal cost schedule changes, he can run right through." Stigler wrote an account of the discussion in his *Memoir of an Unregulated Economist* but I do not think it is entirely accurate. The tale of the vote before and after the discussion is pure fiction although I don't doubt that had there been a vote, it would have come out as he described. His account of how I argued does not strike me being correct, it is just not my style. However, his statement that I used the example of the straying cattle damaging the crops of a neighboring farmer is undoubtedly correct. I suspect that my argument at Aaron Director's home was much the same as that to be found in the first few pages of "The Problem of Social Cost." After the meeting I was asked to write up my arguments for the *Journal of Law and Economics* and that was how "The Problem of Social Cost" came to be written. In that article I did not confine myself to what I have said at the meeting. I illustrated the nature of the problem by references to English nuisance cases. I showed that the conclusion that puzzled the Chicago economists was dependent on the assumption of zero transaction costs although they are in fact quite likely to be large. I discussed the delimitation of property rights. And I ended the article with a discussion of Pigou's views which had been largely adopted by the economics profession and showed that they were erroneous. The article was a great success. It helped to create the modern subject of "Law and Economics." It has been cited more than any other article in the modern economics literature. However, much of this attention does not relate to what I said in that article but to something called "the Coase Theorem." This was invented by George Stigler and stated that: "Under perfect competition, private and social costs will be equal." One of Robert Cooter's reformulations comes closer to what people usually have in mind when they refer to the Coase Theorem: "The initial allocation of legal entitlement does not matter from an efficiency perspective so long as the transaction costs of exchange are nil."

I have never been enthusiastic about Stigler's "Coase Theorem." I don't like the concept of perfect competition nor the assumption of zero transaction costs. To make these assumptions is to have a discussion about a world that does not exist, probably indeed one that could not exist. Of course, in making one's argument, it is quite all right to simplify, but this has to be done sensibly. In discussing the trajectory of a bullet fired from a rifle, it is no doubt reasonable to neglect the effect of gravity, but to make the assumption that gravity did not operate anywhere would mean that you don't have a bullet, a rifle or indeed anything else.

Looking back, it might have been better if, in my FCC article, I have not be influenced by my courses in law and LSE and had not discussed *Sturges v. Bridgman*. I could have confined myself to what I said about a newly discussed cave:

> whether a newly discovered cave belongs to the man who discovered it, the man on whose land the entrance is located, or the man who owns the surface under which the cave is situated is no doubt dependent on the law of property, but the law merely determines the person with whom it is necessary to make a contract to obtain the use of the cave. Whether the cave is used for storing bank records, as a natural gas reservoir or for growing mushrooms depends not on the law of property but whether the bank, the natural gas corporation or the mushroom concern will pay the most in order to be able to use the cave.

This approach makes the same point as does the analysis I made of *Sturges v. Bridgman* but does not involve the kind of argument about *Sturges v. Bridgman* which so upset the Chicago economists. On the other hand, this change of approach would have meant that there was no meeting at Aaron Director's house, no article "The Problem of Social Cost" and very probably no new subject "Law and Economics." Furthermore, since, as has been plausibly argued, it was "The Problem of Social Cost" that drew attention to "The Nature of the Firm," no Nobel Prize in Economics for me and the only bright spot, no Coase Lecture.

But "God moves in a mysterious way, his wonders to perform" and "Law and Economics" did emerge and has flourished, propelled by Richard Posner's *Economic Analysis of Law*.

Many lawyers have learned enough economics to make significant contributions to "Law and Economics." The value of using economic concepts (opportunity cost, elasticity of demand and so on) to aid in the elucidation of legal problems is clear. This work has a solid footing and will continue and develop. The same cannot be said of another part of "Law and Economics," the effect of the legal system on the functioning of the economic system, although it is generally agreed that without a well-functioning legal system you cannot have an efficient economic system. One reason for this lack of interest is that economics has become a theory-driven subject and the need to carry out massive empirical work is not accepted by economists and is certainly not done. That's the bad reason. But there is also a good reason. It is relatively easy for a non-economist to learn the economic concepts. It is very hard for a non-lawyer to learn how the legal system operates, with its doctrines and terminology. I suggest therefore that the study of how the legal system affects the economic system is a task that professors of law should undertake, not all of them, of course, some of them. I don't think this is a diversion from their main task of training the young. Lawyers in business (and there are many of them) are deal-makers. They make it possible for certain transactions to be carried out. Although it may not always seem like this to their clients, they reduce transaction costs. I suggest that research projects be undertaken with the aid of students into how this contracting process actually operates. Some years ago, Professor Kitch, then at this Law School, undertook, with the aid of students, a study of the regulation of taxicabs in Chicago. The result was an excellent study which was published in the *Journal of Law and Economics*. The students proved to be superb investigators. I think much more of this work utilizing the creativity and energy of the young could be done. It would be good training for work that many of them will actually do and the rest of us will benefit from a vastly improved "Law and Economics."